*Three Steps
to Revising
Your writing
for Style,
Grammar,
Punctuation,
and Spelling*

Three Steps to Revising Your Writing for Style, Grammar, Punctuation, and Spelling

Barbara E. Walvoord

Scott, Foresman and Company
Glenview, Illinois
Boston
London

To my mother, Marie Walvoord

Library of Congress Cataloging-in-Publication Data

Walvoord, Barbara E. Fassler
  Three steps to revising your writing for style,
grammar, punctuation, and spelling.

  Includes index.
  1. Authorship—Handbooks, manuals, etc. I. Title.
II. Title: 3 steps to revising your writing for
style, grammar, punctuation, and spelling.
PN147.W34 1988 808'.042   87-28706
ISBN 0-673-18657-1

Copyright © 1988 Scott, Foresman and Company.
All Rights Reserved.
Printed in the United States of America.

123456-KPF-929190898887

CONTENTS

Outline of Steps and Substeps: A Guide to Revising
(inside front cover)

Preface

Acknowledgments

How to Use This Book   1

The Revising Process   8

Introductory Lessons   41

   INTRODUCTORY LESSON A: Identifying Subjects and Verbs   41

   INTRODUCTORY LESSON B: Dependent and Independent Clauses   67

Lessons for Step 1:   102
Read for Meaning and Revise for Style

LESSON 1A: Choose Between Active and Passive Voice Verbs   104
   Exercises   110

LESSON 1B: Add Transitions as Needed   115
   Exercises   124

LESSON 1C: Use Subject/Verb and Sentence Openers for Clarity and Emphasis   128
   Exercises   146

LESSON 1D: Relate Sentence Parts Clearly   153
   Use Parallel Forms for Parallel Ideas   154
   Exercises   158

Revise Distracting Material Between Subject and Verb   159
Exercises   163
Place Modifiers in Clear Relation to What They Modify   163
Clarify Relations Between Other Units   167
Exercises   168
Revise Miscues   169
Exercises for Miscues   172
Exercises for All of Lesson 1D   172
LESSON 1E: Tighten to Achieve Economy   176
Exercises   180
LESSON 1F: Revise Diction (Word Choice)   183
Exercises   191
Exercises for Step 1   195

Lessons for Step 2:   200
Read and Revise for Grammar and Punctuation

Punctuating Sentence Boundaries   202
LESSON 2A: Revise Sentence Fragments as Needed   203
Exercises   206, 213, 217
LESSON 2B: Avoid Run-Ons   221
Exercises   228
Verbs   235
LESSON 2C: Make Verbs Agree with their Subjects   236
Exercises   240, 244
LESSON 2D: Select Verb Tenses Appropriately   249
Exercises   258

LESSON 2E: Use Standard English Verb Forms   263
    Exercises   270
Pronouns   275
LESSON 2F: Select Pronouns   276
    Exercises   280, 284, 287
LESSON 2G: Solve the *Who/Whom, Him and Me* Debate   290
    Exercises   293
LESSON 2H: Give Pronouns Clear Antecedents   297
    Exercises   303
LESSON 2I: Make the Pronoun Agree With its Antecedent   307
Exercises   310
Exercises for All Pronoun Lessons   311
Apostrophe, -s, -es   314
LESSON 2J: Use Apostrophe, *-s*, and *-es* Appropriately   315
    Exercises   317, 318, 322, 327
Interior Sentence Punctuation   330
LESSON 2K: Avoid Commas that Separate the Subject from its Verb or the Verb from its Object   331
    Exercises   338
LESSON 2L: Use Commas After Introducers   341
    Exercises   343
LESSON 2M: Use Commas With Nonrestrictive Interrupters and Modifiers   346
    Exercises   353
LESSON 2N: Use Parentheses and Dashes to Set Off Strong Interrupters   357
    Exercises   362

LESSON 2O: Use Commas to Separate Adjectives in
    a Series 365
 Exercises 368
LESSON 2P: Punctuate Lists and Series with
    Colons, Semicolons, and Commas 371
 Exercises 375, 379
LESSON 2Q: Use Colon or Dash to Announce an
    Explanation 383
 Exercises 385
 Exercises for Interior Sentence Punctuation 386
Quotations 391
LESSON 2R: Punctuate Within and Around
    Quotations 392
 Exercises 401, 406, 411, 415
 Exercises for All of Step 2 415

Lessons for Step 3: 420
Spelling, Names, Titles, and Numbers

LESSON 3A: Spelling 422
 Exercises 430
LESSON 3B: Capitalize, Punctuate, and Abbreviate
    Dates, Numbers, Names, and Titles 432
 Exercises 434, 439, 444, 448
APPENDIX A: How to Use this Book with a
    Computer 453
APPENDIX B: Essays for Revision 457
 Answers to Exercises 465
 Acknowledgments 517
 Index 518

PREFACE

This book shows students how to revise their own writing. It also teaches them the guidelines and conventions they need to use in the revising process.

It is difficult to bridge the gap between a handbook's alphabetized discussions, or a workbook's exercises, and the process of successfully revising one's own prose. "Dangling modifier" is in the handbook under "D," but how are students to know when and how to look for dangling modifiers in their own writing, and how does the search for dangling modifiers fit in with the rest of the writing and revising process? What is the process by which students can effectively revise their own prose for style, grammar, punctuation, and spelling? This book answers those questions for students.

The book is divided into two parts: the first part explains the three steps of the revising process—steps that every student should follow for every piece of writing. The second part contains lessons, keyed to the steps, that teach the conventions and guidelines of style, grammar, punctuation, and spelling. Students use the lessons for reference during the revising process and for systematic study throughout the semester; gradually they become more adept at following the three steps.

THE PLACE OF *THREE STEPS* IN THE TOTAL REVISING PROCESS

Three Steps covers that part of the revision process that occupies the writer's primary attention once the basic theme, structure, and lines of reasoning within the composition are established. The section on "The Revising Process" reminds students that large-scale revisions should be made first, and that later, if a need for further large-scale revisions becomes clear, the writer should temporarily postpone the three steps, returning to them when the basic structure is once again in place. A case study (pp. 28-37) illustrates how one student writer follows the three steps during a typical recursive writing process. She returns at one point to large-scale revisions before once more taking up matters of style, punctuation, grammar, and spelling.

REVISING AS A PROCESS: THE THREE STEPS

Three Steps suggests to students that they reread drafts in three different ways:

Step 1: Read for meaning and revise style
Step 2: Read with attention to grammatical relationships and revise grammar and punctuation
Step 3: Read word by word and revise spelling

The steps are ways to read, ways to look. Current research on the revising process suggests that expert writers make several passes through a manuscript, looking for different aspects each time. The research also indicates that expert revisers use problem-solving strategies, not a random approach. This book formalizes and specifies a process for novices that is based on expert writers' practices. It helps students approach revision purposefully and systematically, rather than rereading their drafts only once, glaze-eyed, trying to identify and solve all the problems at once.

The first part of the book contains "How To Use This Book" and "The Revising Process." The three steps are explained. Students learn to read differently for each step. Further, they learn how to manage the revision process as a whole, how to plan their time, how and when to produce clean drafts and final copies, how to utilize the computer in revising, and how to use classmates, tutors, and instructors legitimately to help them revise and learn.

GUIDELINES AND CONVENTIONS: THE LESSONS

The second part of the book contains lessons that teach the conventions and guidelines of style, grammar, punctuation, and spelling. The lessons are keyed to the steps. For example, Step 1, on style, has six points for students to observe, each covered in a lesson: choosing between active and passive voice (Lesson 1A), using transitions (Lesson 1B), using subject/verb and sentence openers for clarity and emphasis (Lesson 1C), and so on.

Step 2, on grammar and punctuation, is divided into sub-steps in prioritized order, beginning with those problems that researchers have indicated are most distracting to readers. In Step 2, students look first for problems with sentence boundaries (fragments, Step 2A; run-ons/comma splices, Step 2B), then problems with verbs and pronouns (Steps 2C–2I), next apostrophe and -s (Step 2J), then interior sentence punctuation (Steps 2K–2Q), and finally punctuation with quotations (Step 2R). On any given draft, students read for as many of the points of each step as they know and can apply, using the lessons as needed for study and reference. The outline of the steps and lessons on the inside front cover provides a convenient guide to following the steps and locating the corresponding lessons.

Students use the lessons at two points:

1. During the revising process, they look up conventions for reference. (Students use the thorough, heavily cross-referenced index and also the guide to the steps and corresponding lessons located on the inside front cover.)
2. Between papers, students systematically study the lessons they do not yet know or have not been able to apply during revision.

The lessons focus not only on learning the conventions and guidelines but on learning how to identify problems and then how to revise them. The lessons are accompanied by diagrams that illustrate the process of reading, identifying, deciding, and revising for each problem. Numerous examples within the lessons are taken directly from student writing so that they reflect the actual problems of typical student writers. As the students study the lessons, they become more skilled at following the three steps of the revising process.

Three Steps introduces only those grammatical terms necessary to understand the conventions and revise effectively. Two introductory lessons teach the basic grammar needed for understanding the rest of the lessons. Students learn how to identify subjects, verbs, and modifiers, as well as dependent and independent clauses, in their own writing.

EXERCISES

Each lesson contains abundant exercises. About two-thirds of the exercises have answers in the back of the book, so students can study and check them independently. Additional exercises repeat the same forms and demands, this time with answers in the instructor's manual.

Exercises begin with simple phrases or sentences, but work up to the situations in which students make most of their mistakes—when their drafts contain distracting or misleading aspects such as a verbal that looks like a verb or a run-on that unites two closely related ideas. Most of the exercises ask students to identify and remedy problems in actual student writing. Many exercises ask students to combine or compose sentences that test their developing ability to revise and manipulate their own prose. Sentence-combining exercises are especially abundant in the introductory lessons, where one of the goals is to help students increase their fluency with written language.

USING *THREE STEPS*

Three Steps may be taught in class or assigned to students for independent work. It may be used with students across a broad range of ability and preparation. Students are encouraged always to follow the three steps, rereading their drafts in three different ways. Well-prepared students may omit lessons that cover material they already know. The lessons may be studied in any sequence. With this book, a wide spectrum of students, working independently or with classroom help, are able effectively to revise their own prose.

The book was field-tested with more than two hundred students taught by four instructors at five institutions. The instructors used the book in different ways, some teaching it in class, some relying on students' independent use of the book. Comments from students and their instructors contributed to revision of the manuscript. Seventeen students in two classes at very different types of institutions and levels of ability were further tested by administering pretests and posttests and by watching and listening as they composed and revised. These students' experiences were used for further revisions of the text. The pretests and posttests, in which students revised grammar and punctuation in actual college student writing, showed that all but two of the students improved significantly in their ability to revise grammar and punctuation. Those two had become more daring in using punctuation they had not before attempted, and were consequently making mistakes with, for example, the placement of the semicolon. So even these two had stepped ahead onto new ground. On the average, the students were able to identify and remedy three times as many grammar and punctuation errors on the posttest as they had on the pretest.

I wrote this book because my own students were unable to make their way from an alphabetized handbook to successful revising of their own writing. Since I replaced the alphabetized handbook with this book in my own composition classes, both my students and I have been much happier and more successful. That is the outcome that I trust will come, as well, for other instructors and students who use this book.

ACKNOWLEDGMENTS

My greatest debt is to the nearly two hundred students who field-tested this book and who generously shared their problems, responses, and suggestions.

I am deeply indebted to Gail Summerskill Cummins who administered the testing of the manuscript in classes at several colleges and universities. She also gave me invaluable advice based on her own use of the manuscript with her classes at Dundalk Community College and at Towson State University, both in Baltimore. She worked with me in collecting and interpreting data, including think-aloud protocols, showing how our students were learning revising skills and how they were using this manuscript. Her talent and experience as a teacher, scholar, and researcher have contributed significantly to the book.

Others who tested the manuscript in their classes also made important contributions to the book: Frances Alston of Morgan State University in Baltimore and Marianne Spengler of the University of Illinois—Chicago.

I am grateful to those who reviewed the book and offered thoughtful advice: Rosanna Grassi at Syracuse University, Eugene Hammond at the University of Maryland, Kate Kiefer of Colorado State University, Ellen Knodt at Pennsylvania State University—Ogontz, and John Ruszkeiwicz at the University of Texas—Austin. Glynda Hull of the University of Pittsburgh has been extraordinarily helpful, not just through her review of the manuscript, but through her research on student editing processes.

A quiet retreat for working on the book was made possible by H. Mebane and Ava Turner.

My husband, Hoke L. Smith, offered useful critiques of the manuscript and contributed his full support to the writing of the book. By their cooperation and reliability at home, my children, Brian and Lisa Fassler, have helped me find the necessary time and concentration for writing.

Anne E. Smith and Constance Rajala at Scott Foresman have been wonderful editors—knowledgeable, quick to respond, imaginative, and enthusiastic. Mark Grimes, the Project Editor, improved and tightened the manuscript.

HOW TO USE THIS BOOK

OVERVIEW OF THE BOOK

This book is intended for writers who need help revising their writing for style, grammar, punctuation, and spelling. It is for those who need lots of help, those who need only a little help, and everybody in between.

The book is organized into two parts. The first, short part describes the three-step *process of revising* any piece of writing for style, grammar, punctuation, and spelling. You use the three steps every time you revise, even if you're not yet very good at them.

The second part of the book, the lessons, demonstrates how to perform the three steps more skillfully. The lessons explain the guidelines and rules of style, grammar, and punctuation. Exercises in the lessons can be used to help you practice. The lessons can be used for reference while revising or as a systematic, week by week study program.

Using this book is like improving your tennis game. When you're playing a match, you use as much as you know and can execute within the pace of the match. In between matches, you come out to the court and just work on your backhand or on your serve, so that gradually the skills you build through practice will feed back into your game.

WHEN TO USE THE THREE STEPS

Writers revise at both broad and local levels. This book assumes that you have already drafted and revised for content, organization, and lines of reasoning. You are now ready to concentrate on style, grammar, punctuation, and spelling. Experienced writers often postpone these "local" revisions until a later stage of the writing process. Novice writers, on the other hand, may get so distracted, in early drafts, by local worries that they don't have the needed energy and concentration for large-scale concerns. The most effective use of this book, then, is to help you conduct a systematic rereading and revision of your writing after the large-scale concerns have been addressed.

However, the writing process seldom proceeds smoothly. It is recursive—that is, it loops around and doubles back. Like most writers, you may be correcting some spelling or reconstructing some awkward sentences as you write or reread early drafts. Also, like many writers, you may bounce back and forth between large-scale concerns like content and organization, and local concerns like spelling and punctuation. You might *think* the content, organization, and lines of reasoning are all satisfactory and start polishing the prose, only to realize that what seems, at first, to be a single awkward sentence actually is the key to a poorly reasoned passage; when you tug on the sentence, the whole section of the paper comes tumbling down. So back you go to large-scale revisions.

YOU CAN USE THIS BOOK TO LOOK UP A SINGLE ITEM

Suppose you're composing, or revising, and you wonder whether a word should be *peoples'* or *people's*. Try to label the problem—"It's an apostrophe problem" or "It's a problem with possessives"—and use the index to look it up. In the index you'll find both formal grammatical terms and also more common labels.

USE THIS BOOK TO REVISE YOUR WRITING

When you have worked through the large-scale questions and have a draft that basically says what you want it to say, you are ready to follow the three steps.

The Three Steps

Step 1: Read with attention to meaning, and revise for style.
Step 2: Read and revise for grammar and punctuation.
Step 3: Read with attention to individual words, and revise for spelling, capitalization, and abbreviations.

Each step contains substeps. You'll find some you know, some you partly know, some you don't know, and some you know but don't always do. If you have lots of problems, you may, at first, focus on just a few substeps. Your goal is to get better at each of the steps and substeps, so that when you revise a paper, you do the three steps more thoroughly, efficiently, and successfully. The basic plan for using this book is a dual approach: to use the book as a reference each time you write a paper and to study the lessons between papers to become a better reviser. An outline of the steps is on the inside front cover.

HOW TO USE THIS BOOK

1. For each paper:
   a. *Follow the three steps,* doing each as thoroughly as you can. Read your paper through at least once for each step, revising as you find problems.
   b. *Use "The Revising Process"* (pp. 8-40) for detailed guidance in using the steps.
   c. *Use the inside front cover* as an abbreviated guide to the steps and substeps in sequence.
   d. *Use the lessons in the book for reference,* as needed, and as you have time, while you're revising. If you don't have time to learn a substep, skip it for the time being, study the lesson later, and include it in your next paper revision.
   e. *Use the substeps in order of priority.* If many of the substeps are time-consuming and difficult for you, concentrate on the first few substeps in each step, omitting the later ones. (However, do *not* omit any *steps.* Follow all three, as best you can, for each paper.)
2. Between papers:
   a. *Study the lessons you don't know,* completing exercises in each lesson, so you become more knowledgeable and skilled in revision.
   b. *When a paper is returned, put pencil checks on the outline* on the front cover next to the two or three substeps with which you had the most problems. Study the lessons that correspond to those substeps. When you revise a paper, pay special attention to the substeps you've checked.

YOU CAN CHANGE THE SEQUENCE OF STEPS AND LESSONS

The three steps proceed from broader to more local concerns. The substeps in Step 2, on grammar and punctuation, are arranged in priority order beginning with those problems that research has shown are most distracting to readers. You can, however, use any substep or lesson at any time; none assumes prior knowledge. Whenever a lesson refers to a point of grammar covered in an earlier lesson, cross-references will help you turn back easily to the necessary explanation.

How to Use This Book

For each paper:
a. Follow all three steps, even if you are not yet skillful at all of them.
b. Use "The Revising Process" for guidance (pp. 8–40).
c. Use the inside front cover as a summary guide to the steps.
d. Use the lessons for reference.
e. Pay the most attention to the substeps that are earliest in the sequence.

Between papers:
a. Study the lessons you do not know.
b. When a paper is returned, make pencil checks on the inside front cover next to the substeps with which you had the most problems.

USE THIS BOOK TO LEARN OR REVIEW BASIC GRAMMAR

Grammatical explanations are inserted in the lessons, and the basic grammatical skills are explained in Introductory Lessons A and B. These skills are the following:

1. locating subjects and verbs (Introductory Lesson A), and
2. distinguishing between independent and dependent clauses (Introductory Lesson B).

If you already know how to do these two things, skip the Introductory Lessons. Later lessons that rely on the two skills always tell you so, and you can refer back to the Introductory Lessons if necessary.

HOW TO USE THIS BOOK

YOU CAN USE A COMPUTER WITH THIS BOOK

Word processing on the computer can make revision much easier because you can insert, delete, and move passages with ease. "The Revising Process" suggests how best to use word processing with the type of revision in this book. The computer can also help you *flag* problems for revision. Programs that do this are called "Spellers" or "Text Analysis programs." Appendix A suggests how to use such programs with this text.

YOU CAN REVISE
FROM AN INSTRUCTOR'S MARKS

If you get back a paper with instructor marks on it, you can get from your instructor's marks to the relevant pages of this book by using the guide on the inside front cover. For example, if your instructor writes *frag,* find that term on the inside front cover. It means you have a sentence fragment. The front cover tells you where to find this book's lesson on fragments.

YOU CAN ADD YOUR OWN MATERIAL
TO THE BOOK

Add substeps for your own audience's needs. The elements discussed in this book are universal to good writing. For special demands, write your own substeps in the blank spaces provided on the inside front cover and/or in the step/substep outline in "The Revising Process" (p. 18). For example, in one science class, the instructor emphasized that every brand name had to be followed by the trademark sign. In a speech therapy class, students writing client progress reports had to use present and past tenses in certain ways.

Add examples from your own writing. If your instructor finds a problem in your paper that you missed when you were revising, write your own problem sentence, together with the correction, in the space provided at the end of the lesson. Next time, you'll have not only the book's examples, but examples from your own writing as references to help you revise.

ANSWERS TO EXERCISES ARE IN THIS BOOK OR IN THE INSTRUCTOR'S MANUAL

The answers to most of the exercises in the lessons are included at the back of the book. However, each exercise also contains some problems for which the answers appear only in the instructor's manual, so that your instructor can assign them as homework or tests.

THE REVISING PROCESS

This section is based on the previous one, so if you haven't read "How to Use This Book," do so now. This section contains two parts: general advice on the revising process, and then a guide to revising for each of the three steps. Use this section as you revise your writing and as you study and apply the lessons.

ASK THE LARGE-SCALE QUESTIONS

This book helps you revise your writing for style, grammar, punctuation, and spelling. However, you shouldn't think of it as devoted only to helping you "fix errors" on an already solid piece of writing. Instead, you should treat your writing as a whole. Specifically, that means three things:

1. Before beginning the steps in this book, ask and answer the large-scale questions and make large-scale revisions as needed.

2. In following the steps of this book, make decisions in light of your larger message, your audience, and your purpose.
3. Return to large-scale revision any time you realize that content, structure, organization, or lines of reasoning can be improved.

LARGE-SCALE QUESTIONS

1. *Audience.* Who is the audience? What is the reader's level of education? What is the reader's previous knowledge or opinions about the subject? What does the reader expect of this piece of writing? How will the reader use the writing? What will the reader do or think as a result of having read this writing? Is the writing appropriate for the readers and the situation?

2. *Main Idea.* What do I want to say to the reader? Does everything in the piece of writing help to get that point across? Is there material I should add or delete?

3. *Development and Organization.* What are the main sections? What is the topic of each? (List the main ideas of each section, in order.) Are these the points that best help me achieve my purpose for the readers? Are the points in sensible order for my purpose and reader? Are there points that should be added, deleted, or combined? Are the points sufficiently developed with explanation, proof, or illustration?

4. *Coherence.* Is it clear to the reader what the point of each section and each paragraph is and how that section or paragraph fits the main idea and the previous paragraph? (Focus attention especially on the clues given to readers in the first and last sentences of each paragraph.) Does everything in the paragraph serve the point and purpose of that paragraph? Is the order of material in the paragraph sensible and clear to the reader? Working on the coherence of your writing is covered in detail as an aspect of Step 1 on style. However, the essential coherence of your writing is a large-scale concern.

5. *Tone.* The tone is the attitude the writer assumes in the paper. The tone may be terse and businesslike or leisurely and thoughtful. It may be serious or breezy, distant or friendly, formal or conversational. In general, is the tone appropriate to the readers and the purpose?

6. *Quoting and Citing.* Be sure that whenever you use someone else's information or ideas, you give credit through a citation. A citation is needed even if you say another person's idea in your own words. If you quote the person's words directly, you need both a citation and quotation marks. A citation tells the author, title, and other information about your source. Citations differ. A citation may be included in the text of a paper and/or handled as a footnote or list of references. Consult a handbook or your instructor for the citation form appropriate to a particular type of writing.

MANAGE THE REVISING PROCESS

The revising process involves using the three steps and also managing your time, your recopying of drafts, and your use of helpers. Before discussing the process of revising, these are some suggestions for organizing yourself that have been gathered from talking to hundreds of instructors and students in a variety of classes and studying the thinking and writing processes of students.

1. Leave enough time for revision—probably the single biggest problem of a student writer. How much time is enough? Each writer must determine how much time to spend on preparation, writing a first draft, and revision. Some writers do most of their planning before they produce the first draft and then perform minimal revisions. Other writers produce rough first drafts very early in the process and then spend most of their writing time on extensive revisions. Expert writers fit into both of these categories. Ask yourself which style best suits you, the

situation, and the time frame in which you must work. For the best paper you've ever written, how much time did you spend on revision? How much do you wish you'd been able to spend?

A rough guide for students writing academic papers is to leave half of the total time for revision. That means if there are four weeks for a paper, do the research, planning, and make the first draft in the initial two weeks, leaving two weeks for large-scale and local-level revisions. Students often benefit from spending up to three quarters of their total time on revisions if the paper derives primarily from personal reflection, observation, and memory.

Figure out how much time it takes you to follow this book's three steps. Then always leave *double* that amount of time at the end, because as you work on the local revisions, you will almost always find large-scale revisions you didn't see earlier. Also, leave enough time to proofread for typing errors.

2. Concentrate first on the large-scale questions. Be ready to switch to large-scale revisions any time you find problems in content, organization, or reasoning. Use the large-scale questions to check yourself.

3. Don't try to revise a messy draft. Retype or recopy as needed, before you begin your final check through the three steps. If you make major changes in Step 1, on style, you may want to retype or recopy before checking grammar, punctuation, and spelling. In our studies of student writing, many grammar, punctuation, and spelling errors occurred in language that had been written in between the lines or in the margins during revisions. The writer didn't fully integrate the new language with the old or couldn't clearly see grammatical relationships through the messiness of the revision.

Using a word processor saves recopying and gives you a clean, current version of your paper. Most writers find that it's well worth the time it takes to learn word processing.

4. Avoid useless copying. Any time you find yourself re-copying passages with few or no changes, examine your proce-

dures. Many students waste time recopying. For example, one student wrote out a second draft, 95 percent of which was no different from her first draft, and then she wrote another draft for the typist, again making only a few changes. So 90 percent of the words in that paper were written three times in exactly the same form and sequence. If you're going to copy something over with no change, cut it out of its page and tape it onto your new page.

Use the photocopier to help you prepare the final copy of your paper. You can tape typed pieces of former drafts onto sheets of paper, typing in new parts and page numbers. Make sure the lines of type on the taped parts are even with the new lines you type in. Use a high-quality photocopier to duplicate your taped page—the tape won't show and the copy will look as sharp and clear as the original. Use the copy as your hand-in version. You can make it look even better if you insert high-quality typing paper into the photocopier.

5. Use word processing. When people get a new tool, they seem to use it first merely as a substitute for the old tools. Only later do they begin to exploit the real potential of the new tool to do things the old tool could not do. That's probably going to be the way you use a computer. At first it may be a glorified typewriter, used only for the final copy. But if you can, you should train yourself to compose on the computer, or at least to begin using it for your second draft, so that you can move sections, add new pieces, and delete chunks of what you've written without ever having to retype what remains unchanged. You'll also have a clean copy at all times, so you can see what you're doing. We've talked to expert writers who find that, though they know a computer would save them time, they still need their good old number 2 pencils and legal pads for early drafts. Many other expert writers, however, have gradually learned to use the computer early in the writing process and find it saves them significant time and energy.

Eric Batt is a good example. A freshman at Loyola College in Maryland, he had to write a number of papers for composition class and for other classes. He used the computer lab in his school's library for all his papers. He'd begin a paper by entering his rough ideas into the computer. Then he'd add to his list of ideas as he did research, pondered his topic, or talked with teachers and classmates. Gradually he worked the rough lists into drafts. He ran off lots of paper copies so he could see what he had. When he came for a conference with an instructor, he'd bring along a clean copy of his paper in its current form, they'd talk it over, then he'd go back to the computer and change some more, sometimes using what he had as a base, sometimes scrapping whole sections and starting them over. "I just keep pushing them along," he said. During the last part of the semester, as each paper was due, he spent an evening making final changes, putting the paper through the computer's spelling check, and running off a final copy. "I'm doing a paper a night," he said in his last week, "but it's not so bad because the papers have all been in the computer; I've been working on them for a long time. It's kind of fun."

6. Be ready to make changes. Some students believe that having to make major revisions in their writing is a sign of incompetence. On the contrary, expert writers make more extensive changes than novices. As you become more experienced, you will revise more, not less.

Part of being ready to make changes is being able to forsake what you've already written. When you write the words down, make up your mind that you will discard them, move them, or change them, as needed. In early drafts, don't invest more time than necessary in recopying or in fixing up punctuation and spelling, because that investment of time just makes your first draft words more difficult to throw away or change.

Another part of being ready to change is building your revising skills. Then, when you have to cross out some words or pages you've penned, you don't have to fear that the new words you choose may have just as many problems as the ones you discarded. Instead, you can apply the guidelines you've learned to make your revised passages more effective than the previous ones. If you make large-scale revisions in light of the large-scale questions, and local-level revisions using the systematic steps and lessons in this book, you should gradually gain confidence to revise effectively.

USE HELPERS WISELY

A *helper* is anyone who talks with you about your ideas for a paper or who comments on a draft you've written.

You can use helpers in at least three ways:

1. at the beginning, to help you plan and talk through your ideas;
2. to help you as you deal with the large-scale questions in a draft;
3. to help you as you conduct the local revisions.

In this section we'll focus on the third one. One common problem, especially with peer and friend helpers, and sometimes with student tutors, is that they want to focus on grammar and punctuation while there are still major flaws in the paper's content, organization, or reasoning. If this happens, ask the helper to respond to each of the large-scale questions in this section. Once those questions are answered satisfactorily, bring a clean draft for help with the local concerns.

Select appropriate helpers. Your instructor is probably your best source of help when you want to check the large-scale concerns or when you need help with the phrasing, vocabulary, or style that is appropriate for your audience and discipline.

Tutors are another resource. Find out whether your school has a writing center or tutoring service and use it. Writing centers are not for dummies; they're for smart writers. Skilled and experienced writers seek helpers as a matter of course. Writing-center staff are usually glad to help you with large-scale concerns, but, if the tutor is unfamiliar with your class and professor, you're better off going to your instructor. The tutors usually will be well equipped to help you with style, grammar, punctuation, and spelling. If you know you'll need help with those aspects, begin working in the writing center at the beginning of a semester and go there regularly, not just the day before a paper is due.

Classmates, parents, spouses, and friends can help, if you choose them wisely. For testing ideas and for large-scale revising, look for someone who has a logical way of thinking and who writes in a well-organized way. It helps if the person has taken your course or is majoring in the discipline. For help with local revising, look for someone who has a good sense of language and a knowledge of style, grammar, and punctuation.

DO YOUR OWN LOCAL REVISING; THEN GET HELP

Revising your own writing is one of the best ways to learn. If you give your paper to someone who fixes the style, grammar, punctuation, and spelling without your participation, then you've let your helper diminish your education. The following is a suggested procedure:

1. Do your own best revising.
2. Recopy or cut-and-paste as needed to get a reasonably clean copy so your helper can see what's there.
3. Ask your helper to make direct suggestions about style, saying, for example, "This passage seems awkward," or "Is this the word you want?" but don't let the helper phrase your prose for you. For aspects of grammar, punctuation, and spelling, ask the helper to put a pencil check in the margin by any line that has a problem but not to tell you exactly where or what the problem is.

THE REVISING PROCESS

4. See whether you can find and revise the problems.
5. Ask your helper to check the paper again and to discuss with you any remaining problems so you can understand what the helper thinks is wrong. Turn to the relevant lesson in this book and have the helper guide you through it.

Helpers may sometimes give bad advice. Don't be afraid to rely on your own knowledge and on this book, even if your helper is a more advanced student. One freshman followed a friend's very poor advice about what to revise in his paper. When asked why his new draft was so stiff and awkward, and why there were some new errors not present in his old draft, he admitted he'd let his own better judgment be overruled by his friend and hadn't bothered to check his friend's punctuation advice against a handbook.

The last part of this section treats each of the three steps in turn, discussing how to follow each step, and outlining the substeps. Whenever you need explanations for a substep, turn to the corresponding lesson in the next section of the book.

* *A Process Guide to Step One:* Read with Attention to Meaning and Revise for Style *

This section of the book is a guide to the revising process for each of the three steps. A reviser reads differently and notices different aspects for each step.

WHAT IS STYLE?

Good style in writing means prose that reads smoothly, with paragraphs and sentences that are clear and concise. Choices of style are not right or wrong, as with spelling or apostrophes. Style is a matter of judgment—of deciding what will be most clear, most appropriate, and most easy to read.

Some aspects of style may change for different purposes. In one case, your writing may be scholarly and thoughtful, with complex sentences that incorporate fine shades of meaning. In another case, you may write with short, direct sentences that present businesslike units of information to the reader as efficiently and quickly as possible. However, the aspects of style that this book discusses are basic in virtually any context. Here is general advice about revising for style. The substep lessons, in a later section of the book, explain how to follow each substep.

LAY THE PAPER ASIDE

You must have noticed that you can find problems in the writing of someone else more easily than in your own. That's because you're too familiar with your own words. To help yourself get a fresh perspective, lay your writing aside for as long as you can—a week or a few days are ideal. If you're working within a short time frame, even a few hours will probably help, especially if you do something during those few hours that refreshes you, like sleeping, eating, going for a walk, or talking with friends.

READ ALOUD, LISTENING FOR AWKWARDNESS

Read your draft aloud, paying attention to what the sentences and paragraphs would mean to a *first-time* reader. Mark any sentences that seem unclear or awkward. Mark passages where you have to reread to catch the meaning of a sentence or where you stumble or hesitate as you read. A good companion strategy is to ask a friend to read the draft aloud to you, noting every place where the reader stumbles or has to backtrack to understand the paper. Ask your reader also to indicate any sentences or passages that seem awkward, wordy, or unclear.

THE REWRITE STRATEGY—PROS AND CONS

According to research studies, one strategy of both experts and novices, when they find a sentence or passage that sounds awkward, is to rewrite from scratch, without taking the time to diagnose exactly what's wrong with the original. However, if a writer doesn't have a very precise idea of what makes sentences clear or awkward, the rewritten sentence may not be any better than the original. Thus expert revisers also diagnose and apply specific solutions to improve a drafted sentence. The six Step 1 substeps help you look at a sentence, diagnose its problem, and revise it.

USE THE SUBSTEPS AND RELATED LESSONS

The Step 1 substeps call your attention to certain aspects of sentences that most often are the keys to effective style. Each time you revise a paper, use as many of the substeps as you can, referring to the lessons for explanations and guidelines. During a semester, systematically study the lessons and complete the exercises, to become more skillful at using the substeps.

STEP 1A: Choose between active and passive voice verbs (Lesson 1A, p. 104).
STEP 1B: Add transitions and topic clues as needed (Lesson 1B, p. 115).
STEP 1C: Use main subject/verb units and sentence openings appropriately for clarity and emphasis (Lesson 1C, p. 128).
STEP 1D: Relate sentence parts clearly to one another (Lesson 1D, p. 153).
STEP 1E: Tighten to eliminate wordiness (Lesson 1E, p. 176).
STEP 1F: Check word choices for precision (Lesson 1F, p. 183).
STEP 1G:

[In this space, and on the inside front cover, add any guidelines important to a particular situation or type of writing you must do.]

MARK SUBSTEPS FOR EMPHASIS

As you use the substeps to revise a piece of writing, mark those you want to study more thoroughly. When a paper is returned to you, mark the substeps that remained your greatest problems, even after you'd revised. Use pencil marks on the outline on the inside front cover. Your marks can be the basis for your study between papers.

BE WILLING TO MAKE LARGE-SCALE CHANGES

One reason for leaving yourself plenty of time for revision is that some large-scale problems are invisible until you begin local revision; then they suddenly appear. If you're revising an awkward sentence, and you realize that the point of the entire passage isn't clear or well supported, or that you've used a key term in an ambiguous way, be ready to put the local revisions on hold, and go back to large-scale revisions.

 A Process Guide to Step 2: Read and Revise for Grammar and Punctuation

UNDERSTAND GRAMMAR, PUNCTUATION, AND HUMAN LANGUAGE

When people first began to write, everything was capitalized with no punctuation and no spaces: WHENPEOPLEFIRST BEGANTOWRITEEVERYTHINGWASCAPITALIZED WITHNOPUNCTUATIONANDNOSPACESHARDTO READISNTIT

Hard to read, isn't it? You've perhaps never before appreciated that the written sentence, with its capital letters, periods, commas, quotation marks, and other punctuation, is a stunning invention, though it brings lots of grief to writers who have to learn where to put all those commas, capitals, and periods. At first, writers inserted periods and commas wherever they thought a unit of speech had ended or where they wanted the reader to take a breath, but human nature seems to want to regularize language use and make it more predictable. So gradually writers developed a system for punctuation and grammar. When there's a rule, there's also the possibility of an error. So terms were developed to describe a writer's errors. You're the inheritor of this glorious history of human ingenuity. Your ear is not a totally reliable guide to punctuation—you can't just place periods and commas where your reader would pause for breath. You have to know the rules and be able to apply them. If you don't, readers can become annoyed and exasperated, because their sense of order is frustrated and their ability to predict the structure of your language, based on your punctuation, is disrupted. Step 2 helps you learn the rules of written English punctuation.

Unlike punctuation, which pertains only to writing, grammar pertains to both speaking and writing. Children internalize the grammatical rules of the language they hear spoken while growing up and know almost all grammar by the time they're five. So why is grammar such a problem for adult writers? It's a problem because language is always changing. For example, take two groups of people who speak the same language, and put them on two different desert islands with no boats, TVs, telephones, or newspapers. After a couple of generations, both groups will have changed their ways of speaking—developed different accents, added new words to their language, used old words in some new ways. If people from the two groups meet, they will sound strange to one another. Neither group is less intelligent than the other and neither version of the language (called a dialect) is better; they're just different. This ability to change language allows humans to adapt their language to suit new circumstances—an essential and powerful tool for survival. However, since we *do* have TVs and telephones, and we *do* communicate with one another, a Standard English has developed as the language of communication for jobs, schools, civic affairs—places where various groups must understand and be understood.

Nearly everyone uses a slightly different language in the poolroom from the language they use in the classroom. But some American speakers' language is quite different from Standard English. If you've grown up speaking a kind of English different from standard, your own language isn't inherently inferior, and you shouldn't let others make you feel ashamed of it, or of your family, neighborhood, or culture. The rules of grammar set out in this book are the rules for speaking and writing Standard English. Other forms are neither "bad" nor "ignorant." They're just not usually considered appropriate in academic, business, and civic settings.

Teachers, professionals, and employers place heavy importance on grammar and punctuation. Problems in these areas can make a reader think that the writer didn't know or didn't care to polish his or her writing. The reader may become so annoyed, that the ideas, no matter how brilliant, never get through.

In one typical scholarship competition, for example, student applicants were asked to write personal essays. The judges had to select two winners from many applicants. Their first step was to eliminate all applications that did not adhere to Standard English grammar, punctuation, and spelling. That eliminated one third of the applicants! The students had spent a great deal of time gathering transcripts and letters of recommendation, and composing essays, but their work was immediately disqualified because they didn't take the time and care to revise for grammar and punctuation.

STEP 2 SUBSTEPS MAY BE USED IN ANY SEQUENCE

The substeps of Step 2 are arranged in priority order, beginning with problems that are most disturbing to readers. However, in the revising process you may scramble the substeps a bit, revising problems as you encounter them. Also, the Step 2 lessons can be used in any sequence. Whenever a lesson depends on a grammatical point covered in an earlier lesson, you are referred back to the one you need.

MASTER SUBSTEPS GRADUALLY

If the first few substeps give you trouble, you may at first want to limit your attention only to what you can handle. If you check a draft only for the first few substeps, at least you will have dealt with the problems that are most bothersome to readers. Later, as you become more skilled and study more of the lessons, you can revise using more of the substeps.

USING THE SUBSTEPS IN DIFFERENT WAYS

You can use a substep in a variety of ways: you can use it as a reminder for revision, you can study it, or you can skip it altogether.

Take the first substep, Sentence Fragments, as an example. If you never write sentence fragments, then skip this substep and go to the next. If you sometimes write fragments, but you know how to find and revise them, then use this substep as a reminder and check your writing for fragments. If you don't know whether you write fragments, or if you know you sometimes write fragments and don't know how to find and fix them, read the lesson.

HOW TO READ AND REVISE IN STEP 2

In Step 1, rely on your own ear, and on the ears of others, to hear when a sentence or passage is unclear or awkward. To augment that strategy, you use general guidelines, each of which leaves room for individual judgment. In Step 2, your ear is only sometimes reliable as a guide because you may not hear incorrect punctuation and because grammatical forms that are not Standard English may nevertheless sound right to you, since they're often used in informal speaking situations. Thus, in Step 2, you must also learn to spot the forms that differ from Standard written English, even if they sound all right. This requires reading with attention to grammatical relationships and punctuation. As you read your draft, place a mental highlight on those aspects.

USE THE PROCESS DIAGRAMS

The processes of applying rules of grammar, punctuation, and spelling are represented in this text by process diagrams. The diagram outlines the steps used to apply a rule to your own sentences. Figure 2.1 is an example of a process diagram, representing what to do if you're sitting at home and you feel cold.

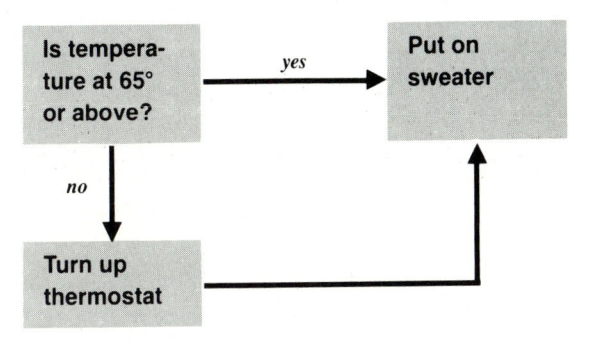

FIGURE 2.1   An Example of a Process Diagram: What to Do If You Feel Cold

Note that you progress from left to right and from top to bottom. You move from one box to another in two ways—by making a decision (such as yes or no) or simply by following the unmarked arrow that leads to the next operation. That's how the diagrams work for grammar and punctuation. You can follow them as you revise. Flip through the Step 2 lessons now, noting the process diagrams. When you study a lesson, use the diagram as an outline of the lesson and a guide to revision.

TWO WAYS TO READ AND REVISE IN STEP 2

An ineffective reviser reads through a draft by looking vaguely for everything at once. Try to get away from this strategy. The key is to read for fewer things at a time, so you can catch more of them.

Within that basic guideline, there are two ways to read and revise in Step 2. You'll want to experiment to discover which is most easy and efficient for you.

1. Read the whole paper for one or two substeps; then read the whole paper for the next substep(s).

2. Read a single sentence or paragraph for *all* the substeps (you may read the paragraph several times, looking for different substeps each time). Then read the next sentence or paragraph for all the substeps.

OMIT SUBSTEPS YOU DON'T NEED OR CAN'T YET HANDLE

Whichever approach you use, you'll want to leave out any substeps you never have to revise for. Some people, for example, never miss apostrophes, even in drafts, so they don't need to check or revise for them. You may also concentrate only on some of the substeps in a given revision.

At first you may be able to read for only one or two substeps at a time. With this system, you'll be reading a sentence or passage a number of times. As you gain experience, you will be able to look for more than one thing at a time, you'll become faster at checking for the substeps, and you'll develop inside your head a system of warning bells that go off automatically when your eyes come across a problem. You may also become better at incorporating Standard English grammar and punctuation as you write, so you won't need to revise so extensively for those aspects.

READING PROBLEMS IN STEP 2

A common problem in revising, especially for grammar and punctuation, is not reading exactly what you've written. If you habitually miss problems, even though you read over your drafts for grammar and punctuation, you may not be seeing exactly what you wrote. One remedy is to use a pointer—a pencil or your finger—to point to each word and punctuation mark individually as you read it. Read slowly, concentrating on what's written. If even this method doesn't work, and you continue to miss problems because you don't *see* them, talk to your instructor, writing-center staff member, or a reading teacher. Sometimes such problems are caused by the way your eyes and brain work together to perceive words on the page. Experts can teach you strategies that will help you read more accurately.

PREVIEW OF STEP 2 SUBSTEPS

The rules of grammar and punctuation can be overwhelming. If you look in a handbook of grammar and punctuation, the rules seem to go on forever. But actually, nearly all the problems writers have when revising fall into just five categories:

THE REVISING PROCESS

1. How to mark the beginnings and ends of grammatical sentences, avoiding fragments and run-ons
2. How to form verbs and pronouns—two types of words that change their form according to their role in the sentence
3. How to form possessives and plurals using apostrophes, -*s,* and -*es*
4. How to use punctuation to separate words or groups of words within a sentence
5. How to mark quoted material

These categories are listed in order of importance. That is, readers are generally more upset over a group 1 problem, such as a fragment, than they are over a forgotten apostrophe.

The following are the substeps in Step 2, arranged under these five categories.

STEP	PAGES	TEACHER MARK
Punctuating Sentence Boundaries		
2A Revise Fragments as Needed	203	Frag
2B Avoid Run–Ons	221	Run On, Comma Splice Fused Sentence
Forming Verbs and Pronouns		
Verbs:		
2C Make Verbs Agree With Their Subjects	236	S/V Agr
2D Select Verb Tenses Appropriately	249	Tense
2E Use Standard English Verb Forms	263	Vb Form

Pronouns:

2F	Select Pronouns	276	Pro
2G	Solve *Who/Whom, Him and Him and Me* Debate	290	Case
2H	Give Pronouns Clear Antecedents	297	Antec
2I	Make the Pronoun Agree With Its Antecedent	307	Pro Agr

Apostrophe, -s, and -es

2J	Use Apostrophe, -*S*, and -*ES* Appropriately	315	Plural Apos

Interior Sentence Punctuation

2K	Avoid Commas To Separate Subject/Verb, Verb/Object	331	No Com
2L	Use Comma after Introducer	341	Com-Intro
2M	Use Commas With Nonrestrictive Interrupters and Modifiers	346	Com-Nonrest
2N	Use Parentheses and Dashes With Strong Interrupters	357	( ) Dash
2O	Use Commas to Separate Adjectives in a Series	365	Com-Adj
2P	Punctuate Lists and Series With Colons, Semicolons, and Commas	371	List
2Q	Use Colon or Dash to Announce an Explanation	383	Colon Dash

Quotations

2R	Punctuate Within and Around Quotations	392	Quot

* *A Process Guide to Step 3:* Read with Attention to Individual Words and Letters, and Check Spelling *

HOW TO READ IN STEP 3

Step 3 requires special strategies that help a writer focus on individual letters in words. Many writers like to read their drafts backward. This technique keeps them from gliding along with the meaning of the sentences and helps them concentrate on the individual words and letters. Some writers also like to use a pointer—a pencil or finger—under each word as they read, again to help them focus on each word singly.

Spelling is the most common area where computer software can help you. Appendix A shows how to use a computer to check spelling and other aspects of grammar and punctuation.

A STUDENT'S REVISING PROCESS

The previous sections have suggested strategies for the revision process as a whole and for each of the three steps. To illustrate the revision process in an actual paper, the following is an account of the way a college student, Triana D'Orazio, revised an assignment. D'Orazio's composition class had read Mark Twain's *Adventures of Huckleberry Finn* and had discussed why the novel has been banned in some of our nation's schools. The class was asked to imagine that they were parents, writing to their child's school about a pending decision to ban the novel. For purposes of research, the students also agreed to keep records of how they composed and revised. This case history is compiled from those records.

D'Orazio's first piece of writing was a list of ideas, in which she wisely paid no conscious attention to grammar or punctuation. Her total attention was concentrated on her ideas. That list of ideas is on p. 29.

Next D'Orazio wrote a first draft, again wisely concentrating on her ideas, organization, and lines of reasoning. As she

A STUDENT'S REVISING PROCESS

worked on this draft, she established the sequence of ideas, placing first the request for an open forum, which appears third on her list. During the drafting, and during the rereading immediately after drafting, she read for meaning and concentrated on large-scale issues and issues of style. This was her first round of revision. It included several readings. In the following draft, the changes of her first round are indicated by crossing

D'ORAZIO'S FIRST LIST OF IDEAS

-set up meetings w/ teacher who will be teaching

-ask the students & parents

-invite parents — open forum

what I think Huck is:

    -good reading

    -insightful — comments on racism satirically

-apply it when studying irony or satire

-not for elementary kids

-teach it in advanced courses at the 8th and/or 9th

out the typewritten words and by showing her additions in italics. The handwriting on the draft indicates her *second* round of revision. In that round, which included at least two readings of the draft, she concentrated primarily on style and also began some grammar and punctuation revisions. The draft and the summary of her changes illustrate clearly how she progressed from large-scale revisions through style and into grammar and punctuation.

D'ORAZIO'S FIRST ROUND REVISIONS
(print; additions in italics)
AND SECOND ROUND REVISIONS (handwriting)

Dear Mrs. Rogers:

~~It~~ ~~Mrs.~~ Smith and I received the notice today ~~that~~ *concerning* the Parents and Teacher's Association, ~~along~~ the school board, and administrative officials' ~~have~~ ~~has~~ ~~have~~ ~~decided~~ *decision* to remove Mark Twain's <u>Huckleberry Finn</u> from the library, as well

5 as from the classroom. This is insane! No prev*i*ous notice was given *to us. and* ~~I~~ ~~have~~ ~~consulted w/ other~~ ~~parents~~ Mrs Smith and I missed the Jan 15th meeting due to a previous engagement—I assume th*i*s~~at~~ was when the decision was reached. I consulted with a few

10 parents who do not belong to the PTA, and they were *also* not aware of the situation until now. Only 22 parents ~~comprise the PTA~~ regularly attend PTA meetings, and, when such a decision is reached, I believe it is an injustice to the remaining 64 fathers and mothers. ~~The~~

15 ~~parents are concerned w/ their children & wish to involve themselves in~~ How can such a decision be ~~reached~~ *made* w/out the approval of all? I believe, or rather, I insist, that a meeting be scheduled and formatted as an "open-forum". All parents should be invited to attend

20 and offer their views and on whether H.F. *as well as our childrens' education* should be

> banned, ~~and our children's education banned~~. [The draft continued with a discussion of the reasons for the writer's objection to banning *Huck Finn*. She signed her letter with a pseudonym, "Bettina Smith."]

In the summary that follows, the revisions are classified by type.

You can see that D'Orazio is progressing from large-scale questions to local revisions and that she gives her draft several readings, first concentrating primarily on meaning and style, and then more heavily on grammar and punctuation. You should go through the same sequence, focusing your rereading

SUMMARY OF D'ORAZIO'S FIRST AND SECOND ROUND REVISIONS

FIRST ROUND OF REVISION (in type; additions in italics)	SECOND ROUND OF REVISION (handwritten changes)
Large-scale —Changed the gender of the letter's writer (l. 1). —Crossed out 3 sentence openings and began new ideas (ll. 1, 6, 14).	(No large-scale changes)
Style —Changed "comprise" to "regularly attend" for clarity (l. 12). —Changed "this" to "that" (l. 8).	*Revised structure of last sentence (l. 20). *Added "also" for clarity (l. 10).

THE REVISING PROCESS

—Corrected facts
(ll. 2, 6).

*Changed "reached" to "made" (l. 17).

Grammar/Punctuation
—Changed "have/has" for subject-verb agreement (l. 3).

*Restructured first sentence to avoid agreement problem.

*Deleted a comma (l. 18).

*Changed place of a comma (l. 12).

Spelling/Abbreviation
—Corrected spelling of "previous" (l. 5 Not clear when this change occurred).

---

upon limited concerns and trying not to look for everything at once. Like D'Orazio, you may mix the steps together a bit—for example, if you're reading for style and you see a misspelled word or a misplaced comma, you may fix it right away. You should read initially for meaning and for sentence structures and word choices that affect meaning, then read for punctuation and grammar. Later, D'Orazio concentrated heavily on spelling and abbreviations as a last step. Before she got to that stage, however, she realized she needed to return to large-scale revision.

D'Orazio took her draft to a conference with her instructor who helped her see that, although she had been doing local revising and thought her letter was almost finished, her draft still had major problems in content and tone. Her instructor asked her how she thought the principal would react to having the school's actions termed "insane." The instructor urged D'Orazio to acknowledge and discuss the disadvantages of the recommendations she was urging on the school, and to deal with what was probably the principal's worst fear—the fear of adverse publicity about the school in the public media.

SUMMARY OF D'ORAZIO'S FIRST AND SECOND ROUND REVISIONS

Spurred by these thoughts, D'Orazio realized that her draft was, as she put it, "rather bombastic and insultive." To suddenly realize that major changes are still needed is a rather common experience for writers, even after they've begun revising a draft for local concerns. D'Orazio made the right move at this point—she temporarily abandoned her local revising and returned to large-scale revisions. In all, her changes affected nearly half the total lines in her paragraph.

Now D'Orazio moved into her fourth and final stage of revision. As she wrote her second draft, the one she would hand in, she gave her primary attention to small details: style (but only single-word substitutions), grammar, punctuation, and spelling/abbreviations. As necessary, she used this book to look up questions such as where to place the apostrophe in *children's,* and where to put the period after *open-forum.*

D'ORAZIO'S THIRD ROUND REVISIONS
(Also Shown As Printed Crossouts and Italics in Draft, Next Page)

Large-Scale

—Removed the accusatory sentence, "This is insane!"

—Added material to show she sympathized with the principal's difficult job.

—Added material to acknowledge a possible drawback in her recommendation.

—Omitted irrelevant material about missing the January meeting.

(No revisions in style, grammar, punctuation, or spelling.)

THE REVISING PROCESS

The following is the final version of the first paragraph. D'Orazio's third round (large-scale) changes are indicated by print cross-outs, with her additions in italics. Her fourth round revisions, all for grammar, spelling, and punctuation, are indicated in this draft by handwritten corrections. The draft is arranged this way so you can clearly distinguish round 3 from round 4 revisions. However, what D'Orazio actually did was try to produce her final copy directly from her original draft, with all its messy additions and deletions, including the extensive round 3 revisions, which were written on the back of her paper, with asterisks to indicate where they should be inserted in her draft. This attempt to go directly from a very messy draft to her final draft left D'Orazio with some awkward sentences in her hand-in version.

D'ORAZIO'S FOURTH ROUND REVISIONS
(Also Shown as Handwriting in Draft, Below)

Style

—Removed an unnecessary "that is."

—Substituted "be" for "act as."

—Substituted "realize" for "know."

Grammar, Punctuation

—Corrected "your" to "you are."

—Corrected "childrens'" to "children's."

—Corrected punctuation with quotation marks.

Spelling, Abbreviations

—Wrote out the numbers twenty-two and sixty-four, instead of using numerals.

—Wrote out and underlined title of *Huck Finn.*

—Added periods within abbreviation of P.T.A.

SUMMARY OF D'ORAZIO'S FIRST AND SECOND ROUND REVISIONS

D'ORAZIO'S THIRD ROUND (print, additions in italics)
AND FOURTH ROUND REVISIONS (handwriting)

Dear Mrs. Rogers:

Mr. Smith and I received the notice today concerning the Parents and Teachers' Association, the school board, and administrative officials' decision to remove Mark Twain's Huckleberry Finn from the library, as well as from the classroom. ~~This is insane!~~ No previous notice was given to us. ~~Mrs. Smith and I missed the Jan 15th meeting due to a previous engagement. I assume that was when the decision was reached.~~ I consulted with a few parents who do not belong to the ~~PTA~~ *P.T.A.*, and they were also not aware of the situation until now. *I understand and sympathize w*/~~*ith*~~ *the position you are in*~~*your in*~~. *You must* ~~*act as*~~ *be a neutral mediator and compromiser and assure everyone's satisfaction—* ~~*that is*~~ *a most certainly difficult job. However, when* ~~*O*~~ *only* ~~22~~ *twenty-two parents regularly attend PTA meetings and, when such a decision is reached, I believe it is an injustice to the remaining* ~~64~~ *sixty-four mothers and fathers. How can such a decision be made without the approval of all? I believe, or rather, I insist that a meeting be scheduled and formatted as an "open-forum." All parents should be invited to attend and offer their views on whether* ~~H.F.~~ *Huck Finn, as well as our children's education, should be banned. I realize* ~~*know*~~ *this might create unwanted publicity, but it must be done. The banning of the book will eventually reach the media, and so may the displeasure of many unhappy parents. This is not a threat, but a fact.*

35

The strong points of D'Orazio's revision process were the following:

1. She made her first list and her first draft with maximum concentration on the large-scale problems.

2. Once she saw further large-scale problems, she returned to large-scale revision, even though she had already invested time in local revisions.

3. In conducting her local revisions, she reread her paper a number of times, reading aloud and listening to her own language.

4. In general, she first read for meaning and concentrated primarily on style. In later rereadings, she made changes in grammar, punctuation, and spelling.

Had D'Orazio been a more experienced reviser, she probably would have done some things differently:

1. She might have asked the large-scale questions earlier in her revising process, before she began revising for style and punctuation, instead of waiting for her instructor to push her into the large-scale questions.

2. To help her with the large-scale questions, she might have sought her instructor's help as soon as she had her rough draft penned, before she invested time in local revision.

3. She might have focused her rereadings even more specifically, checking certain aspects each time. That way, she would not have been trying to fix awkwardness, spelling, and punctuation, all in the same reading.

4. She might have looked up rules instead of guessing. For example, instead of looking up subject-verb agreement rules in her first sentence, she changed to an awkward construction that created problems with apostrophes, which she never completely straightened out.

5. Several of the more serious local problems remaining in her final paper occur at points where she earlier made revisions

between the lines or on a separate sheet. Preliminary results from the large research project, of which D'Orazio's records are only a part, indicate that errors in final drafts cluster around points where a student has revised a draft. Because the words become so messy, it is difficult to see sentence relationships. Knowing this, D'Orazio might have given special attention to the style, grammar, and punctuation of her revised passages, recopying as needed to give herself a clean draft.

6. In fact, probably her wisest move would have been to make one more draft, after her large-scale revisions in round 3. Then she could have read that clean draft carefully for style, grammar, and punctuation, before trying to produce her final draft for handing in.

CHAPTER SUMMARY

This chapter has presented suggestions for the writing/revising process in general and for each of the three steps. Also, a student's revising process illustrated how to use the suggestions.

Writers can increase their effectiveness and efficiency if they manage the revising process carefully: ask the large-scale questions first, leave enough time for revising, avoid working with drafts that are too messy to see what's happening, avoid useless recopying, use word processing if possible, and be ready to make changes—even extensive changes—when necessary. Writers should choose helpers wisely and use helpers as teachers, not as mere fixers.

Each of the three steps requires different strategies for rereading and revising. For Step 1 revision, read for meaning, read aloud, rely on your ear to indicate awkwardness, ask helpers to read and notice where they stumble or misread. An unclear or awkward passage may be rewritten from scratch, but skilled revisers also learn how to diagnose and revise awkward or unclear sentences.

THE REVISING PROCESS

For Step 2 revision, writers must understand that nonstandard forms are not "bad English," but that readers expect and demand orderliness in language, including the use of standard grammar and of conventional spelling and punctuation. If grammar and punctuation are still difficult, master the substeps gradually, concentrating initially on the first substeps in Step 2. When rereading for Step 2, focus on grammatical relationships and on marks of punctuation, comparing what you see to conventional standards, rules, and forms. The process diagrams show how to perform these comparisons. Mastery of grammar and punctuation is easier when you realize that the rules fall into five major categories: sentence boundaries; forming verbs and pronouns; using apostrophes, -s and -es; separating units within the sentence; and marking quoted material.

To revise for Step 3—spelling and abbreviations—reread backwards or with a pointer, to focus on individual letters.

A student's revising process should begin with the large-scale issues, then follow the same sequence as the steps: matters of style, and, in later rereadings, grammar, punctuation, and spelling. The writer, like the student D'Orazio in the case study, must be ready to return to large-scale revisions at any time. Be willing also to create a clean draft when needed, so that messiness in drafts does not lead to errors.

The next section of the book contains the lessons. Each lesson explains a substep and offers practice in revising for that substep.

EXERCISES

1. Answer the following:

(Answers in instructor's manual)
   a. Five suggestions this chapter makes for the writing process are
   b. In revising, you should *not* use helpers to
   c. In revising, you can benefit by using helpers to
   d. The three steps for revising are

CHAPTER SUMMARY

   e. You should follow the three steps to revising a paper only when you have had a chance to do the lessons for all three steps (T F).
   f. In reading for style, you should read for
   g. It is wasteful to let your draft sit without working on it (T F).
   h. A strategy used by both experts and novices to revise style is
   i. A strategy used primarily by experts to revise style is
   j. The six substeps for Step 1 are
   k. Once you have started revising for grammar and punctuation, you should not return to large-scale revisions (T F).
   l. Some dialects or languages are inherently better than others (T F).
   m. Children do not learn the grammar of their language until they study grammar in school (T F).
   n. Some ethnic groups in America speak bad English (T F).
   o. When you hand in an important piece of writing, readers will concentrate on your ideas and will ignore grammar and punctuation (T F).
   p. The substeps under grammar and punctuation are arranged in a sequence determined by
   q. If the first grammar/punctuation substeps give you great trouble, it is all right to concentrate on the first ones and leave the succeeding ones for later (T F).
   r. Revisers always read exactly what they have written (T F).
   s. Nearly all grammar/punctuation problems for writers fall into these five categories:
   t. In Step 3 revision, you should only read the draft forward, not backward (T F).
2. Imagine that D'Orazio is your friend. She has shared with you her drafts, records, and revising process, as presented in this section. Write her a letter, telling her the strong points of

her revising process and suggesting improvements for her future writing. Revise your letter as needed for large concerns, style, grammar, and punctuation.
3. Take a recent paper you have received back from an instructor and analyze it for problems in style, grammar, punctuation, and spelling. In light of that paper, put check marks on the inside front cover of this book, next to the lessons you most need to study.
4. For the next assignment you write, keep all drafts and notes. If you make more than one round of revisions on a draft, use different colored pencils for each, or, if you're working on a word processor, run a paper copy after each round of revision, and label the copies with date and time of day. In a separate notebook or on tape, keep a careful record of your thoughts and actions as you write and revise the paper. Write in your notebook, or talk on tape, immediately after every session in which you work on the paper. Try to record exactly what you did, what you thought about, what kinds of changes you made and why, what confused or bothered you, what you felt confident about, and why you moved to each different draft or type of revision. Once the paper is finished, write the story of your revising process. In your write-up, include copies of your drafts, with analysis of the kinds of changes you made at each stage of the revision process. At the end of your report, analyze the strong points and weak points of your revision process.
5. Do the same as number 4, but use a classmate as your subject. Begin by asking the classmate to keep all notes, outlines, and drafts and date them. The classmate should also keep a daily record of his or her revising process. Once the classmate has completed the paper, conduct an interview. In the interview, ask the classmate to show you the drafts, telling you how he or she revised the writing, and why. Then write the classmate's story.

INTRODUCTORY LESSON A

IDENTIFYING SUBJECTS AND VERBS

For several kinds of revision treated in this book, you must know how to identify the subjects and verbs in your writing.

Definition: A SUBJECT is a word or group of words that names the person or thing that is performing the action or that is in the state of being named in the verb.

Definition: A VERB is one to four words that name the action or state of being of the subject.

Examples:
   In the following examples, the subject and verb are marked.

      S   V
John bought a cone.
             S   V
The dirty kitten jumped onto the table.

In the second example, the subject, *kitten,* has two modifiers—words that describe it or limit its meaning. The two modifiers are *the* and *dirty.*

Definition: A MODIFIER is a word or group of words that describes or limits the meaning of another word or group of words in the same sentence.

SUBJECTS AND VERBS NEED ONE ANOTHER

You can see from the definitions that subjects are not subjects unless they have verbs, and vice versa. You can never confidently say that a certain word is the subject of a sentence until you've also found the verb that goes with it. Likewise, you can never be sure of the verb until you have found the subject. (A few kinds of sentences have a verb or a subject that is not stated but understood—more on that later.) This book refers to a subject-verb unit, a subject and verb that belong to each other.

DON'T CONFUSE SUBJECTS WITH NOUNS

A common mistake in identifying subjects is to confuse subjects with other nouns, especially nouns appearing early in the sentence.

Definition: A NOUN is a word or group of words that names a person, place, concept, or thing.

You can't just find the first noun, or any noun, in a sentence and assume it is the subject. A noun may *become* a subject in a particular sentence *only if it has a verb in that sentence.* Otherwise, the noun serves some other role. The following are some sentences where the first noun is *not* the subject. The subject is only one of the nouns in the sentence. Subjects, nouns, and verbs are marked. Note that *rings* is both a noun and the subject.

    N   S,N V   N
In the box, seven rings lay wrapped in tissue paper.

HELPING VERBS

A verb can be a word or a phrase having as many as four words. (However, other words may intermingle with the verb words, so the verb words are not always all together). A verb includes the word that names the action or state of being, plus the "helping" verbs. The helping verbs are the following:

Helping Verbs

Forms of *do*
Forms of *will, would, shall, should, can, could, may, might, must, ought, do*
Forms of *have*
Forms of *be* (including *is, are, were, was*)

Verbs form predictable patterns that can have as many as four parts.

Verb Patterns

	Form of did, will, would, could, shall, may	Form of have	Form of be	Main Verb
She	did			eat.
He	could			swim.
The bike	should		be	checked.
The day		has		passed.
Eclipses			were	occurring.
The rug	might	have	been	finished.
Roger				was.
Yes, he				could.

INTRODUCTORY LESSON A

As the last two examples show, any of the helping verbs can also act as main verbs.

EXAMPLES

The family* will start *for California tomorrow.
***He* could have gone *to the picnic, but he* did *not* have transportation.**

(The sentence has two subject-verb units. Note that a modifying word, such as *not,* may appear in the midst of verb words.)

A horse* will *usually* become *frisky in cold weather.

(*Frisky* is a modifier describing the horse; it is not part of the verb. This construction is common with verbs of being, seeming, and becoming. For example, the horse *seems* frisky, *acts* frisky, *appears* frisky, and *was* frisky. These verbs differ from verbs that express an action influencing the subject: The ball *was hit.*)

DON'T CONFUSE VERBS WITH OTHER WORDS THAT NAME ACTIONS OR STATES OF BEING

A typical sentence will have several words that name actions or states of being, but not all of them will be verbs. To be a true verb in a sentence, an action/being word must have a subject. The following sentence has several action/being words, only one of which is a verb.

      S   V
Running around from store to store is not my idea of a relaxing holiday.

Running is not a verb; it has no subject word. Instead, *running* is the subject of the verb *is*. *Relaxing* is not a verb, again because it has no subject word that tells who is relaxing. A reader of this sentence can determine who is running and relaxing, but that's not good enough. There must be an actual word that names the person or thing that is doing the action or is in the state of being named in the verb.

WORDS WITH *-ING*, WITHOUT HELPERS, ARE NOT VERBS

Another way to tell that *running* and *relaxing* are not being used as verbs is that they have no helpers. If an *-ing* word is without a helper, it is not a verb.

Exception: Sometimes an *-ing* word is the second or third verb in the subject-verb unit, and the *-ing* word is understood to use the first verb's helper.

The farm hands were feeding the livestock and breaking the horses.

(The helping verb *were* serves both parts of the verb—*were feeding* and [*were*] *breaking*. Both the *-ing* words are verbs.)

ACTION/BEING WORDS PRECEDED BY *TO* ARE NOT VERBS

She wanted to have a party.

In the preceding sentence, *to have* is not a verb. Any action/being word that has *to* in front of it is not a verb in its sentence. The verb in the sentence is *wanted*. The subject is *she*.

INTRODUCTORY LESSON A

THE VERB MAY PRECEDE THE SUBJECT

In many sentences, the subject comes first. In the following sentence, the verb comes first.

      V   S
Above the door was a sprig of mistletoe.

A SUBJECT-VERB UNIT MAY HAVE MULTIPLE SUBJECTS AND VERBS

A subject-verb unit may have more than one person or thing as a subject and more than one action or state of being as a verb.

    S   S   V
The team and the coach celebrated the victory.

(Two subjects belong to the same verb.)

      S   V
The exuberant swimmers picked up their coach and
  V
dunked her in the pool.

(Two verbs belong to the same subject.)

    S   S   V   V
Then the players and the coach showered, dressed, and
  V
went to the victory party.

(Two subjects belong to the same group of three verbs. The sentence contains only one subject-verb unit, because all of the subjects as a group belong to all of the verbs as a group.)

Once you have two or more verbs, *each with a different subject,* then you have two or more subject-verb units.

IDENTIFYING SUBJECTS AND VERBS

    S1   S1 V1
Some swimmers and officials went to take their showers,
  S2   V2
but Donna stayed to talk to fans.

(There are two subject-verb units: *swimmers/officials went* and *Donna stayed.*)

SEPARATING THE SUBJECT FROM ITS MODIFIERS

A subject is often surrounded by its modifiers. To find the subject, first locate the verb, then ask who or what is doing/being what the verb names.

          V
The bear caught in the trap was unharmed.

(Identify *was* as the verb, then ask "who/what was?" The answer is *bear,* so *bear* is the subject.)

OBJECT OF A PREPOSITION IS NOT THE SUBJECT

Definition: A PREPOSITION is a word, usually short, that shows direction or relation. It has an object following it; together the preposition and its object (with any modifiers) are called a prepositional phrase.

The following are some prepositional phrases.

SAMPLE PREPOSITIONAL PHRASES

 after the ring dance
 about Cinderella
 around the large room

between the devil and the deep blue sea (The preposition has two objects.)
from dancing
in the act
near me (However, *near* may sometimes function not as a preposition, but as a modifier, as in *He was a near neighbor.*)
on my honor
over my dead body
to the barricades (*To* is different from the *to* that may be used in front of a verblike word, as in *to play.*)
under the drinking age
up the staircase
with my doctor's help

A word that is the object of a preposition is never the subject of a verb.

A group of people ran toward the park.

(*People* is not the subject because it is the object of the preposition *of.* Instead, *group* is the subject.) Be sure the word is actually being used as a preposition. In the following sentence, *after* is not a preposition.

After the people left, we relaxed on the couch.

(*After* is *not* a preposition. Instead, it modifies the verb *relaxed,* telling *when* we relaxed. The sentence has two subject-verb units: *people left* and *we relaxed.* The only preposition is *on.* Its object is *couch.*)

THE SUBJECT MAY BE A PRONOUN

Pronouns are words that substitute for nouns.

Some Common Pronouns

I, we, you, he, she, they, who, which, that, this

Any of these words may (but does not necessarily) act as a subject in a sentence. In the following example, the subjects are underlined.

Although we knew that man, he didn't speak to us.
That was very rude.

(The first *that* is not a subject but merely modifies *man*.)

A SUBJECT MAY BE MORE THAN ONE WORD

A subject is usually a single word. Sometimes, however, a subject may be a group of words. That group may even contain its own subject and verb.

Subject as a single word: Near our mountain cabin, icy *water* from a spring tumbles down a tiny waterfall.

Subject as a verblike phrase: Merely *having survived* was an amazing feat.

Subject as a group of words containing its own subject-verb unit: *That he recovered* was a miracle.

USE OF *IT, THERE*

It is often a subject.

It was a good game.
It was raining.
It was hard *to decide on a color.*
It was clear *that he had won the race.*

In the last two examples, the *it* postpones the real subject (in italics). You can identify these kinds of sentences because they make sense when turned around: *To decide on a color was hard.* The verb is *was*. What *was?* The subject is *to decide on a color.*

There is almost never a subject.

There were nine pigs in the pen.
Verb: *were*
What were?
Subject: *pigs*

INTRODUCTORY LESSON A

EXAMPLES

The following are sample sentences to help you find subjects.

Beauty of face and body is not as important as generosity of spirit.

Verb: *is*
Subject: *beauty*
(*Face* and *body* cannot be subjects because they are the objects of the preposition *of.*)

After basking in the sun on shipboard for half the day, the royal guests, by then thoroughly relaxed, took an invigorating swim in the pool.

Verb: *took*
(*Swim* is not the verb because it describes what the guests took. The reader knows that the guests swam, but there is no word in the sentence that acts as a subject for the word *swim.* Instead, *guests* is the subject of the verb *took.*)
Subject: (Who took?) *guests*

To win requires patience and strength.

Verb: *requires*
Subject: (What requires?) *to win*
(The subject is a verblike word formed with *to.*)

Winning requires patience and strength.

Verb: *requires*
Subject: (What requires?) *winning*
(The subject is a verblike word ending in -*ing.*)

Whoever wants to win must have patience and strength.

Verb: *must have*
Subject: *whoever wants to win*
(The entire group of words acts as a subject. That group has its own subject, *whoever,* and its own verb, *wants.*)

FINDING SUBJECTS AND VERBS IN YOUR WRITING

The goal of this lesson is for you to identify the subjects and verbs in your own writing, so you can become a more effective reviser. The process diagram (Figure Intro A.1) shows how to proceed. Start at the upper left and move with the arrows. The following example shows how the process works with an actual piece of writing. The passage is quite complex in its sentence structure. If you can distinguish the subjects and verbs in this passage, you can handle almost any kind of writing. The sentences are numbered for reference.

> (1) Scientists say, simply, that the tiger is a large, graceful, brightly colored cat that lives in jungles and eats meat. (2) Scientists, hunters, and animal handlers have come to know how strong a tiger can be. (3) In fact, people who know both the tiger and the lion say that the tiger is more powerful. (4) Residents of isolated villages in tiger territory know the fear of a tiger that, because it is old, diseased, or unable to hunt its normal prey, has turned to killing domestic livestock or even people. (5) Wounded, a tiger is very dangerous, especially when protecting its young. (6) A tiger who has been shot but not killed will attack a hunter. (7) Even if the hunter is seated on an elephant, a wounded tiger has been known to leap onto the elephant's back and attack the hunter. (8) All of this is perfectly natural, self-protective behavior by an animal that is merely trying to survive, eat, and protect itself from enemies; however, story and legend have transformed the tiger into an almost supernatural creature of cruelty and mystery. (9) For example, Rudyard Kipling, in his *Jungle Books,* tells of a scarred tiger called Shere Khan, who is the outlaw of the jungle, killing not only for food, but also for the love of blood. (10) The other animals hate him for his treachery, and they fear him

INTRODUCTORY LESSON A

```
Does word name action or state of being?
  │ no → Not a verb
  │ yes ↓
Preceded by to?
  │ yes → Not a verb
  │ no ↓
-ing without helper?
  │ yes → Not a verb
  │ no ↓
Subject word(s) in the sentence?
  │ no → Subject understood, as in commands/requests?
  │                                │ no → Not a verb
  │                                │ yes → It is a verb
  │ yes ↓
It is a verb
```

FIGURE INTRO A.1 How to Identify Verbs

for his viciousness and cruelty. (11) If you've grown up reading Kipling, as many of us have, it's difficult to be objective about tigers.

The following is a process you can follow as you identify the verbs and subjects in this passage. Begin by identifying every word that names an action or state of being. Not all of these words will be verbs, but at least you have a guide to words that may be verbs. Next, look for a subject for each verb, asking

IDENTIFYING SUBJECTS AND VERBS

whether the sentence provides a word that names the person or thing that is doing the action or is in the state of being named in the verb. The following are examples from the passage you've read:

Sentence 1
First action/being word: *say*
Who says?
Subject: *scientists*
Verb: *say*

Next action/being word: *is*
Who is?
Subject: *tiger*
Verb: *is*

Next action/being word: *lives*
Who lives?
Subject: *that* (The subject is not *cat;* in the sentence the word *that* is provided as the subject word for *lives.*)

Next action/being word: *eats*
Who eats?
Subject: *that (Eats* is part of the same subject-verb unit as *lives* because they share the same subject—*that.)*

Sentence 2
First action/being words: *have come to know (To know* is not technically part of the verb because the verb *know* is preceded by *to.)*
Who have come?
Subject: *scientists, hunters, handlers* (Three subject words belong to the same verb.)
Verb: *have come*

Next action/being words: *can be*
Who can be?
Subject: *tiger*
Verb: *can be*

INTRODUCTORY LESSON A

Sentence 3 First action/being word: *know*
Who know?
Subject: *who (People* is not the subject of *know* because the sentence uses *who* as the subject word. *People* is the subject of the later verb, *say.)*
Verb: *know*

Next action/being word: *say*
Who say?
Subject: *people*
Verb: *say*

Next action/being word: *is*
Who is?
Subject: *tiger*
Verb: *is*

Sentence 4 First action/being word: *know*
Who know?
Subject: *residents (Isolated villages* and *tiger territory* are not the subjects because they are objects of prepositions.)
Verb: *know*

Next action/being word: *fear*
Who fear?
There is no word that names the subject of *fear*. The word *people* is not the subject because *people* is the subject of *know*. The word *fear* is not a verb in this sentence.

Next action/being word: *is*
Who is?
Subject: *it*
Verb: *is*

Next action/being word: *to hunt*
It is not a verb because it is preceded by *to*.

Next action/being word: *has turned*
What has turned?

IDENTIFYING SUBJECTS AND VERBS

Subject: *that (Tiger* is not the subject because the sentence provides the word *that* as the subject word for *has turned.)*

Next action/being word: *killing*
It is not a verb because it is an *-ing* word used without a helping verb.

Sentence 5

First action/being word: *wounded*
Who wounded?
Wounded is not a verb because it has no subject. Instead, it modifies *tiger*.

Next action/being word: *is*
Who is?
Subject: *tiger*
Verb: *is*

Next action/being word: *protecting*
It is not a verb because it is an *-ing* word used without a helping verb.

Sentence 6

First action/being word: *has been shot*
What has been shot?
Subject: *who*
Verb: *has been shot*

Next action/being word: *killed*
Who killed?
No one killed. The tiger *has been killed. Killed* and *shot* share the same helpers—*has been*. The subject of both verbs is *who*.
Who has been killed?
Subject: *who*
Verb: *[has been] killed*

Next action/being word: *will attack*
Who will attack?
Subject: *tiger*
Verb: *will attack*

INTRODUCTORY LESSON A

Sentence 7　First action/being word: *is seated*
Who is seated?
Subject: *hunter*
Verb: *is* (*Seated* is not part of the verb, but is an adjective modifying *hunter*.)
Next action/being word: *wounded*
Who wounded?
Wounded is not a verb, but a word modifying *tiger*.
Next action/being word: *has been known to leap*
To leap is a form with *to,* so is not a verb.
Who has been known?
Subject: *tiger*
Verb: *has been known*
Next action/being word: *attack*
Who attack?
There is no subject word for *attack*. *Attack* is a companion for *to leap,* and both share the word *to.* Thus the real action word is *to attack,* which is not a verb.

Sentence 8　First action/being word: *is*
What is?
Subject: *all* (*This* is not the subject because it is the object of a preposition.)
Verb: *is*
Next action/being word: *is*
What is?
Subject: *that* (not *animal*)
Verb: *is*
Next action/being word: *trying*
At first, you may think *trying* is an *-ing* word used alone without a helping verb, hence not a verb. However, look back a few words. *Merely*

IDENTIFYING SUBJECTS AND VERBS

interrupts the parts of the verb *is trying*.
Who is trying?

Subject: *that*

Verb: *is trying*

Next action/being words: *to survive, eat, protect*
These all share the same *to*. Thus all are forms with *to*, and cannot be verbs.

Next action/being words: *have transformed*
What have transformed?

Subject: *story, legend* (Two subjects share the same verb.)

Verb: *have transformed*

Sentence 9　First action/being word: *tells*
Who tells?

Subject: *Rudyard Kipling*

Verb: *tells*

Next action/being word: *scarred*
Who scarred?
No one scarred. *Scarred* is not a verb, but a word modifying *tiger*.

Next action/being word: *called*
Who called?
No one called. *Called* is not a verb, but a word modifying *tiger*.

Next action/being word: *is*
Who is?

Subject: *who* (not *tiger*, not *Shere Khan*)

Verb: *is*

Next action/being word: *killing*
Killing is not a verb because it is an -*ing* word used alone without a helping verb. The previous *is* does not act as a helping verb for *is killing*, but acts as its own verb.

Next action/being word: *love*

INTRODUCTORY LESSON A

                    Who love?
                    Love is not a verb, but a noun naming the thing that Shere Khan kills for.

Sentence 10 First action/being word: *hate*
                    Who hate?
                    Subject: *animals*
                    Verb: *hate*

                    Next action/being word: *fear*
                    Who fear?
                    Subject: *they*

Sentence 11 First action/being words: *have grown*
                    Who have grown?
                  Subject: *you*

                    Next action/being word: *reading*
                    Reading is not a verb because it is an *-ing* word used alone without a helping verb.

                    Next action/being word: *have*
                    Who have?
                    Subject: *many* (*Us* is not the subject because it is the object of the preposition *of.*)
                    Verb: *have* (Actually, the verb is *have grown*. The *grown* is understood.)

                    Next action/being word: *is* (Do not neglect action/being words that are part of a contraction—two words combined with an apostrophe to indicate the missing letters.)
                    What is?
                    Subject: *it*

                    Next action/being words: *to be*
                    To be is not a verb because it is formed with *to.*

    This discussion of the tiger passage has tried to show the process a person would actually go through when identifying subjects and verbs in a piece of writing. The following exercises ask you to identify subjects and verbs in your own and others' writing.

IDENTIFYING SUBJECTS AND VERBS

EXERCISES

Answers in back of book: 2a-g, 3a-j, 4a-s, 5a, 7a-c, 8a-c, 9a-h
Answers in instructor's manual: 2k-q, 4t-y, 5b, 7d-f, 8d-f, 9i-l

1. Write definitions for the following. Refer back to the lesson for answers.   verb   helping verb   subject   modifier   noun   preposition

2. Answer the following:

   (Answers in back of book)

   a. Every word that names an action or a state of being is a verb. (T F)
   b. The first noun in a sentence is the subject. (T F)
   c. An *-ing* word is a verb only when it has a helper with it. (T F)
   d. Action/being words preceded by *to* are never verbs. (T F)
   e. A subject always comes before the verb. (T F)
   f. A subject is never the object of a prepositional phrase. (T F)
   g. A subject always has only one word. (T F)

3. For the following sentences, write each verb and its subject. The first one is done for you as an example.

   The rabbits have been fed.
   Verb: have been fed   Subject: rabbits

   (Answers in back of book)

   a. Roger went to the store.
   b. Alice, my neighbor, brought some cookies.
   c. The city zoo has acquired a new hippo.
   d. After resting, the players will resume the match.
   e. This afternoon, the children have been quiet.
   f. Our lawn has been mowed.
   g. These apples have been carefully selected for their color and quality.
   h. Rachel will take her driving test tomorrow.

INTRODUCTORY LESSON A

    i. By Thanksgiving, we will have been in our new home for several months.
    j. Driving carefully, we arrived home safely.

(Answers in instructor's manual)
    k. The workers were skilled.
    l. The bridge across the stream was well built.
    m. My brother has found a new girlfriend.
    n. When lighted, sparklers can be dangerous.
    o. The day of graduation will be very hot.
    p. Before Christmas, I will have lost five pounds.
    q. Wagging happily, Bowzer greets me at the door.

4. For the following sentences, write each verb and its subject. The first one is done for you as an example.

The dog dug under the fence and ran about the neighborhood until a neighbor caught him.

Sample answer:
Verbs: dug, ran   Subject: dog
Verb: caught   Subject: neighbor

(Answers in back of book)
    a. We played hard.
    b. Six clown costumes lay crumpled on the floor.
    c. An old tin can, dented and dirty, had caught some rainwater.
    d. Tired, the workers returned home, but they couldn't rest yet.
    e. You and Bob can come in and eat supper as soon as you finish the game.
    f. In an insurance company, computers can provide the competitive advantage, but management must know how to manage both computers and people.
    g. Since they installed sophisticated computers, several companies have been able to develop improved information systems.
    h. One firm, which last year experienced a 32 percent increase in business applications, acknowledged that the

IDENTIFYING SUBJECTS AND VERBS

computers were the key to keeping up with all those new applications.
i. Like everything else in the United States, the traffic ticket business has entered the computer age.
j. Some towns are using the Ticketwriter, a handheld computerized device for producing tickets that are instantly recorded in a memory system.
k. Because the computer does the paperwork, the officers can spend more time on the streets giving tickets.
l. The device also provides a way to catch people who have ignored tickets and owe the department money for fines.
m. When the officer punches in the numbers of a car's license, the machine automatically searches the list of delinquent fine payers.
n. If the license matches a delinquent, the device beeps and flashes.
o. Whenever I go camping, I always have to take along my sister because there's no one else to stay with her.
p. There in the window was the most beautiful pair of gold earrings I had ever seen.
q. The officer who had jumped out of the car when the shooting started now ran zigzagging between the walls and leapt up onto the roof.
r. It was hard for me to hold down a job, go to school, and take care of my children.
s. The boss said that I would be recommended for a promotion.

(Answers in instructor's manual)

t. A single glass of water was all he had to drink.
u. Before my prom, I spent the whole day getting ready, having my hair done, polishing my nails, deciding what jewelry to wear, pressing my dress, and being nervous.
v. The lawn we had so carefully seeded was now a lovely expanse of smooth, green turf.

INTRODUCTORY LESSON A

w. Whoever had been employed by the bankrupt airlines now had to look for a new job.
x. Fortunately, it was not difficult to find work, and most of the workers were soon employed once more.
y. After Ron and his friends had swept through the kitchen, there were only three cookies left in the jar.

5. In the following paragraphs, write each verb, then its subject.

(Answers in back of book)

a. (1) The pier was crowded with all sorts of people. (2) Old men were patiently waiting for fish to bite their lines, and children were playfully running around while their parents kept a close eye out for them. (3) Nevertheless, I felt as if I were alone with Carleton. (4) It was a rough day out in the ocean, with a strong wind blowing. (5) The pier creaked and shifted beneath us. (6) We stood arm in arm gazing at the ocean, wondering if maintaining our relationship would be as rough as the water below. (7) It felt safe to be in his arms, protected and secure, yet I was scared. (8) Perhaps our love would not survive the separation we were about to face. (9) An entire year of college 1200 miles away was an overwhelming thought. (10) Tears streamed down my face that day on the pier, the day we had to say good-bye.

(Answers in instructor's manual)

b. (1) When I first saw Melissa's bracelet, I thought it was one of the most interesting things I had ever encountered. (2) Yarns of orange, green, blue, and white were woven together, forming an intricate design that encircled Melissa's wrist. (3) She explained to me how important the bracelet was. (4) Handmade by a Guatemalan refugee, the bracelet represented one person's desire for freedom. (5) The contributions of people who purchased the bracelets aided refugees in their plight. (6) The name of the creator, attached to the bracelet, told Melissa whom she had helped. (7)She was so touched by the whole program that she contributed more than her five dollars, and later she sold bracelets at school and at fairs in Baltimore.

6. Take a paragraph you have written—perhaps part of a school paper, an application essay, or a letter. Underline each verb and draw an arrow to that verb's subject(s).
7. For each of the following, write three sentences. In one sentence, use the given word as a verb (you may add helping verbs as needed). In another sentence, use the word as a subject (you may have to add one or more words to make a group of words that acts as a subject). In a third sentence, use the word as neither verb nor subject. After each sentence, write the subjects and verbs. If there is more than one subject-verb unit, number the units. The first one is done for you as an example.

guarding

Sample answer:
1. I was guarding the house.
   Verb: was guarding   Subject: I
2. Guarding the empty factory at night was a job I hated.
   Verb #1: was   Subject #1: Guarding
   Verb #2: hated   Subject #2: I
3. Guarding the cake, I had to fight off all the hungry kids.
   Verb: had   Subject: I

(Sample answers in back of book)
a. running
b. have laughed
c. track
(Sample answers in instructor's manual)
d. swimming
e. have found
f. catch

INTRODUCTORY LESSON A

8. In the following sentences, change the underlined word so that it functions as a verb. Revise other words or add words as needed. The first one is done for you as an example.

   <u>Skipping</u> school, she spent the day on the beach.
   Sample answer: She skipped school and spent the day on the beach.
   OR When she skipped school, she spent the day on the beach.
   (Sample answers in back of book)
   a. <u>Laughing</u> hard, he fell against the table.
   b. <u>Having brushed</u> their teeth and <u>washed</u> their faces, the children were ordered to bed.
   c. <u>Teased</u> by some children, the little dog came home <u>to hide</u>.
   (Sample answers in instructor's manual)
   d. <u>Lying</u> out in the sun, we got a severe burn.
   e. <u>Having worked</u> all day in the broiling heat, the workers went home to relax.
   f. <u>Blown</u> by the wind, the papers scattered across the pond.

9. For each of the following, combine all the ideas into a sentence that has two subject-verb units, and then into a sentence that has one subject-verb unit. (Each unit may have multiple subjects and/or multiple verbs.) After the sentence, write your subject(s) and verb(s). The first one is done for you as an example.

   Ideas to include:
       The horses heard the shots
       The horses smelled the powder
       The horses stampeded
       They stampeded across the field
       They broke down the fence
   Sample sentence with two subject-verb units: When the horses heard the shots and smelled the powder, they stampeded across the field, breaking down the fence.
   Verbs #1: heard, smelled   Subject #1: horses
   Verb #2: stampeded   Subject #2: they

IDENTIFYING SUBJECTS AND VERBS

Sample sentence with one subject-verb unit: Hearing the shots and smelling the powder, the horses stampeded across the field and broke down the fence.
Verbs: stampeded, broke   Subject: horses

(Sample answers in back of book)
a. The farm hands had been practicing with their guns
   The farm hands had been shooting at tin can targets
b. The farm hands did not realize they were so near the horses
   The horses were grazing in a nearby pasture
c. The horses ran into the woods
   The horses scattered through the trees
d. The farm hands ran after the horses
   The farm hands called to the horses
   The horses were panicked
e. Finally the farm hands gave up
   They stopped the chase
   They left open the barn door
   They put oats into the mangers in the barn
f. The night was dark
   The night was cold
   There was no food or water in the woods
g. The horses came into the yard
   They came slowly
   They stamped their feet
   They snuffled softly to each other
h. The horses smelled the grain
   The grain was in the barn
   The horses saw the door to the barn
   The door to the barn was open
   The horses slipped into their stalls

(Sample answers in instructor's manual)
i. The farm hands went in
   The farm hands talked gently to the horses
   The farm hands closed the stall doors
j. Horses are frightened of any loud noise

INTRODUCTORY LESSON A

      Horses are apt to panic
      Horses will barge over fences and gates
      Horses are very strong
k. One student tells a story
      The story is about her horse
      She was riding her horse on the road
      The horse became frightened by a car
l. The horse bolted
      The horse ran up onto the porch of a house
      The owners of the house were surprised

GRAMMATICAL TERMS IN THIS LESSON

Subject: A word or group of words that names the person or thing that is performing the action or that is in the state of being named in the verb

Verb: One to four words that name the action or state of being of the subject

Helping Verb: A verb that accompanies another verb and that is a form of *to be, to have, to do,* or of words such as *could, may,* and *should.*

Modifier: A word or group of words that describes or limits the meaning of another word or group of words in the same sentence

Noun: A word or group of words that names a person, place, concept, or thing

Preposition: A word, usually short, that shows direction or relation. The preposition and its object form the prepositional phrase.

Pronoun: A word that substitutes for a noun: for example, *I, she, you, who, which, this,* and *that.*

INTRODUCTORY LESSON B

DEPENDENT AND INDEPENDENT CLAUSES

WHY STUDY CLAUSES?

As a writer, you need to understand clauses for the same reason that a housebuilder needs to understand rooms. Clauses are the basic units of language. Here are four reasons for studying clauses.

1. Clauses are the basic units of sentences. A sentence always contains one or more clauses. As you learn to compose, revise, and manipulate clauses, you become a more sophisticated and flexible writer. The exercises at the end of this section offer practice in composing, combining, and revising clauses.

2. Changing a clause to a different type of clause or to a group of words that is not a clause is often the key to making a sentence smoother, clearer, and more economical (Step 1 lessons, especially 1E).

3. If you recognize and handle the main clause appropriately, you have the basis for clarity and precision in your writing (lesson for Step 1C).

INTRODUCTORY LESSON B

4. Whether a group of words is a clause or not often determines the use of punctuation. Punctuation problems often occur between clauses. For that reason, later lessons, especially 2A (fragments) and 2B (run-ons), depend on your understanding clauses.

Subjects and verbs are the keys to identifying clauses. If you are not sure how to identify subjects and verbs, review Introductory Lesson A. This section also uses the term *modifier*, which is introduced in Introductory Lesson A, but explained again here.

This lesson keeps grammatical terminology to a minimum; however, five new terms are essential: *clause, complement, independent clause, dependent clause,* and *coordinating connector.* Begin by studying the first three definitions.

Definition: A CLAUSE is composed of a subject-verb unit, together with that unit's modifiers and complements.

Definition: A MODIFIER is a word or groups of words that describes or limits the meaning of another word or group of words in the same sentence. (To review modifiers, see Introductory Lesson A, p. 41.) The following is a representative (not complete) list of how modifiers function.

MODIFIERS TELL . . .

What kind: The *successful* businesses received grants.
Which one(s): Our *blue* car is now gray.
When: *At sunset,* she went to the fields.
Why: *Because of the flu,* the school closed.
For what purpose: *To help me,* they cleaned the barn.
In what way: She climbed *courageously* up the cliff.

Definition: A COMPLEMENT is a word or group of words that completes the meaning of the verb.

***The doctor gave* me pills.**

In this sentence, the verb has two complements. *Pills* receives the direct action of the verb *gave*. (This kind of complement is called a direct object.) *Me* receives the action indirectly. *Me* is the person or thing to whom or for whom the action is done. (This kind of complement is called an indirect object.) The complement of a verb of being/seeming/becoming describes or renames the subject:

***The sprinter was* fast.**
***My friend looks like* a runner.**

(These complements are called predicate nouns or predicate adjectives.) For this lesson, you need not know the grammatical terms, but only be able to recognize when a word or group of words is a complement.

MODIFIERS AND COMPLEMENTS MAY BE OTHER CLAUSES

In the previous examples, we've used the most simple single-word or several-word modifiers and complements. However, modifiers and complements may be clauses.

MODIFIERS THAT ARE CLAUSES:

The businesses *that were successful* received grants.
Our car, *which was blue,* is now gray.
As the sun set, she went to the fields.
Because the flu was so widespread, the school closed.
Since they wanted to help me, they cleaned the barn.
As she gained courage, she climbed up the cliff.

COMPLEMENTS THAT ARE CLAUSES:

I asked the doctor for *whatever would help my toothache.*
The winner is *whoever holds ticket number 131.*

A PREVIEW OF THE LESSON:
TWO METHODS FOR IDENTIFYING
DEPENDENT AND INDEPENDENT CLAUSES

This lesson shows two methods for identifying dependent and independent clauses:

1. analyzing the role of the clause in its sentence; and
2. examining words and punctuation that open clauses or that connect clauses to one another. Openers and connectors are often clues to the dependence or independence of clauses.

The process of using the two methods to identify dependent and independent clauses is summarized in Figure Intro B.1. Follow the diagram as you read this chapter and as you analyze clauses and sentences.

ANALYZING THE CLAUSE'S ROLE
IN ITS SENTENCE

The common definitions for independent and dependent clauses in a sentence are as follows:

Definition: INDEPENDENT CLAUSES can stand alone.

Definition: DEPENDENT CLAUSES cannot stand alone.

Main clause means the same as *independent clause*. *Subordinate clause* means the same as *dependent clause*.

When you read a dependent clause, it sounds incomplete; you wait for something else to complete the thought. For that reason, a dependent clause does not appear alone as a sentence.

DEPENDENT AND INDEPENDENT CLAUSES

Analyze the Clause's Role in a Sentence and
Examine Openers and Connectors

```
Does clause modify    no    Complement verb    no    Act as a noun in
something in                in another                another clause?
another clause?             clause?
     |                         |                         |
    yes                       yes                       yes    no
     |                         |                         |     |
     v                         v                         v     |
  Dependent                Independent  <-----------------------+
     ^                         ^
     |                         |
```

Openers:
Relative Pronoun, Nonmovable Connector (except Coordinating Connector)

Openers:
Coordinating Connector, Movable Connector

Connectors Between Two Independent Clauses in the Same Sentence:
  ;
  ; + movable connector
  , + coordinating connector

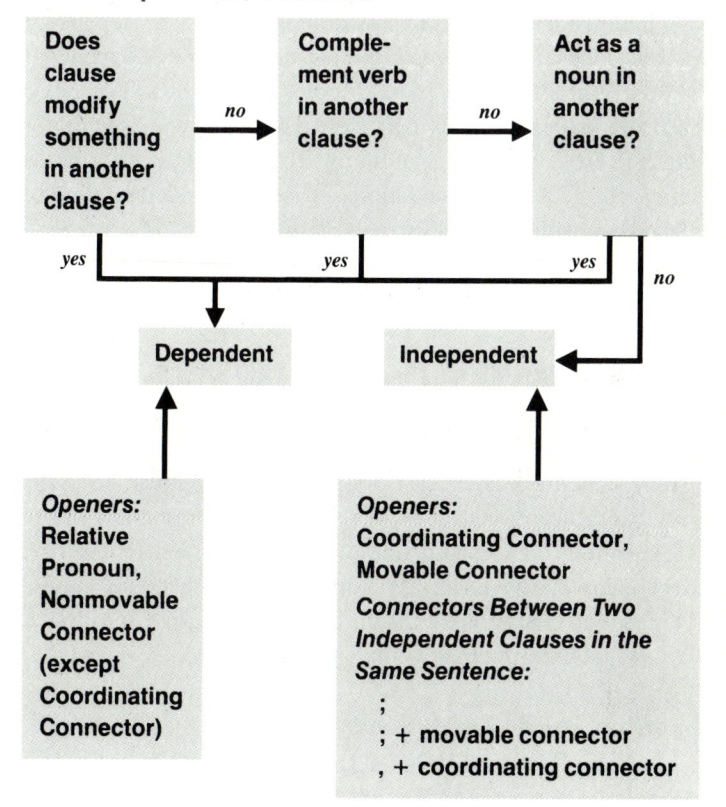

FIGURE INTRO B.1 How to Identify Dependent and Independent Clauses

A dependent clause should be part of an independent clause in the same sentence. For example, the following clause reads like an incomplete thought:

    Dependent clause: when I was elected
    Reader asks: when I was elected—then what?
    Place the dependent clause within an independent clause:
    When I was elected, we had a party.

Now the sentence sounds complete. The independent clause makes it a grammatically complete sentence. In this sentence, the independent clause is the whole sentence. The dependent clause, *when I was elected,* is now part of that independent clause. Whether a clause sounds complete or not will be a clue to its dependence or independence. However, you may find it difficult to develop an ear for something as vague as "sounds complete." Thus you need a more thorough understanding of the relationships among subjects, verbs, clauses, and sentences. These relationships are summarized in Figure Intro B.2.

A SENTENCE HAS AT LEAST ONE INDEPENDENT CLAUSE

Every sentence has at least one independent clause. (See the following exceptions, p. 75.) A sentence may have one or more independent clauses and one or more dependent clauses. A dependent clause is always part of an independent clause. Dependent clauses nest inside other clauses like the nested boxes that children play with.

DEPENDENT CLAUSES SERVE THREE FUNCTIONS

Every dependent clause serves one of three functions in relation to the clause in which it nests. In the examples, independent clauses are underlined once, dependent clauses are underlined twice, and subjects and verbs are marked *I* when they belong to an independent clause, *D* when they belong to a dependent clause.

1. A dependent clause may *modify something* in another clause.

DEPENDENT AND INDEPENDENT CLAUSES

Two Types of Clauses

Subject and Its Modifiers	Verb and Its + Complements and Modifiers

Independent (Can stand alone)

OR

Subject and Its Modifiers	Verb and Its + Complements and Modifiers

Dependent (Cannot stand alone)

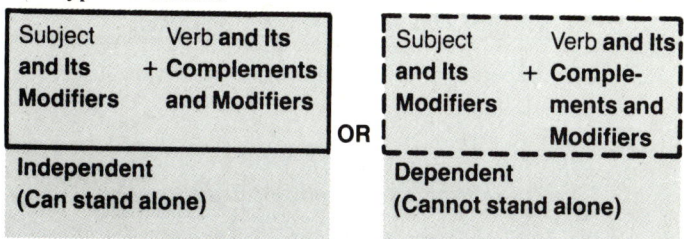

Combining Clauses in Sentences

Simplest Sentence: (One Independent Clause)
The kitten slept soundly.

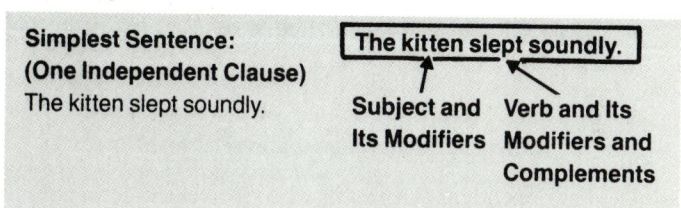

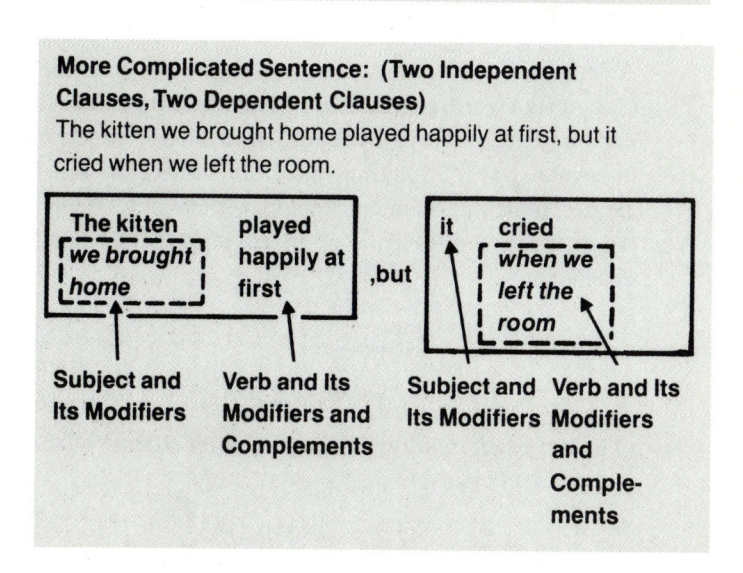

The kitten slept soundly.
- Subject and Its Modifiers
- Verb and Its Modifiers and Complements

More Complicated Sentence: (Two Independent Clauses, Two Dependent Clauses)
The kitten we brought home played happily at first, but it cried when we left the room.

The kitten *we brought home* played happily at first ,but it cried *when we left the room*

- Subject and Its Modifiers
- Verb and Its Modifiers and Complements
- Subject and Its Modifiers
- Verb and Its Modifiers and Complements

FIGURE INTRO B.2 Relationships of Subjects, Verbs, Clauses, and Sentences.

INTRODUCTORY LESSON B

<pre>   S-I S-D   V-D   V-I</pre>
<u>The girl</u> <u>who danced</u> <u>was</u> <u>my daughter.</u>

(The dependent clause modifies *girl,* the subject of another clause.)

<pre> S-I V-I   S-D   V-D</pre>
<u>I went</u> skating <u>after I had finished</u> shoveling.

(The dependent clause modifies *went,* the verb of another clause.)

2. A dependent clause may *complement the verb* in another clause.

<pre>   S-I   V-I   S-D   V-D</pre>
<u>The police</u> <u>will help</u> <u>whoever is lost.</u>

(The dependent clause tells who receives the action of the verb *will help.*)

3. A dependent clause may *act as a noun* in another clause. (A noun is a word, group of words, or clause that names a person, place, concept, or thing.) Noun clauses function in several ways. Sometimes they are subjects of other clauses, sometimes complements, sometimes other things. Any clause acting as a noun in another clause is dependent.

<pre>   S-I
       S-D   V-D   V-I</pre>
<u>Whatever</u> <u>will be</u> <u>will be.</u>

(The dependent clause acts as the noun subject of the independent clause.)

<pre>   S-I   V-I   S-D V-D</pre>
<u>The boss</u> <u>knew</u> <u>that he was</u> absent.

(The noun clause acts as a complement, telling what received the action of the verb *knew.*)

      S-I   V-I   S-D   V-D
The crown is placed on the head of whoever has written

the silliest limerick.

>   (The dependent clause acts as a noun because it names the person/thing that is the object of the preposition *of* [to review objects of prepositions, see Introductory Lesson A, p. 47].)

The Functions of Dependent Clauses

1. To modify something in another clause
2. To complement the verb in another clause
3. To serve as a noun in another clause

Exceptions: Occasionally a writer may use a dependent clause by itself, punctuated as a sentence. If there is not a good reason, the sentence, called a *fragment,* needs revision (see Lesson 1A). Also, some clauses have the subject or verb missing or understood. The most common example is a request ("Pass the salt" has an understood "you" as its subject). Exceptions will be treated in other lessons as needed.

OPENERS AND CONNECTORS ARE CLUES TO DEPENDENT AND INDEPENDENT CLAUSES

As you identify clauses by their function, you can use clause openers and connectors to help you. This is the second group of procedures in Figure Intro B.1.

    The terms *opener* and *connector* are used loosely to refer to words (and punctuation) that open the clause and/or form a connection to another clause. You need not worry about differences between openers and connectors. There are certain typical ways to open clauses and to connect clauses to one another within a sentence. These are summarized in Figure Intro B.3.

INTRODUCTORY LESSON B

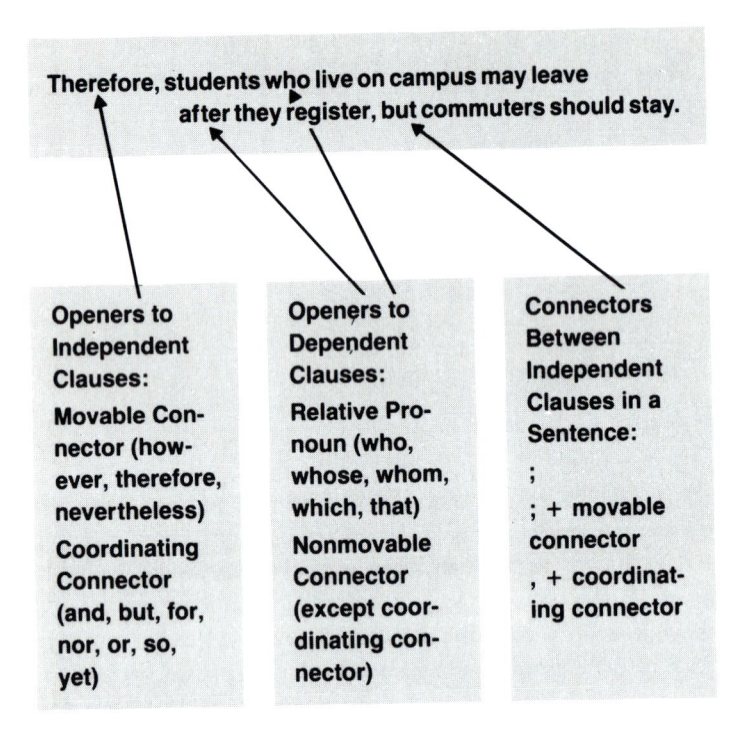

Therefore, students who live on campus may leave after they register, but commuters should stay.

Openers to Independent Clauses:	Openers to Dependent Clauses:	Connectors Between Independent Clauses in a Sentence:
Movable Connector (however, therefore, nevertheless)	Relative Pronoun (who, whose, whom, which, that)	;
Coordinating Connector (and, but, for, nor, or, so, yet)	Nonmovable Connector (except coordinating connector)	; + movable connector , + coordinating connector

FIGURE INTRO B.3   Openers and Connectors Are Clues to Dependent and Independent Clauses

CLAUSES THAT OPEN WITH RELATIVE PRONOUNS ARE DEPENDENT

Clauses that are not questions and that open with relative pronouns are always dependent.

Relative Pronouns

who whom whose which that whoever whomever

Clauses that *open* with relative pronouns are dependent. *Open* means that the relative pronoun is the first word, or the first word after an opening noun. If a clause is not a question, and if it opens with *who, whom, whose, whoever,* or *whomever,* it is dependent. If it opens with *which* or *that,* it *may* be dependent, but only if the *which* or *that* is acting as a relative pronoun. When *which* and *that* act as relative pronouns, they refer back to a noun in that sentence or another sentence. Check your sentence by asking whether the clause serves one of the three dependent clause functions listed earlier.

In the following two examples, clauses can be identified by using two methods—noting the function of the clause and the opener of the clause.

S-I   S-D   V-D   V-I
The clerk who relieved me found my watch.

You know that *who relieved me* is dependent because it opens with a relative pronoun and because it modifies something (the subject, *clerk*) in another clause.

S-I V-I   S-D V-D
I know whose shoes these are.

You know that *whose shoes these are* is dependent because it opens with a relative pronoun and because it acts as a complement by naming the thing that receives the action of the verb—the thing that is known.

THE RELATIVE PRONOUN IS SOMETIMES OMITTED

A relative pronoun is sometimes omitted. Restoring it helps you see the nature of the clause.

S-I   V-I   S-D V-D
She knew the same people whom I knew (or that I knew).

S-I   V-I   S-D V-D
She knew the same people I knew.

In the examples, the dependent clause modifies the noun *people* by telling *which* people. However, in the last example, there is no relative pronoun. Because of the common omission of the relative pronoun, you must be able to recognize such clauses by imagining a relative pronoun, or by recognizing that the clause serves one of the three functions of a dependent clause.

THAT MAY BE DECEPTIVE

The word *that* has been used in two different ways in dependent clauses. In the previous example about relative pronouns, *that* is a relative pronoun—*the people that I knew*. *That* stands in for the noun *people*. In the discussion of clauses that may be subjects or complements earlier in this section, *that* also signals a dependent clause—this time a clause used as a noun. (I knew that he was late.) *That* has other uses, too. It is one of the trickiest words in the English language. For example, an opening *that* is not necessarily a clue to dependence when used as a modifer to a noun:

That stream has flooded three times this year.

(*That* is merely a modifier for the subject, *stream*. The sentence has only one clause—independent.)

Nor is *that* a clue to dependence when used as a pronoun subject of an independent clause:

That was a real victory.

That can be used in many different ways. One might say it is the wildcard of the English language. While *which* does not have as many uses, it also may be used as a relative pronoun or in other ways. Thus when a clause opens with *which* or *that*, take it as a *possible* clue to dependence, but be sure it is being used as a relative pronoun or as an opener to a noun clause. To be certain, ask whether the clause serves any of the three functions of a dependent clause.

CONNECTORS MAKE A CLAUSE DEPENDENT

Connectors that are words (rather than punctuation) can make a clause dependent. Sometimes you cannot tell the function of the clause except by looking at its opening word, which is the only reason the clause is dependent. Remove the opening connecting word, or substitute another type of word, and the clause will change from dependent to independent or vice versa. The connecting words that determine a clause's dependence or independence are listed in the following box.

Three Types of Connecting Words

This connector	makes the clause....
Coordinating Connector	Independent
and, but, for, nor, or, so, yet	
Movable Connector	Independent
(can change position in its clause)	
however, nevertheless	
Nonmovable Connector	Dependent
(cannot change position in its clause)	
after, because	
(except coordinating connectors)	

MOVABLE AND NONMOVABLE CONNECTORS

It rained all night; however, we had the party.
It rained all night; we had the party, however.

In these examples, the *however* can be moved to a later point in its clause without changing the meaning. It is a *movable* connector. It introduces an *independent* clause. In the next example, an independent clause changes to a dependent clause when its connecting word is changed.

INTRODUCTORY LESSON B

```
           S-I  V-I                  S-I  V-I
It rained all night; however, we had the party.
    S-I  V-I                S-D  V-D
It rained all night after we had the party.
```

The *after* cannot change its position. You cannot say *we had the party after,* and keep the same sense and meaning. Thus *after* is a nonmovable connector. The clause is dependent—it modifies the verb *rained* by telling *when* it rained.

LEARNING THE CONNECTORS

To learn the connectors, first memorize the seven coordinating connectors (see box, p. 79). Other connectors you can generally distinguish by their movability. A few nonmovable connectors, such as *though,* may be confusing. *Though,* in its meaning of *although,* is not movable, even if it sounds movable.

I swam, though the doctor had forbidden it.

(*Though* means *although.* It is a nonmovable connector. The clause is dependent.)

The following are some common movable and nonmovable connectors:

Common Movable (Adverbial) Connectors
(Open or Connect Independent Clauses)

also	however	otherwise
besides	likewise	therefore
consequently	moreover	then
furthermore	nevertheless	though (meaning *however*)
		thus

DEPENDENT AND INDEPENDENT CLAUSES

Common Nonmovable* (Subordinating) Connectors (Open Dependent Clauses)

after	ever since	than
although	if	though
as	in order that	(meaning *although*)
because	since	unless
before	so (only when it	until
even if	means *so that*)	when
even when		while

*The coordinating connectors are also nonmovable, but they open/connect independent clauses.

SUMMARY SO FAR

This lesson has shown you two ways of identifying dependent and independent clauses. You can analyze the structure of your sentence and the relations among its clauses. You can also use the openers and connectors to identify dependent and independent clauses. The following example illustrates the actual process of identifying dependent and independent clauses in a passage of writing.

IDENTIFYING DEPENDENT AND INDEPENDENT CLAUSES

The following passage, nearly the same as in Introductory Lesson A, is used to demonstrate the process of identifying dependent and independent clauses.

> (1) Scientists say, simply, that the tiger is a large, graceful, brightly colored cat that lives in jungles and eats meat. (2) Scientists, hunters, and animal handlers have come to know

INTRODUCTORY LESSON B

how strong tigers can be. (3) In fact, people who know both the tiger and the lion say that the tiger is more powerful. (4) Residents of isolated villages in tiger territory know the fear of a tiger that, because it is old, diseased, or unable to hunt its normal prey, has turned to killing domestic livestock or even people. (5) Wounded, a tiger is very dangerous, especially when protecting its young. (6) A tiger who has been shot but not killed will attack a hunter. (7) Even a hunter who is seated on an elephant. (8) Wounded tigers have been known to leap onto the elephant's back and attack the hunter. (9) All of this is perfectly natural, self-protective behavior by an animal that is merely trying to survive, eat, and protect itself from enemies; however, story and legend have transformed the tiger into an almost supernatural creature of cruelty and mystery. (10) For example, Rudyard Kipling, in his *Jungle Books,* tells of a scarred tiger called Shere Khan, who is the outlaw of the jungle, killing not only for food, but also for the love of blood. (11) The other animals hate him for his treachery, and they fear him for his viciousness and cruelty. (12) If you've grown up reading Kipling, as many of us have, it's difficult to be objective about tigers.

This next section outlines the process of identifying independent and dependent clauses in each sentence of the tiger passage. Independent clauses are underlined once; dependent clauses twice. This means that for grammatically complete sentences, everything in the sentence will be underlined once because everything is part of an independent clause. (See Figure Intro B.2, p. 73.) Dependent clauses, which are always part of those independent clauses, will get an additional line. Subjects and verbs are marked. Links between independent clauses are circled.

   Sentence 1

   S-I   V-I   S-D V-D
   Scientists say, simply, that the tiger is a large, graceful,

DEPENDENT AND INDEPENDENT CLAUSES

<u>*brightly colored cat* <u>*that*</u> <u>*lives in jungles* </u> *and* <u>*eats meat.*</u></u>
                S-D   V-D   V-D

The clue to the dependent clauses is that both open with *that*. In the first dependent clause, *that* is an opening connector; in the second dependent clause, *that* is a relative pronoun.

Sentence 2

    S-I   S-I   S-I   V-I
<u>*Scientists, hunters, and animal handlers have come to*</u>
         S-D   V-D
<u>*know how strong tigers can be.*</u>

The dependent clause complements the verb by naming *what* scientists and others have come to know. (Actually, because *know* is preceded by *to*, it is not technically part of the verb, but it can take a complement, as it does here.)

The dependent clause has no *that* or other typical opener, though the *how* makes the clause sound incomplete.

Sentence 3

         S-I   S-D   V-D   V-I
<u>*In fact, people who know both the tiger and the lion say*</u>
   S-D V-D
<u>*that the tiger is more powerful.*</u>

Both dependent clauses have typical openers: *who* and *that*. The first dependent clause serves as a modifier telling which people. The second dependent clause serves as a complement to the verb, naming *what* people say.

Sentence 4

      S-I   V-I
<u>*Residents of isolated villages in tiger territory know the*</u>
    S-D   S-D V-D
<u>*fear of a tiger that, because it is old, diseased, or unable to*</u>

INTRODUCTORY LESSON B

<u>**V-D**
hunt its normal prey, **has turned** to killing domestic live-

stock or even people.</u>

One dependent clause is embedded within another dependent clause. The *because* clause modifies the verb of the other dependent clause *(has turned)* by telling *why* the tiger has turned. Both dependent clauses open with dependent openers: *that* and *because*. *That* is a relative pronoun. *Because* is a nonmovable connector.

Sentence 5

<u>**S-I V-I**
Wounded, a tiger is very dangerous, especially when pro-

tecting its young.</u>

The *when* does not open a clause because no subject-verb unit follows the when.

Sentence 6

<u>**S-I   S-D   V-D   V-I**
A tiger who has been shot but not killed will attack a

hunter.</u>

The dependent clause opens with the relative pronoun *who*.

Sentence 7

Even a hunter who is seated on an elephant.

This group of words does not follow the rules for an independent clause, because what seemed to be a subject—*hunter*—has no verb in the sentence. The clause *who is seated on an elephant* has a subject and a verb, but is dependent because it opens with a relative pronoun *who*. This is a sentence fragment.

DEPENDENT AND INDEPENDENT CLAUSES

Though sometimes used deliberately for good reason, usually fragments should be revised. Lesson 1A covers fragments in more detail.

Sentence 8

      S-I   V-I
<u>**Wounded tigers have been known to leap onto the elephant's back and attack the hunter.**</u>

To leap and *[to] attack,* because of the *to,* are not acting as verbs. Instead, the sentence has one verb *(have been known)* and one independent clause.

Sentence 9

S-I   V-I
<u>**All of this is perfectly natural, self-protective behavior by**</u>
   S-D V-D   V-D
<u>**an animal that is merely trying to survive, eat, and protect**</u>
              S-I   S-I   V-I
<u>**itself from enemies; (however,) story and legend have transformed the tiger into an almost supernatural creature of cruelty and mystery.**</u>

   The part of the sentence after *however* is a second independent clause, because the clause does not fulfill any of the three functions of dependent clauses: it does not act as part of the subject-with-modifiers, nor modify/complement the verb, nor act as a noun in another clause. Also, the clause begins with a semicolon plus a movable linking word—*however.*

Sentence 10

                   S-I   V-I
<u>**For example, Rudyard Kipling, in his Jungle Books, *tells***</u>

INTRODUCTORY LESSON B

<u>S-D</u> <u>V-D</u>
<u>of a scarred tiger called Shere Khan, who is the outlaw of</u>

<u>the jungle, killing not only for food, but also for the love</u>

<u>of blood.</u>

 The dependent clause opens with a relative pronoun *who*. Neither *called* nor *killing* are verbs, so the words connected with them do not form clauses, but instead modify other elements in the sentence.

Sentence 11

    S-I V-I   S-I
*The other animals hate him for his treachery, **and** they*
V-I
fear him for his viciousness and cruelty.

 The sentence has two independent clauses. The second clause does not modify or complement, or act as a noun, within another clause. The second clause opens with one of the typical connectors between independent clauses—a comma plus a coordinating connector *(and)*.

 Length is not an appropriate guide to the number of independent clauses a sentence will have. This sentence is shorter than most in this passage, yet most of the other sentences, even the longest ones, have only one independent clause. Though the second clause is not grammatically part of the first, words in the second clause may be pronouns that refer back to words in the first clause *(they, him, his)*.

Sentence 12

  S-D V-D   S-D   V-D
If you've grown up reading Kipling, as many of us have,
V-I [is]   S-I
it's difficult to be objective about tigers.

The two dependent clauses both open with nonmovable connectors: *if* and *as*. The *it* acts as a kind of filler, which postpones the true subject—*to be objective about tigers.*

This discussion has explained the steps a person might go through in order to identify dependent and independent clauses in a passage of writing. This process, diagrammed in Figure Intro B.1, can guide you in making those identifications in your own writing. The following exercises will help you both to identify clauses and to increase your ability to compose, revise, and manipulate clauses and sentences.

When you have finished this and Introductory Lesson A, you will be able to identify verbs and subjects, as well as dependent/independent clauses in your own writing. You will be able to use the terms *modifier, complement, noun, pronoun,* and *coordinating connector* to help you understand sentences and clauses. With these understandings, you are equipped to begin the lessons that help you follow the three steps. Those lessons begin next. Their numbers are keyed to the steps: Lesson for Step 1A, Lesson for Step 1B, and so on through Steps 2 and 3.

EXERCISES

Note: This lesson contains far more exercises than any of the other sections. This is where your basic understanding of sentence structure is formed. Use the exercises to practice constructing and revising clauses and sentences. If you are an inexperienced writer, you may want to spend considerable time working with the exercises, to provide a solid base before beginning the next lessons.

Refer back to lesson for answers: 1, 2, 3, 4, 6
Answers in back of book: 5a-b, 8a-i, 9a-e, 10a-s, 11a-j, 12a, 20a-c, 21a
Answers in instructor's manual: 5c-d, 7, 8j-o, 9f-i, 10t-y, 11k-n, 12b, 20d-f, 21b

INTRODUCTORY LESSON B

1. Write definitions for the following. Refer back to the lesson for answers.
   subject   verb   modifier   complement   clause
   independent clause   dependent clause   noun   pronoun
2. List five movable connectors and five nonmovable connectors. Refer back to the lesson for answers.
3. List the coordinating connectors. Refer back to the lesson for answers.
4. Write the two types of openers/connectors for dependent clauses. Refer back to the lesson for answers.
5. Use each of the following words in one sentence as a dependent clause opener, and in another sentence in a different function. The first one is done for you as an example.
   when
   Sample answers:
   Sentence with *when* as dependent clause opener:
      When I went to the dump, I found this old chest.
   Sentence with *when* as something else:
      When going to the dump, always keep your eyes open for treasures.
   (Answers in back of book)
   a. after
   b. because
   (Answers in instructor's manual)
   c. that
   d. which
6. Write the ways to open independent clauses and/or connect independent clauses to one another. Refer back to the lesson for answers.
7. Answer the following: True or False

DEPENDENT AND INDEPENDENT CLAUSES

(Answers in instructor's manual)
   a. Every word in a sentence is part of some dependent clause. (T F)
   b. Movable connectors make a clause independent. (T F)
   c. A clause beginning with *that* is always dependent. (T F)
   d. A coordinating connector makes a clause dependent. (T F)
   e. A dependent clause can be linked to an independent clause by a semicolon. (T F)
8. For each of the following sentences, underline the independent clause once and the dependent clause(s) twice. Mark subjects and verbs of each clause, as has been done throughout this lesson. Each of these sentences has only one independent clause, though they may have any number of dependent clauses. The next exercise (number 9) includes sentences that have more than one independent clause. A sample is done for you.

                 S-I   V-I
As the whistle blew, my mother gathered up her packages,
  S-D   V-D
which contained Christmas presents for all the cousins,
         V-I
and boarded the train.

(Answers in back of book)

   a. The Titanic was a British steamer that was supposed to be unsinkable.
   b. However, the Titanic sank on its first voyage.
   c. On the night of April 14–15, 1912, as it was sailing through icy seas about 1600 miles northeast of New York City, the ship struck an iceberg.

INTRODUCTORY LESSON B

    d. When it tore through the ship's hull, the iceberg made a 300-foot gash.
    e. On board ship, crew members and passengers struggled to fill and release the lifeboats.
    f. The lifeboats, which had room for less than half the passengers, took on mostly women and children, leaving fathers and husbands behind.
    g. Launching the lifeboats was risky and difficult because the decks were sloping and wet.
    h. No one knows exactly how many lives were lost.
    i. The sinking of the Titanic was one of the greatest tragedies in shipping history.
(Answers in instructor's manual)
    j. Sunken treasure probably attracts more treasure seekers than any other kind of treasure.
    k. Diving for treasure has become a popular pastime.
    l. Robert Louis Stevenson's *Treasure Island* is famous among treasure stories.
    m. Though some experts would disagree, I believe that the discovery of treasure is possible, even for the amateur diver.
    n. In the Great Lakes alone, there are an estimated 8000 sunken ships, whose total cargo is valued at more than a million dollars.
    o. New types of diving equipment and demolition tactics offer increased possibility of discovering some of those buried riches.

9. For each of the following sentences, follow instructions for Exercise 8. These sentences all contain two or more independent clauses. Circle the connecting words/punctuation between independent clauses. Some of the independent clauses have embedded dependent clauses. A sample is done for you.

                V-I   S-I   S-I

In most cases there is little reason to fear snakes(;)only 8
   V-I
percent are poisonous to humans.

(Answers in back of book)

a. Worms are wet and slimy, but snakes are dry.
b. A transparent cap keeps a snake's eyes always open, so it is impossible to tell whether a snake sleeps.
c. The snake is deaf to sound carried by air; it hears by sensing vibrations from the ground.
d. Popular belief holds that the snake stings with its tongue; however, the tongue is harmless.
e. A snake's body is always about the same temperature as the air; it has great trouble withstanding cold; therefore, snakes abound in the tropics, but few are found in arctic climates.

(Answers in instructor's manual)

f. A healthy snake can live without food for a year, but snakes usually eat regularly.
g. A snake must swallow its food whole; thus the bones of its lower jaw are hinged so that it can separate its jaws widely.
h. Animals with long bodies are easiest to swallow, so lizards and other snakes are favorite foods for snakes.
i. Most snakes hatch from eggs, but others are born alive, like mammals; in either case, the young snakes can take care of themselves.

10. For this exercise, use the sentences in Exercise 4 in Introductory Lesson A, p. 60. Follow the instructions for Lessons 8–9. (You may already have identified subjects and verbs if you did the exercise for Introductory Lesson A). The sentences may have any number of independent and dependent clauses.

INTRODUCTORY LESSON B

11. For each of the following sentences, follow the instructions for Exercises 8–9. Each of these sentences may contain any combination of independent and dependent clauses.
    (Answers in back of book)
    a. Spices were used by the Egyptians 4500 years ago to embalm bodies.
    b. Today, even cat litter and dolls often contain scent.
    c. The smell of smoke that has permeated a building after a fire can linger for years.
    d. In today's market, companies have discovered that consumers will more readily buy a product that smells nice than a product that has no smell.
    e. Dogs leased by private owners help find drugs, termites, and lost children.
    f. The campers wisely set up tents and slept out the blizzard.
    g. When a recipe calls for vanilla, the chef inserts a knife into a long vanilla bean and scrapes tiny seeds into the pot.
    h. The tent was crowded; tempers flared.
    i. About 65 million years ago, large numbers of living things became extinct, and as many as half of all genera disappeared.
    j. Ancient people valued meteorites for their metals; however, in modern times meteorites are valued as sources of information about the cosmos.
    (Answers in instructor's manual)
    k. Salt was first mined from the sea when people scooped out shallow holes along the seashore.
    l. Waves filled the holes with salty seawater; the sun dried up the water, leaving the salt behind.
    m. Each gallon of seawater contains more than a quarter pound of salt; however, water from the Dead Sea contains even more salt.

n. Salt is still taken from the sea, but most salt in the U.S. comes from salt wells, which are drilled much as a water or oil well is drilled.
12. For this exercise, use the paragraphs in Exercise 5 of Introductory Lesson A, p. 61. Follow the instructions in Exercises 8–9. (You may already have identified subjects and verbs if you did the exercise as part of Introductory Lesson A.) Each sentence may contain any combination of independent and dependent clauses.
13. Compose sentences using the following specifications:
    a. A sentence 20 words long, opening with "when," and containing one independent clause and one dependent clause
    b. A sentence 20 words long, containing one independent clause and no dependent clauses
    c. A sentence 20 words long, containing two independent clauses and no dependent clauses
    d. A sentence 20 words long, containing two independent clauses and one dependent clause
    e. A sentence 6 words long, containing 3 independent clauses
14. For the following list of subjects, write at least ten words to modify each subject, as though you were going to write a full sentence. However, do not write any part of the sentence that would be a verb or that would modify or complement the verb. (You may write modifiers for the subject that are dependent clauses.) A sample is done for you.

    Subject: toboggan

    Sample Answer: The banged up, old toboggan that we had borrowed from our neighbors
    Incorrect: After we had finished our run, our shiny new toboggan *(After we had finished our run* would modify the verb.)

a. robin
b. screen
c. lipstick
d. anger
e. chimney
(For the following, use both words as subjects that would take the same verb.)
f. sticks, stones
g. pizza, sodas
h. I, The Incredible Snowman

15. For each of the subject-plus-modifiers you composed in number 14, add a verb with modifiers and complements. Your addition should contain at least ten words and include at least one dependent clause.

16. Use the exercise in number 14 as a game with two or more classmates. Each person must add at least one word to the sentence's subject, without beginning any part of a verb, or anything that would modify or complement a verb. In one turn, a person may add only words that are connected to one another, and may insert words at only one point in the part of the sentence that has been written. Pass the sentence subject around the circle until no one can add any more words. Each person receives a point for each word she or he can add. Whoever adds words that would have to be part of the sentence's predicate receives no credit for the words, and has a 1 point penalty for each attempted word.

    Example: One student begins: *The box*   2 points.

    Second student adds: The *long, narrow, red* box   3 points.

    Third student (or back to the first student, if there are only two players) adds: the long, narrow, red box *that my mother gave me*   5 points.

    Next student adds: The long, narrow, red box that my mother gave me *after my ring dance*   4 points.

Next student adds: The *very* long, narrow, red box that my mother gave me *the day* after my ring dance (Only one entry is accepted—a player may not add words in two places in the same turn.) 2 points for *the day*. *Very* is deleted.

Next student adds: The long, narrow, red box that my mother gave me the day after my ring dance *had to be burned* Receives 4 point penalty because the added words would have to be part of the predicate. Turn passes to next student.

If you have access to a computer, this game can be played through electronic mail. Each person adds his/her words, initials them, and sends the passage to the next person. If you do not have electronic mail, give each person access to the file that has the passage. The file could be a mainframe file to which everyone has the access code, or it could be a floppy disk that is available for everyone to check out on individual microcomputers.

17. Write a sentence, at least twenty-five words in length, that has only one independent clause. You may use only two words as the subject-with-modifier (for example, *the elephant*). All the rest must be verbs and modifiers and complements of the verb. Your modifiers and complements may contain dependent clauses. Your sentence may not depend on repetition for length (for example, you may not write, The firecrackers went bang, bang, bang . . .).

18. Write a sentence, at least twenty-five words in length, that has only one independent clause. You may use only two words as verb-plus-modifiers/complements (for example, *laughed softly*.) All the rest must be the subject with its modifiers. Your subject and its modifiers may contain dependent clauses. Your sentence may not depend on repetition for length (for example, you may not write, The very, very, tiny, tiny . . .).

INTRODUCTORY LESSON B

19. For each of the following phrases, write two sentences. In the first sentence, make the phrase part of the subject or its modifiers. In the second sentence, make the phrase part of the verb, or modifiers and complements to the verb. A sample is done for you.

Phrase: running away

Answers: As subject: Running away is foolish. OR as modifier to subject: Randy, who was running away from home, had only fifty cents in his pocket.

As verb/modifiers/complements: The boys were running away. OR: A funny cartoon showed a little boy who was running away from home, pulling along his TV set on a little red wagon.

a. having
b. presented with a gift
c. tied to a post
d. had been seen

20. For each of the following (1) change the second independent clause to a dependent clause, and then (2) change the whole sentence to a sentence that has only one independent clause and no dependent clauses. A sample is done for you.

Sentence: The Freedman's Bureau was established in 1865; it was the end of the Civil War.

Sample Answers:

1. The Freedman's Bureau was established in 1865, which was the end of the Civil War.
2. The Freedman's Bureau was established in 1865, the end of the Civil War.

(Sample answers in back of book)

a. The Freedman's Bureau was a federal agency; it was created by Congress.

b. The Freedman's Bureau staffed hospitals; the hospitals were the only source of medical treatment for many Blacks.
c. Many Blacks in the war-torn South were hungry; the Freedman's Bureau distributed food to them. (Hint: try making Freedman's Bureau the subject of an opening independent clause.)

(Answers in instructor's manual)

d. The Freedman's Bureau established an educational program; that program became its largest.
e. Within five years after the Civil War, the Freedman's Bureau created and administered more than 4,000 schools; the schools eventually had enrollment of more than ¼ million Blacks.
f. Army officers came to the schools; they gave lectures to Blacks about civil rights. (Hint: try starting the sentence with "To the schools came . . . .")

21. For each of the following groups of ideas, compose sentences using the following specifications. Each sentence must use all the information, but you may change the forms or the order of words and ideas, and you may omit words. Mark your sentences following the instructions for Exercises 8-9. A sample is done for you.

Specifications:
  A sentence with three independent clauses
  A sentence with two independent clauses and two dependent clauses
  A sentence with two independent clauses and one dependent clause
  A sentence with two independent clauses
  A sentence with one independent clause and one dependent clause
  A sentence with one independent clause

INTRODUCTORY LESSON B

Ideas to Combine:
The Freedman's Bureau was a federal agency
It was created by Congress
It was created in 1865
That was the year the Civil War ended
The purpose of the Freedman's Bureau was to help Blacks

Sample sentences:

Three independent clauses:

     S-I V-I   S-I V-I
The Freedman's Bureau was a federal agency; it was set up by Congress in 1865, at the end of the Civil War, and its
 S-I V-I
purpose was to help Blacks.

Two independent clauses, two dependent clauses:

       S-I S-D V-D
The Freedman's Bureau, which was a federal agency,
 V-I   S-D   V-D
was created in 1965, the year the Civil War ended; the
    S-I V-I
agency's purpose was to help Blacks.

Two independent clauses, one dependent clause:

      S-I V-I
The Freedman's Bureau was a federal agency whose
 S-D V-D   S-I V-D
purpose was to help Blacks; it was established in 1865, at the end of the Civil War.

Two independent clauses:

     S-I   V-I
The Freedman's Bureau, a federal agency, was created by
                S-I
Congress in 1865, at the end of the Civil War; its purpose
V-I
was to help Blacks.

One independent clause, two dependent clauses:

     S-I   S-D V-D
The Freedman's Bureau, whose purpose was to help
 V-I
Blacks, was a federal agency created by Congress in 1865,
     S-D V-D
the year the Civil War ended.

One independent clause, one dependent clause:

     S-I   S-D V-D
The Freedman's Bureau, whose purpose was to help
 V-I
Blacks, was a federal agency created by Congress in 1865,

at the end of the Civil War.

One independent clause:

  S-I   V-I
To help Blacks was the purpose of the Freedman's

Bureau, a federal agency created by Congress in 1865, at

the end of the Civil War.

INTRODUCTORY LESSON B

(Sample answers in back of book)
a. It was the end of the Civil War
Only 10 percent of U.S. Blacks could read or write
Five years passed
Then 21 percent could read and write
The difference was largely due to the Freedman's Bureau Schools

(Sample answers in instructor's manual)
b. The Freedman's Bureau resettled Blacks
The Blacks were homeless after the havoc of the Civil War
The Freedman's Bureau had only a little land at its disposal
The Freedman's Bureau parcelled out its land to Blacks

GRAMMATICAL TERMS IN THIS LESSON

Noun: A word or group of words that names a person, place, concept, or thing

Subject: The word or group of words that names the person or thing that is performing the action or that is in the state of being named in the verb

Verb: One to four words that name the action or state of being of the subject

Clause: A subject-verb unit together with that unit's modifiers and complements

Modifier: A word or group of words that describes or limits the meaning of another word or group of words in the same sentence

Complement: A word or group of words that completes the meaning of a verb

Dependent Clause: A clause that cannot stand alone
Independent Clause: A clause that can stand alone
Sentence: A group of words punctuated with an opening capital and closing period. A grammatically complete sentence always contains at least one independent clause.
Fragment: A group of words punctuated as a sentence that does not contain any independent clauses
Coordinating Connector: *and, but, for, nor, or, so* (in its meaning *therefore*), *yet*
Relative Pronoun: *who, whose, whom, which, that,* and any of these words with *-ever*

LESSONS FOR STEP ONE

READ FOR MEANING

AND

REVISE FOR STYLE

LESSON FOR STEP 1A

CHOOSE BETWEEN ACTIVE AND PASSIVE VOICE VERBS

PREVIEW OF THE LESSON

The six lessons in Step 1 help you revise your language so that it is clear and smooth. The aspects treated in Step 1 are sometimes included under the term *style*. Use these lessons in conjunction with the process guide for Step 1 revision, pp. 16–19. The place of Step 1 revision within the writing process as a whole is discussed on pp. 8–16.

Choosing between active and passive voice verbs is important because your choices can significantly affect the tone of your writing. Writing with a great deal of passive voice usually sounds much more formal, scientific, and/or official than writing that primarily uses active voice verbs. If you're overusing the passive, you often must go back to rewrite a whole passage.

LESSON 1A: CHOOSE BETWEEN ACTIVE AND PASSIVE VOICE VERBS

Also, your choice between active and passive voice establishes your subjects and verbs, which will come under closer scrutiny later in this section.

For this lesson, you must be able to identify subjects and verbs. Review Introductory Lesson A if necessary.

Definition: In ACTIVE VOICE, the grammatical subject of the verb performs the action named by that verb.

Definition: In PASSIVE VOICE, the grammatical subject of the verb is acted upon.

                     S   V
        Active: **John hit the ball.**
                        S   V
        Passive: **The ball was hit by John.**

DETERMINE WHETHER YOUR VERBS ARE ACTIVE OR PASSIVE

The following steps help to determine whether any verb is active or passive. Remember that a sentence may have more than one verb (see Introductory Lesson A). A sentence may contain both active and passive verbs. The process of deciding whether a verb in your draft is active or passive is diagrammed in Figure 1A.1.

Does the verb contain a form of *to be* plus a main verb?	→ Yes →	Can the subject become the object?	→ Yes →	Passive
↓ No		↓ No		
────────────────────────────────→				Active

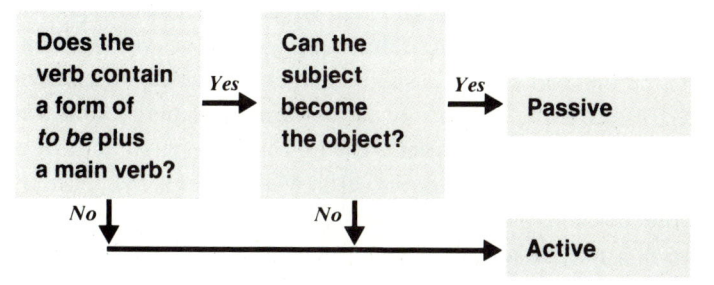

FIGURE 1A.1: Identifying Passive/Active Verbs

STEP ONE: READ FOR MEANING AND REVISE FOR STYLE

1. LOOK FOR A FORM OF *TO BE* PLUS A MAIN VERB

In looking for passive voice verbs, you need to consider only those verbs that have helping verbs and that contain some form of *to be*. The passive voice always contains a form of *to be* (and sometimes another helper) plus the main verb.

Helper	*Sample Passive Verb*
is, am, are	is hit
will be, will have been	will have been eaten
was, were	were rescued
has been, have been, had been	has been amended
could be, would be, should be, might be, etc.	could be destroyed

The presence of a *to be* helper does not automatically mean the verb is passive, only that it might be passive. If there is no *to be,* however, you know the verb is active. Notice that passive verbs often end in *t, en,* or *ed.*

2. DISTINGUISH REAL PASSIVES FROM LOOK-ALIKES

If a verb has a helper, as in the previous examples, the last test is to decide whether you have a real passive voice verb or only a counterfeit. The counterfeit is a *to be* verb plus a word that tells a subject's state of being. The real passive voice verb tells an action that was done to a subject. To determine the difference, ask whether the sentence could be turned around so that the subject becomes the object. (The object is the person or thing that receives the action of the verb.) Make *X* the subject. Make your possible passive voice verb (without its *to be* part) the verb. Make the subject of the old sentence the object of the new sentence. If the essential meaning of the sentence remains the same, the original verb was passive.

LESSON 1A: CHOOSE BETWEEN ACTIVE AND PASSIVE VOICE VERBS

Sentence	Make X the subject; make the old subject the object.	Original verb passive?
S V The ball is hit.	S V O X hits the ball.	Passive
S V The woman is tired.	S V O X tireds the woman?	New sentence does not make sense, so original verb is active, not *passive*.
S V The bill was passed by the legislature.	S V O X passed the bill.	Passive

Notice that in some sentences the new subject *X* is named in the original sentence, often following the word *by,* as in the example where you might say *X passed the bill* or *the legislature passed the bill.*

APPLYING THE TWO STEPS

In the following examples, the two tests are applied to determine whether the verb is active or passive.

All the workers quit yesterday.

(There are no helpers, so the verb is active.)

The report was excellent.

You may recognize immediately that *excellent* is not a verb but merely describes the report. If in doubt, apply the second test: *X* excellented the report? The new sentence makes no sense, so the original verb is active, not passive.

STEP ONE: READ FOR MEANING AND REVISE FOR STYLE

The report was praised.

The verb is *was praised*. *Praised* in this sentence is different from *excellent* in the previous sentence because *excellent* described the report; *praised* tells what happened to the report, so it is part of the passive verb. If in doubt, apply the second test: *X* praised the report. The sentence makes sense, so the original verb is passive.

The firm's investment opportunities will be restricted by this legislation.

The verb is *will be restricted*. Apply the second test: *X* will restrict the firm's investment opportunities. The original verb is passive.

The manager said he was sorry the machine had been broken, but nothing could be done.

Was is active because *sorry* describes the manager, rather than telling what was done to the manager. *Had been broken* is passive. *Could be done* is passive. Apply the second test: *X* broke the machine; *X* could do nothing.

The manager said he was sorry the machine had broken, but he could do nothing.

All verbs are active. *Had broken* is active because the machine is the subject of the full verb, *had broken*. That verb lacks a helper based on *to be,* so does not qualify as passive.

REASONS FOR CHOOSING PASSIVE VOICE

Passive voice may eliminate the actor. For example, the sentence *The ball was thrown* does not state who threw the ball. Alternately, passive voice may place the actor toward the end of the sentence *(The ball was thrown by the boy).* Thus passive

LESSON 1A: CHOOSE BETWEEN ACTIVE AND PASSIVE VOICE VERBS

voice deemphasizes the actor and emphasizes the action. It also allows a concept or topic to appear at the beginning or end of a sentence. For example, in the next sentence, *passive voice* appears at the beginning because that is the topic and because opening a new paragraph with that term helps the reader quickly to recognize that the sentence says something else about passive voice and its uses.

Passive voice is heavily used in scientific and technical writing to deemphasize the role of the researchers or the research team. Thus a report may say "Technique X was applied" rather than "We applied technique X." Also, the passive voice may be used to elevate certain concepts to the front of a sentence and bury others at the back. Thus, writing about a particular type of cancerous tumor, a medical researcher, writing for a professional journal, puts the type of tumor and the size of the research sample right up front by using a passive voice verb (underlined):

Five Type C cancers <u>were studied</u> *by light and electron microscopy.*

Heavy use of the passive voice is common in scientific and technical fields, but active voice is becoming more widespread. To balance the previous example, where passive voice was used to bury the identity of the researcher, in the same issue of this medical journal, authors refer to themselves variously as "we" or "the authors," or they give the name of the research group as the subject of an active voice verb (underlined). The following are examples:

The Southwest Oncology Group <u>tested</u> *three combinations of drugs.* . . .
Using FAB criteria, we <u>classified</u> *195 adult leukemia cases.* . . .
The authors <u>reviewed</u> *the 150 patients.* . . .

STEP ONE: READ FOR MEANING AND REVISE FOR STYLE

DO NOT OVERUSE PASSIVE VOICE

A common tendency is to overuse the passive voice, as in the following paragraph, which discusses some actions that the Department of Youth Service in Massachusetts took to develop new alternatives to juvenile prisons.

Draft: The creation of new alternatives *was approached* by the department by having humane homes instead of the juvenile prisons. The use of small, community-based programs instead of large institutions, and the purchase of services from private community groups rather than state-operated programs *were* also *incorporated* into the reform. (50 words)

The passive voice leads to awkward and wordy sentences. Changing to active voice helps the writer tighten the passage and make it more direct and clear. The revision makes *department* the subject. In this essay, that was an appropriate choice, since the department was, in fact, the instigator and since the essay emphasized the department's role in changing juvenile services.

Revision: As new alternatives, the department *created* humane homes instead of juvenile prisons. It *instigated* small, community-based programs in place of large institutions, and it *purchased* services from private community groups instead of using state-operated programs. (37 words)

EXERCISES

Answers in back of book: 1 a-k, 2
Answers in instructor's manual: 1 l-t, 3, 4

1. In the following list, change all passive voice verbs to active voice. Supply a subject if needed. Those that already are active, simply mark *A*.

LESSON 1A: CHOOSE BETWEEN ACTIVE AND PASSIVE VOICE VERBS

(Answers in back of book)
a. The ball was hit.
b. The ball was blue.
c. Air flowed into the chamber.
d. The bait had settled by a large rock.
e. Seven experienced welders were applying for the job.
f. They were all experienced.
g. They were all hired.
h. By Christmas, I will have been working six months.
i. She wanted to know whether all salespeople had been hired by the personnel office.
j. The firm has recently closed its downtown office because profits have been small.
k. A routine that has generally been followed is for the children to be allowed into the hallway only when an assembly is being presented.

(Answers in instructor's manual)
l. Ann's car was painted gray.
m. The symphony traveled to Europe.
n. We had run by the river.
o. Christmas cards were sent by the company.
p. The children were called.
q. The children were cold.
r. Eight banks have recently located their offices in Delaware because taxes are lower.
s. The picnic is greatly appreciated and should be continued.
t. Questions about how and why Chuck had left school were asked among groups of friends, but they remained unanswered.

2. In the following student writer's passage, change all passive verbs to active. If necessary change verb tenses for consistency. Sentences are numbered for reference. (Sample revision in back of book)

111

STEP ONE: READ FOR MEANING AND REVISE FOR STYLE

(1)The decision was made by the company to make sure that all wastes were disposed of according to federal regulations. (2)However, the government has recently closed the only nearby approved toxic waste dump, so a problem is faced by the company. (3)They have been unhappy in the past about government regulation of toxic waste disposal; now they are even more dissatisfied.

3. The following is part of a letter from a fast food restaurant employee to his employer, asking that the management allow more freedom in scheduling work hours. As you think appropriate, change passive voice to active voice and tighten as necessary to make the letter crisp and to highlight the changes the employee wants to make. The first paragraph acknowledges what the writer appreciates about the firm's policy. The second paragraph presents the problem. Sentences are numbered for reference. (Sample revision in instructor's manual)

(1)In the past, management has been fair in regard to allowing time off to its employees. (2)It is asked that requests be made two weeks in advance and the request is granted. (3)This practice is much appreciated and should be maintained.

(4)Some complaint can be made concerning weekly scheduling procedures. (5)Commonly, one will be assigned to work 5 P.M. to 2 A.M. Saturday night and 8 A.M. to 5 P.M. Sunday. (6)Another schedule that has been commonly assigned is 5 P.M. to 2 A.M. both Friday and Saturday nights. (7)With eighty employees, it is not understood why management finds it necessary to schedule a worker with only six hours between shifts, or on both weekend nights. (8)It would seem that there are enough workers for there to be some variation in the schedule.

4. The following paragraph is part of a student's humorous fantasy about the way literature students will have to study

LESSON 1A: CHOOSE BETWEEN ACTIVE AND PASSIVE VOICE VERBS

current twentieth-century literature in the twenty-second century. Where you think advisable, change passive to active voice. Sentences are numbered for reference. (Sample revision in instructor's manual)

(1) Watching a movie such as *E.T.* for homework could become as dreaded as reading the *Merchant of Venice*. (2) *E.T.* could be researched for its plot structure, conflicts, and mood. (3) What about symbolism? (4) Will the Reese's Pieces, the glow of E.T.'s finger, and E.T.'s little plant represent life? (5) Then there is the director to be considered. (6) Perhaps the life of Steven Spielberg will be studied so that more insight to the character of E.T. will be gained. . . . (7) Just imagine trying to find the complete *Cliff Notes* to *E.T.* and its director. (8) A twenty-second century student may learn to hate our beloved *E.T.* as much as we hate the sixteenth century's beloved *Romeo and Juliet*.

REVISING YOUR OWN WRITING

In the space provided, enter sentences or passages from your own writing, where you've inappropriately chosen passive or active voice. Write the revision. Then write five other sentences or passages that follow similar patterns.

Your Sentence(s)

_____
_____
_____
_____
_____

Your Revision

_____
_____

STEP ONE: READ FOR MEANING AND REVISE FOR STYLE

Five Other Sentences in the Same Pattern

GRAMMATICAL TERMS IN THIS LESSON

Subject: A word or group of words that names the person or thing that is performing the action or that is in the state of being named in the verb

Verb: One to four words that name the action or state of being of the subject

Helping Verb: A verb that accompanies another verb and that is a form of *to be, to have, to do, will, would, shall, should, can, could, may, might, must, ought*

Active Voice: In active voice, the grammatical subject of the verb performs the action named in the verb

Passive Voice: In passive voice, the grammatical subject of the verb is acted upon

Object: The word or words that name the person, thing, or concept that receives the action of the verb (direct object) or to whom or for whom the action of the verb is performed (indirect object)

LESSON FOR STEP 1B

ADD TRANSITIONS AS NEEDED

PREVIEW OF THE LESSON

Transitions are the connective tissue of good writing. Without them, even well-organized writing may seem disconnected or choppy to readers. As you revise, put yourself in the reader's place, asking whether you have made clear and explicit the links between ideas in your writing. This lesson shows how transitions work and how to provide them in your writing.

Definition: A TRANSITION is a word or group of words that clarifies relationships between ideas.

These are three common types of transitions:

1. a word, phrase, or sentence that makes the relationship explicit
2. the repetition of words or ideas
3. repeated structures, such as a series of sentences that open with *to*

STEP ONE: READ FOR MEANING AND REVISE FOR STYLE

In a section of Martin Luther King, Jr.'s "I Have a Dream" speech, the transitions work in many ways. King made this speech at the Capitol, in 1963, having led a band of marchers there to commemorate the one hundredth anniversary of Lincoln's Emancipation Proclamation, which freed the slaves. (The sentences are numbered for reference.)

FROM "I HAVE A DREAM"
—MARTIN LUTHER KING, JR.

(1) Five score years ago, a great American, in whose symbolic shadow we stand, signed the Emancipation Proclamation. (2) This momentous decree came as a great beacon light of hope to millions of Negro slaves who had been seared in the flames of withering injustice. (3) It came as a joyous daybreak to end the long night of captivity.

(4) But one hundred years later, we must face the tragic fact that the Negro is still not free. (5) One hundred years later, the life of the Negro is still sadly crippled by the manacles of segregation and the chains of discrimination....

(6) In a sense we have come to our nation's capitol to cash a check. (7) When the architects of our republic wrote the magnificent words of the Constitution and the Declaration of Independence, they were signing a promissory note to which every American was to fall heir. (8) This note was a promise that all men would be guaranteed the unalienable rights of life, liberty, and the pursuit of happiness.

How does King use transitions to link Abraham Lincoln, slaves, people today, the issues of segregation and discrimination, the Constitution, and the metaphor of the check?

Sentence 1 begins with the same words and the same eloquent language as Lincoln's Gettysburg Address. That famous speech that commemorated the Civil War dead begins, "Fourscore and seven years ago, our fathers brought forth on this continent a new nation, conceived in liberty, and dedicated to the proposition that all men are created equal." Already King has created a link, in this case by evoking something with which his audience is already familiar. The job of a transition is to make a connection explicit, but transitions often draw upon a body of shared knowledge and expectation common to both writer and reader. By the implied connection here, King puts himself and his readers in the tradition of American freedom and in the tradition of great American speeches about liberty. He also prepares for his explicit reference, at the end of the sentence, to the Emancipation Proclamation. The first sentence also links King's present audience to America's past. His first use of *we* in the passage is tightly linked, in the sentence, to Lincoln and Lincoln's shadow.

The second sentence begins with a direct reference to the previous sentence: *This momentous decree.* Then the sentence goes on to add new information. This structure is one of the most common kinds of transitions: a sentence opens with reference to what has just been said, then goes on to add new material. The next sentence also opens with a reference to the decree: *it.* These two sentences are both formed in the same way, each with the *decree* as subject. Their similar structure reinforces the fact that they both make statements about the effects of the decree.

The next paragraph begins with a specific transitional word *but,* which shows the oppositional relationship between what has just been said and what will now be said. If you were to read only the word *but,* you could probably predict the content of what King will say in the paragraph.

The *we* enters here for a second time. Now, however, *we* is not simply inserted in a parenthetical phrase wedged into a secondary spot in the sentence; *we* becomes the subject of the sentence. King has given the reader and himself responsibility for what is happening in the present.

Both sentences in the second paragraph begin with an echo of the very first sentence: *Five score years ago* becomes the more colloquial *one hundred years later,* and that phrase is repeated to link the two sentences in the second paragraph. Each of those two sentences tells a condition of the present, one hundred years after Lincoln.

In the third paragraph, King introduces the check metaphor. He links this paragraph to the others by making *we* the subject of his first sentence, and by the phrase *have come to our capitol.* King has moved from one hundred years ago to the general conditions of blacks today, and now to the specific reason why he and his followers have marched to the Capitol. Sentence 7 begins with a reference to the nation's founders. At first the reader may not know what point King is trying to make; however, the sentence ends with *promissory note,* a kind of check. The link to the paragraph's first sentence is clear. The statement *to which every American was to fall heir* faintly echoes the very first relationship King established between us and Lincoln—*in whose shadow we stand.* Sentence 8 opens, again, with an explicit transition, *This note.*

You can see that an explanation of transitions in a well-written passage includes the three specific types of transitions previously listed. However, an explanation must go beyond the list to discuss how the transitions work. The explanation must show how transitions evoke and connect ideas, weaving a network within which a reader can be led smoothly toward the conclusion.

HOW TO PROVIDE TRANSITIONS AS NEEDED

One good way to see whether a piece of writing has sufficient transitions is to read the first sentence of each paragraph. For most academic papers and other informational and persuasive writing, the first sentence often provides a link to the previous ideas and a clue about the new topic. In fact, for many term papers, reports, and other informational or persuasive writing, readers may be able to outline the main ideas of a paper just by reading the first sentences of the paragraphs. (For purposes of surprise, suspense, or to give background information, or in more imaginative or philosophical writing, writers may not follow this guideline strictly.)

This strategy may remind you of the term *topic sentence.* Topic sentences often serve as transitions because they not only state the new topic, but show how it connects to the previous one. The straightforward opening topic sentence, that states the paragraph or section topic outright, is one good way to lead the reader. However, in real-world writing, many effective paragraphs do not open with a strict topic sentence.

Perhaps a better term is *topic clue.* The first sentence of a paragraph usually gives the reader a clue about the direction of the paragraph. If a clue is misleading, the writer has established a false expectation and must then fight that expectation all the way through.

For example, one student was writing a paper to counter a classmates' assertions that their rural county was boring. The writer's goal was to overwhelm her readers with vivid descriptions of the many enjoyable things for teens to do in St. Mary's County. One of her paragraphs began this way:

Draft: One of the programs designed to keep teenagers away from alcohol and drugs is Project Graduation, a program that St. Mary's County initiated three years ago. The object of Project Graduation is precisely to keep teenagers away from alcohol and drugs and to make sure they survive their graduation night. The county gives each high school $2,000 to throw a big party for its seniors on their graduation night. The students have a say as to how the money will be used. The only provision is that no drugs or alcohol be involved. [The paragraph continues with a description of the graduation party the writer's high school class organized with its $2,000—the wonderful band, luscious food, the elegant country club, and the night of dancing that ended with a sunrise breakfast on the terrace of the country club.]

If you read the first sentence of this paragraph without knowing the context, you would think that the paper was about programs designed to keep teenagers away from alcohol and drugs. Thus when the writer finally focuses on her real point, she will be fighting a misleading impression that her first sentences have already established. The writer, instead, should open with a focus on Project Graduation as one of the ways teens have fun in St. Mary's County. The opener may be straightforward or imaginative, but it must give an accurate *topic clue.*

Revision: Another way to have fun in St. Mary's County is to have an elegant party, and, on graduation night, the county will even help the graduates pay for the party.

Alternate revision: Would you call a county boring if the county government gave you and your friends $2,000 for an elegant party?

Alternate revision: Dancing all night, swirling around an elegant, country-club ballroom, with your favorite band playing, near a candle-lit table full of crab sandwiches and little, spicy sausages wrapped in pastry—does that sound boring?

Just as you read the beginnings of paragraphs to check transitions, likewise read within each paragraph. The reader should feel that the direction of thought is easy to follow. Does each sentence maintain a clear link to previous ideas?

The following are the first few paragraphs of a much longer paper. As you read the opening of the paper, try to make an outline of the main ideas of each paragraph. (Paragraphs are numbered for reference.)

DRAFT OF PAPER ON MEN'S ROLES

(1) Men suffer the effects of traditional gender roles more than women. Behavioral patterns that are innate come into conflict with the assigned roles that culture attempts to instill in its youth. Culture expects boys to mature faster than girls even though boys actually mature more slowly than girls. An act of opposite sex behavior carried out by a boy is frowned upon to a greater degree than if performed by a girl. Similar behavior of a boy and of a girl is often met with scorn for the boy and acceptance for the girl. The concept that only men must achieve and be aggressive is a prime cause of their suffering.

(2) If it is true that the central nervous system differs between males and females, then it should cause differences in the behavior of male and female children. There should be differences in behavioral patterns even before the environment takes hold on the two sexes.

(3) It is difficult to conduct a study of young infants under six months of age because of their lack of body control and inability to communicate effectively. Therefore, the study subjects must be at least six months old in order to perform a relevant study.

(4) A study of infants which was conducted by J. Kagan and M. Lewis (1965) produced the following results of innate differences. [table of differences follows]

The paper confuses the reader because there is no relationship beween the first and second sentences. Nor does the reader know how any of the other sentences are related to one another or to the main structure of the paper. Actually, however, the writing is logical. In paragraph 1, the thesis is stated in the first sentence, and then the four subpoints of the paper are stated in order. The first subpoint is covered in two sentences (2 and 3). Each other subpoint is stated in one sentence. All the subpoints represent reasons why men suffer more than women. The

STEP ONE: READ FOR MEANING AND REVISE FOR STYLE

writer's thoughts are well organized, but the reader can't tell. Further confusion results when the reader begins paragraph 2. The reader has no way of knowing how the central nervous system relates to the topics mentioned in paragraph 1. The first sentences of paragraphs 2 and 3 waste the subject and verb in ways that provide little real information. Notice how long the writer makes the reader wait, in each case, for any word that names the *topic* of the coming paragraph. The following revision shows how transitions and sentence openers can make the progression of ideas more clear. (Added transitional material is underlined. A few wordy passages have been tightened.)

REVISION

(1) Men suffer the effects of traditional gender roles more than women. <u>One reason men are so disadvantaged is that their</u> innate behavioral patterns conflict with the assigned roles that culture attempts to instill in its youth. <u>For example,</u> culture expects boys to mature faster than girls even though boys actually mature more slowly than girls. <u>A second reason for the difficulties of boys</u> is that an act of opposite sex behavior carried out by a boy is frowned upon to a greater degree than if performed by a girl. <u>In addition,</u> similar behavior of a boy and of a girl is often met with scorn for the boy and acceptance for the girl. <u>Finally,</u> the concept that only men must achieve and be aggressive is a prime cause of boys' suffering.

(2) <u>Society expects boys, more than girls, to overcome their innate biological characteristics.</u> If it is true that the central nervous system differs between males and females, then it should cause differences in the behavior of male and female children. There should be differences in behavioral patterns even before the environment takes hold on the two sexes.

(3) <u>Such evidence of differences does, in fact, exist,</u> <u>based on six-month-old infants.</u> <u>The reason for using six-month-olders is that</u> it is difficult to conduct a study of young infants under six months of age because of their lack of body control and inability to communicate effectively. Therefore, the study subjects must be at least six months old in order to perform a relevant study.

(4) <u>One such</u> investigation of six-month-old infants, which was conducted by J. Kagan and M. Lewis (1965), produced the following results of innate differences [table].

The added material uses two important strategies for making sentence openers serve transitional functions:

1. To specify relationships *(one reason; for example)*.
2. To repeat earlier ideas and link them to new ideas *(men are so disadvantaged; such evidence; one such investigation)*.

Notice that the first sentence of paragraph 2 repeats the key word *innate* from paragraph 1, to show the reader that the essay is now taking up that point which was announced in the first paragraph. These are two important ways of making sentence openers serve transitional functions.

The passage needs revision for word choice and wordiness, but the point is to illustrate how the addition of transitional material, especially at sentence and paragraph openings, can make a writer's network of ideas clearer to the reader. At the end of the revised passage, the reader knows that the paper will present four reasons why men are more affected than women by gender expectations. The reader knows that the writer has begun the first point by discussing the difficulties of research in that area. Then the writer has presented the first research study he will use as support for his claim.

STEP ONE: READ FOR MEANING AND REVISE FOR STYLE

EXERCISES

Answers in back of book: 3a
Answers in instructor's manual: 1, 3b

1. The following passage is the paragraph of King's "Dream" speech that immediately follows the passage printed in this lesson. Write a discussion of the way the transitions work. Follow the example earlier in the lesson. Sentences are numbered for reference. (Sample discussion in instructor's manual)

(1)It is obvious today that America has defaulted on this promissory note insofar as her citizens of color are concerned. (2)Instead of honoring this sacred obligation, America has given the Negro people a bad check; a check which has come back marked "insufficient funds." (3)But we refuse to believe that the bank of justice is bankrupt. (4)We refuse to believe that there are insufficient funds in the great vaults of opportunity of this nation. (5)So we have come to cash this check—a check that will give us upon demand the riches of freedom and the security of justice. (6)We have also come to this hallowed spot to remind America of the fierce urgency of *now*. (7)This is no time to engage in the luxury of cooling off or to take the tranquilizing drugs of gradualism. (8)*Now* is the time to make real the promises of Democracy. (9)*Now* is the time to rise from the dark and desolate valley of segregation to the sunlit path of racial justice. (10)*Now* is the time to open the doors of opportunity to all of God's children. (11)*Now* is the time to lift our nation from the quicksands of racial injustice to the solid rock of brotherhood.

(12)It would be fatal for the nation to overlook the urgency of the moment and to underestimate the determination of the Negro. (13)This sweltering summer of the Negro's legitimate discontent will not pass until there is an invigorating autumn of freedom and equality. (14)1963 is not an end,

LESSON 1B: ADD TRANSITIONS AS NEEDED

but a beginning. (15)Those who hope that the Negro needed to blow off steam and will now be content will have a rude awakening if the nation returns to business as usual.

2. Write a short paper about three of the ways in which people your age have fun where they live. Your audience is your class. Your goal is to counter other peoples' claims that the place you live is "boring." Concentrate especially on effective transitions.

3. In the following paragraphs, supply transitions between the sentences as needed. You may want to rearrange or combine ideas. Improve each paragraph in as many ways as you can, but pay particular attention to the transitions.

(Sample revision in back of book)
 a. The following paragraph opens an essay in which a student, a New York City native, tells other students how to travel and sightsee safely in New York. Sentences are numbered for reference.

(1)Who is afraid of New York City? (2)Of course you know what a great city it is—the Empire State Building, Madison Square Garden, Broadway, Chinatown, Fifth Avenue, Carnegie Hall. (3)The average tourist does not want to experience or witness the disgusting violence on the six o'clock news. (4)It is true that the city is filthy, congested, and overpopulated with thieves, murderers, and other unpleasant elements. (5)This does not suggest that the chances of surviving a day in the city are as delicate as if playing Russian roulette. (6)New York City may be both safe and exciting if you know how to travel and how to act like a New Yorker.

(Sample revision in instructor's manual)
 b. The following paragraph opens an essay in which a student proposes that there be no classes at her college the day after Easter. To understand her argument, you need

STEP ONE: READ FOR MEANING AND REVISE FOR STYLE

to know that a "day of obligation," to Catholics, is a day in which they have an obligation to attend Mass. (The names of the college and academic vice-president have been changed.) Sentences are numbered for reference.

(1)Classes should not be held the Monday after Easter at Saints Philip, Matthew, James and John College. (2)I investigated the situation by interviewing Thomas S. Gowtamass, Academic Vice-President of the college. (3)He is given a specific number of school days to work with. (4)He had a choice of holding classes either Holy Thursday or the Monday after Easter. (5)Saints Philip, Matthew, James and John College, being a Catholic school, takes religious holidays into considerable account. (6)The Academic Vice-President chose Holy Thursday as the day off so that students and faculty can attend Mass services. (7)Holy Thursday is not even a day of obligation. (8)He scheduled classes Monday to meet the required number of school days. (9)Other administrators, like Vice-President Gowtamass, also hold the same belief: that classes should not be held on a holy day, especially on Holy Thursday. (10)I feel Thursday should be counted as a required school day while classes should be cancelled on the Monday after Easter. [The writer continues with the reasons for cancelling classes on Easter Monday: students want to spend the full day Easter Sunday with their families, Easter evening traffic is heavy and difficult, and so on.]

REVISING YOUR OWN WRITING

In the space provided, enter passages from your own writing, where you've needed better transitions. Write the revision. Then write five other sentences or passages that follow similar patterns.

Your Sentence(s)

_____
_____
_____
_____

Your Revision

_____
_____
_____
_____

Five Other Sentences in the Same Pattern

_____
_____
_____
_____
_____

GRAMMATICAL TERMS IN THIS LESSON

Transition: A word or group of words that clarifies relationships between ideas

Topic clue: A word or group of words that helps the reader understand the topic of a paragraph or passage

LESSON FOR
STEP 1C

USE SUBJECT/VERB AND SENTENCE OPENERS FOR CLARITY AND EMPHASIS

PREVIEW OF THE LESSON

Subjects and verbs are the "guts" of your writing. Sentence openers orient the reader. If these two aspects are strong, you're a long way toward clear, forceful, effective writing. In this step, consider how your choices about main subject-verb units and sentence openers contribute to emphasis and clarity in your writing. First identify the subject-verb units of the independent clauses (also called main clauses). Also examine the sentence openers. Then revise as needed.

LESSON 1C: USE SUBJECT/VERB AND SENTENCE OPENERS

If you need help identifying subjects and verbs, see Introductory Lesson A. To identify independent clauses, see Introductory Lesson B.

UNDERLINE THE OPENING WORD OR PHRASE IN EACH SENTENCE

In each sentence, underline the first unit of importance to the reader. Sometimes it's a word, sometimes a group of words. Use your own judgment about what to underline.

UNDERLINE SUBJECT-VERB UNITS OF INDEPENDENT CLAUSES IN EACH SENTENCE

Next, underline the subject and verb of each independent (main) clause. For help identifying subjects and verbs, see Introductory Lesson A. For help identifying independent clauses, see Introductory Lesson B. (If you find a sentence that has no independent clause, it is a fragment. Unless it serves a special purpose, it should be revised. See Step 2A.) Of course, if your main clause subject is the sentence's first unit, you've already underlined it.

THREE GUIDELINES FOR REVISING SUBJECT-VERB UNITS AND SENTENCE OPENERS

The underlined sections of your paragraphs are the most important parts of your writing for your readers. It is as though your paragraph were a scene on a stage, with the brightest spotlights on the parts you've underlined. Your goal is to use your main subject-verb units and your sentence openings to

STEP ONE: READ FOR MEANING AND REVISE FOR STYLE

emphasize your most important ideas and to create a smoothly flowing piece of writing. So as you revise your sentences, keep the following guidelines in mind.

1. Use the main subject-verb unit for the most important idea in a sentence. Less important ideas should be relegated to secondary *(subordinate)* sentence elements.

Exception: Writers may disregard this principle in order to begin or end a sentence with a specific idea that needs emphasis, begin a sentence with a clear link to preceding sentences, achieve a certain order of information within a sentence, or create surprise, suspense, or humor.

2. Use the first few words in the sentence or the paragraph to:
   a. orient the reader to the subject of the new sentence/paragraph,
   b. establish the relationship between the sentence/paragraph to come and the sentence(s) just completed (also see transitions, Lesson 1B),
   c. emphasize important ideas by giving them the prominent opening position.
3. Check whether the subject, verb, and object words are appropriate for one another. (The object is the person or thing that receives the action of the verb. For example, John hit *the ball.*)

HOW TO SHAPE MAIN SUBJECT-VERB UNITS

One idea may be written many different ways. To apply the three guidelines, you need to know how to shape the main subject-verb units in a sentence. In the following sentences, the writer changes the emphasis of the ideas by revising the subject-verb unit (underlined) of the independent (main) clause.

LESSON 1C: USE SUBJECT/VERB AND SENTENCE OPENERS

Writing about the impact of environmental concern on the development of technology, a writer might use the main subject-verb unit to say that environmental concerns have stalled certain projects:

                S   V

Environmental <u>protectionists succeeded</u> in stalling even such important projects as the trans-Alaska pipeline, despite the efforts of engineers, developers, and industry.

In another context, the writer might want to emphasize the supporters:

    S   S   S   V

<u>Engineers, developers, and industry supported</u> the Alaska pipeline, which was being stalled by environmental protectionists.

In still another context, the writer might wish to emphasize the pipeline:

                   S   V

The trans-Alaska <u>pipeline was stalled</u> by environmental protectionists, despite the efforts of engineers, developers, and industry.

To see how subject and verb choices can change the emphasis of a passage, read the following two reports of the same biological experiment, written by two different writers. (At a nearby lake, students had performed a test of the lake's productivity. The students used technical terms, which have been changed in the passages. The students gathered surface water in light and dark-colored bottles. Then they suspended the bottles at various depths in the lake. After a day, tests of the suspended water revealed something that is referred to here as the lake's *productivity*.)

STUDENT 1'S REPORT

To estimate the productivity of Lake Roland, we used the light/dark bottle technique. Surface water was collected and resuspended in dark and light bottles at several depths. After one day's time, the bottles were then recollected and taken to the lab for measuring. The values received led to the conclusion that Lake Roland is a productive lake.

STUDENT 2'S REPORT

The light and dark bottle method is an extremely useful method to learn indirectly about a lake's productivity. In this experiment, it was used to determine the nature of Lake Roland and its tributary, Jones Falls. The results clearly indicate that Lake Roland is a very productive lake.

The first report opens with a statement of the experiment's purpose, *to estimate the productivity of Lake Roland*. The main subject-verb unit emphasizes the procedures used for that purpose. No sentence has *bottle method* as its subject. Only one sentence has *bottles* as its subject, and that sentence is buried in the middle of the paragraph. The final sentence states the conclusion in relation to the earlier stated purpose: *Lake Roland is a productive lake*. Note the subjects and verbs:

Subject	*Verb*
we	used
water	was collected and resuspended
bottles	were recollected and taken
values	led

In the second report, the first sentence places emphasis immediately upon the bottle technique. The second sentence also has the bottle method *(it)* as its subject.

Subject	Verb
[bottle] method	is
it [bottle method]	was used
results	indicate

Both reports end with a variation of *the results indicate Lake Roland is productive.* However, in the first report, the final sentence has greater impact because the question about the lake's productivity has been posed early, as the experiment's purpose, and has been the focus throughout. In the second report, the productivity of Lake Roland seems almost a by-product of the writer's focus on the bottle technique. These examples illustrate how significantly the choice of subject-verb units and sentence openers can shape what the reader perceives as the main point of your writing.

SUBORDINATING SENTENCE ELEMENTS

Revising subject-verb word choices may sometimes include demoting a subject-verb unit to a less important status in a sentence. You can change a main (independent) clause into a dependent clause. (Exercises 20 and 21 in Introductory Lesson B give you practice in doing that.) You can also change a clause to a phrase that has no subject-verb unit. Some clauses can even be changed to one or two words. As you review the subject-verb units in independent clauses, ask whether they are equally important, or whether some of them are secondary to others. For example, in the following sentences, the revisions change an independent clause into a dependent clause.

Draft: A glider has no engine and the pilot has fewer things to think about while flying.

In this draft, the fact that the glider has no engine is preliminary, but not equal, to the writer's real point—the pilot has fewer things to think about. The revision subordinates the first point and highlights the second.

Revision: Because a glider has no engine, the pilot has fewer things to think about while flying.

In the following example from a paper about German castles, the writer debates two choices.

Draft: The castle was built by King Ludwig II and is a fairy-story palace.

The two statements about the castle are not of equal importance and seem incongruous linked together as verbs of the independent clause. One of them can be subordinated. The choice depends upon whether the writer wants to emphasize the castle's builder or its fairy-tale quality.

Revision: The castle, built by King Ludwig II, is a fairy-story palace. OR The fairy-story castle was built by King Ludwig II.

In the following sentence, the repetition of *and* is a clue that the sentence strings together too many independent clauses and that some should be subordinated.

Draft: You stepped into one of those theaters and you could escape for just a few hours into a dream world and anything you could possibly imagine would be yours.

Revision: When you stepped into one of those theaters, you could escape for just a few hours into a dream world where anything you could possibly imagine would be yours.

CHECKING SUBJECT-VERB-OBJECT WORD CHOICES

As you examine subjects and verbs, examine also the objects. Ask whether the words you've chosen for subject, verb, and object fit together.

Definition: The OBJECT is the person or thing that receives the action named in the verb.

There are two kinds of objects: direct and indirect. The following sentence illustrates the difference between them.

Subject	Verb	Direct Object	Indirect Object
Jill	*threw*	*the ball*	*to me.*

There's no further explanation or practice on direct and indirect objects here, because for now, you don't need to be perfectly accurate in identifying direct objects or distinguishing them from indirect objects. You just need to look at the main clause of your sentence—the part that tells who is doing what to whom—and ask whether the words you've chosen make sense together.

The following examples illustrate some problems with subject-verb-object word choices. The writer is arguing for the relocation of a city's stadium.

Draft: This area would also reduce the crime around a new stadium.

The area would not reduce crime. Rather, the choice of the area, or the security, or the middle-class nature of the area would minimize crime.

Revision: The security of this area would also reduce crime around a stadium.

STEP ONE: READ FOR MEANING AND REVISE FOR STYLE

In the following essay, the author responds to columnist George Will's criticism of people who wear designer clothing. She maintains that dressing in a particular way can increase self-esteem by making people feel comfortable, helping people fit in with peers, and enabling people to express individuality. The following paragraph develops her first point—clothes offer personal comfort, thus increasing self-esteem.

Draft: Although we subconsciously choose the clothing that gives us the most self-satisfaction, the genesis of such contentment stems from the comfort of our clothes. Aside from a sizable comfort, the clothing includes outward appearance. Some accept the cliché, "You feel as good as you look," and dress accordingly. Dressing in freshly pressed clothes of the latest styles make these people feel better about themselves. I, too, am one of those perfectionists who can't bear to have any clashing colors, any nibbled nails, or any snagged stockings. To me, trekking across campus with messy hair, old clothes and docksiders compares with a malignant disease for which the only therapy is curlers, the latest fashions and high-heeled shoes. A neat appearance increases my self-image. When I look good, I feel good. Others, however, prefer a more casual appearance. An old pair of Levis may be their medicine for a bad day. Not worrying about wrinkling pants or dirtying a new blouse is their idea of being comfortable. Thus, since their wardrobe makes them feel more relaxed, their daily performance increases. Although their comfort is different from mine and others, it is unfair to pass cynical judgments. In essence, the ideal of comfort is an individual trait where applying an alteration would strip one's character and decrease their self-image.

Suppose this writer checked this passage for the word choices of her subjects, verbs, and objects. She might start with the first sentence. Can genesis stem from comfort? The writer

LESSON 1C: USE SUBJECT/VERB AND SENTENCE OPENERS

actually intends to emphasize the *subconscious* element. We choose our clothes subconsciously, but behind that choice is our desire for comfort. In the next sentence, can clothing include appearance? The writer actually means that her definition of *comfort* includes peoples' feelings of comfort with their outward appearance. In the sentence that begins *Thus,* can a performance increase? In the sentence that begins *To me,* the writer's subject, verb and direct object state that *trekking compares with a disease,* an awkward comparison. In the last sentence of the paragraph, can an *ideal* be a *trait?* Can one's *character* be *stripped?* Can self-image be *decreased and increased?* A revision of the paragraph might well include some changes in other aspects, but to illustrate this lesson, the following revision includes only changes in subjects, verbs, and objects.

> *Revision:* Our choice of clothing is subconscious, but the genesis of that choice is comfort, including comfort with our outward appearance. Some accept the cliché "You feel as good as you look," and dress accordingly. Dressing in freshly pressed clothes of the latest styles makes these people feel better about themselves. I, too, am one of those perfectionists who can't bear to have any clashing colors, any nibbled nails, or any snagged stockings. When I trek across campus with messy hair, old clothes and docksiders, I feel like I have a malignant disease for which the only therapy is curlers, the latest fashions and high-heeled shoes. A neat appearance enhances my self-image. When I look good, I feel good. Others, however, prefer a more casual appearance. An old pair of Levis may be their medicine for a bad day. Not worrying about wrinkling pants or dirtying a new blouse is their idea of being comfortable. Thus, since their wardrobe makes them feel more relaxed, their daily performance improves. Although their comfort is different from mine and others, it is unfair to pass cynical judgments.

STEP ONE: READ FOR MEANING AND REVISE FOR STYLE

In essence, all of us find comfort in our own ways. To make us change would diminish our individuality and damage our self-image.

SAMPLE REVISIONS USING THE THREE GUIDELINES

The following sentences show how the guidelines are specifically applied. Notice the importance of transitions (Lesson 1B).

Writing about a novel's main character and her escapes from danger, the author begins a discussion of one such narrow escape with this sentence:

Draft: Jane's intended marriage to Rochester was a near disastrous mistake but represented another barely escaped danger.

The writer underlined the subject, *marriage,* and two verbs: *was a mistake* and *represented another danger.* He asked himself whether the subject and verbs highlighted the main point and whether the sentence contained a clear indication of the true topic of the coming paragraph. He realized that the opening subject-verb unit, *Jane's marriage was a mistake* might mislead the reader. The real topic is not Jane's mistakes, but Jane's escapes from danger. The writer revised to make that idea clearly primary.

Revision: Jane's intended marriage to Rochester was another barely escaped danger.

The fact that the intended marriage was a mistake is taken up later in the paragraph, since it is a subordinate idea. The revised opening sentence gives the reader a clear reminder of the general topic—escapes from danger. It announces the topic of this paragraph—Jane's marriage. It shows the relationship

LESSON 1C: USE SUBJECT/VERB AND SENTENCE OPENERS

between this paragraph and the larger topic—the intended marriage is one of the escaped dangers.

In the next example, about using a certain kind of medical chart, the writer finds that her two main subject-verb units do not represent two equally important ideas. One idea can more accurately be captured in a subordinate structure.

Draft: The chart should be used only as a guideline and medical tests and a personal history are essential to diagnose the disease.

The writer underlined her two main subject-verb units: *chart should be used* and *medical tests and history are essential*. She asked herself whether these two ideas deserved equal prominence in the sentence, and whether *and* was the appropriate connector. She realized that what she wanted to say was that the chart should be used only as a guideline. The second subject-verb unit, she realized, explained *why* the chart should be used only as a guideline. That is a subordinate idea. Next, she realized that the concept of *diagnosis* was the most important idea in the second part of the sentence. The information about medical tests and personal history make sense only when the reader understands that diagnosis is the goal. She decided to place *diagnosis* earlier:

Revision: The chart should be used only as a guideline, since a firm diagnosis of the disease also requires medical tests and a personal history.

To see how revision of subject and verb choices and sentence openings can sharpen clarity and emphasis in longer passages, analyze the following two paragraphs. They form the opening of an essay in which the writer invites the reader to share her alarm at the spread of drug use to educated, professional people, and the impact of that spread upon young people in America.

STEP ONE: READ FOR MEANING AND REVISE FOR STYLE

DRAFT

While lying in my bed, unconsciously listening to the television, the news flashed on. Another story was being reported of a top businessperson under arrest for drug use and dealings worth millions. Today, drug busts aren't against your average lowlife junkie; no, what is present here is your typical businessperson, athlete, actor, and about a dozen other top notch people in our society. The businesspeople producing our many services, the political leaders running our country, and the athletes who influence the youth are the headlines concerning drug abuse today.

Sixty Minutes was interviewing a Pittsburgh Pirate who was a drug user. This player used drugs his entire twelve-year career. He openly admitted to millions of viewers that he pitched a no-hitter game while on LSD! During that entire game he was never aware of how fantastic he had pitched. I sat watching this man in disbelief. Aren't these the people who are supposed to be in control of themselves? Why are they allowing drugs to take control of them? Athletes need to obtain control and concentration to win a game; this baseball player didn't even know he was playing a game!

The following is the list of main (independent clause) subject-verb units in the previous passage:

Subject	*Verb*
news	flashed
story	was being reported
drug busts	aren't
what	is
business people/political leaders/athletes	are
Sixty Minutes	was interviewing
player	used

LESSON 1C: USE SUBJECT/VERB AND SENTENCE OPENERS

Subject	Verb
he	admitted
he	was never aware
I	sat watching
these	aren't
they	are allowing
athletes	need
player	didn't know

Analyzing this list shows that the writer used the subjects and verbs of the first two sentences to describe the reporting of the news, not the content of the news—a heavy investment for background information. The reader is a long way into the paragraph before the real emphasis becomes clear. Further, the first sentence might catch a reader's attention more effectively if its verb portrayed the writer in startled attention. A revision, then, might focus on the actions of the writer and the actions of drug users, unobtrusively inserting that the information about drug users came from a news broadcast:

Revision: Lying on my bed, unconsciously listening to the television news, suddenly I snapped to attention. Another top businessperson was under arrest for drug use and dealings worth millions.

The third, fourth, and fifth sentences all have forms of *to be* as verbs. Whenever you use forms of *to be* or *to have,* ask yourself whether there is a more precise and vivid substitute. In this case, the three sentences can be condensed into two, to eliminate the repetition of the list of people (more on this kind of tightening in Lesson 1E). Then each sentence can be given a sharp, precise verb. (No other changes have been made.)

Revision: Today, drug busts don't hit your average lowlife junkie. No, the businesspeople producing our many services, the political leaders running our country, and the athletes influencing our youth dominate the headlines concerning drug abuse today.

The second paragraph opens with a subject and verb that do not effectively link its ideas to the ideas of the previous one. The baseball player is the real focus of attention, not the fact that *Sixty Minutes* was interviewing him. The writer should select a subject and verb for the sentence that puts the opening emphasis squarely on the Pirate, and links him to the business people, political leaders, and athletes who dominate our attention at the end of the previous paragraph. A revision might be the following:

Revision: A Pittsburgh Pirate interviewed on *Sixty Minutes* had used drugs his entire twelve-year career.

The opening sentence of the second paragraph now establishes the important subject—the Pirate. The reader understands immediately how that paragraph relates to the previous one. The subsidiary information *interviewed on Sixty Minutes* is slipped in unobtrusively. The single, straightforward verb, *had used drugs,* substitutes for the writer's original two repetitious verbs, *was a drug user* and *used drugs.*

The writer's analysis of the subject-verb choices in the next example showed where the paragraph had gotten off track. The writer could then make changes in the order of ideas within the paragraph. The following is the original paragraph recommending a new location for Baltimore's sports stadium.

Draft: Approximately thirty years ago, a new stadium complex was being constructed in the heart of Baltimore. Who would have ever expected that, today, Memorial Stadium would be that popular landmark in our city. With the increased popularity of sports and the expansion of the city, it is time that we considered other possible locations for a new stadium.

LESSON 1C: USE SUBJECT/VERB AND SENTENCE OPENERS

The main subjects and verbs are shown in the following solid-line boxes, with dependent clauses in broken-line boxes, to make a visible representation of the paragraph's structure:

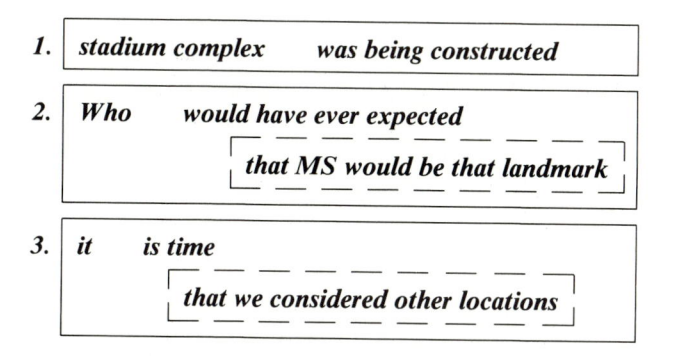

1. | *stadium complex* *was being constructed* |

2. | *Who* *would have ever expected* |
      | *that MS would be that landmark* |

3. | *it* *is time* |
      | *that we considered other locations* |

The outline shows that sentence 2 emphasizes an irrelevant and confusing point—*who would have expected?* Further, Memorial Stadium as a landmark is not clearly related to the writer's main point about location. The writer meant to contrast people's original satisfaction with the stadium to their current realization that the old stadium is no longer adequate.

Revision: Approximately thirty years ago, great excitement surrounded the construction of a new stadium complex in the heart of Baltimore. Memorial Stadium served the city well and became a beloved landmark. Today, however, with the increased popularity of sports and the expansion of the city, we must consider other possible locations for a new stadium.

The writer changed the first sentence to make *excitement* the subject—an emphasis more in keeping with his purpose. The confusing *who would have expected* disappears. The second sentence focuses upon the stadium as the subject; the verb emphasizes the past success of the stadium. The third sentence clearly indicates the switch in time *(today)* and the

STEP ONE: READ FOR MEANING AND REVISE FOR STYLE

transition to a view different from the earlier one *(however)*. The subject of the last sentence becomes *we*. That choice eliminates the wordy *it is time that* and emphasizes the need for readers to participate in the action the writer is recommending.

The next example shows a writer's reasoning in revising a passage of writing where many decisions have been appropriate, but where some improvements can be made. The following passage is from a booklet for students and faculty at a college. The booklet, entitled "Access to Computing Facilities," explains the computer facilities available on campus. (Sentences are numbered for reference.)

Draft: (1)Academic computing facilities may be used by members of the academic community for research and instruction. (2)There is no charge for the use of any of the facilities although some departments may impose a lab fee associated with specific courses. (3)To use the VAX, you must obtain an account from Academic Computing Services in 415 Harrison Hall. (4)Students must apply in person with proof of student status and student number to obtain accounts. (5)There is no account associated with the use of the microcomputers. (6)However, users may be asked to show their college ID before using the equipment.

In reviewing this passage, the writer should examine each sentence, marking sentence openers and main subject-verb units. This is how the writer's thinking might proceed: The present opening words establish *academic computing facilities* as the subject of the paragraph. However, the earlier paragraphs, as well as the title, have already established that topic. This particular section is about *access,* and the reader's logical first question is *who* may have access. The writer decides to lead with the answer to that question. The answer, in its current version, is phrased, *members of the academic community.* Will all student readers, even freshmen, be sure that that phrase includes them? The writer decides to clarify. Now the sentence reads:

Revision: (1)Any member of the academic community—student, faculty, or staff—may use the academic computing facilities for research and instruction.

The second sentence has two key ideas: *no charge* and *lab fees.* Should those ideas logically go next? The writer decides they should, since the question of charge is likely to be an important one to readers who have just been told they may use the facilities. Is *no charge* more important than *lab fees?* The writer decides that it is. Thus the current sentence, which places *no charge* as the first idea and as the idea that comprises the sentence's main subject and verb, seems effective.

Sentences 3 and 5 are a pair. They answer the question, *How do I get access to the computers?* The two different types of computers require different accessing procedures. The writer decides to make the differences clear by opening each sentence with the type of computer that will be explained: *To use the VAX,* do X, and *To use the microcomputers,* do Y. The writer now asks whether the subject of sentence 3, *you,* is as precise as it needs to be. Probably it would be better to specify *all users,* so that readers understand that this rule applies to everyone. Sentence 4 explains the specific regulations for students. The opening of that sentence, *Students must apply,* does not immediately make clear what is the context, and how this idea relates to the previous one. The writer decides to lead with *To obtain an account,* which clearly establishes *how* to obtain an account since the earlier sentence told *who* may obtain an account. Next, the writer realizes that regulations for faculty and administrators should also be explained. Sentences 3 and 4 now read:

Revision: (3)To use the VAX, all users must obtain an account from ACS in 415 Harrison Hall. (4)To obtain an account, students must apply in person with proof of student status and student number; faculty and staff can request an account in person, by telephone, or in writing.

STEP ONE: READ FOR MEANING AND REVISE FOR STYLE

Sentence 5 opens with words that give little or no information or orientation: *There is no account.* The reader must wait too long before learning that the sentence is telling how to get an account for *microcomputers.* The writer decides to lead with the distinction *To use microcomputers,* establishing a clear relationship with the previous *to use the VAX.* The writer also decides that *no account* should be first, followed by the *show ID* information. The writer determines that the *However,* as the opener to sentence 6, provides an accurate and useful clue to the relationship between the two sentences. Thus sentences 5 and 6 now read:

Revision: (5) To use the microcomputers, no account is required. (6) However, users may be asked to show their college ID before using the equipment.

This lesson has examined the process by which a writer makes choices about sentence openers, subjects, and verbs. In this instance, the writer's goal was to make the passage easy and clear for readers who are reading as fast as they can to obtain the necessary information from the passage. When goals and context vary, however, you can use the same sort of thinking process.

EXERCISES

Answers in back of book: 1a-e, 2a, 3a, 4, 5a
Answers in instructor's manual: 1f-i, 2b, 3b, 5b

1. Revise the following sentences for subject-verb-object word choice and for placement of ideas in independent (main) subject-verb units.
   (Sample revisions in back of book)
   a. The present site for the new stadium is city owned. Thus financial arrangements in that respect are foregone.
   b. The onset of alcoholism has been classified into four

LESSON 1C: USE SUBJECT/VERB AND SENTENCE OPENERS

stages. These include the Pre-alcoholic stage, the Early-alcoholic stage, the Crucial stage, and the Final stage.
c. The fake personality of a candidate usually doesn't get elected because, through the long hard campaign, his or her real personality will show.
d. Jane would be a puppet under Rochester's rule and this would totally defeat the very purpose of her own self-sufficiency.
e. The record industry cannot control what songs play on the radio because that jurisdiction is under the guidance of the Federal Communication Commission (FCC).

(Answers in instructor's manual)

f. Actions must be done to help.
g. Another possible step toward cleaning up the mess could be brought about by the music industry itself.
h. The experience of working at a soup kitchen shed a new light on my attitude toward my own life and the world around me.
i. Such men as Mozart, Bach, and Beethoven wrote the music that would leave an impact stronger and finer than any other composer could dare to write.

2. Revise the following passages.

(Sample revision in back of book)

a. Clearly teens have sex, and without birth control, and many become pregnant. In fact, every thirty seconds, another unwed teenager becomes pregnant. Naturally, this hurts the Church's stand on premarital sex and damages its teaching against birth control.

(Sample revision in instructor's manual)

b. However, prejudices and misconceptions are against teenagers. It is a common myth that the less teens know about sex, the less likely they are to have it. This is not only unfounded and wrong, but also leads to ignorance in the prevention of unwanted pregnancies.

STEP ONE: READ FOR MEANING AND REVISE FOR STYLE

3. Revise the following paragraphs, focusing on sentence openings, main subject-verb units, and word choices for subjects, verbs, and objects.

The following is part of a paper detailing recent developments in the writer's small but growing town of Howell. This paragraph is about the improvements in roads. The writer's thesis is that though many people complain about the coming of the new development, it has significant advantages for the town. Two paragraphs are printed here, to give you the tone and flavor. Revise the *second paragraph* only. Sentences are numbered for reference.

(Sample revision in back of book)

a. (1)Howell has started to develop better roads. (2)There has been major improvement in old roads as well as the development of new ones. (3)The old jokes about getting lost on the backroads trying to find Howell are becoming extinct. (4)Interstate I95, developed within the last five years, has made it easier to get to Howell. (5)Before this time you would have to take another highway and get off in another town and then you had the task of finding Howell. (6)In past years if you needed help on your journey people were not always sure where Howell was, or always eager to admit that they knew of Howell.

(7)Then there is the illustrious Route 9 which has always been a major road not only in Howell but also in neighboring towns to the north and south. (8)Route 9 has always been thought of as a life-threatening road to travel on but even more so in Howell. (9)Presently Route 9 is under a dualization process while others have dualized several years previously. (10)Maybe this will finally stop the Route 9 killer.

(Sample revision in instructor's manual)

b. The following paragraph is part of an essay in which the writer wants to assess the differences between the graded and the nongraded school. The audience is fellow stu-

LESSON 1C: USE SUBJECT/VERB AND SENTENCE OPENERS

dents in an upperclass education course. This particular paragraph deals with the intellectual differences between students in the two curricula.

(1)Pupils in the nongraded curriculum seem to be more advanced in some areas of reasoning than those in the graded curriculum. (2)There is no significant difference between the two curricula other than in this area. (3)The reason for this may be that these students are exposed to a variety of choices that will help them attain the goal of mastering the task. (4)They experiment and figure out the best method for them. (5)The children in the graded curriculum are limited by their structured classrooms. (6)Barbara Nelson Pavan (1979) supports McLoughlin (1974) by stating that the children in the nongraded curriculum acquire greater conceptual maturity than those in the graded curriculum. (7)This was proven true by the results on the Draw-a-Person test, where the children in the nongraded curriculum scored higher in this test which is a measure of abstract thinking.

4. Following is the first sentence of each paragraph in a newspaper feature article. To get the information for the article, the writer interviewed Brenda Gottesman, staff assistant for *Milwaukee Magazine*. [Names of people and publications have been changed.] Among her other duties, Ms. Gottesman plans articles. Rewrite first sentences so that the article will focus upon Ms. Gottesman.

   (Sample revisions in back of book)

   (1) In planning an article, the audience must always be kept in mind.

   (2) Potentially touchy subjects, such as the recent article on the relation between upperclass Milwaukee women and their maids, must be handled carefully.

   (3) A magazine article needs durability, Ms. Gottesman said.

STEP ONE: READ FOR MEANING AND REVISE FOR STYLE

(4) Ms. Gottesman would like to see *Milwaukee Magazine* "key into the culture scene more," to be "making trends."

5. The following is a list of facts about *Milwaukee Magazine* and Ms. Gottesman. Using as many of them as are relevant, write two lead paragraphs: (a) a lead paragraph for an article that will emphasize how *Milwaukee Magazine* is working for growth and (b) a lead paragraph for an article featuring Ms. Gottesman.
(Sample revisions: (a) in back of book, (b) in instructor's manual)

Ms. Gottesman was hired as a staff assistant in 1972.

In 1972, *MM* had a circulation of 9000 and was owned by the Milwaukee Chamber of Commerce.

During the first few years, Ms. Gottesman's duties were typing, filing, making phone calls, and doing research for articles.

In 1977, the *Capital News* bought *MM*.

Between 1977 and this year, circulation has more than quadrupled, to 39,000.

With the growth has come a deluge of office work, and new and higher responsibilities for staff members, including Ms. Gottesman.

Ms. Gottesman now plans articles, revises articles sent in by free-lancers, and writes her own monthly column.

MM has none of its own staff writers, but relies on free-lancers.

MM has only four editors.

MM editors have pleasant, roomy offices.

One of the staff's chief goals is to sell 55 percent of their space to advertisers.

Ms. Gottesman says that *MM*'s growth depends on its advertisers, and that successful magazines sell fifty-five percent of their space to advertisers and use their remaining forty-five percent for copy.

LESSON 1C: USE SUBJECT/VERB AND SENTENCE OPENERS

Ms. Gottesman believes that the key to success for *MM* is the quality of its articles—a quality achieved by careful planning.

Ms. Gottesman has a B.A. in English from Appleton College.

REVISING YOUR OWN WRITING

In the space provided, enter sentences or passages from your own writing, where you've inappropriately chosen main subject-verb units and sentence openers. Write the revision. Then write five other sentences or passages that follow similar patterns.

Your Sentence(s)

_____
_____
_____
_____

Your Revision

_____
_____
_____
_____

Five Other Sentences in the Same Pattern

_____
_____
_____
_____
_____

STEP ONE: READ FOR MEANING AND REVISE FOR STYLE

QUESTIONS TO ASK ABOUT MAIN SUBJECT-VERB UNITS AND SENTENCE OPENINGS

1. Do my main subject-verb units incorporate ideas I want to emphasize, or do they give undue importance to minor ideas?
2. Do the openings of my sentences and paragraphs place undue emphasis on subsidiary ideas while ignoring more important ideas?
3. Do the openings of my sentences and paragraphs give readers a sufficiently early and accurate clue about the relationship of the coming sentence to previous ideas and to the primary subject of my paragraph?
4. Do my word choices for the subject, verb, and object fit together?

GRAMMATICAL TERMS IN THIS LESSON

Verb: One to four words that name the action or state of being of the subject

Subject: A word or group of words that names the person or thing that is performing the action or that is in the state of being named in the verb

Clause: A subject-verb unit plus that unit's modifiers and complements

Independent (Main) Clause: A clause that can stand alone

Dependent Clause: A clause that cannot stand alone

Object: The word or words that name the person, thing, or concept that receives the action of the verb (direct object) or to whom or for whom the action of the verb is performed (indirect object)

Modify: To limit or describe. A MODIFIER is a word or group of words that describes or limits the meaning of another word or group of words in the same sentence.

LESSON FOR STEP 1D

RELATE SENTENCE PARTS CLEARLY

PREVIEW OF THE LESSON

In the previous lesson, a paragraph was likened to a play on a stage, in which the brightest spotlights are trained on the subject-verb unit and on the sentence openings. Now it's time to check that the subordinate actors, who stand in the dimmer lights, are also doing their job, and that the whole configuration is pleasing and meaningful. Your goal is to allow the reader to follow your sentences smoothly, without getting confused or misled, even momentarily. The following is a preview of the issues you should examine in your sentences.

1. Use parallel forms for parallel ideas.
2. Revise distracting material between the subject and verb.
3. Place modifiers in clear relation to what they modify.
4. Clarify relationships among other elements.
5. Revise forms that miscue the reader.

STEP ONE: READ FOR MEANING AND REVISE FOR STYLE

This step does not contain any fast rules, only guidelines that you must adapt to the situation, tone, and goals of your particular piece of writing. This step asks you to do much more than look for *errors*. It asks you to actively shape your language. Consider not, "What mistakes have I made?" but "Are the relationships between sentence parts as clear as I can make them in this context for this audience?"

The remainder of the section discusses these five guidelines in sequence. Each guideline is followed by an exercise so you can practice that guideline before going on to others. Exercises at the end of the lesson offer practice in applying all the guidelines.

1. USE PARALLEL FORMS FOR PARALLEL IDEAS

In this context, the term *parallel ideas* means that two or more ideas have equal importance in a sentence. In its simplest form, parallelism means that a list of similar items or concepts should be similar in grammatical form.

Draft: Good salespeople are persistent, liking people, and to be able to work hard.

Revision: Good salespeople are persistent, outgoing, and hard working.

The three qualities of salespeople are all equally important; that is, they are parallel ideas. To convey their parallelism efficiently to the reader, the writer uses similar grammatical forms. Frequently in revising for parallelism, the writer also discovers how to condense the passage, as the previous revision illustrates.

In the following sentence, the writer lists several parallel functions for political parties.

Draft: The political parties in the United States perform such functions as electing candidates to run for

LESSON 1D: RELATE SENTENCE PARTS CLEARLY

	public office, helping organize the government, provide opposition to the party in power, raise funds needed to conduct election campaigns, and inform voters about public affairs and problems that need governmental action.
Revision:	The political parties in the United States perform such functions as *electing* candidates to run for public office, *helping* organize the government, *opposing* the party in power, *raising* funds for election campaigns, and *informing* voters about public affairs and problems that need governmental action.

In the first draft, the writer switches from *-ing* words *(electing, helping)* to present tense verbs *(raise).* The switch is probably caused by *helping organize,* which introduces the new verb form. The writer forgets that the sequence began with *-ing* words. The sheer number and length of the items adds to the confusion. In the revision, the writer restores the *-ing* pattern to all the elements and shortens some of the elements by eliminating unnecessary words.

ADDING WORDS TO CLARIFY PARALLEL STRUCTURES

Sometimes a sentence can be made more readable by adding a word to clarify the parallelism of the relationship. The next sentence is from a paper about the growth of Chicano political power.

Draft:	The Chicano population, in order to achieve substantial success in meeting its needs, will have to opt either for an alliance with other minority organizations to form a third party or a continued bartering process with the major parties.

There are two options for the Chicano population: an alliance or a bartering process; however, so many words are

STEP ONE: READ FOR MEANING AND REVISE FOR STYLE

included in the *alliance* part that the reader may be lost by the time he or she reads *bartering process*. One remedy is to add a clue—repeat the word *for* to reestablish the *opt for* construction:

Revision: The Chicano population, in order to achieve substantial success in meeting its needs, will have to opt *either for* an alliance with other minority organizations to form a third party *or for* a continued bartering process with the major parties.

USING EITHER/OR, NEITHER/NOR, NOT/BUT

Note in the previous example that when you are using *either/or* and similar constructions, the *either* comes *just before* the point at which the two forms will diverge. A common mistake is to place the *either* too early in the sentence.

Draft: Computer owners can either get help from their local self-help groups or from a dial-in hotline.

Notice that *get help* is still part of the common core of the sentence. The two parallel options do not split off until *from . . . groups or from . . . hotline*. The *either* should wait until just before the first parallel phrase.

Revision: Computer owners can get help *either from* their local self-help groups *or from* a dial-in hotline.

PLACING SHORTER UNITS BEFORE LONGER UNITS

A sentence is often more readable (and sometimes more rhythmic) if the longer units in a series are moved to the end. The shorter units at the beginning do not as easily interrupt the reader's sense of the structure of the series. For example, in the previous Chicano example, the sentence could be made more readable by moving the shorter *bartering process* phrase to the

LESSON 1D: RELATE SENTENCE PARTS CLEARLY

first position and saving the longer and more complex *alliance* phrase for the end. While making this change, the writer might also see that the *bartering* unit could be shortened even more by removing the unnecessary word, *process*.

Further revision: The Chicano population, in order to achieve substantial success in meeting its needs, will have to opt either for continued bartering with the major parties or for an alliance with other minority organizations to form a third party.

MOVING SENTENCE PARTS TO MAKE PARALLEL RELATIONSHIPS CLEAR

A writer not only may add words to make parallel relationships clear but also may move sentence parts.

Draft: Under this plan, the present site would hold the stadium and 30 percent of the parking while the remainder would use the new parking facility at the high-school area and the surrounding streets.

One problem is that the sentence leads the reader to expect a parallel pattern. The pattern begins, *the present site will do X, while* .... The reader expects next to read, *while another site will do Y*. However, *remainder* does not refer back to *site*. So the two parallel items *(site would hold* and *remainder would use)* do not both refer to the same core idea. *Remainder* may seem to refer to *parking,* but then the rest of the clause doesn't make sense, because *parking* can't *use* a lot.

Another problem in the sentence is that *at the high-school area and* establishes the expectation that the sentence will conclude, *and at X*. The present ending, *and the surrounding streets,* leaves the reader unsure whether the new parking facility is in the surrounding streets or whether the writer means that the remainder of the cars will park in the surrounding streets. A subsidiary problem is that *at the area* sounds awkward.

STEP ONE: READ FOR MEANING AND REVISE FOR STYLE

The remedy for the first problem is to place the two physical locations—the present site and the surrounding streets/high school area—into a clear parallel relationship. Alternately, the writer can place the two functions—stadium/30 percent parking and remainder of parking—into a parallel relationship.

The second problem may be amended by putting *and the surrounding streets* first in its phrase, since it is the shortest unit. Then *the new parking facility at the high school* becomes clearly a separate alternative, placed at the end of the sentence. Finally, *at the high-school area* may be shortened to *near the high school*.

Revision: Under this plan, the present site would hold the stadium and 30 percent of the parking, while the surrounding streets and the new parking facility near the high school would accommodate the remaining parking.

Alternate Revision: Under this plan, the stadium and 30 percent of the parking would be located on the present site, while the remaining parking would be accommodated on the surrounding streets and at the new parking facility near the high school.

EXERCISES

Answers in back of book: 1a-e
Answers in instructor's manual: 1f-h

1. Revise each of the following sentences for parallelism. (Sample revisions in back of book)
   a. We need to discover who is in control and their goals.
   b. The college student must often hold down a job at night and borrowing money to stay in college.
   c. As I drive over the bridge connecting the island to the mainland, I remember the long drives my family took to our beach home and arriving with armloads of luggage.

d. The 1940's also saw the rise of political organizations in addition to the formation of youth groups for juvenile problems and securing education reform for the Chicano.
e. At the beginning of the night, there may be more than enough students to build stage sets, but as it gets later, students leave because they either have class the next day or with other things to do.

(Sample revisions in instructor's manual)

f. The system of government the Constitutional Convention intended to frame concentrated all power with the national government and major control being maintained in the hands of a few selected officials.
g. The news of the doctor's mistake not only devastated my family but the whole school as well.
h. An organization's desire to relocate may be stimulated by a growth in demand, a desire to expand market influence, the plant and its equipment being outdated, or operating at a different site may be more profitable.

2. REVISE DISTRACTING MATERIAL BETWEEN SUBJECT AND VERB

Connect each verb with its subject, either in your mind or by drawing arrows on your paper. (For help with identifying subjects and verbs, see Introductory Lesson A.) Is there material between the subject and the verb that is confusing? The subject and verb need not be next to each other. In fact, sometimes ten or fifteen words can separate a subject from its verb, provided those words are clearly structured so that the reader does not lose track of the relationship between the subject and verb. If your reader has lost the meaning of the sentence, then revise. If you can't tell, ask a couple of friends to read the sentence aloud—you can usually hear from their stumbles or their tone whether they have a confident understanding of the sentence or have lost their way.

STEP ONE: READ FOR MEANING AND REVISE FOR STYLE

Some decisions about the amount of material to place between related elements like subjects and verbs will depend upon the sophistication of your readers and the nature of your writing. In simple, direct writing meant for people who are reading rapidly, for unsophisticated readers, or for situations where you want to sound terse and efficient, you will generally place related items close to one another. Sentences will often be short, following a simple subject-verb pattern, with one important idea to a sentence. The following sentence may be revised in several ways, depending upon how short and simple the writer wants the sentences to be.

Draft: *Close examination*[S] *of the construction of the managerial team and the board, the extensive powers granted to the vice-presidents, and the principle upon which the whole was based led*[V] *the consultants to this conclusion.*

The subject is *examination;* the verb is *led*. In between, the writer does clearly delineate three phrases, separated by commas. However, the double *of* in the first phrase adds to the complexity of the material, and just the sheer number of words may cause the reader to lose track of the sentence before the verb appears.

FOUR OPTIONS FOR REVISING DISTRACTIONS BETWEEN SUBJECT AND VERB

Four solutions are commonly used to clarify the relationships, not just between subject and verb, but between any related elements.

LESSON 1D: RELATE SENTENCE PARTS CLEARLY

1. Change the subject or verb, creating a clearer sentence.
2. Shorten the intervening elements.
3. Create two or more sentences from one sentence.
4. Move parts of the sentence so the related elements are closer together.

The writer might choose a new subject and verb for the sentence, placing the long list of items at the end of the sentence, where it doesn't interrupt the relationship between any two elements. This option gives the hurried or unsophisticated reader a simple subject-verb-object opener.

                          S   V
Revision: ***The consultants reached this conclusion through closely examining the construction of the managerial team and the board, the extensive powers granted to the vice-presidents, and the principle upon which the whole was based.***

Alternately, the sentence may be revised using the second option—keeping the original structure but shortening the elements:

                        S
Revision: ***Close examination of the managerial team's and board's construction, of the vice-presidents' extensive***
                                            V
powers, and of the originating principle led the consultants to this conclusion.

Both of these options are still complex. The writer may decide to divide the sentence into two sentences:

STEP ONE: READ FOR MEANING AND REVISE FOR STYLE

                                     S   V

Revision: *The consultants reached this conclusion through closely examining the construction of the mana-*
                          S   V
gerial team and the board. They also reviewed the extensive powers granted to the vice-presidents and the principle upon which the whole was based.

The next example illustrates option four: simply moving sentence parts—in this case the verb—to make relationships clearer. The sentence also illustrates a variation of the subject-verb problem. The confusion is not between the subject and verb, but between the two verbs that belong to the subject *I*.

Draft: Using the Nelson-Denny Form A exam, I *contacted* all seniors at the college who had begun their college careers there *and tested* them.

By the time the reader reaches *and tested,* it is not clear whether that verb belongs with *contacted* or with the intervening *had begun.* The writer began the revision by bringing together the two parts of the verb:

First   Using the Nelson-Denny Form A exam, I *con-*
Revision: *tacted and tested* all seniors at the college who had begun their college careers there.

When the two verbs were brought together, the writer realized that if the seniors were tested, they would also naturally have been contacted. Thus the word *contacted* is unnecessary. The repetition contained in *at the college, college,* and *there* also needs revision. Another repetition lies within *exam* and *tested.*

Further   I administered the Nelson-Denny Form A exam to
Revision: all seniors who had started as freshmen at that college.

LESSON 1D: RELATE SENTENCE PARTS CLEARLY

Frequently, revisions for the relationship of sentence parts will highlight wordiness and repetition. More about those kinds of revisions in Lesson 1E.

EXERCISES

Answers in back of book: 2a
Answers in instructor's manual: 2b

2. Revise the following sentences to bring the verb closer to its subject. To get practice in moving sentence parts, make these revisions even if you think that, in some contexts, the sentence is acceptable as it stands.

   (Sample revision in back of book)
   a. The purpose of the new government, according to the final thoughts of the general convention, which included delegates from all the colonies, was to provide for "common defense, security of liberty and general welfare."
   (Sample revision in instructor's manual)
   b. Many misconceptions, based on fears, superstitions, and misunderstandings dating back to early beliefs about devils and evil spirits exist today about the mentally retarded.

3. PLACE MODIFIERS IN CLEAR RELATION TO WHAT THEY MODIFY

Definition: A MODIFIER is any word or group of words that describes or limits the meaning of another word or group of words in the same sentence.

Short adjective modifiers like "the *furry* kitten" usually are placed next to the word they modify and don't cause problems. You should be most interested in modifiers that are longer groups of words, because they can often interfere with the flow of a sentence when placed awkwardly or when dangled at the

STEP ONE: READ FOR MEANING AND REVISE FOR STYLE

end of a sentence, where their relationship to what they modify is not clear. The following sentences show common types of modifiers (underlined):

The sculptor, <u>**who had lived so long in obscurity**</u>**,** ***was now famous.***

(A clause, with its own subject and verb, modifies another word—*sculptor*. For discussion of clauses, see Introductory Lesson B.)

<u>**Accustomed to living in poverty**</u>**,** ***she at first could not imagine how to use her new-found wealth.***

(A phrase modifies another word—*she*.)

She thanked her benefactors <u>**generously**</u>**,** <u>**by giving each of them a fine miniature wood carving.**</u>

(One single word—*generously*—and one phrase both modify the verb, *thanked*.)

In each of your clauses, mark the modifiers that include several words, and all the modifiers that modify verbs (because they're especially likely to cause trouble). Ask yourself whether the modifier's relationship to what it modifies will be clear to the reader. The elements need not be next to each other, but readers should be able to see the relationship clearly.

Just as for subject-verb relationships, discussed in the previous section, some decisions about the amount of material to place between related elements will depend upon the sophistication of your readers and the nature of your writing. In simple, direct writing (meant for people who are reading rapidly, for unsophisticated readers, or for situations where you want to sound terse and efficient), you will generally place related items close to one another. Sentences will often be short, following a simple subject-verb pattern, with one important idea for each sentence. Longer modifiers may be taken out of a sentence and made into additional sentences.

LESSON 1D: RELATE SENTENCE PARTS CLEARLY

In the following example, both a *that* clause and another modifying phrase cause problems because they are not clearly related to the words they modify:

Draft: He showed a pattern of self-destructive behavior for at least one month that limited his ability to get along with people and to do his work.

The phrase *for at least one month* modifies *showed,* because it tells *when* he showed. The clause *that limited his ability . . .* modifies *behavior* because it tells what kind of behavior. The remedy is to move each modifier closer to the word it modifies:

Revision: For at least one month, he showed a pattern of self-destructive behavior that limited his ability to get along with people and to do his work.

In the next example, *advertisements* and its modifier, *such as . . . ,* are too far apart. The remedy is to move some of the confusing material to the beginning of the sentence.

Draft: One can find advertisements in the back of *Seventeen Magazine* and several others such as "Send for Your Official American Identification Card."

Revision: In the back of *Seventeen Magazine* and several others, one can find advertisements such as "Send for Your Official American Identification Card."

The following example is about the framing of the U.S. Constitution and the views of Sherman, a delegate to the Constitutional Convention. In the draft, the phrase *by stating* is far from the word it modifies, *opposed.* Further, the two *by's* are awkward. The remedy is to rewrite the sentence:

Draft: Sherman opposed election by the people by stating, "The people should have as little to do as may be."

Revision: Sherman, opposing election by the people, stated, "The people should have as little to do as may be."

STEP ONE: READ FOR MEANING AND REVISE FOR STYLE

OR Opposing election by the people, Sherman stated, "The people should have as little to do as may be."

REVISING A DANGLING MODIFIER

A dangling modifier is a modifier that is placed so its relationship to what it modifies is not clear. The most common form of the dangling modifier occurs with a phrase that contains a *participle*—a verb-like word usually ending in *-ing, -ed,* or *-t* (*jumping* for the ball, fully *satisfied, caught* in the act). In these cases, the next person or thing named after the participial phrase should be the person or thing doing the action described in the participle. Failure to follow this rule creates a dangling modifier.

Draft: Jumping for the rebound, the umpire called a foul on me.

As is often the case with dangling modifiers, the passage as a whole still makes the meaning clear. The reader knows that the umpire did not jump for the rebound; however, grammatically, the reader expects a certain structure. The reader's expectation is overturned; the dangling modifier may cause a momentary hesitation in reading. Thus a careful writer revises to remove dangling modifiers.

There are two ways to amend a dangling modifier:

1. Change the first noun after the phrase.

Revision: *Jumping* for the ball, *I* heard the umpire call "foul!"

OR

2. Make the modifier into a clause with its own subject. (For help identifying clauses, see Introductory Lesson B.)

Revision: As I jumped for the rebound, the umpire called a foul.

In the next sentence, the writer is describing his ball-catching dog.

Draft: Poised like an outfielder, she waits to catch a high pop that is tossed or hit to her. Like any selfish child, however, once caught it is almost impossible to get it back without a chasing game.

The participial phrase, *poised like an outfielder,* is correctly followed by *she* [the dog], because it is *she* who is poised. But the next sentence gets into trouble with the modifier *like any selfish child.* This is not a participial phrase, but a different kind of modifier. Like the participial phrases discussed so far, however, this modifier lacks a word to specify *who* is doing the action—in this case, *who* is like any selfish child. The two uses of *it* in the last sentence cause further awkwardness.

Revision: Like any selfish child, however, she puts us through a chasing game to get the ball back.

4. CLARIFY RELATIONS BETWEEN OTHER UNITS

Guidelines 2 and 3 discussed relationships between subject and verb and between a modifier and what it modifies. A variety of other relationships also must be clear in the sentence. In the following example, the problem is a long and confusing group of words between *you would think that* and the words that explain what you would think: *the person was talking to a human.*

Draft: Our dog Charli is treated just like a human. If in another room someone is talking to Charli, *you*

STEP ONE: READ FOR MEANING AND REVISE FOR STYLE

> would think that, with them not being able to be seen, by the person's tone of voice and kind words that *the person was talking to a human.*

The remedy is to shorten some of the intervening material, and move some of it to a different point in the sentence. In the revision, a more digestible amount of material occurs between *you would think* and the words describing what you would think.

Revision: Our dog Charli is treated just like a human. If an unseen person in another room is talking to Charli, *you would think,* by the person's tone of voice and kind words, *that the person was talking to a human.*

An alternate revision places the two sentence parts shoulder to shoulder:

Alternate Revision: If an unseen person in another room is talking to Charli, the person's tone of voice and kind words *make you think that he or she is talking to a human.*

EXERCISES

Answers in back of book: 3a-d
Answers in instructor's manual: 3e-g

3. Revise the following to make the sentences clearer.
   (Sample revisions in back of book)
   a. Severe medical problems have been caused by the massive quantity of drugs consumed, which are complicated by malnutrition.
   b. Brief periods of forgetfulness, occurring during or after the trauma, called amnesia, become frequent.
   c. Another consideration is that the new site should be located close to local businesses that are geared to serve the public like restaurants and hotels.

LESSON 1D: RELATE SENTENCE PARTS CLEARLY

    d. On the vanity I have a two week old cup of tea which the also two week old lemon in it has begun drawing fruit flies by the swarm.

(Sample revisions in instructor's manual)

    e. As we began our climb up the rocks, the child started to cry. We tried to tell him how easy it was, and that there was nothing to be afraid of, for a good fifteen minutes.

    f. If the boss thought your reason was passable, he would permit you to have off, which was seldom.

    g. Pledged to continue negotiations, an agreement was reached between the strikers and management.

---

5. REVISE MISCUES

Any word that you write down establishes expectations for the reader. Problems arise when you as a writer fail to meet those expectations. You can locate these sorts of problems by having someone else read your writing or by reading it yourself, stopping frequently to ask two questions:

1. How would I expect this sentence to continue?
2. What would I expect to have read prior to these words?

Try this method with the following sentence:

Draft: The developmental reading course played no significant . . . .

What would you expect to follow? Probably the word *role* and then a phrase beginning with *in*. Instead, this is the way the original sentence read:

Draft: The developmental reading course played no significant assistance in the test results.

The word *assistance* is a surprise to the reader. It doesn't appear to belong with *played*. The remedy is to rewrite the sentence, using a consistent pattern:

STEP ONE: READ FOR MEANING AND REVISE FOR STYLE

Revision: The developmental reading course played no significant role in the test results.

In this last example, the use of a *word (played)* established expectations. In the next example, a *construction* establishes expectations. The writer is discussing the reasons for changes in American political parties over the years.

Draft: A number of factors have been associated with the weakening of the party organizations and also of party loyalty among voters . . . .

What would you expect to follow? Nothing. The sentence so far has contained a subject *(factors)*, a verb *(have been associated)*, and modifying phrases telling about the association. The reader is surprised, therefore, when the writer adds another phrase, *are widely appreciated.*

Draft: A number of factors have been associated with the weakening of the party organizations and also of party loyalty among the voters are widely appreciated.

Any sentence that ends with *are widely appreciated* should open with the subject words: *X and Y are widely appreciated.* One option for revision is to adopt this pattern.

Revision: The factors associated with the weakening of party organizations and also of party loyalty among voters are widely appreciated.

This revision contains a large number of words between the subject, *factors,* and the verb, *are appreciated.* One remedy is to make the verb active (see Lesson 1A), and begin with the subject and verb. The long phrases about party organizations and party loyalty can then be placed at the end of the sentence where they do not interrupt other relationships.

LESSON 1D: RELATE SENTENCE PARTS CLEARLY

Further A wide range of observers have appreciated the
revision: factors associated with the weakening of party organizations and also of party loyalty among voters.

In the next sentence, about the creation of the U.S. Constitution, false expectations mislead the reader again.

Draft: Actually it is ironic that the Constitutional Convention did not intend for the common people to participate but . . . .

Now what would you expect? Perhaps *but did intend for the people to X.* The following is the writer's original draft:

Draft: Actually it is ironic that the Constitutional Convention did not intend for the common people to participate but were to elect their superiors to represent them.

If you read a sentence that ended *but were to elect their superiors to represent them,* how would you expect that sentence to have begun? Perhaps with something like, *The common people were not to X, but were to elect . . . .*

The remedy is to follow just one of the two patterns or to select a new pattern and rewrite the sentence to meet the reader's expectations.

Revision: Actually it is ironic that the Constitutional Convention intended for the common people not to participate but to elect their superiors to represent them. OR Actually it is ironic that the Constitutional Convention intended not that the common people participate but that they elect their superiors to represent them.

Part of the solution is to recognize that the *did not intend . . . but intended* pattern is repetitive and awkward. A single verb,

STEP ONE: READ FOR MEANING AND REVISE FOR STYLE

intend, can introduce both parallel pieces, followed by a *not/but* construction. Note that the *not . . . but* appears at the point where the common structure ends and the divergent structures begin (see p. 156).

EXERCISES FOR MISCUES

(Note: Exercises 1-3 appear earlier in the chapter.)
Answers in back of book: 4a-b
Answers in instructor's manual: 4c-d

4. Revise the following sentences to eliminate miscues.
   (Sample revisions in back of book)
   a. Do you often wonder what makes us appreciate certain things when they're not around than when they are?
   b. Well, once at college, you realize even as early as three days of eating the food there, that the food is only disgusting because it's being compared to what you are used to eating at home, which is your mom's home cooking.
   (Sample revisions in instructor's manual)
   c. But senioritis is not as long lasting, and can often be cured by a parent-child talk or in severe cases a removal of car keys is needed.
   d. In this area, the racetrack would be placed far enough away from residents to prevent irritation of lights and pollution from traffic and noise to affect homeowners.

EXERCISES FOR ALL OF LESSON 1D

Answers in back of book: 5a-d, 6a-b
Answers in instructor's manual: 5e-g, 6c

5. Revise the following paragraphs for all the aspects of sentence relations in this lesson. You may change words or change the order of elements in the sentences to make them

LESSON 1D: RELATE SENTENCE PARTS CLEARLY

flow smoothly. You may also change verbs from passive to active (Lesson 1A).

(Sample revision in back of book)
   a. I was tossed into the center of the raft as we rode over a partially submerged rock, and I was very lucky to get only a bruise on my knees and my head got bumped.
   b. When I was called to eat with that stern, strict tone at dinnertime by my mom I knew something was wrong. As I sat down, Dad would slowly look up from his plate and send a bleak smile in my direction.
   c. These women often had children to provide and care for, and many of the same problems arose in this care which will be faced by us in the years ahead.
   d. Using the same warning labels as the movie raters, the "R" label on record albums would force distributors to think twice about carrying the particular album and therefore restricting sales.

(Sample revisions in instructor's manual)
   e. If it's one thing I learned from that memorable day is that the heart truly sees better than the eyes.
   f. The Snake River, which flows through the Appalachian Mountains from a height of 7,000 feet, is very swift and provides for a good white water run. These mountains are very rocky and this is the reason for the white water. White water is a combination of rapids with turbulence, the water is foamy, and obstacles.
   g. One major problem that has arisen since the higher drinking age has been in effect is the sudden awareness of its illegality by the younger generation and the more appealing it is to drink.

6. For each of the following groups of ideas, form a single sentence in which all parts are related clearly.

(Sample sentences in back of book)
   a. Ralph Morrison is a ship analyst at the U.S. Navel Intelligence Center in Feester, Virginia.

STEP ONE: READ FOR MEANING AND REVISE FOR STYLE

    Morrison noticed three photos of a Soviet aircraft carrier.
    The photos were lying on a desk.
    The desk belonged to a colleague.
    Morrison thought the photos might be of interest to the press.
    Morrison gave the photos to the *American Defense Weekly*.
  b. Digital Equipment Corporation won an award.
    The award is the Business in the Arts Award.
    The award has brought national recognition.
    The award is sponsored by the Business Committee for the Arts.
    The award is also sponsored by Forbes Magazine.
    The award is the only national program to honor businesses for sponsoring the arts.
(Sample sentences in instructor's manual)
  c. Goering has an office.
    The office is in his home.
    His home is in Beverly Hills.
    His office has a clutter of toys, masks, board games, and books.
    Goering works in his office.
    He works on six projects at a time.
    Some projects are novels.
    Some projects are nonfiction prose.
    Some projects are film scripts.

REVISING YOUR OWN WRITING

In the space provided, enter sentences or passages from your own writing, where you have not clearly shown relationships between sentence elements. Write the revision. Then write five other sentences or passages that follow similar patterns.

Your Sentence(s)

___

Your Revision

___

Five Other Sentences in the Same Pattern

___

GRAMMATICAL TERMS IN THIS LESSON

Parallel: Having the same importance, the same function in the sentence, and/or the same grammatical structure
Participle: A verb-like word usually ending in *-ing, -ed,* or *-t,* but not used as a verb in its sentence
Participial Phrase: A phrase that depends on a participal
Modifier: A word or group of words that describes or limits the meaning of another word or group of words in the same sentence
Dangling modifier: A modifier whose relationship to what it modifies is unclear

LESSON FOR STEP 1E

TIGHTEN TO ACHIEVE ECONOMY

PREVIEW OF THE LESSON

Sentences should not be inflated with unnecessary words. Many of the steps already covered have helped with tightening—for example, in clarifying the relationships between sentence parts, you may have shortened intervening material or rewritten sentences to make relationships clear and to eliminate unnecessary words. Now continue to tighten your writing for greater economy.

READ FOR WORDS THAT CAN BE ELIMINATED AND CONSTRUCTIONS THAT CAN BE SHORTENED

As you read your writing, ask at the end of each word, "Can that word be eliminated?" At the end of each group of words, ask, "Can that idea be said more briefly?" Especially scrutinize

LESSON 1E: TIGHTEN TO ACHIEVE ECONOMY

the following words and constructions, which are often keys to wordiness:

1. forms of *to be (is, are, am, was being)*
2. forms of *have* and *do*
3. a verb plus a noun where just a verb will do *(make a decision* instead of *decide)*
4. a clause that can be reduced to a word or a phrase (For identification of clauses, see Introductory Lesson B.)
5. verbs like *proceed to* and *begin to*
6. pronouns, especially *who, which, that,* and *this*
7. *there is/are,* and *it is*
8. *I feel, we believe,* and similar statements (Normally, if the writer states something, the reader assumes the writer believes it.)
9. passive voice (see Lesson 1A)

The following examples show the way these elements can indicate wordy constructions.

Draft: The uprising *was in protest of* recent legal proceedings.

Revision: The uprising *protested* recent legal proceedings.

(The verb-noun combination *was in protest* can be replaced by just the verb *protested.*)

Draft: We pick *who* our leaders will be by *what* we see in the candidates' campaigns, but is *what* we see the real picture?

Revision: We pick our leaders by what we see in the candidates' campaigns, but do we see the real picture? OR We pick our leaders by the candidates' campaigns, but do we see the real picture?

(The clause *who our leaders will be* can be replaced by two words, *our leaders.* The clue to the wordiness is not only the clause but also the word *who.*)

STEP ONE: READ FOR MEANING AND REVISE FOR STYLE

Draft: It is clearly seen that *there are* several causes for cheating.

Revision: Clearly, several factors cause cheating.

(The passive voice verb *is clearly seen* as well as the phrases *it is* and *there are* alert the writer to wordiness.)

Draft: *I feel that having* a new and modernized facility in this area would be convenient for most people.

Revision: A new and modernized facility in this area would be convenient for most people.

(Since the writer has asserted an idea, we assume she or he *feels* it. The unnecessary *having* can be deleted.)

TIGHTEN ENTIRE PASSAGES

Sometimes when you begin to tighten individual sentences, you find that a whole paragraph or a whole section needs tightening on a larger scale. In the following draft, sentences are numbered for reference.

Draft: (1) Approximately six months ago, *Twenty/Twenty* aired a fifteen-minute documentary concerning the hazards of earphones. (2) A test was taken by ten, randomly picked volunteer students. (3) They were required to listen to any type of music for three continuous hours with the volume set at five. (4) Astonishingly, seven out of ten students did not regain their full hearing capabilities until three hours later. (5) Each student took a hearing test before and after the listening session occurred. (6) This data was used in determining when the full hearing capabilities were regained. (7) The other three students remaining from the test ranged between forty-five and sixty minutes before they were back to their original hearing state.

Following the first explanation of the test and its results, in sentences 2-4, the writer doubles back, in sentences 5-7, to give less important information about the test; however, that information takes up nearly half the total words and captures the crucial final spot in the paragraph. The writer decided to try to insert the minor information earlier, leaving the final climactic spot in the paragraph for the most important information—the results (sentence 4). A check of the main subject-verb units revealed to the writer that in sentence 2 he had used a whole sentence for *a test was taken*—a subordinate idea that could be shortened and integrated with other sentences.

Revision: Approximately six months ago, *Twenty/Twenty* aired a fifteen-minute documentary concerning the hazards of earphones. Ten randomly picked, volunteer students were required to take a hearing test, then to listen to any type of music for three continuous hours with the volume level set at five, and finally to retake the hearing test. Three students took forty-five to sixty minutes to return to their original hearing. Astonishingly, the other seven did not regain their full hearing until three hours later.

In another context, this writer might have wanted to tell the astonishing results at the beginning of the paragraph. Such procedures are common in writing for newspapers and in much business reporting or correspondence, when some readers will be skimming or will want to know the bottom line very quickly. In such a context, the writer might have led with the astonishing results and filled in further information as economically as possible, saving the least important until last.

Alternate Revision: In one test of the hazards of earphones, ten students listened to three hours of music with the level set at five. Astonishingly, seven of the ten students did not regain their full hearing for three hours. The remaining three students took forty-five to sixty minutes to regain

STEP ONE: READ FOR MEANING AND REVISE FOR STYLE

their full hearing. The results were based on hearing tests administered to the students before and after the music listening sessions. The tests were reported as part of a fifteen-minute documentary on the hazards of earphones, aired on *Twenty/Twenty* approximately six months ago.

EXERCISES

Answers in back of book: 1a-g
Answers in instructor's manual: 1h-k

1. Revise the following for economy.
   (Sample revisions in back of book)
   a. The Chicano Service Organization is still in existence today, but, because of its nonpartisan platform, it does not hold much power within the Chicano community.
   b. If the source of electricity is near the stadium, costs will be less in the way of wiring.
   c. A possible solution that is being discussed is making a requirement of a C average for all students receiving federal assistance.
   d. Due to the harsh treatment my car experiences on a daily basis, I found myself petting and consoling my faithful companion.
   e. The consideration of the traffic aspect is a major one so the stadium must be accessible by major roadways.
   f. The existing theater is terribly insufficient in the availability of parking space which causes transportation problems.
   g. Although there is probably no ideal design for the location for the stadium, the newspapers, television, and city officials must realize that there are many considerations that must be taken account of before any decisions can be made.
   (Sample revisions in instructor's manual)
   h. Recently it has been found that it is the quality not the

LESSON 1E: TIGHTEN TO ACHIEVE ECONOMY

quantity of time spent with children which is most important.
i. In earlier times, women worked in the fields and with the livestock, which provided them with food on which to survive.
j. Because of the tremendous changes and mental pressures of divorce, this causes the child to be able to deal with problems in more adult ways in the future.
k. The best evidence that exists for this change can be seen through recent popular media.

REVISING YOUR OWN WRITING

In the space provided, enter passages from your own writing where you have used unnecessary words. Write the revision. Then write five other sentences or passages of the same type, that could be wordy, but that you have revised.

Your Passage

_____
_____
_____
_____
_____

Your Revision

_____
_____
_____
_____
_____

Five Other Sentences in the Same Pattern

_____
_____

STEP ONE: READ FOR MEANING AND REVISE FOR STYLE

_____
_____
_____

GRAMMATICAL TERMS IN THIS LESSON

Clause: A subject-verb unit plus that unit's modifiers and complements

Verb: One to four words that name the action or state of being of the subject

Pronoun: A word that substitutes for another word or group of words

Passive Voice: In passive voice, the grammatical subject of the verb is acted upon

LESSON FOR STEP 1F

REVISE DICTION (WORD CHOICE)

PREVIEW OF THE LESSON

In Step 1B, you examined your word choices for subjects, verbs, and objects. In tightening for economy, Step 1E, you sometimes replaced a group of vague words with a single, more precise word. Now focus your attention on all the words you've chosen and revise as needed for clarity and precision.

For each of your words and phrases, ask yourself, "What are other alternative words? Is this the most precise and effective word for this context?"

USING A THESAURUS

A thesaurus is a special kind of dictionary that lists synonyms (words similar in meaning) and antonyms (words opposite in meaning). Entries are alphabetized. For example, if you look under *s* for *stubborn,* you will find words such as *obstinate* that are similar in meaning, and the words like *compliant* that are opposite in meaning.

A thesaurus can be a useful tool for writers; however, you should not use a thesaurus to find the longest, most obscure words you can, and substitute them for your own words. In most situations, plain, straightforward words will be easier for readers to understand. Use the thesaurus, therefore, *only* to suggest other words that you know are clearer and more precise than the ones you already have. Do not use a thesaurus only to substitute six-syllable words for two-syllable words.

TRITE WORDS AND PHRASES

Trite words and phrases are overused formulas such as *easy as pie* or *lived to a ripe old age*. Often the words and phrases are based on an implied comparison (between *easy* and *pie*, between *old age* and *ripe* fruits). Because these comparisons are so common, they are stacked on the front shelves of our minds, and as we run along the shelves looking for the next words of a sentence, these trite phrases come to mind easily, without much thinking. Slapping down such prefabricated phrases is all right in the first stages of generating ideas and drafting, because then you are just trying to capture the idea on paper. However, later in the revision process, reexamine trite phrases and make the passages fresher and clearer. Either find a more original comparison or substitute straightforward, concrete words.

Draft: Opportunities for advancement were few and far between.

Revision: Opportunities for advancement were scarce. (The revision replaces the trite phrase with a single, direct word.)

Draft: Once again, racial violence had reared its ugly head in our small town.

Revision: Once again, racial violence had erupted in our small town.

Alternate revision: The town discovered, to its surprise, that it was situated on an active volcano of racial prejudice. (A more original metaphor replaces the trite phrase.)

CONCRETE AND ABSTRACT WORDS

Broad, abstract words are useful to express broad concepts. However, a common problem in drafting is that the writer chooses words too broad or vague, where precise, concrete words would be more effective. Make your words fit your meaning tightly and precisely. For example:

Abstract words: The horse ran across the field.

Concrete words: The filly galloped across the pasture.

A helpful vision for writers is to imagine a *ladder of abstraction,* with the broader, more abstract words at the top and the more concrete words at the bottom. The following is a ladder for a noun, *horse,* and for a verb, *run.* (For definitions of noun and verb, see Introductory Lesson A). From these two fairly abstract words, the writer may go up or down.

Most abstract:	animal	move
	herbivore	go
	horse	run
	filly	gallop
Most concrete:	Misty	

As you read each word in a paragraph, ask, "Am I as low on the abstraction ladder as I need to be to achieve concreteness and precision?" In the previous sample sentence, the writer has chosen the bottom level for her verb *(gallop),* but not quite the bottom for *filly,* preferring in that situation not to give the filly a name. A writer decides, then, where to stop on the ladder, depending upon the tone and meaning he or she wants to convey.

CONNOTATION AND DENOTATION

Two useful concepts in discussing word choice are connotation and denotation. A word's denotation is its straightforward meaning. Its connotation is the meanings and associations that surround it, given a particular context. For example, the words *dumb* and *intellectually limited* describe the same basic concept; however, calling someone *dumb* conveys a different attitude than *intellectually limited*.

EXAMPLES

The following are some alternative word choices taken from various parts of an essay about the grueling work involved in competitive swimming. The writer's original choice is in brackets; the revised choice is underlined.

I [go] glide into my flip-turn as I [reach the end of] finish the first two laps. My toes [hit] strike the edge.
My brain is [telling] urging every inch of my body to keep moving as I [get to] approach the wall.
My heart is palpitating and I can't seem to [get] inhale enough oxygen.
Two to five hours of practice a day can wear [any] the fittest person down.
Practice is [hard] grueling.
Your arms barely [come] lift out of the water.
Your mouth [is dry] feels like cotton.
With all this work, you may be able to [take] trim half a second from your time.

In the next example, from a sociology paper, the meaning of a passage is unclear because of several ineffective word choices, which are italicized in the draft. The writer is announcing his topic for a paper on a mental institution called Springdale.

Draft: This is a sociological *writing* of the problems that the *people* of Springdale faced and the solutions that they *had* to overcome the pressures of the outside world.

Revision: This is a sociological *view* of the problems Springdale *residents* faced and the solutions they *adopted* to overcome the pressures of the outside world.

Notice that the revision results in greater economy (see Step 1E). The two types of revision are often closely related.

TECHNICAL WORDS AND JARGON

Technical terms are often the lowest possible level of abstraction, but a writer pays a price for their specificity. For example, horse trainers have specific, technical words for horses, indicating their breed, their purpose, or their body type. They also have technical terms for the various running gaits. In writing a technical book on horse training for trainers, a writer would need to use those technical terms, but, for a general audience, the specificity isn't needed. The density of technical language would present an unnecessary barrier for a reader. When you use technical terms unnecessarily or ostentatiously, the reader is likely to accuse you of *jargon*—technical language used inappropriately. Simpler language would convey your meaning more effectively and easily.

The basic guideline is to use only as much technical language as is needed in a situation to achieve precise communication with your reader. Otherwise, use simple, common words. In the following example, there are three versions of the same information—a description of the learning disability dyslexia. The first version is from a technical source written by an expert to other professionals in the field.

FROM *DYSLEXIA DEFINED*
—MACDONALD AND EILEEN CRITCHLEY

Dyslexia is a learning disability which initially shows itself by difficulty in learning to read, and later by erratic spelling and lack of facility in manipulating written as well as spoken words. The condition is cognitive in essence, and usually genetically determined. It is not due to intellectual inadequacy or to lack of sociocultural opportunity, or to faults in the technique of teaching, or to emotional factors, or to any known structural brain defect. It probably represents a specific maturational defect which tends to lessen as the child grows older, and is capable of considerable improvement, especially when appropriate remedial help is afforded at the earliest opportunity.

If we were to revise this paragraph for the same technical audience, we would have to retain many of the technical terms. For example, *facility* and *remedial* and *cognitive* have specific meanings for speech therapists and educators—meanings the writer may want to retain.

Other words are not necessarily technical terms, but words appropriate to a technical or scholarly context. For example, *intellectual inadequacy* is similar in meaning to the colloquial word *dumb,* but a writer would not use that word in this context because it would sound out of place and might carry with it some unwanted implications.

Even for its technical audience, however, this passage might be tightened and simplified a bit. The phrase *in essence* (second sentence) might be omitted. *Faults in the technique of teaching* could be shortened to *faulty teaching.* The last verb, *is afforded,* might be simplified to *is offered* or *is given*. Basically, however, this passage represents competent writing for a technical audience. In general, the writers have resisted the temptation to use unnecessarily long and complex words. For example, in sentence 1 they use *shows itself,* rather than *exhibits itself* or *is manifested.* In sentence 3, they use the straightforward *It is not due to,* rather than an unnecessarily stiff alternative such as *The condition does not proceed from.*

Many writers, when they use appropriately technical language in a school or job setting, overshoot the mark and obscure their meaning with inappropriately stilted language that makes reading difficult. One writer, Ken Macrorie, calls this kind of language *Engfish*. Unfortunately, you'll sometimes see this kind of language in library sources you use for a paper. The following is a version of the dyslexia essay with unnecessarily stiff and bureaucratic language.

ENGFISH VERSION OF PASSAGE ON DYSLEXIA

Dyslexia has been found to be a learning disability which initially is exhibited by difficulty in the learning of reading skills, and later by erratic spelling and lack of facility in manipulating written as well as oral discourse. The condition exhibits a cognitive essence and usually is found to be determined by genetic factors. It does not take its origin from intellectual inadequacy, or from diminishment of sociocultural opportunity, or from infelicities in pedagogical technique, or from emotional dysfunctions or from any currently ascertained structural brain defect. It probably exhibits the proclivities of a specific maturational defect which shows a tendency to exhibit decline as the child advances in age, and tends to be capable of considerable improvement, especially when appropriate remedial help is afforded at the earliest possible opportunity.

To avoid this sort of writing, first of all imagine yourself looking your reader directly in the eye. Then write as simply as possible, using technical terms when necessary for precision, but otherwise sticking to straightforward nouns and verbs. Next, tighten your writing for economy, and ask of each word, "Can this be said more simply?"

When you change audiences, you must make different choices about language. The following is a student writer's version of the essay on dyslexia. The writer wants to encourage fellow students to accept and support their peers who have dyslexia, rather than mocking or ostracizing them. It would be a mistake to use the technical language from the first selection, even though that language is appropriate for a technical or academic setting where a specialist is talking to other specialists. When writing an informal essay for peers, however, the writer must choose a more suitable language. The writer is working from the specialist's description in the first example, but she translates the concepts for her own audience and purpose. (She should use a citation, nevertheless, to credit the source of her description.)

EXPLANATION OF DYSLEXIA FOR STUDENT AUDIENCE

Dyslexia is a learning problem. It first shows up when a child has a hard time learning to read. Later, the dyslexic child is a poor speller, and can't write or speak fluently. The problem lies in the brain and is usually inherited. A dyslexic is not dumb, nor culturally disadvantaged, nor crazy, and there is nothing structurally wrong with the person's brain. Rather, dyslexia seems to be a problem of maturation. As the child grows older, the dyslexia tends to diminish. Dyslexics can improve considerably, especially if they get the right kind of early help.

Notice that in this version, sentences and words are much shorter than in the source. The writer chooses language for a peer audience. *Dumb* and *crazy* work in this context. They represent the actual words peers use to tease dyslexics—the words the writer wants to abolish. Notice, too, that the subjects of sentences have changed. The technician writing the first selection is concerned with describing the disease, so *dyslexia* (or some word that means dyslexia) is the subject of all the sentences. The student writer, however, focuses on the *person* who must be accepted and supported by other students, so the subject more often is *the dyslexic*.

EXERCISES FOR DICTION

Answers in back of book: 1a-d, 2a-d, 3a
Answers in instructor's manual: 1e-f, 2e-g, 3b

1. In the following statements, word choices are inappropriate, trite, too abstract, or not precise. In revising, you'll find that issues of economy (Step 1E) are often connected to issues of diction. You may make any changes you think necessary for clarity and economy.

   (Sample revisions in back of book)
   a. Space at stadium concession stands is absolutely horrendous.
   b. When little Bobbie asked to play, it was the last straw.
   c. By having the new stadium built in a less congested area with more parking facilities, we could avoid the problems of parking inconveniences between the residents and the sports fans.
   d. Within the last six to eight years, there has been a substantial educational and legal sophistication of the Chicano population.

   (Sample revisions in instructor's manual)
   e. Rumsford had a father who had been a grocer, and his

STEP ONE: READ FOR MEANING AND REVISE FOR STYLE

grandfather had been a grocer, but Rumsford himself had strayed from the straight and narrow.

f. [about drunk driving] Another analysis was done between New York and Massachusetts, leaving out all the counties except the ones which border the two states, to see if crossing over the border for alcohol was a factor in the accident figures. Less than two percent of the teenage fatality rate in car accidents were from the opposite state; therefore, this is not even close to being a radical statistic.

2. Rewrite the following technical statements so that they can be incorporated into an informal essay addressed to an audience of students. Use a dictionary to look up technical terms unfamiliar to you.

(Sample revisions in back of book)

a. In 50 percent of the cases of dyslexia, the impairment is genetic in origin.
b. The first symptom of dyslexia is impaired visual and auditory perception.
c. Dyslexia is a symptom resulting from one or more various neurological impairments.
d. The dyslexic manifests reversals and related scrambling difficulties in reading, writing, and spelling, despite adequate emotional and educational stimulation.

(Sample revisions in instructor's manual)

e. When dyslexic children are of high intelligence, their prospects of developing neurotic reactions are enhanced, as they perceive their retarded progress in relation to siblings and peers.
f. In a study of 500 dyslexic children, only 2.6 percent of the children were socially maladjusted in the sense of being chronically dishonest or guilty of theft, truancy, or other types of delinquent or criminal conduct.
g. A more objective picture of the relation between learning failure and social maladjustment could be gained by investigating how many maladjusted youngsters are se-

verely retarded readers with normal intelligence and relatively normal early childhood development.
3. Revise the following passages so they can fit into an essay addressed to student peers.
(Sample revision in back of book)
   a. [From a paper about the framing of the U.S. Constitution. The writer makes the point that many framers of the Constitution did not trust the people to have good judgment and wanted to limit the people's role in government.]
Sources considering the history and development of the framing of our constitution are embellished with the incompetencies and degrading descriptions of the inabilities of the common people to participate in their government, specifically regarding election.
(Sample revision in instructor's manual)
   b. [about stutterers]: This feeling of inferiority and self-criticism slowly withdraws them from others and has them believing they are victims of society. They remain to be low in dominance and have an even poorer self-image. The only thing the stutterer really wants is acceptance. However, all of these different emotional factors make any real feelings for himself become lost. As a result alienation from self sets in and dominates his whole personality.

REVISING YOUR OWN WRITING

In the space provided, enter sentences or passages from your own writing, where you have not used the most precise and effective word choices. Write the revision. Then write five other sentences or passages that follow similar patterns.
Your Sentence(s)

STEP ONE: READ FOR MEANING AND REVISE FOR STYLE

_____
_____
_____

Your Revision
_____
_____
_____
_____
_____

Five Other Sentences in the Same Pattern
_____
_____
_____
_____
_____

GRAMMATICAL TERMS IN THIS LESSON

Subject: A word or group of words that names the person or thing that is performing the action or that is in the state of being named in the verb

Verb: One to four words that name the action or state of being of the subject

Object: The word or words that name the person, thing, or concept that receives the action of the verb (direct object) or to whom or for whom the action of the verb is performed (indirect object)

Noun: A word or group of words that names a person, place, concept, or thing

Synonym: A word similar in meaning

Antonym: A word opposite in meaning

Connotation: The implied meaning of a word

Denotation: The straightforward, literal meaning of a word

LESSON 1F: REVISE DICTION (WORD CHOICE)

EXERCISES FOR STEP 1

Answers in back of book: 1a-d, 2a, 3a
Answers in instructor's manual: 1e-g, 2b, 3b

1. Combine each of the following groups of ideas into one sentence that follows the guidelines for effective style.
   (Sample sentences in back of book)
   a. There is a definition of loneliness
      It is the best definition of loneliness I have ever read
      The definition was written by the poet May Sarton
      Sarton says that people are lonely when they have no one with whom to exchange the deepest part of themselves
   b. The definition helps to explain why married people may feel lonely
      The definition helps to explain why single people may not feel lonely
   c. Sometimes I have no private time
      Then I tend to lose sight of myself
      I enter conversations with others
      I hear myself parroting their points of view
      That experience can be lonely and depressing
   d. I spend hours alone
      Those times do not make me feel lonely
      Those times keep me from feeling lonely
      Those times help me know an essential self
      Then I can share that essential self with others
   (Sample sentences in instructor's manual)
   e. The earth is made of rock
      One hundred miles below the surface the rock is hot
      The rock is hotter than a burner of a stove at its highest setting
   f. Rock at the depths of the earth shifts
      It shifts slowly
      It shifts a few centimeters a year
      That is the same rate at which fingernails grow

STEP ONE: READ FOR MEANING AND REVISE FOR STYLE

    g. The molten rock flows deep
       The flows have relentless force
       The force pushes the continents
       The force cracks the ocean floors

2. Revise the following passages for all aspects of Step 1. At the end of your revision, select two phrases or sentences you think were among the original author's most effective, and explain why you think so. Sentences are numbered for reference.

(Sample revision in back of book)

    a.   (1)For four years I had always wanted to visit France. (2)Ever since I began studying French I wanted to visit and explore their culture first hand. (3)I had always been impressed with their culture. (4)It had always seemed attractive to me. (5)During my fourth year of French I was offered the opportunity to go and of course I was elated. (6)I then became a bit apprehensive. (7)Everyone I knew who had visited previously told me how awful their trip was because the French people were so rude and nasty. (8)This, needless to say, put a slight damper on my plans. (9)So the French hate Americans. (10)What do I do now?

(Sample revision in instructor's manual)

    b.   (1)On a typical weekend with the clique, I would call them—they rarely called me—to find out what the plans were for that particular night. (2)After deciding what we were going to do, I would usually get a phone call saying something like "I can't drive. Can you?" (3)The sucker that I am, more times than not, I ended up driving. (4)To feel less used, my conscience would make up excuses for why I was driving. (5)"You have the biggest car" or "Everyone else will be drunk so you need to drive" were the most common excuses. (6)Looking back at this, I realize the clique was depriving me of my fun. (7)Even if I wanted

LESSON 1F: REVISE DICTION (WORD CHOICE)

to drink and loosen up, I couldn't. (8)Being the driver, my main concern was getting everyone home on time and in a decent condition. (9)Too busy worrying about everyone else, I was never able to enjoy myself.

(11)Once at the party, my so-called friends headed straight for the keg of beer. (11)That is the last I would see of them until time to go. (12)When the time came to leave, they would all flock to me—unless I had to track someone down who was too drunk to make it back to the car on their own. (13)In the car, whoever was able to would talk about whom they met and whatever else they deemed important. (14)I never had anything to share. (15)Staring at the lonely road ahead of me, I sat in silence.

3. Revise the following passage, keeping in mind all the aspects of Step 1. At the end of your revision, select two phrases or sentences you think were among the original author's most effective and explain why you think so. The writer's purpose is to analyze the dangers of white water rafting. You may make any changes you think necessary to improve the essay's effectiveness.

(Sample revision in back of book)

a. Imagine being swept down a river by rushing white water totally under mother nature's control. This is a very exhiliarating and exciting experience, but it can be very dangerous.

Three years ago I went white water rafting for the first time. I was very frightened, but I was looking forward to a physical obstacle. I went rafting on the Snake River in the last week of June, 1983.

My parents, my brother and I left for Wild Rock State Park on a Saturday morning with almost forty other people. We were all very excited but very weary because no one knew what to expect. It took close to four hours to get to our campground. When we arrived, we pitched tents and got ready to sleep. That night before bed, our group had a meeting around the fire. There were only eight experienced people in this group, and everyone listened intently to what was said.

First everyone was told that this is a very dangerous sport and many deaths are caused because of carelessness or mere stupidity. Everyone was told never to get excited or frightened because you will be caused to do dumb things.

We were told that the water is very dangerous. The whole river is covered by rocks and many accidents can occur. We were never to kneel or sit on the bottom of the raft because if rocks are ridden over by the raft you could be injured. Also we were warned to hold our hands over the end of the paddle because if the other end hits a rock the end you are holding might be knocked into your face.

Many drownings have occurred from careless white water rafters. Very often people are thrown from their raft. This is a very crucial time. You must not try to get back in the raft because you may get sucked under it, caught between the raft and a rock. While in the water, you must float on top of the water with your feet downstream to push off of rocks. You must not try to stand up because your feet may become wedged between rocks in the bottom, and the force of the water will push you under, and you will drown.

(Sample revision in instructor's manual)

b.   A very common occurrence in white water rafting is a hydraulic. A hydraulic is produced by rushing water being pushed back upstream by underwater rocks. These hydraulics are very dangerous because you can get caught in them. The way to get out, we were told, is to make yourself into a ball. This will force the hydraulic to pop you out.

LESSON 1F: REVISE DICTION (WORD CHOICE)

The guide told us the most obvious danger is from a capsized raft, but that hardly ever happens because of the raft's great buoyancy. If a raft does turn over, this is a dangerous time. A capsized raft almost always occurs when two boats collide. A good precaution is to keep distance between rafts while going through rapids. Keeping distance between rafts is very tough because it takes a lot of strength and togetherness to control one of these rafts. It takes even more to make a raft slow down. While attempting to slow down, usually the raft will turn sideways and get hung up in the rapid. The one and only way to get a raft free is for all rafters to move to the part of the raft being pushed with the most water.

LESSONS FOR STEP TWO

READ AND REVISE

FOR GRAMMAR

AND PUNCTUATION

PUNCTUATING SENTENCE BOUNDARIES

LESSON FOR STEP 2A

REVISE SENTENCE FRAGMENTS AS NEEDED

Definition: A FRAGMENT is a group of words that is punctuated as a sentence (opening capital letter, closing period), but that is not a grammatical sentence.

PREVIEW OF THE LESSON

Writers may occasionally use fragments deliberately for specific purposes, but most kinds of fragments can be highly annoying to readers. In one study, where readers were asked to rank the seriousness of various grammar and punctuation problems, fragments ranked in the top group. Step 2 begins with fragments for that reason.

To understand this lesson, you need to know how to identify subjects and verbs and dependent and independent clauses (Introductory Lessons A and B).

Exercises for this lesson are interspersed throughout, so you can practice one concept before going on to the next.

STEP TWO: READ AND REVISE FOR GRAMMAR AND PUNCTUATION

IGNORE SENTENCE LENGTH

A sentence fragment has nothing to do with length. Nor does it have very much to do with putting periods where your voice makes a significant pause while reading. To know when and how to punctuate a sentence, you have to apply a grammatical test.

THE TEST FOR FRAGMENTS

Everything you punctuate as a sentence (opening capital letter, closing period) must have at least one independent clause. If not, the group of words is a fragment. The procedure for determining whether a sentence meets this criterion is summarized in Figure 2A.1.

WHICH SENTENCES SHOULD YOU CHECK?

You may find that when you write or check your writing, your intuition will alert you to sentence fragments. If you wonder whether a sentence is a fragment or not, put it through the test. If you have not developed any intuition yet, you may have to check every sentence, at least for a while.

A good strategy is to check the kinds of sentences that writers most often punctuate as fragments:

1. Sentences that have verb-like words but not a real verb. The most common are *-ing* words without helpers. (See Introductory Lesson A, p. 45.)
2. Sentences that begin with any of the typical openers/connectors of dependent clauses:
   a. Relative pronouns: *who, whom, whose, which, that* (Introductory Lesson B, pp. 76–78).
   b. Nonmovable connectors such as *although* and *because* (Introductory Lesson B, pp. 79–81).

LESSON 2A: REVISE SENTENCE FRAGMENTS AS NEEDED

Test any group of words you have punctuated as a sentence (opening capital, closing period), especially if it opens with any of the typical openers/connectors of dependent clauses (p. 75).

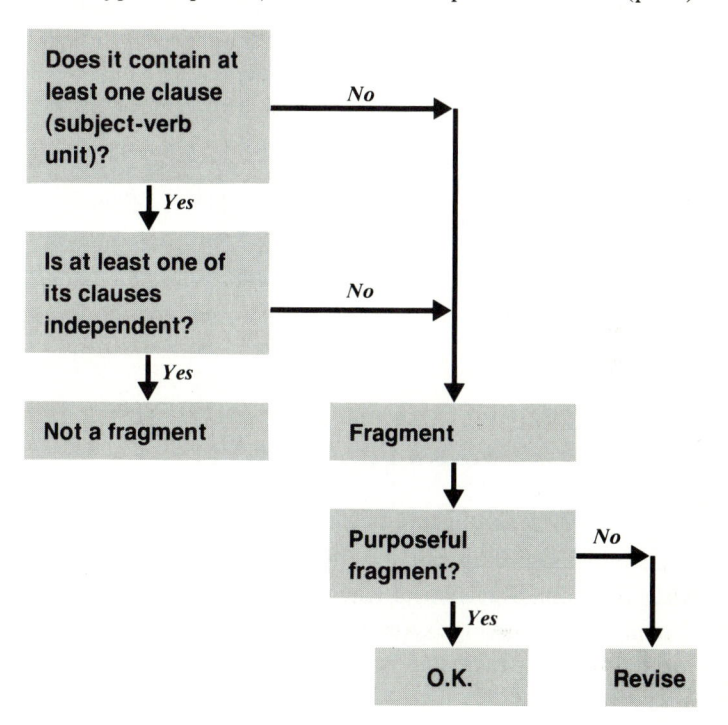

FIGURE 2 A.1 Test for Fragments

FIRST PART OF THE TEST: IS YOUR SENTENCE A CLAUSE?

Since a sentence must contain at least one independent clause, start by asking yourself whether it contains a clause. A clause is a subject-verb unit together with that unit's modifiers and complements. Try to find a subject-verb unit in the following example. (See Introductory Lesson A for help if needed.)

STEP TWO: READ AND REVISE FOR GRAMMAR AND PUNCTUATION

Group of words: Thinking about the end of the summer.

Look for a subject-verb unit. "Thinking" may sound like a verb, but it has no subject (*who* was thinking?). "End of the summer" may sound like a subject, but it has no verb. (The end of the summer *does or is* what?) The group has no subject-verb unit. It is a fragment.

Exceptions:

Commands (Pass the ketchup.):   The subject is understood to be *you*.

Sentences that are already questions (Who is coming?) rarely give trouble as fragments. In many contexts, a question may legitimately be a fragment (Who?).

MARK FRAGMENTS

If any group of words you've punctuated as a sentence lacks even one subject-verb unit, it is a fragment. Mark it for possible later revision. (Revision of fragments is covered later in this lesson.) The following exercises will help you identify groups of words that are fragments because they have no subject-verb unit.

EXERCISES

Answers in back of book: 1a-i, 2a
Answers in instructor's manual: 1j-l, 2b

1. List the sentences that are fragments.
   (Answers in back of book)
   a. Thinking carefully about the proposed plan.
   b. Thinking about this plan is difficult.
   c. Trapped with no escape.
   d. They were trapped.

LESSON 2A: REVISE SENTENCE FRAGMENTS AS NEEDED

    e. The traps lying on the ground.
    f. Ice cream dripping all over the place, running down her arms, making a mess on the floor.
    g. Ice cream dripped all over the place, running down her arms, making a mess on the floor.
    h. A modest communication center set up in three rooms and operated by students.
    i. Without a doubt was there in the hotel but couldn't be located.
    (Answers in instructor's manual)
    j. Helping the handicapped each Tuesday afternoon after work.
    k. Anxious to go but waited another hour just hoping for her arrival.
    l. Waiting is difficult.

2. List the sentences that are fragments.
    (Answers in back of book)
    a. (1)The managers are always after the workers, trying to find something to complain and scream about. (2)Hurting the pride and good will of the workers. (3)Instead of explaining their point kindly.
    (Answers in instructor's manual)
    b. (1)Aware of the weaknesses of this argument, the boss questioned the workers' right to seniority. (2)Stating that seniority had been gained under a discriminatory system.

3. Compose the longest fragment you can that has no subject-verb unit. The words must make sense and must not rely on repetition for length. (Not allowed: "Shooting again and again and again and again.") If you write a really wonderful fragment, send it to the book's author at the following address. The next edition will print the longest, most varied and imaginative fragment, together with the name of the student who submitted it.
Loyola College, 4501 N. Charles St., Baltimore, MD 21210.

STEP TWO: READ AND REVISE FOR GRAMMAR AND PUNCTUATION

SECOND PART OF THE TEST: DOES YOUR SENTENCE CONTAIN AN INDEPENDENT CLAUSE?

So far you've identified fragments that are not clauses (that is, they lack a subject–verb unit). But some groups of words that *are* clauses are still not grammatical sentences because the group of words contains no *independent* clause. So the next procedure is to ask whether your sentence contains at least one *independent* clause. Use the procedures in Introductory Lesson B, pp. 67–87.

The following are sample fragments that have only dependent clauses. The clauses open with nonmovable connectors (p. 79) that make them dependent:

because the manager has just quit
ever since the flood of 1984
whenever there is a loss of power

Not all sentences that open with these words are fragments. The following is an example:

Because I hurt my elbow, I couldn't play.

This sentence contains a dependent clause, *because I hurt my elbow,* and an independent clause, *I couldn't play.* Even though the sentence opens with *because,* it is not a fragment, since it contains at least one independent clause.

The following are examples of dependent clauses that begin with relative pronouns (p. 76) and that are dependent because they modify (describe or limit the meaning of) a noun or they act as a noun (p. 72). They cannot stand alone.

the electrician who came to our office this morning

Electrician is a noun. *Who came to our office this morning* modifies the noun by telling *which* electrician. The group of words has no verb to tell what the electrician who came to our office this morning *did* or *was*.

> *whichever animals were weakest*

The entire group of words acts as a noun by naming a thing. There is no verb to tell what happened to whichever animals were weakest.

> *that the weather is very cold here in winter*

The clause is dependent because it opens with the relative pronoun *that*. The clause acts as a noun. The sentence lacks a verb to tell *what about* that the weather is very cold here in winter. The sentence needs another part, such as "*I regret* that the weather is very cold here in winter" or "*He told us* that the weather is very cold here in winter."

> **With the start of college many of us leave old and familiar friends at home. People with whom we've shared the experiences of growing up.**

The first sentence is grammatically complete. The second is a fragment. One indicator is the relative pronoun *whom*. Note that the relative pronoun need not be the very first word. In this case, the clause *with whom we've shared the experience of growing up* modifies the noun *people* by telling which people. There is no verb to tell what the people with whom we've shared the experiences of growing up *are or do*.

NOT ALL SENTENCES OPENING WITH RELATIVE PRONOUNS OR NONMOVABLE CONNECTORS ARE FRAGMENTS

The following are some examples of complete sentences that are not fragments, even though they open with nonmovable connectors or with relative pronouns.

STEP TWO: READ AND REVISE FOR GRAMMAR AND PUNCTUATION

That the machine wouldn't work was obvious.

The clause *that the machine wouldn't work* acts as the noun subject. The verb is *was*. Thus the group of words contains an independent clause.

Whatever I wanted, I got.

Whatever I wanted is a dependent clause naming the thing that I got. The sentence has an independent clause whose subject is *I* and whose verb is *got*.

THE YES-NO QUESTION TEST

The yes/no question test* is a useful method to help distinguish groups of words that are not independent clauses. Try to turn the group of words into a question, to which the answer can be *yes* or *no*. You may not add any words except a form of *do* or *it*. You may not omit any words. You may move parts of the verb to make the question sound more natural. If the question can be answered *yes/no*, the group of words contains at least one independent clause.

That the machine wouldn't work.

Yes/No
Question: That the machine wouldn't work?
Conclusion: The question cannot be answered *yes/no*, so the group of words contains no independent clause. It is a fragment.

---

*Adapted from a test developed and tested by Robert de Beaugrand, "Yes, Teaching Grammar Does Help," *English Journal* 73:2 (Feb. 1984), 66–69.

LESSON 2A: REVISE SENTENCE FRAGMENTS AS NEEDED

That the machine wouldn't work was obvious.

Yes/No Question:	Was it obvious that the machine wouldn't work?
Conclusion:	Question can be answered *yes/no,* so the group of words contains an independent clause and is not a fragment.

Who would volunteer to bring the refreshments.

Yes/No Question:	Who would volunteer to bring the refreshments?
Conclusion:	Question cannot be answered *yes/no,* so group of words contains no independent clause. It is a fragment.

MORE COMPLICATED FRAGMENTS

Sometimes the word that makes the clause dependent does not come at the beginning of the sentence. In the following sentences, fragments are in italics:

> I doubt I'd have been able to cope with my illness as well as I have, without friends beside me through the hard times. *The times when I felt so lost and afraid I didn't know how I could bear it.*

The word *when* is a nonmovable connector that indicates the clause's dependence, but the *when* does not come directly at the beginning of the sentence.

Sometimes a sentence is a fragment because within it is a group of words that the reader expects to be an independent clause but is not. Such a sentence may fool the reader because it has one independent clause that is complete.

Draft:	The story then tells how Princess Leia, after having stolen the plans of the Empire's most formidable weapon, a giant battle station.

The sentence opens with an independent clause: *the story then tells.* The problem arises in the second clause—the one that indicates what the story tells. After *how Princess Leia,* the reader expects some words that answer the question, "how Princess Leia *did what?"* The reader, in other words, expects a verb for the subject *Princess Leia.* Instead, the sentence inserts a group of words without a true verb: *after having stolen....* The sentence never provides a verb to tell the reader what Princess Leia *did* after having stolen the plans.

BLOCKING OUT MODIFYING PHRASES AND CLAUSES

The following passage illustrates another tricky fragment.

Therefore, allowing teams who'd made mistakes to start over provided a satisfactory resolution. Although for some people, for example the teams that had made no early mistakes, the resolution was not welcome.

The student who wrote this passage wondered about the second sentence, but found the subject and verb *(resolution was)* and concluded the sentence was complete. However, if she had tried to frame a yes/no question, she would have seen that the second sentence is a fragment because the question doesn't make sense. She also would have discovered the clause's dependence if she had eliminated the middle modifiers. In the example, two modifiers separate the *although* from the subject and verb. The modifiers are *for some people* and *for example the teams that had made no early mistakes.* Because the *although* is so far separated from the subject and verb, the writer missed the fact that the central clause of the sentence really is *although the resolution was not welcome*—clearly a dependent clause because it opens with the nonmovable connector *although.* To avoid this kind of confusion, try blocking

LESSON 2A: REVISE SENTENCE FRAGMENTS AS NEEDED

out the modifying phrases and clauses, leaving just the central words. Sometimes this procedure helps you see whether the central clause in your group of words is dependent or independent.

EXERCISES

Answers in back of book: 4a-o, 5a-d, 6a
Answers in instructor's manual: 4p-s, 5e-g, 6b

4. List the sentences that are fragments.
   (Answers in back of book)
   a. That the airplane was damaged.
   b. Who wanted my scarf.
   c. Which I loved.
   d. Even though he laughed.
   e. Because the ice was too thick.
   f. Whenever the customers became too demanding.
   g. The pennies that were tossed into the fountain.
   h. My brother, whom I dearly loved.
   i. The guard who wanted my scarf to use as a flag.
   j. The danger of going too far.
   k. However, he laughed.
   l. My brother gave me a pair of earrings that I treasure.
   m. Sailing jauntily into the harbor, while the flags waved and the people cheered.
   n. Because of the storm, we left a day late.
   o. That flag was shredded in the wind.
   (Answers in instructor's manual)
   p. The omelet that I had just ordered.
   q. The wind that whipped across the lake, raising waves that slapped against the pier.
   r. When the glacier blocked the inlet, many seals were trapped.
   s. Because of my elbow, which had been injured in the match when I hit a hard backhand.

STEP TWO: READ AND REVISE FOR GRAMMAR AND PUNCTUATION

5. List the sentences that are fragments.
   (Answers in back of book)
   a. (1)This forces a shoot-out. (2)Which has the spectators hanging on the edges of their seats.
   b. (1)Next the server must take the heavy tray into the kitchen. (2)He or she then rushes back to reset the tables before the boss seats the next customers. (3)And this is very difficult to do when there isn't enough silverware, plates, or glasses. (4)Sometimes because other servers decided to make use of them.
   c. (1)For some reason, many people think that louder and slower speech is the key to understanding different languages. (2)When in fact shouting makes the situation seem almost ridiculous. (3)Especially if you're the "foreigner" watching a person yelling in vain and getting nowhere.
   d. (1)How we handle the pollution of our lakes is an important political issue. (2)An issue that each individual must consider carefully and knowledgeably.
   (Answers in instructor's manual)
   e. (1)While individual employers look for different character traits, most agree that energy is a key characteristic in a prospective employee. (2)Especially in jobs that require initiative and self-direction.
   f. (1)Most kidney stones are only the size of a dime. (2)However, removing them used to require major surgery. (3)Including a long hospital stay.
   g. (1)I fail to see the difference between a drunk driver who is eighteen or nineteen years old and one who is twenty-one or forty-one. (2)Except that the one who is eighteen wasn't blind enough to let his problem go on for years and years without doing a thing about it.
6. List the sentences that are fragments.
   (Answers in back of book)
   a. (1)The director of the county animal shelter told me that the rabies epidemic, after having increased greatly during

the past decade, especially in the city's wild animal population. (2)When wild animals are infected, they spread the disease to domestic animals who sniff them, fight with them, or play with them. (3)The director said that, even after a well-publicized campaign to get people to have their pets vaccinated, only an estimated 60 percent of the pets in the city are vaccinated against rabies.
(Answers in instructor's manual)
b. (1)The director of the school for the handicapped said that after the efforts of many parents and citizens, over a period of years. (2)New playground equipment has been purchased for the school. (3)And installed in a lot next to the school.

USING PURPOSEFUL FRAGMENTS

Even in formal types of writing, fragments sometimes serve useful purposes. The following are some examples:

Exclamations:	Hooray!
Answers to questions:	Has the issue been settled? Hardly.
For emphasis:	Five long months and eighteen operations later, Warren was ready. Not ready to leave the hospital, but to learn to walk again.

To give language a punchy, informal, conversational, telegraphic, or urgent tone (most common in advertising and promotional writing; used sparingly in academic or other types of writing):

> Soothe your spirits in the cerulean skies of Barbados, Jamaica, or Aruba. Splash down in the turquoise surf of Martinique or Antigua. Or settle for doing absolutely nothing in the aquamarine splendor of St. Croix. All at prices that won't make you blue.
> —advertisement for Eastern Airlines

STEP TWO: READ AND REVISE FOR GRAMMAR AND PUNCTUATION

MAKING THE FRAGMENT A COMPLETE SENTENCE

To make your fragment into a sentence, you can add or change elements in two ways:

1. Remove a word that makes the clause dependent

   At the wedding where my sister broke her leg.
   BECOMES At the wedding, my sister broke her leg.

2. Add a subject or a verb

   The director of the county animal shelter told me that the rabies epidemic, after having increased greatly during the past decade, especially in the city's wild animal population. BECOMES The director of the county animal shelter told me that the rabies epidemic has become a major problem, after having increased greatly during the past decade, especially in the city's wild animal population.

JOINING THE FRAGMENT TO ANOTHER SENTENCE

You can also join the fragment to another sentence:

At the wedding. The fugitive hid among the guests.
BECOMES At the wedding, the fugitive hid among the guests.
Because we conducted three separate experiments. We were reasonably sure of our accuracy.
BECOMES Because we conducted three separate experiments, we were reasonably sure of our accuracy.
We spent the whole night searching. Riding around in the ranger's truck.
BECOMES We spent the whole night searching, riding around in the ranger's truck.

LESSON 2A: REVISE SENTENCE FRAGMENTS AS NEEDED

To avoid wordiness, watch for chances to shorten the fragment as you integrate it with other elements.

> *The room was cold. Being on the north side.*
> *MIGHT BECOME The north room was cold.*
> *With the start of college, many of us leave old and familiar friends at home. People with whom we've shared the experiences of growing up.*
> *MIGHT BECOME With the start of college, many of us leave at home familiar people with whom we've shared the experiences of growing up.*
> *And this is very difficult to do when there isn't enough silverware, plates, or glasses. Sometimes because other servers decided to make use of them.*
> *MIGHT BECOME This is difficult when other servers have used all the silverware, plates, or glasses.*

Lesson 1E contains a further discussion of tightening for economy.

PUNCTUATING YOUR REVISED SENTENCES

When your fragment is incorporated into another sentence, you may have a question about its punctuation. Other lessons, especially the lessons for steps 2K-2N, on interior sentence punctuation, answer such questions.

EXERCISES

(Note: Exercises 1–6 appear earlier in the lesson.)
Answers in back of book: 7a-o, 8a-d, 9a, 10a-b
Answers in instructor's manual: 7p-s, 8e-g, 9b, 10c

7. In Exercise 4, p. 213, write two revisions for each fragment you marked. In one revision, make the fragment into a complete sentence, with as few additions as possible. You

STEP TWO: READ AND REVISE FOR GRAMMAR AND PUNCTUATION

may omit words in the fragment. In another revision, leave the fragment unchanged, and add words and ideas to create a complete sentence. Answers are in back of book or in instructor's manual, as marked for that exercise.

8. In Exercise 5, p. 214, write revisions for all fragments you marked. When possible, combine the fragment with another sentence, condensing if necessary. Answers are in back of book or in instructor's manual, as marked for that exercise.

9. In Exercise 6, p. 214, revise the passage to remove fragments, condensing if necessary. Answers are in back of book or in instructor's manual, as marked for that exercise.

10. In the following passages, mark all fragments and revise. When several types of revision are possible for the same group of words, try to compose one that is smooth and not wordy. Sentences are numbered for reference.

(Sample revisions in back of book)

a. (1)One element that contributes to the slavery of the server is poor equipment. (2)The bread oven isn't useful at all. (3)It is probably as old as the restaurant. (4)Serving the bread hot is a must. (5)But since so many people go to Tio Rancho restaurant, the bread doesn't get enough time to heat. (6)Making the server take a tray of bread to the ovens that the cooks use in the kitchen. (7)Then the cooks start to protest. (8)The server interfering with their jobs.

b. (1)The burning of coal brings serious pollution problems. (2)Coal may shortly be limited for use. (3)It damages human lungs and kills many other forms of life. (4)It contains sulfur and some metals. (5)Which are very expensive to remove. (6)Acid rain comes from the burning of coal. (7)This rain damages buildings and kills the life in many ponds, lakes, and streams. (8)Also from the burning of coal and other fossil fuels, carbon dioxide is

LESSON 2A: REVISE SENTENCE FRAGMENTS AS NEEDED

emitted and can accumulate in the atmosphere, holding heat on the earth's surface and leading to the Greenhouse Effect. (9)A great meltdown of the polar ice caps, which would cause destruction and cost many lives.
(Sample revisions in instructor's manual)
c. (1)The issue of reverse discrimination became publicized in the Webber case. (2)Brian Webber, a white man who had worked for Kaiser Aluminum for the past ten years. (3)Webber applied for an on-the-job training program. (4)Due to dual seniority lists, some Blacks with less seniority than he were admitted to the program. (5)While Webber himself was not. (6)Webber sued on the grounds that his constitutional and civil rights had been violated.

REVISING YOUR OWN WRITING

In the space provided, enter sentence fragments you have missed in your own writing, and write the correction. Then write five other sentences that follow similar patterns, punctuating them correctly.

Your Fragment

_____
_____
_____
_____

Your Revision

_____
_____
_____
_____
_____

STEP TWO: READ AND REVISE FOR GRAMMAR AND PUNCTUATION

Five Other Sentences in the Same Pattern
_____
_____
_____
_____
_____

GRAMMATICAL TERMS IN THIS LESSON

Subject: A word or group of words that names the person or thing that is performing the action or that is in the state of being named in the verb

Verb: One to four words that name the action or state of being of the subject

Clause: A subject-verb unit plus that unit's modifiers and complements

Modifier: A word or group of words that describes or limits the meaning of another word or group of words in the same sentence

Complement: A word or group of words that completes the meaning of the verb

Dependent Clause: A clause that cannot stand alone

Independent Clause: A clause that can stand alone

Fragment: A group of words punctuated as a sentence that does not contain any independent clauses

Noun: A word or group of words that names a person, place, concept, or thing

LESSON FOR STEP 2B

AVOID RUN-ONS

Definition: A RUN-ON is a sentence in which independent clauses are improperly joined, usually with no punctuation or with a comma only.

For this substep, you will need to know how to identify subjects and verbs (Introductory Lesson A) and independent and dependent clauses (Introductory Lesson B). If you do not link one independent clause to another in a legitimate way, you create a run-on. The terms *comma splice* and *fused sentence* are also used, but this book simply will use the word *run-on* to refer to any sentence in which independent clauses are not properly joined to each other.

RUN-ONS HAVE NOTHING TO DO WITH LENGTH

Note that run-ons have nothing to do with length. Run-ons are not created by making the sentence too long, but rather by linking the independent clauses in the wrong way. Run-ons are

STEP TWO: READ AND REVISE FOR GRAMMAR AND PUNCTUATION

revised not necessarily by shortening the sentence but by fixing the link. Shortening the sentence may of course be advisable in some situations.

PREVIEW OF THE LESSON

Step 2B asks you to identify every sentence with two or more independent clauses, then to check whether those clauses are properly joined and revise for run-ons. This lesson covers three procedures:

1. Find your sentences with two or more independent clauses
2. Join independent clauses appropriately
3. Identify run–ons and revise

The procedures for checking run–ons are summarized in Figure 2B.1.

FIND YOUR SENTENCES WITH TWO OR MORE INDEPENDENT CLAUSES

Find every group of words that you have punctuated as a sentence and that contain *two or more independent clauses.*

Whenever we went to the beach, Alex got sunburned.

The preceding sentence has two clauses whose subject-verb units are *we went* and *Alex got.* The first clause is dependent because of the nonmovable opener *whenever* (pp. 79–81). The clause modifies *got sunburned.* The sentence cannot be a run-on because it has only one independent clause.

The paint was peeling, and the walls were water-stained.

The preceding sentence has two independent clauses whose subject-verb units are *paint was peeling* and *walls were.* Each

LESSON 2B: AVOID RUN-ONS

```
                    ┌─────────────┐
   ┌───────────┐    │ Does        │    ┌─────────────┐
   │Not a run-on│◄──│ sentence    │───►│Check links  │
   └───────────┘ No │ have two or │ Yes│between      │
                    │ more        │    │independent  │
                    │ independent │    │clauses      │
                    │ clauses?    │    └─────────────┘
                    └─────────────┘
```

| Semi-colon only | Semi-colon with movable connector | Comma with coordinating connector | Comma only, no connector | No punctuation |

| Semicolon placed correctly? | | Three or more clauses or two short clauses? | |

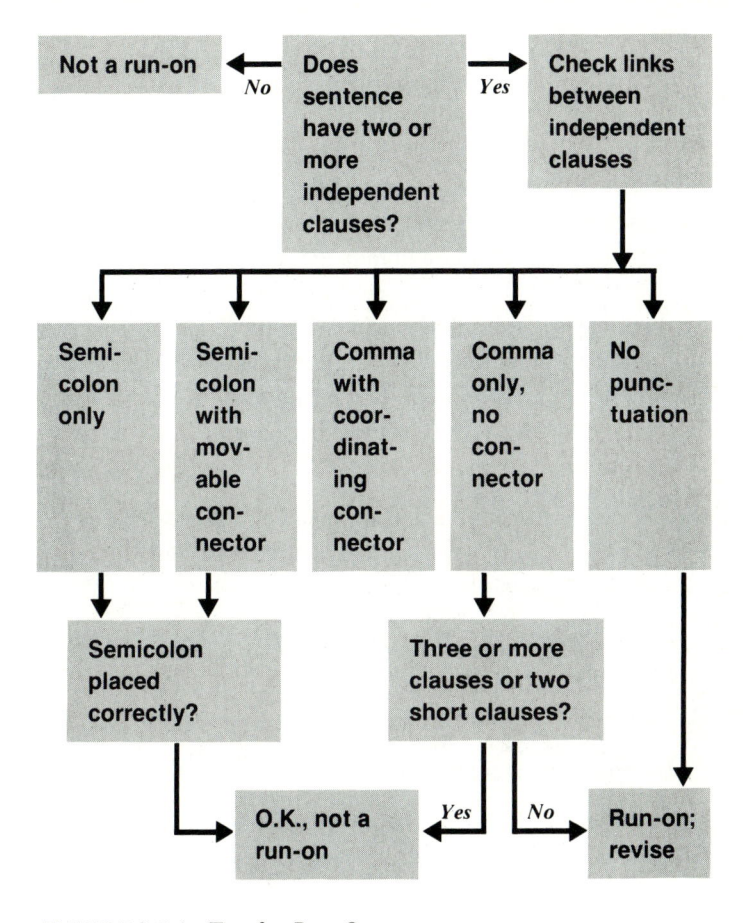

O.K., not a run-on ◄── Yes | No ──► Run-on; revise

FIGURE 2 B.1   Test for Run-Ons

clause stands on its own. Neither opens with a relative pronoun or with one of the nonmovable connectors that can make a clause dependent (pp. 79–81). Neither one acts as a noun in another clause (pp. 72–74). Thus the sentence has two independent clauses. There is the possibility of a run-on (though this sentence is punctuated correctly).

STEP TWO: READ AND REVISE FOR GRAMMAR AND PUNCTUATION

JOIN INDEPENDENT CLAUSES APPROPRIATELY

Test whether independent clauses are joined appropriately. To punctuate between two independent clauses, you have five options. Three of these options are only briefly listed here because they are presented in more detail in Introductory Lesson B (p. 67). That lesson presented the ways of joining independent clauses within the same sentence. The other two options are to break the independent clauses into two sentences or to make one of the clauses into a dependent clause or into a group of words that is not a clause. The five options, therefore, are as follows:

Option One: Link the clauses by a comma plus one of the coordinating connectors: *and, but, for, nor, or, so, yet* (p. 79).

The President was angry, so he sent a message to the Senate.

Option Two: Link the clauses by a semicolon alone (p. 76).

The President was angry; he sent a message to the Senate.

Option Three: Link the clauses by a semicolon plus a movable connector such as *however* or *therefore* (p. 79).

The President was angry; however, Congress still refused to follow his recommendations.

In the following sentence, the movable connector *however* is moved to a different position:

The President was angry; Congress, however, still refused to follow his recommendations.

Note that the semicolon comes at the point where the two clauses join, *not necessarily* at the point where the movable connector is placed.

Option Four: Punctuate each clause as a sentence with a capital letter and a period.

The President was angry. He sent a message to the Senate.

Option Five: Make one of the clauses a dependent clause or a group of words that is not a clause.

The President sent a message to the Senate because he was angry.

One independent clause is reduced to a dependent clause.

Angrily, the President sent a message to the Senate.

One independent clause is reduced to a single word, *angrily*.

REVISE RUN-ONS AS NEEDED

When you link two independent clauses with a comma alone or with no punctuation at all, you create a "run-on sentence," also called a "run-together sentence," a "fused sentence," or a "comma splice." A related error is to misplace the semicolon.

Incorrect: This spring the dogwood died, it had been diseased for a long while.

(Two independent clauses joined by a comma alone)

Incorrect: Some alcoholics are able to function in a job some are not.

(Two independent clauses joined with no punctuation)

Incorrect: Some alcoholics are able to function in a job, however; some are not.

(Misplaced semicolon)

Incorrect: Though some alcoholics are able to function in a job; some are not.

(A semicolon should not be used because the clauses are not both independent. The first is dependent because of its opener, *though*. See Introductory Lesson B, p. 80).

STEP TWO: READ AND REVISE FOR GRAMMAR AND PUNCTUATION

ACCEPTABLE RUN-ONS

You should never join two independent clauses without linking words or punctuation. Commas alone may be used to link independent clauses under the following conditions:

1. There are three or more independent clauses similar in form and function, so that the clauses form a series. They may then be separated by commas like other elements in a series. (Rules for series: Lesson 2P.) If the clauses have internal commas, however, beware of confusion and misreading. Use semicolons when in doubt.

   The army arrived, tents went up, a food line opened, and doctors began to treat the injured.

   Four short independent clauses are used in a series with no chance of misreading, so they may be separated by commas.

   Bob brought his mother breakfast in bed while she was ill; Mark delivered her messages, typed papers, and took her dictation; and Karen kept her supplied with books and crossword puzzles.

   Semicolons are needed because one of the independent clauses has internal commas.
2. The clauses are similar in form and closely related, and there is no chance of a misreading.

   He came, he left again.

   The choice of commas to separate two independent clauses, even if they are both short, as in number 2, is a matter of judgment and preference. Some readers are reluctant to accept this practice. When in doubt, use semicolons.
3. Elements of a clause are understood, not stated.

Some of the barns were red, some white, some unpainted.

The verb *were* is understood, but not stated in each clause. The elements may be joined by commas.

REVISING RUN-ONS

One way to revise run-ons is to use one of the options previously described to join the two independent clauses.

Run-on: The president was angry, he sent a message to Congress.
BECOMES The president was angry; he sent a message to Congress.
OR The president was angry. He sent a message to Congress.
OR The president was angry, so he sent a message to Congress.

Sometimes in revising independent clauses in a sentence, you see that the sentence could be tightened by shortening one of the independent clauses to a dependent clause or to just a few words. The following are some examples:

Draft: The workers are poorly educated, and because of this fact their opportunities to move to other jobs are limited.

Revision: Because the workers are poorly educated, their opportunities to move to other jobs are limited.
OR The workers' inadequate education limits their opportunities to move to other jobs.
OR The workers, poorly educated, have limited opportunities to move to other jobs.

Draft: It is obvious that the members have a strong influence on each other; this fact is evident by observing their behavior toward a young boy.

STEP TWO: READ AND REVISE FOR GRAMMAR AND PUNCTUATION

Revision: The members' strong influence on each other is evident in their behavior toward a young boy.
OR The members' behavior toward a young boy illustrates their strong influence on each other.

EXERCISES

Answers in back of book: 1a-g, 2a-q, 3a-b
Answers in instructor's manual: 1h-k, 2r-v, 3c

1. In the following sentences, add correct punctuation. (Answers in back of book)

   a. The dogwood died this spring it had been diseased for a long while. (Use two different options without adding any new words.)
   b. The dogwood had been diseased for a long while unfortunately it died this spring.
   c. The dogwood had been diseased for a long while and it died this spring.
   d. Her brothers and sisters are all investment bankers Monica admits to being the odd-ball in the family. (Use two different options without adding any new words.)
   e. Her brothers and sisters are all investment bankers but Monica admits to being the odd-ball in the family.
   f. Italians, Poles, Ukranians, and Scandinavians brought to America their love of the variety of mushrooms they had known in Europe however most Americans knew only the supermarket button mushrooms.
   g. Now, however, mushroom mania has overtaken Americans mushroom hunting associations are flourishing as people gather to scour their local woods, fields, and marshes for the delicious fungi.

   (Answers in instructor's manual)
   h. My grandmother baked cookies we children ate them in the orchard under the apple trees. (Use two different options, without adding any new words.)

LESSON 2B: AVOID RUN-ONS

    i. My grandmother baked cookies and we children ate them in the orchard under the apple trees.
    j. My grandfather let my sisters ride the old draft horse however I was afraid to try.
    k. Since some mushrooms can be poisonous, the safest way to hunt them in the wild is to join a local organization such clubs are forming in almost every part of the country.

2. In the following passages, list all run-ons. Then suggest revisions or justify keeping the run-on. Some passages may not contain any run-ons. Some passages may contain misplaced semicolons you should revise. Sentences are numbered for reference.
(Answers in back of book.)

    a. (1)What really surprised me is that, after all the chaos, my dad bought the dress for me. (2)He had no choice, he was dealing with a very dramatic child who loved getting everything she wanted.
    b. Don't get me wrong, Americans do not hate their country, they just feel differently now about patriotism and dying for their country.
    c. Kelly knew how to carry herself, she knew what to say and when to say it.
    d. You can make lots of money in your own business, you might set up a service grooming pets, polishing furniture, or running errands.
    e. She had a way of making people smile; of making me smile.
    f. There are several causes for cheating, it is not always a simple situation.
    g. If I asked the question and you responded as a typical teenager, you would answer yes, however, is this a thoughtful response?
    h. Some people are for the legislation, some against it, some undecided.

i. The other type of diabetes is maturity onset diabetes, it responds more satisfactorily to oral drugs.
j. Greer is not making up any excuses for women, and she definitely is not putting women down, she is just trying to show how women are equal to men.
k. The intent is for the President to represent the people, he is to be their defender, but that role is often blurred.
l. I have learned that by turning to my inner strengths and a higher power; I can be happy.
m. You have a right to believe what you want to believe, you have a right to take that risk.
n. (1)The most difficult part of taking care of our money was forcing ourselves to put some aside every week for bills at the end of the month. (2)We were constantly tempted to cash our checks and head to the ocean, or pick up that extra case of beer for the weekend, but we had bills to pay. (3)We both had enough sense to realize that we needed a list of priorities so we would be able to meet our debts at the end of the month, then if we had a little left over, we would plan some type of weekend activity. (4)Of all the survival techniques that I learned, money management was the most important.
o. (1)The worst accident that could occur at a nuclear plant is a meltdown, which occurs when, because normal and emergency methods have failed, the radioactive material escapes from the reactor into the environment. (2)The possibility of this happening, though, is very small, because there are many emergency back-up systems available either to stop fusion or to cool down the fuel so that it cannot melt through the reactor.
p. Many did not live through the ordeal, some emerged with serious injuries, and all were emotionally scarred.
q. When my job ended; the empty feelings were overwhelming.

(Answers in instructor's manual)

r. I can't blame her for liking Andrew, he's just the kind of guy that everyone likes.
s. (1)Ardrey states that early humans were poorly adapted for scavenging, they could not digest the grains of grasses, and thus they were forced rapidly into hunting. (2)Gradually their feet adjusted, their stance became more erect, and they discovered the value of tools in the hunt.
t. When the general surrendered, he begged the enemy to guarantee humane treatment for the soldiers, Nakayama would promise nothing.
u. (1)Strolling the aisle of the toy store, I felt as though I were under a constant surveillance. (2) Observing me through cellophane windows in their boxes were hundreds of little robots. (3)Raising one of the boxes to examine it, I found that each box had the name of its inhabitant, record of its lifetime missions, and illustrations of various configurations it can take. (4)The one that I was holding was called Roboto-Blackbird, it had just been synthesized and could take the form of anything from a man-like robot to an F–14 fighter plane.
v. In addition to regulating my activities in various ways; I also began to think differently about my handicap.

3. Put each group of ideas together in a single sentence. Then write two more sentences that combine the material in different ways. In your sentences, link independent clauses correctly, without creating run-ons. The first example is done for you, showing four options; you need compose only three.

Ideas to be joined:
I am not pleased with the new material.
I ordered the material from Sed's.
I am returning the material.

Option one: I am not pleased with the new material that I ordered from Sed's, so I am returning it. (The two independent clauses are linked by a comma plus *so*. The first independent clause contains a dependent clause, *that I ordered from Sed's*.)

Option two: I ordered the new material from Sed's; I am not pleased with it; therefore, I am returning it. (The three independent clauses are joined by a semicolon alone and by a semicolon plus *therefore*.)

Option three: Though I ordered the new material, I am returning it to Sed's because I am not pleased with it. (The independent clause is in the middle, flanked by two dependent clauses.)

Option four: I am not pleased with the material I ordered from Sed's; I am returning it. (The two independent clauses are linked by a semicolon. The first independent clause contains a dependent clause, *I ordered from Sed's*. Note the *that*, which might open the dependent clause, has been omitted—compare to Option 1.)

(Sample revisions in back of book)
a. The settlers arrived in February.
   It was very cold.
   They had very little food with them.
   That winter, 30 percent of the settlers died.
b. The flood came in June.
   Rain filled the mountain gullies.
   Rain caused flash floods and mud slides.
   Three parties were known to be campinig in the mountains.
   The rangers went out to look for the campers.
(Sample revisions in instructor's manual.)
c. Two parties of campers returned on their own.
   One party of campers was not found until the third day.
   Their camp had been washed away by floods.
   They had escaped to high ground.
   They were wet and cold.
   They were otherwise unharmed.

4. Compose a sentence that exhibits all three ways of joining independent clauses within the same sentence.
5. Compose a sentence that is at least thirty words long but does not become a run-on. Do not rely on repetition for length. (You may not write "The firecrackers went bang, bang, bang. . . .")
6. Compose the shortest run-on you can.

REVISING YOUR OWN WRITING

In the space provided, enter run-on sentences you've found in your own writing, and write the correction. Then write five other sentences in the same pattern, making corrections where necessary.

Your Sentence

Your Revision

Five Other Sentences in the Same Pattern

STEP TWO: READ AND REVISE FOR GRAMMAR AND PUNCTUATION

GRAMMATICAL TERMS IN THIS LESSON

Run-on Sentence: A group of words punctuated as a single sentence where independent clauses are joined incorrectly with a comma alone (sometimes called a comma splice) or with no punctuation (sometimes called a fused sentence)

Subject: A word or group of words that names the person or thing that is performing the action or that is in the state of being named in the verb

Verb: The one to four words that name the action or state of being of the subject

Clause: A subject-verb unit plus that unit's modifiers and complements

Independent clause: A clause that can stand alone

Dependent clause: A clause that cannot stand alone

Relative Pronoun: Who, whom, whose, whoever, whomever, which, or that, when they are used not to open a question or to modify a noun, but to refer back to a noun in the same or another sentence

Noun: A word or group of words that names a person, place, concept, or thing

Connector: A word that connects a word or group of words to another

Coordinating Connector: And, but, for, nor, or, so (when it means therefor), yet

Nonmovable Connector: A connector that cannot change its place in its clause

VERBS

LESSON FOR STEP 2C

MAKE VERBS AGREE WITH THEIR SUBJECTS

PREVIEW OF THE LESSON

Because verbs are so variable and so central to your writing, they often need revision. In this lesson, you will check whether each of your verbs agrees with its subject. The next substeps, 2D and 2E, also deal with verbs. For this lesson, you will need to know how to identify verbs and their subjects. (See Introductory Lesson A.)

This lesson covers four procedures:

1. How to Identify Each Verb in Your Writing
2. How to Identify the Single Word Subject(s) of Each Verb
3. How to Determine Whether the Subject is Singular or Plural
4. How to Check Whether the Verb Agrees with the Subject and Revise as Needed.

These procedures are summarized in Figure 2C.1

LESSON 2C: MAKE VERBS AGREE WITH THEIR SUBJECTS

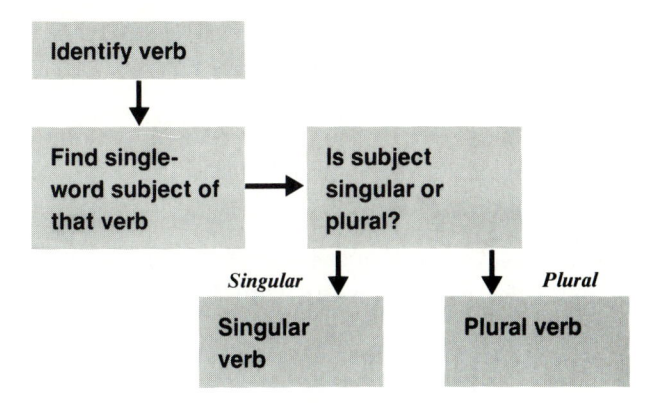

FIGURE 2C.1 Check Subject-Verb Agreement

BE READY TO REVISE VERBS IN OTHER WAYS

As you check verbs for their grammatical qualities, you may also realize that a verb should be changed from passive to active voice (Step 1A) or that you should rewrite the sentence's subject-verb unit (Step 1C) to make your writing clear and forceful.

THE AGREEMENT RULE

If the subject is singular (referring to one only), the verb must be singular; if the subject is plural (referring to more than one), the verb must be plural.

The cat [singular subject] runs [singular verb].
The cats [plural subject] run [plural verb].

STEP TWO: READ AND REVISE FOR GRAMMAR AND PUNCTUATION

SITUATIONS THAT CAUSE AGREEMENT PROBLEMS FOR WRITERS

In most situations, native English speakers automatically form the verb correctly to agree with its subject. Problems occur, however, when the writer:

1. Loses track of what is the real subject of the verb and makes the verb agree with a word that is not the subject OR
2. Does not know whether the subject is singular or plural (occurs with certain subject words such as *anyone* and *crowd* or when a single verb has two subjects, one singular and one plural) OR
3. Knows the real subject of the verb but uses a form of the verb other than the Standard English form (for example, "My mother *work* at the store" rather than the Standard English "My mother *works* at the store"). See pp. 268-70 for further discussion of standard and other forms of language.

IDENTIFY VERBS

Introductory Lesson A covers identification of verbs. For this substep, you should particularly check verbs whose subjects seem complex in any of the following ways, because these are the kinds of subject-verb units where agreement is usually a problem.

1. There are many intervening words between the subject and verb.
2. The subject is a word like *group* or *crowd* where you are not sure whether it is singular or plural.
3. There is more than one subject for the same verb.
4. If you sometimes have trouble forming Standard English verbs (for example remembering to add *-ed* or *-s*), you probably should check all your verbs.

LESSON 2C: MAKE VERBS AGREE WITH THEIR SUBJECTS

IDENTIFY THE SINGLE WORD SUBJECT(S) OF EACH VERB

Introductory Lesson 1A covers identifying subjects. For this substep, it is important to identify just the *single word* subject for a verb (pp. 47–49). You need the subject without its modifiers (other words that describe it or limit its meaning). Also, remember that the subject is never the object of a preposition (p. 47).

Sometimes a verb has two or more subjects: *"Bob, Jake, Harry, Louise,* and *Sally* own the restaurant." It is important to identify all the subjects, and reduce each to its single word. Sometimes a subject is two words. *("To forgive* is divine.") Sometimes a subject is a whole clause. (*"That he was not killed* was a miracle." See Introductory Lesson B on clauses.) This lesson deals with subjects stripped of their modifiers, usually leaving one word.

The reason for being so careful to identify the single word subject of your verb is that most errors in subject–verb agreement appear because the writer loses track of the real subject. The writer then forms the verb to agree with some other word that is not that verb's real subject.

DO NOT BE DISTRACTED BY WORDS BETWEEN THE SUBJECT AND VERB

Writers often lose track of the real subject because other words intervene between the subject and the verb. The following are some examples; italics mark the subject(s).

Jim walks to the bridge.
Jim, the contractor for several construction jobs, walks to the bridge.
One of the contractors walks to the bridge. (Rule out *contractors* as the subject, because it is preceded by a preposition—a word showing direction or relationship.)

Jim, the contractor's son, walks to the bridge. (Do not be distracted by *the contractor's son*. It describes the subject by renaming it.)
Jim, one of the contractor's sons, walks to the bridge.
Not until morning was *Jim* going to walk to the bridge.
Jim and a *group* of young children walk to the bridge. (If two subjects are joined by *and, or, nor,* or *plus,* count both as subjects.)
Among the best walkers is *Jim*. (The verb precedes the subject.)
Jim, after a talk with the contractor and a luncheon with some guests, walks to the bridge.
Jim is one of the men *who* walk to the bridge. (There are two clauses, each with a subject and a verb: *Jim is, who walk*.)

EXERCISES

Answers in back of book: 1a-j
Answers in instructor's manual: 1k-m

1. In the following sentences, underline each verb; draw a line from each verb to its subject.
   (Answers in back of book)
   a. This subject is important.
   b. With very simple means she could obtain striking results.
   c. Following the identification of the culprit, management moved quickly.
   d. The doctor lives frugally, but Gordon is a spendthrift.
   e. The grand jury hands down indictments, signs subpoenas, and may even play the role of investigator.
   f. The 1978 decision to repeal the state's mandatory helmet laws has directly influenced the number of serious motorcycle accidents.
   g. The body of the car is in very good shape; it's the transmission and engine that cost me money.

h. Scientific reasoning was the process that gave birth to the concept that neutrinos must exist.
i. Leaders who fail to take social forces into account and yet try to change their organizations resemble nothing so much as Canute, the legendary Danish monarch who stood on the beach and commanded the waves to stand still as proof of his power.
j. While this task may be shared and developed with other key members of the organization, it remains the core responsibility of the manager and cannot be delegated.

(Answers in instructor's manual)

k. I have grown to love my job because the atmosphere is friendly and the owners treat employees with respect.
l. In general, however, unless some unusual problem exists, the leaders encourage the campers to stick it out and complete their journey.
m. At International Motors, developing the new vision was the direct responsibility of Arthur Handy, and while it took a great amount of staff work and literally dozens of mission papers, the vision was shaped by Handy's philosophy and style.

DETERMINE WHETHER A SUBJECT IS SINGULAR OR PLURAL AND REVISE THE VERB IF NECESSARY

Once you have located your single word subject, you can usually figure out which verb form is appropriate; however, some words may give you trouble—words such as *group* and *team,* and instances where a single verb has both a singular and a plural subject. The following are guidelines for cases where you may be in doubt:

WHEN SUBJECT(S) ARE:	VERB IS:
each, neither, either, and subjects ending in *-one, -body,* and *-thing*	singular

    Example *Somebody wants the contract.*

all, any, most, more, none and *some*	either singular or plural depending on the word they refer to

    Example *Plural: All of the rabbits were dead.*
    Singular: All of the coal was high in sulphur.

when two or more subjects are joined by *and*	plural

    Example *The contractor and her helpers walk to the bridge.*

if two subjects are joined by *or* or *nor* and both of them are singular	singular

    Example *Neither the treated patient nor the untreated patient shows any change.*

if two subjects are joined by *or* or *nor* and one is singular, one plural	follow the one nearest the verb

    Example *Neither the white rabbit nor the brown rabbits were harmed.*
    Neither the brown rabbits nor the white rabbit was harmed.

a collective noun, referring to a group of persons or things as a unit *(jury, crowd, audience, herd, group)*	plural when the individual members of the group are acting separately, singular when they act as a group

    Example *The jury adjourns today.* **(singular)**
    The jury have been leaving the room in pairs. **(plural)**

LESSON 2C: MAKE VERBS AGREE WITH THEIR SUBJECTS

WHEN SUBJECT(S) ARE:	VERB IS:
the title of a novel or play, or a word used as a word	singular, even when the title or the word is plural

    Example   Antony and Cleopatra *is a fine play.*
                      "Children" *is not the word you want.*

nouns that are plural in form but singular in meaning	singular

    Example   *Home Economics is my field.*
              The news is on at 7 P.M.
    Seven miles seems too high an estimate.

fractions, numbers, dollars, measurements, and distance	singular, except for the following

    Example   *One fifth of the original forest survives today.* **(Singular verb)**
    Twenty dollars is too much for that set of earphones. **(Singular verb)**

if the items that make up the quantity are thought of as separate parts rather than as a single unit	plural

    Example   *Of one hundred four victims, fifty percent survive today.* **(Plural verb)**
    Seventy grueling miles separate them from the finish line. **(Plural verb)**

who, which, and *that*	singular when the subject refers to something singular, plural when the subject refers to something plural

    Example   *All my friends, who are in the car with me, come from Michigan.*
        (*Who* **refers to** *friends,* **so it takes a plural verb.)**

STEP TWO: READ AND REVISE FOR GRAMMAR AND PUNCTUATION

> *One of the workers, who is in the car with me, comes from Michigan.*
> (*Who* refers to *one*, so it takes a singular verb.)

WHO, WHICH, THAT: SINGULAR OR PLURAL?

Who, which, and *that* are singular or plural depending on the words they refer to. To help yourself decide what the *who, which,* or *that* refers to, turn the *who* clause into a question: "Who is in the car with me?" In the preceding example, the answer is "One [worker] is in the car with me." Thus the *who* refers to *one,* which is singular, so it takes a singular verb.

SPECIAL NOTE ON ADDING "S" TO SINGULAR VERBS

If you grew up hearing and saying "The manager shout at the workers," you may know that a verb is singular but not always form it by the rules for Standard English. Lesson 2E reviews the rules for forming Standard English verbs.

EXERCISES

(Note: Exercise 1 appears earlier in the lesson.)
Answers in back of book: 2a-q, 3a-o
Answers in instructor's manual: 2r-w, 3p-v

2. Label the following subjects *S* for singular or *P* for plural. For those that can be either, give them both labels, and explain when they would be singular and when plural. (Answers in back of book)
    a. Saccho and Venezetti
    b. neither Paul nor the others

LESSON 2C: MAKE VERBS AGREE WITH THEIR SUBJECTS

    c. the crowd
    d. all
    e. three quarters of the loaves
    f. one of the instruments
    g. anybody
    h. something
    i. "mice" (used as a word, as in this sentence: She didn't know that *"mice"* [is/are] plural for "mouse.")
    j. who
    k. economics (as a school subject)
    l. "The Owl and the Pussycat" (poem)
    m. more than half a bushel of apples
    n. children
    o. the crowd that
    p. managers who
    q. the manager who
    (Answers in instructor's manual)
    r. everyone
    s. the jury
    t. which
    u. half a loaf
    v. *Farewell to Arms* (novel)
    w. "geese" (used as a word, as in this sentence: She didn't know that *"geese"* [was/were] the secret password.)

3. In the following sentences, correct any errors in subject-verb agreement.
   (Answers in back of book)
   a. Any cheerleader still on the benches or in the locker rooms get two demerits.
   b. Every one of the potatoes have sprouted already.
   c. Rugby and lacrosse are two of the most violent sports I know.
   d. The group of hikers meet every Saturday.
   e. The trails and the mountain lookout needs maintenance.

STEP TWO: READ AND REVISE FOR GRAMMAR AND PUNCTUATION

f. Only about half the people bring umbrellas.
g. Half the milk was spilled.
h. The team, with Brent in the lead, win the final victory.
i. Each Saturday, a group of men go to the market.
j. Ralph is one of the men who goes to the market every Saturday.
k. I was afraid she would tumble off one of the boulders that separates our yard from the river.
l. The profit from our sale of the restaurants have paid for the new house.
m. The result of our strenuous efforts, long hours, and vigorous sales campaign over the past months have been impressive gains in every area of the business that are under our control.
n. A cactus or some other desert plant survive nicely in this dry, sunny location.
o. The recollection of the due dates, which just happen to be within twenty-four hours, give John a sick feeling in his stomach.

(Answers in instructor's manual)

p. A student who plans to enter any of the health-related professions enter a field of great opportunity and need.
q. In our small suburb, town politics was the focus of conversation on Sunday mornings at the local Bagel Depot.
r. All the kids played in the neighborhood softball league, which were coached by parents.
s. Each of the players who need first aid should come to the office.
t. The problem with our toboggans were severe.
u. Dirt or sand blow into the machine through the grill.
v. The loss that resulted from the fires were paid by insurance.

REVISING YOUR OWN WRITING

In the space provided, enter passages from your own writing where you've missed problems with subject-verb agreement. Write the correction. Then write five other sentences that follow similar patterns, forming verbs appropriately.

Your Sentence(s)

_____
_____
_____
_____
_____

Your Revision

_____
_____
_____
_____

Five Other Sentences in the Same Pattern

_____
_____
_____
_____
_____

GRAMMATICAL TERMS IN THIS LESSON

Subject: A word or group of words that names the person or thing that is performing the action or that is in the state of being named in the verb

Verb: The one to four words that name the action or state of being of the subject

STEP TWO: READ AND REVISE FOR GRAMMAR AND PUNCTUATION

Clause: A subject–verb unit plus that unit's modifiers and complements

Singular: Referring to one

Plural: Referring to more than one

Preposition: A word, usually short, that shows direction or relationship and that is accompanied by an object

Object of a preposition: The word that completes the preposition, answering the question *for what? to what? near what?*

Prepositional Phrase: A preposition plus its object and modifiers.

Modifier: A word or group of words that describes or limits the meaning of another word or group of words in the same sentence

LESSON FOR STEP 2D

SELECT VERB TENSES APPROPRIATELY

PREVIEW OF THE LESSON

For Step 2C, you identified verbs and made them agree with their subjects. A second factor that can change the form of a verb is tense (how a verb indicates past, present, or future time). First review verb tenses and then you'll consider the choices a writer must make.

THE STANDARD ENGLISH TENSE SYSTEM

Standard English has six different verb tenses.

Present tense:	I hunt.
Future tense:	I will hunt.
Future perfect tense:	I will have hunted.
Past tense:	I hunted.
Present perfect tense:	I have hunted; he has hunted.
Past perfect tense:	I had hunted; he has hunted.

249

In each of the preceding categories, variations of *to be* may be added to express continuing action. These tenses are called the *progressive* tenses:

Present Progressive:	I am hunting.
Future Progressive:	I will be hunting.
Future Perfect Progressive:	I will have been hunting.
Past Progressive:	I was hunting.
Present Perfect Progressive:	I have been hunting.
Past Perfect Progressive:	I had been hunting.

CHOOSE A DOMINANT TENSE

In choosing tenses, your first job is to decide whether your dominant tense should be past, present, or future. Not all your verbs will be in the dominant tense, but most of them will be. It will usually be obvious when you should choose future, but the choice between past and present may be more difficult. Sometimes, in reciting past events such as a historical incident or the events described in a novel, you can use the present tense to describe past events. Present tense makes the events sound more immediate and vivid. You can also use the present tense when you are analyzing something that exists in the present—for example, a work of art, a piece of writing, a factory, a machine. For instance, you might say, "Shakespeare *repeats* the reference to blindness in the play's next scene." (Use present tense because the item being analyzed—a play—is in existence now.)

In revising your writing, identify the dominant tense and ask three questions:

1. Does my choice of a dominant tense make sense?
2. Have I kept the same dominant tense throughout, without making unnecessary changes?

3. If the dominant tense changes at some point in the paper, does the change occur at a logical point that will sound natural to the readers?

The process of deciding whether to use present or past as the dominant tense is summarized in Figure 2D.1.

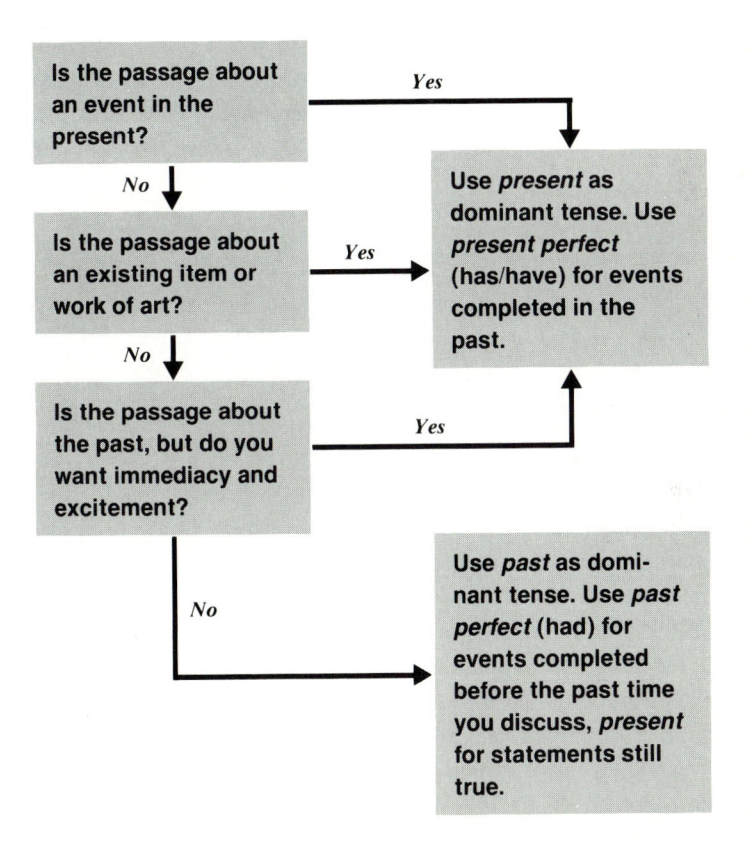

FIGURE 2D.1   Choosing Between Past and Present as Dominant Verb Tense

SHIFT TENSE FOR SPECIFIC PURPOSES

Even though you have chosen a dominant tense, not every verb in the passage will be in that tense. There are legitimate reasons for using verbs that are not in the dominant tense. Those reasons are explained later in this lesson. Most problems, however, arise when you unnecessarily shift one or more verbs out of the dominant tense. If your dominant tense is past, do not shift an individual verb to present just to give it more vividness. If your dominant tense is present, do not shift an individual verb to past just because you describe a specific event in the past. For example, note the awkward shift in verb tenses in the following essay about Mark Twain's *Huck Finn:*

> In a similar way, Twain creates sympathy for Miss Watson. Huck describes her as "a tolerable slim old maid." Without a family of her own, she generously shelters Huck. She tried to teach Huck how to spell. But Huck couldn't stand it, and "got fidgety."

The writer begins the passage with present tense as the dominant tense: *creates, describes, shelters.* Then, however, the writer switches to the past tense: *tried, could stand,* and *got.* She switches for two reasons, both *in*appropriate. She thinks she should switch to past because the spelling lesson is a specific incident in the novel, whereas Miss Watson's sheltering and Huck's evaluation are more generally true over a period of time in the novel. She is also influenced by the past tense of the words she quotes from the novel: *got fidgety;* however, these are *not* valid reasons for changing the verb tense. When describing the events of a novel in present tense, retain present tense as the dominant tense for all events (some individual verbs, though, may be written in future, past, or present perfect, as explained later in this lesson). In a revision of the *Huck Finn* passage, the writer puts the spelling incident in present tense to make it

LESSON 2D: SELECT VERB TENSES APPROPRIATELY

match the rest of the passage. She also revises to make the quoted words fit the rest of her passage. The following example shows three options for correcting the passage:

Revision: In a similar way Twain creates sympathy for Miss Watson. Huck describes her as "a tolerable slim old maid." Without a family of her own, she generously shelters Huck. She *tries* to teach Huck how to spell. But Huck *cannot* stand it, and *gets* "fidgety."

Alternate Last Sentence: But Huck *cannot* stand it, and, as he says, "I got fidgety."

Alternate Last Sentence: But Huck *cannot* stand it, and "[gets] fidgety."

KEEP TENSES CONSISTENT WITH QUOTATIONS

When you are quoting a source that uses a verb tense different from the one you're using (as in the *Huck Finn* example), there are three common ways to handle the problem:

1. Put the verb outside the quotation marks and change to the dominant tense. This works well only when there is a single verb that comes at or near the beginning or end of your quotation, so you can leave the verb out of the quotation marks. You would not do that if the verb itself were unique and important to your point. In that case, you would want to include the verb in the quotation marks to acknowledge that it was directly quoted and to preserve it as a basis for your discussion. For example, one writer quotes an educator who is discussing the current U.S. Secretary of Education: "The Secretary seems more interested in sparring with us than in sitting down and solving problems." The verb *seems* is important to the educa-

tor's meaning. You would not want to leave it out of the quotation. If you needed to change its tense, you would use one of the other options.

2. Add words to introduce the quoted verb.

The words the writer adds repeat the writer's dominant tense and sets the quoted words, with their different tense, into a distinct context.

3. Change the verb in the quotation and enclose the changed verb in brackets.

Readers trust that whatever you have enclosed in quotation marks is *exactly* what the original source said. Thus if you change the tense of a quoted verb, enclose that verb in brackets—the standard way of showing a reader that the bracketed material preserves the sense of the quotation but does not exactly reproduce the original source.

Further guidance for handling quoted material is included in Lesson 2R.

GUIDELINES FOR COMBINING TENSES

Being consistent in your dominant tense does not mean that every verb in your passage will be in the same tense. If you have chosen one tense as your dominant tense, some individual verbs will be in other tenses. The following are four guidelines for combining tenses. (See also Figure 2D.1.)

1. If you are using past tense, shift to present tense to express things that are still true.

The explosion *occurred* at 7 P.M., and, since that *is* the moment at which the night workers *begin* their shifts at the plant, there *were* twice the usual number of people in the building. (*Is* and *begin* are present tense, because the shifts at the plant are the same today. If the incident happened

LESSON 2D: SELECT VERB TENSES APPROPRIATELY

long ago, or if shifts have changed, you would use past tense for every verb.)

2. Use the present perfect tense (with *has, have*) to show an action completed in the recent past, that has an impact on the present.

I am *well now, but I* have been *ill for the past two weeks.*

Choices between present perfect and simple past tenses are often a matter of judgment. In the preceding example, *I was ill* would be acceptable, but the present perfect conveys a finer shade of meaning.

3. Use the past perfect tense to show action that was completed before a time described with a past tense verb.

Writers sometimes underutilize the past perfect tense, missing the fine distinctions of time that would help readers understand a sentence more easily.

Draft: I discovered I was without a calculator, but John *brought* his.

Revision: I discovered I was without a calculator, but John *had brought* his.

The revision clarifies that John had brought the calculator earlier, not that he went out and got it after the speaker's dilemma had become apparent.

4. When the main part of the sentence uses *would have, could have, should have, might have,* or a similar form, a dependent clause that begins with a word like *if* or *when* does not repeat the *would* form, but simply takes a past perfect verb. (To identify dependent clauses, see Introductory Lesson B.)

Draft: The plan *would have worked* if the salespeople *would have been* more aggressive.

Revision: The plan *would have worked* if the salespeople *had been* more aggressive.

SELECTING TENSES TO PRESENT RESEARCH DATA

Sometimes choice of tense reflects a writer's confusion about the extent to which evidence gathered in the past can be used to make statements about what is true in the present. The following passage from a report on rape suffers from this type of confusion.

DRAFT OF STUDENT PAPER ON RAPE

> Rapists usually work alone and attack only lone women. In completed rapes, 95% of the victims were alone, and in attempted rapes 91% of the victims were alone. About 60% of completed rapes and 80% of attempted rapes involve one victim and one offender.
>
> The time and place of occurrence of rapes are very rarely the stereotype of a woman being attacked in a dark alley. More than 30% of rapes occur during the daytime (6 A.M. to 6 P.M.).
>
> About 20% of all reported rapes occur in the victim's home, and an additional 14% took place nearby. More than 65% of rapes occurred in open outdoor places.
>
> [The paper continues the discussion of women's feelings after rape.]

LESSON 2D: SELECT VERB TENSES APPROPRIATELY

The writer needs first to add appropriate information and citations for the research studies. Then she can use present tense for conclusions that are still valid, and past tense for reporting the results of individual studies.

REVISION

Rapists usually work alone and attack only lone women. One large-scale study (Smith, 1978) showed that in completed rapes 95% of the victims were alone, and in attempted rapes 91% of the victims were alone. Robinson (1980), with a smaller sample, found that about 60% of completed rapes and 80% of attempted rapes involved one victim and one offender.

The time and place of occurrence of rapes are very rarely the stereotype of a woman being attacked in a dark alley. Brown (1982) found that, in Cleveland between 1975 and 1980, more than 30% of rapes occurred during the daytime (6 A.M. to 6 P.M.). Other studies (King, 1981; Wassail, 1982) indicate that about 20% of all reported rapes occur in the victim's home, and an additional 14% take place nearby. The same studies reveal that 65% of rapes occur in open outdoor places.

STEP TWO: READ AND REVISE FOR GRAMMAR AND PUNCTUATION

EXERCISES

Answers in back of book: 1a, 2a-e, 3a, 4a, 5a
Answers in instructor's manual: 1b, 2f-g, 3b, 4b, 5b

1. In the following passage, the writer is telling the story of how one student handled an essay assignment in a literature class. Verb tenses are well chosen. In the passage, identify the tense of each verb. What is the dominant tense? Which verbs are not in the dominant tense? Why? Note that the passage has a number of verb-like words that, since they are not being used as verbs, have no tense (see outline of the tense system, p. 249, and Introductory Lesson A.)

   (Answers in back of book)

   a. Bob Tuinstra (not his real name) began by reading the three possible essay questions, assessing them carefully. Then he read the short story, William Faulkner's "Barn Burning," pondering which of the questions he could answer best. The story concerns a young boy whose father continually moves about the country, in each location provoking a fight with neighbors, and then vengefully setting someone's barn on fire. Through the course of the story the boy struggles to separate himself from this cycle of destruction. Finally, in one town he alerts a barn owner to his father's impending act, and runs away from home as the barn's owners shoot his father in the act of setting fire to their barn.

   (Answers in instructor's manual)

   b.   When he finished reading the story, Bob chose the question that asked students to analyze point of view in the story. He spent a few minutes pondering what one can say about point of view in literature. He knew that "point of view" means the characteristics of the voice that tells the story or poem. He knew the various points of view one finds in literature.

LESSON 2D: SELECT VERB TENSES APPROPRIATELY

2. In the following passages, revise verb forms to make appropriate use of the perfect tense.
   (Sample revisions in back of book.)
   a. At the beginning of the year, I went to the lab and listened to a French dialogue that was read in class. I answered dialogue questions that I already answered.
   b. I looked around the crowded locker room as the coach began his pre-game pep talk. Everyone seemed calm and under control except me. Something was wrong. My body felt weak and I was light-headed. Was I nervous? I didn't think so because I was involved in games like this before.
   c. Kelly's watch was like new. It was expertly repaired by her grandfather, a jeweler.
   d. The designer came to the party in a leopard mask decorated with rhinestones. She studied the uses of masks in other cultures and decided to promote masks for her own parties.
   e. The mask she wore was not her first. She made masks for more than eight years.
   (Sample revisions in instructor's manual)
   f. My teacher looked very serious. I heard from former students that on the last day of class he usually gave a word of advice, but this was looking ridiculous.
   g. When the surgery failed, Jim finally realized his problem was real and smoking was the main cause. Jim regretted that he didn't listen to everyone's advice to quit smoking.
3. In the following passage, revise the verb tenses.
   (Sample revision in back of book)

   The passage is an excerpt from an analysis of Henrik Ibsen's play, *Enemy of the People*. The crafty and selfish Aslaksen's actions are being described. Dr. Stockman is the humane person who leads the town's efforts to improve its mineral baths.

STEP TWO: READ AND REVISE FOR GRAMMAR AND PUNCTUATION

    a. Aslaksen came out to support Dr. Stockman to enhance his own reputation in the community. Aslaksen also supports Dr. Stockman because he knows Stockman's proposal to improve the baths would eventually improve Aslaksen's own business.

        Thus, in this scene, Aslaksen is not only there for support, he was also looking out for himself. He gives that away when he says, "We shall all make our living out of them [the baths], especially those of us who are householders. That is why we will back up the project as strongly as possible" (Act 2, p. 309).

(Sample revision in instructor's manual)

    b.   Aslaksen also likes to be in the spotlight. When he was trying to tell the doctor how much power he really had: "I have a certain influence in the town, a little bit of power, if I may be allowed to say."

4. In the following passage, revise the verb tenses. As part of his essay on procrastination, the writer is drawing an imaginary portrait of a typical procrastinator. Sentences are numbered for reference.

(Sample revision in back of book)

    a.   (1)John, a high school senior and typical put-it-off-to-the-last-minute-and-hope-it-gets-done person, received today his list of calculus problems due next week. (2)"Whew, one whole week! No problem." (3)Now he can devote all of his time to that English paper that was assigned a few weeks ago. (4)John spends his day snoozing in class and his night lounging in front of the television. (5)As for that English paper—well, in his own immortal words, "It loses!" (6)Inevitably, his catch-up weekend finally comes; however, homework is last on his weekend's schedule. (7)He decides it is time to pay a visit to the ocean; he has never seen it in winter. (8)He always wondered if the waves froze. (9)If he should happen to return home in time, he really wanted to catch the Colt game Sunday afternoon and of course, he simply could

LESSON 2D: SELECT VERB TENSES APPROPRIATELY

not miss *Rocky III* on cable that night. (10) At the conclusion of the weekend's escapades, the grim thought of that English paper, his calculus problems, his chemistry lab, his biology lab, and his Spanish dialogue battered his memory. (11) The recollection of the due dates which just happened to be within the next twenty-four hours gives rise to a football-sized lump in his throat. (12) It would seem that it was a bit late to be starting at this point, but not for John. (13) It's like a race for John; his mother yelling at him to get to work is just like the starting gun.
(Sample revision in instructor's manual)
[continuation of same paper]
b. (14) So John sets out on his journey to "dawn's early light." (15) He glances at the stack of textbooks on his desk, and they leer back as if to say, "I wonder who will win this time?" (16) As his pencil comes to life, he takes a quick look at the clock, which reads 10:30 p.m. (17) "Uh-oh," he thinks to himself as a sudden sensation of nausea comes upon him. (18) The next time his glazed and bloodshot eyes left his work, not counting the fifteen minutes that he spent watching the last half of "The Benny Hill Show," it was 4:38 A.M. (19) His biology is halfway finished; every other sentence from his Spanish lesson is translated; his English paper is done—there were only sixteen spelling mistakes, seven fragments, and just one little "t" where there was supposed to be a capital "T." (20) There was also one skipped paragraph, but John wasn't particularly fond of that one anyway. (21) He was rather impressed with his paper: fifty-two minutes was his all-time record. (22) He finally gives in to his sagging eyelids after reasoning that calculus simply did not have enough eternal significance for him to continue this masochistic endeavor.

5. Write a revision of the Bob Tuinstra case study in Exercise 1, making the present tense dominant.
(Sample revision of first paragraph in back of book, second paragraph in instructor's manual.)

STEP TWO: READ AND REVISE FOR GRAMMAR AND PUNCTUATION

REVISING YOUR OWN WRITING

In the space provided, enter passages from your own writing where you have missed problems with verb tenses. Write the correction. Then write five other sentences that follow similar patterns, forming verbs appropriately.

Your Sentence(s)

_____
_____
_____
_____

Your Revision

_____
_____
_____
_____

Five Other Sentences in the Same Pattern

_____
_____
_____
_____

GRAMMATICAL TERMS IN THIS LESSON

Clause: A subject-verb unit plus that unit's modifiers and complements

Dependent Clause: A clause that cannot stand alone

Verb Tense: The way in which a verb is formed to indicate time. Tenses in English are: Present, Past, Future, Present Perfect, Past Perfect, Future Perfect. All six categories have progressive forms (with "to be").

LESSON FOR
STEP 2E

USE STANDARD ENGLISH VERB FORMS

PREVIEW OF THE LESSON

Verbs are a part of language that changes as people move from one situation to another, from informal to formal settings, and from spoken to written language. Thus many writers must reread their writing to make sure they have used verb forms that are appropriate for written Standard English. If necessary, see Introductory Lesson A to identify verbs and Lesson 2D to establish tenses. This lesson discusses some of the most common problems writers face when forming verbs.

DO NOT WRITE *OF* FOR *HAVE* IN FORMING VERBS

Because *of* and *have* sound alike, writers sometimes confuse the two. Only *have* is used as a helping verb.

Incorrect: I should *of* gone with him.
Correct: I should *have* gone with him.

STEP TWO: READ AND REVISE FOR GRAMMAR AND PUNCTUATION

USE APPROPRIATE VERB FORMS FOR PAST AND PERFECT TENSES

Most verbs in English form the past tense by adding -ed. However, many verbs are irregular—they form the past and perfect by changing their interior spelling and pronunciation: for example *catch* (present), *caught* (past), *has/had caught* (perfect). If you are not sure what the past and perfect forms of a verb are, use a dictionary. For example, suppose you are wondering whether to write *he swam* or *he swum*. Look it up in the dictionary under the present tense form, *swim*. This is what you will find:

> **swim** (swim), *v.i.* [SWAM (swam) or *archaic* or *dial.*
> SWUM (swum), SWUM, SWIMMING], (ME. *swimmen;* AS.
> *swimman;* akin to G. *schwimmen;* IE. base *swem-*
> *Webster's New World Dictionary,* College Edition, 1962.

If there are two entries for a word, select the one that has *v.* or *v.i.* or *v.t.* after the word, not the one that has *n.* (for noun) or any other letter. Ignore for now what the *i.* or *t.* means. You are only interested in the *v.* (for verb). Read the definition to make sure you have the word you want. After *v.i.,* or *v.t.,* in capital letters, is the past tense form. Then, in parentheses is the pronunciation for that form.

Normally, the next word would be the form you use with perfect tenses, but in this case, there is additional information: the past tense has another form—an archaic (very old) or dialect (regional or ethnic) form, *swum*. That form, too, is followed by a guide to its pronunciation, in parentheses. (Sometimes a dictionary will use the word *obsolete* for outdated forms of words and *rare* for forms infrequently used. A dictionary may also give the region where a verb form is used: for example, *British and regional* means that British speakers and some regional speakers in America use that form.) If a dictionary simply gives two forms separated by the word *or,* it means that both forms are equally acceptable.

Next is the form you would use with perfect tenses. If the

LESSON 2E: USE STANDARD ENGLISH VERB FORMS

past and perfect forms are the same, some dictionaries print only one form. This is followed by the *-ing* form. In some dictionaries, this form is followed by the present tense form you would use with he/she/it—the form that normally adds *-s (swims).* Using the dictionary, you have discovered that you would form the verb this way:

Present tense:	He swims.
Future tense:	He will swim.
Past tense:	He swam. (But the old forms, and some dialects, use *swum*.)
Present perfect tense:	He has swum. (Uses the perfect form).
Past perfect tense:	He had swum. (Uses the perfect form.)
Future perfect tense:	He will have swum. (Uses the perfect form.)
-ing form:	He is swimming.

CHOOSE, CHOSE, LOOSE, LOSE

Another problem is the spelling of *choose* (pronounced like *chews*), *chose* (rhymes with *rose*), *loose* (rhymes with *moose*), and *lose* (rhymes with *chews*). The dictionary will tell you the forms of these verbs:

FORMS OF *CHOOSE* and *LOSE*

Present	Past	Perfect	*-ing*
I choose (he/she/it chooses)	I chose	I have/had chosen	choosing
I lose (he/she/it loses)	I lost	I have/had lost	losing

Loose is rarely used as a verb, and when it is it means to untie or unbind. Almost always, *loose* is a modifier meaning the opposite of tight. (My shoelaces were *loose*.)

STEP TWO: READ AND REVISE FOR GRAMMAR AND PUNCTUATION

LIE/LAY, SIT/SET, RISE/RAISE

Writers frequently confuse the various forms and meanings of these pairs of similar verbs. In daily conversation, the forms are often used interchangeably. In writing, however, it is important to choose the correct form. The following is a series of steps for figuring out and remembering which verb to use. The procedures are summarized in Figure 2E.1.

Begin by identifying the one verb in each pair that has an *i* in its present tense form: *sit, lie, rise*. This leaves out *set, lay,* and *raise*. (In the case of *rise/raise*, you will have to remember that, though both contain *i*, the form that counts—*rise*—has an *i* standing alone.) Any time you have a direct object or are using the verb in the passive voice, you must *not* use an *i* verb. All other situations take the *i* verbs.

Definition: A DIRECT OBJECT is the person or thing that directly receives the action of the verb.

In the sentence, *I hit the ball to Mark, ball* is the direct object. *To Mark* is not the direct object, because Mark did not get hit; he did not receive the *direct* action of the verb. The following direct objects are underlined.

I set the <u>bread</u> *on the table.*
He lays his <u>coat</u> *on the bench.*
Farmers raise <u>corn</u>.

Does the verb have a direct object?	→ No →	Is the verb in passive voice?	→ No →	Use *i* verb: sit, lie, rise
↓ Yes		↓ Yes		set, lay, raise

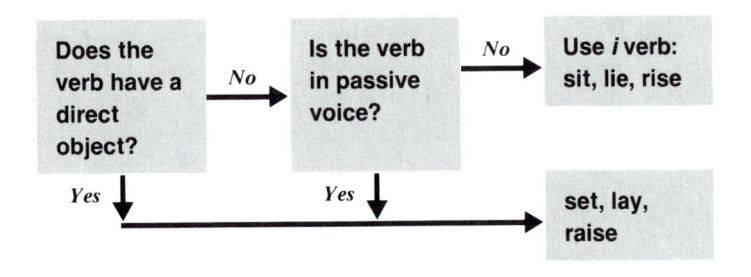

FIGURE 2 E.1   Choosing Lie/Lay, Sit/Set, Rise/Raise

LESSON 2E: USE STANDARD ENGLISH VERB FORMS

When you are dealing with *sit/set, lie/lay,* and *rise/raise,* ask first whether the verb has a direct object. If so, use *set, lay,* and *raise*.

If your verb does not have a direct object, it still may take either form depending upon whether it is in the passive voice. (See Lesson 1A.) When a verb is passive, use forms of *set, lay, raise*.

The milk had been set *on the table*.
Roses were laid *on the casket*.
(*Laid* is a form of *lay*.)

Cotton was raised *in the South*.

Once the choice of the verb is made, you need to know the correct past and perfect forms of the verb. The following table presents them.

VERBS THAT NEVER TAKE DIRECT OBJECTS OR PASSIVE VOICE

	Present	*Past*	*Perfect*
sit	I sit.	I sat.	I have/had sat.
lie	I lie.	I lay.	I have/had lain.
rise	I rise.	I rose.	I have/had risen.

VERBS THAT ALWAYS TAKE DIRECT OBJECTS OR PASSIVE VOICE

	Present	*Past*	*Perfect*	*Passive*
set	I set the book on the table.	Yesterday I set the book on the table.	I have/had set the book on the table.	The book was set on the table.
lay	I lay the book on the table.	Yesterday I laid the book on the table.	I have/had laid the book on the table.	The book was laid on the table.
raise	I raise corn.	Last year I raised corn.	I have/had raised corn.	The corn was raised by farmers.

Lie and *lay* are complicated because the past tense of *lie* is the same as the present tense of *lay*. The best strategy is to imagine the verb in the present tense and select the correct present tense verb according to the rule about *i* and the direct object/passive. Then consult the table to move as needed into past or perfect tenses.

The correct *-ing* forms of these verbs use the spelling of the present tense core:

-ing Forms

sit	sitting	set	setting
lie	lying	lay	laying
rise	rising	raise	raising

DO NOT USE A DIALECT VERB FORM WHERE STANDARD ENGLISH IS EXPECTED

People who say "Last year we learn the Morse code," or "We come a long way to be at this party," or "My mother work at the hospital" are not speaking *bad* English. Instead, they're speaking a dialect, or form of language, whose rules are just as specific as the rules of Standard English.

If you form verbs using Standard English, skip this section. If your dialect is different, and you sometimes aren't sure which forms to use when you're writing Standard English, the following is a guide to Standard English verb forms. The procedure for deciding which form to use is summarized in Figure 2E.2.

ADDING -*S* OR -*ES* TO SOME PRESENT TENSE VERB FORMS

Standard English adds *-s* or *-es* to present tense verbs whose subjects are singular and not "I" or "you." It does *not* add *-s* or *-es* to any other present tense verbs.

LESSON 2E: USE STANDARD ENGLISH VERB FORMS

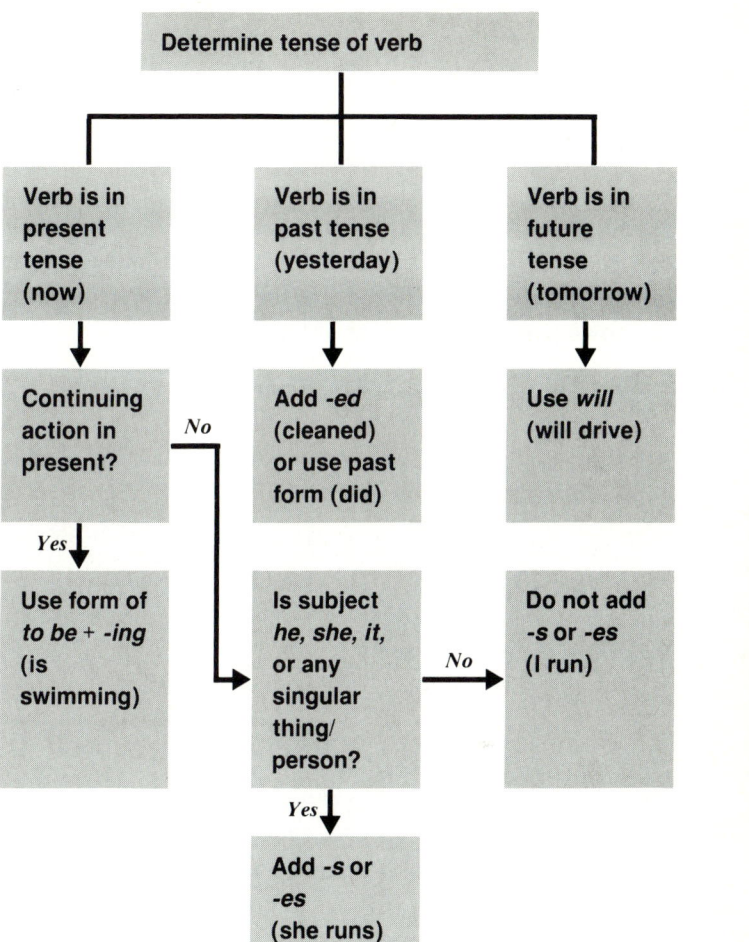

```
                    Determine tense of verb
            ┌───────────────┼───────────────┐
      Verb is in        Verb is in       Verb is in
      present           past tense       future
      tense             (yesterday)      tense
      (now)                              (tomorrow)
          │                 │                 │
          ▼                 ▼                 ▼
      Continuing   No   Add -ed          Use will
      action in  ─────  (cleaned)        (will drive)
      present?         or use past
          │            form (did)
       Yes│
          ▼                 
      Use form of      Is subject
      to be + -ing     he, she, it,
      (is              or any       No   Do not add
      swimming)        singular    ────  -s or -es
                       thing/            (I run)
                       person?
                           │
                        Yes│
                           ▼
                       Add -s or
                       -es
                       (she runs)
```

FIGURE 2 E.2   Standard English Verb Forms

STEP TWO: READ AND REVISE FOR GRAMMAR AND PUNCTUATION

Standard English *Dialect*
I try.   I tries.
She marries the bartender.   She marry the bartender.

ADDING -*ED* TO PAST TENSE VERBS

In editing your writing, identify every past or perfect tense verb, and be sure you have added -*ed* if needed (I hunted; I had hunted). Some verbs do not add -*ed* for the past tense; they have their own past tense forms, as in *brought* and *did*.

USING -*ING* VERB FORMS

Standard English uses *is* or *are* together with an -*ing* form to express continuing action in the present.

Standard English *Dialect*
We are having a picnic.   We having a picnic.
She is working at the store.   She be working at the store.
OR She works at the store.
It is supposed to snow.   It suppose to snow.

EXERCISES

Answers in back of book: 1a, 2a-j, 3a-d, 4a, 5a
Answers in instructor's manual: 1b, 2k-r, 3e-h, 4b, 5b

1. In your dictionary, look up the given words and answer the following questions:
   What is the past tense form?
   What is the perfect form?
   Are there archaic, obsolete, rare, or dialect forms? What are they?
   Are there forms that are equally acceptable? What are they?
   Fill in the blanks:
   Present tense: She
   Future tense: She

LESSON 2E: USE STANDARD ENGLISH VERB FORMS

    Past tense: She
    Present perfect tense: She
    Past perfect tense: She
    Future perfect tense: She
  a. (Answers in back of book) slink
  b. (Answers in instructor's manual) wake

2. Write the Standard English form of the verb.
   (Answers in back of book)
   a. I think I will go (lie, lay) down for a nap.
   b. Look at the women (setting, sitting) on the porch.
   c. The pie was (setting, sitting) on the counter.
   d. Yesterday I (lay, laid) the pen on the desk.
   e. The cook (sat, set) the pie on the counter.
   f. I (raised, rose) from my bed to see what was the matter.
   g. Last year we (choose, chose) Bill as captain.
   h. This year we want to (choose, chose) someone else.
   i. Randy grabbed the horse and (led, lead) it away from the road.
   j. I don't want to (loose, lose) a friendship.
   (Answers in instructor's manual)
   k. That dog has (lain, laid) there for an hour.
   l. Randy went to (set, sit) down on the porch.
   m. A heavy log was (lain, laid) to mark the boundary.
   n. After his nap, my grandfather (raised, rose) from the couch.
   o. She (set, sat) the lamp squarely in its place.
   p. Last year she (led, lead) the work crew.
   q. I wanted to (choose, chose) my own colors.
   r. The children always (lose, loose) their mittens.

3. Revise the following verbs.
   (Answers in back of book)
   a. He might of gone to bed already.
   b. Of all the things that could of happened, this one was the best.
   c. The court should have been convinced of his guilt.

271

STEP TWO: READ AND REVISE FOR GRAMMAR AND PUNCTUATION

  d. If I hadn't of caught him, he'd of fallen into the water.
  (Answers in instructor's manual)
  e. He had to of returned, or his sweater wouldn't be here.
  f. Andrew should of shoveled the driveway.
  g. The officers have been relieved of their duties.
  h. If the boss hadn't been looking, I'd of gotten away with it.
4. In the following passage, revise verb forms to conform to written Standard English. Since this is an informal essay, the contractions may remain. However, when a contraction contains a verb form that differs from Standard English, change it. Refer to a dictionary for meanings and forms of "wake," "awaken," and "awake." Sentences are numbered for reference.

(Sample revision in back of book)
  a. (1)It was 4:30 A.M. early Saturday morning, the beginning of a five day escapade, a weekend we would never forget. (2)We, the class of 1986 of Jones Harbor High School, having just graduated the night before, were all awakening and getting set to go to the paradise on the beach, with good times, parties, and most important of all no parents. (3)"Ocean, here we come," was our motto that night. (4)I woke up to the loud sounding alarm and cool morning breeze coming in through the open window behind my headboard. (5)It's a wonder I could get up. (6)I felt myself tossing and turning the whole three hours I laid in my bed. (7)I had to have woken up at least ten times in the three hours I slept. (8)It's like that feeling you get on the night before Christmas.

(Sample revision in instructor's manual)
  b. [Same essay continues] (9)Your blood is racing up and down your veins at a hundred miles an hour. (10)If I'd of known that this trip was going to lead to a broken friendship, I would rather have stayed in bed and bagged the trip than loose my best friend.

LESSON 2E: USE STANDARD ENGLISH VERB FORMS

5. The following passage is deliberately written in a dialect. Change verbs to Standard English forms. Keep the first three sentences in the present tense, then switch to past tense as the dominant tense (remember that not every verb need be in the past.) For a review of tense choices, see Lesson 2D. Sentences are numbered for reference.

   (Answers in back of book)

   a. (1)Every day when I hear the mail carrier come around the neighborhood, I be waiting to see if anything come for me. (2)Usually nothing come. (3)But yesterday a big, fat envelope come rattling into the mail chute. (4)I opens it. (5)What it be? (6)Nothing but a piece of cardboard. (7)Every once in awhile, Samantha send me a picture she take of the kids.

   (Answers in instructor's manual)

   b. [same paragraph continues] (8)But this time, she forget to put the picture in the envelope. (9)So all I gets is the piece of cardboard that suppose to keep the picture from getting bent.

REVISING YOUR OWN WRITING

In the space provided, enter passages from your own writing where you have had problems with verb forms. Write the corrections. Then write five other sentences that follow similar patterns, forming the verbs appropriately.

Your Sentence(s)

_____
_____
_____
_____
_____

STEP TWO: READ AND REVISE FOR GRAMMAR AND PUNCTUATION

Your Revision
_____
_____
_____
_____

Five Other Sentences in the Same Pattern
_____
_____
_____
_____
_____

GRAMMATICAL TERMS IN THIS LESSON

Verb: The one to four words that name the action or state of being of the subject

Subject: A word or group of words that names the person or thing that is performing the action or that is in the state of being named in the verb

PRONOUNS

LESSON FOR STEP 2F

SELECT PRONOUNS

PREVIEW OF THE LESSON

In Steps 2C–2E you checked verbs which frequently cause problems for writers because verbs change according to their role in a sentence. Another type of word that changes its form according to its role is the pronoun. Like verb problems, problems with pronouns are very distracting to readers. In this step you will identify pronouns and make choices about using *I, you, one,* and *a person.* You will also establish a policy about sexism in pronouns. In Step 2G, you will make pronoun decisions like *who/whom* and *him and me.* In Step 2H you will check that each pronoun has a clear antecedent—a word to refer back to. In Step 2I you will make pronouns agree with antecedents.

BE READY TO MAKE BROADER CHANGES

Pronouns are often a source of ambiguity, awkwardness, and wordiness. So as you work with the grammatical aspects of pronouns, be ready also to revise whenever a pronoun seems vague, awkward, or unnecessary. For further help in tightening your writing, see Step 1E.

THE SUBSTITUTION TEST FOR PRONOUNS

Before you can consider revision of your pronouns, you must be able to identify them in your writing. Begin with the following definitions:

Definition: A PRONOUN is a word that substitutes for another word or group of words.

Definition: An ANTECEDENT is the word to which the pronoun refers.

Since pronouns stand in for, or refer to, other words, you can identify a pronoun by temporarily substituting the name of the thing it replaces. If the substitution works, the word is a pronoun. A word or group of words the pronoun refers to is called the pronoun's antecedent. The antecedent may appear in the same sentence or in another sentence. Usually the antecedent comes first and the pronoun follows, but occasionally the pronoun appears first, then the antecedent. In the following examples, the pronoun is in capital letters; the antecedent is underlined.

Mary wrenched **the handle** *and broke IT.*

Substitution Test: Mary wrenched the handle and broke the handle.

Conclusion: *it* is a pronoun.

The **plumbers** *took THEIR tools with THEM.*

(Two pronouns refer to the same antecedent.)

Substitution Test: The plumbers took the plumbers' tools with the plumbers.

Conclusion: *their* and *them* are pronouns.

STEP TWO: READ AND REVISE FOR GRAMMAR AND PUNCTUATION

<u>Jack</u> and <u>Angela</u> *took THEIR vacation last week.*
(The pronoun refers to a double antecedent.)

Do YOU have control of the accounting division?
(The antecedent is understood to be the person addressed.)

I was confused.
(The antecedent of the pronoun *I* is understood to be the speaker.)

This umbrella is YOURS.
(The antecedent is understood to be the person addressed.)

The <u>tree</u> *THAT fell yesterday is being removed.*
(*That* is used as a pronoun referring to *tree*.)

The <u>boys</u> *WHO came to the fair were all younger. Here are two* <u>nets</u>. *WHICH is the best?*
(The pronoun refers to the antecedent in previous sentence.)

THESE are the most efficient <u>methods</u>.
(The pronoun comes before the antecedent.)

<u>Running this machine</u> *is hard. IT requires quickness and strength.*
(The pronoun refers back to an antecedent that is more than one word.)

MEMORIZE PRONOUN WORDS

Since the number of pronoun words is limited, you can help yourself recognize pronouns by memorizing the following list of the words that are always pronouns. The asterisked words are sometimes used as pronouns.

PRONOUNS

Singular	Plural
I, me, my, mine	we, us, our, ours
you, your, yours	you, your, yours
he, his, him	they, them, their, theirs
she, her, hers	
it, its	
any of the above forms with -*self* (myself, herself)	
who, whom, whose	who, whom, whose
*which, *what	*which, *what
*this, *that	*these, *those

You can remember the list if you recognize that it contains:

1. variations of *I, you, he/she, it, they*
2. variations of *who*
3. *which* and *what*
4. variations of *this* and *that*

The preceding list leaves out several pronouns—*each, either, neither,* and words ending in *one (someone, no one, anyone)*. For writers, it does not matter that these words are technically classified as pronouns. They rarely cause trouble as pronouns. They only become problems when they act as antecedents of other pronouns; more on that in Lesson 2I.

In the list of pronouns, the asterisked words *which, what, this, that, these,* and *those* are sometimes not used as pronouns. Sometimes they *are* used as pronouns, but without a clear antecedent, so the substitution test does not clarify their status as pronouns. The following are some examples.

It is the ice we fear, not the snow.

It is serves as an indefinite phrase to postpone the subject and verb, *we fear*. There is no clear antecedent for *it*. The same is often true for *there is* and *there are*.

I know that I have been assigned to this department.

That introduces a clause. (A clause is a group of words containing at least one subject-verb unit.) The *that* does not specifically refer to an antecedent. *This* modifies (describes) the department by telling *which* department.

PRONOUNS MAY ALSO BE ADJECTIVES.

An adjective describes or limits the meaning of a noun. *("Her* truck delivered *our* furniture.") *Her* and *our* are adjectives because they describe *truck* and *furniture;* however, they are also pronouns, because they stand in for the nouns that would actually name the people. Because they are pronouns, they must follow the rules about antecedents described later in this lesson.

EXERCISES

Answers in back of book: 1a
Answers in instructor's manual: 1b

1. Write each pronoun and its antecedent. Sentences are numbered for reference.

   (Answers in back of book)
   a. (1)My friend talked me into it. (2)It wasn't really my idea to bike the 157 miles from my house to Ocean City. (3)But I agreed. (4)"It will be a cinch!" we assured ourselves. (5)The trip, which lasted from 5 A.M. one morning until long after dark that night, was lots of things—but it was surely no cinch.

   (Answers in instructor's manual)
   b. [A later paragraph of the same essay as above.] (6)The

Chesapeake Bay Bridge is a blessing for motor vehicles that need to get across the bay to the ocean. (7)It is a discouraging and illegal barrier, however, for bikers with the same intention. (8)To get yourself and your bike over the bridge you must engage in something I find very embarrassing and time consuming—begging. (9)You must flag down a pick-up truck at the tollgate and beg the driver to take you across. (10)The nice ones say "no." (11)Others say "Drop dead," "Get lost," or "Swim across if it's that important." (12)After a good half hour, a sympathetic driver stops. (13)"That will be $10," he says. (14)It's pretty frustrating to pay a stranger $10 for a $1.25 toll and a ride across a bridge of which you can see the other side. (15)But at least you are over the bridge and one of the many problems is behind you.

SELECTING PRONOUNS

Now that you can identify pronouns, you are ready to make choices. When selecting pronouns, use your common sense and be consistent. If common sense tells you that a certain pronoun choice sounds awkward or wrong for your audience and purpose, review your choice. Whatever you choose, be consistent throughout a paper.

WHEN TO USE *I*

You may have heard somewhere that you should never use *I* in writing. Some types of formal writing avoid *I,* but you should use *I* when it is the most appropriate pronoun for a particular audience. Do not make your writing sound stiff and awkward to your reader, just to avoid using *I.*

STEP TWO: READ AND REVISE FOR GRAMMAR AND PUNCTUATION

However, don't overuse *I*. Avoid the unnecessary use of phrases such as *I believe* or *I feel*. If you state an idea as your own, the reader assumes you believe it. Thus, usually such statements are not necessary, unless you particularly want to distinguish your belief from that of someone else (Rusk has stated that *x*, but I believe that *y*. . . .). Also, sometimes you may use the *I believe* to show the level of certainty of a conclusion (The evidence is not plentiful, but *I believe* we should rely on it.).

WHEN TO USE *YOU, ONE,* OR *A PERSON*.

In situations where *you* sounds appropriate for your audience, don't be afraid to use it. Giving instructions, for instance, you can address the reader as *you,* as in this sentence:

In your right hand, hold the reins. With your knees, urge the horse forward.

In all writing, however, avoid the overuse of the pronoun *you*. For example:

Draft: If the solution is too acidic, you add. . . .
Revision: If the solution is too acidic, add. . . .

It is usually preferable to use *one* or *a person* instead of *you* in the following situations:

1. when you are stating a general truth or principle

Draft: The Germans believe that salt is bad for your health.
Revision: The Germans believe that salt is bad for one's health.

2. when you are stating conditions where the reader is not one of those referred to

Draft: In medieval England, you had to get an education through the church.

Revision: In medieval England, a person had to get an education through the church.

When you choose *you, one,* or *a person,* be consistent. In the following paragraph, the writer has two options for pronoun choice, but must be consistent in using one or the other, not mixing them as in the draft.

Draft: Of course, bodybuilding is not easy. One must maintain concentration and discipline when he* begins to train. There will be times when you won't feel like pushing yourself any more, when you feel depleted of energy and your body grows listless.

Revision: Of course, bodybuilding is not easy. You must maintain concentration and discipline when you begin to train. There will be times when you won't feel like pushing yourself anymore, when you feel depleted of energy and your body grows listless.

Alternate Revision: Of course, bodybuilding is not easy. One must maintain concentration and discipline when he* begins to train. There will be times when he won't feel like pushing himself anymore, when he feels depleted of energy and his body grows listless.

The first revision sounds slightly more informal, and includes the reader in the group of potential bodybuilders the writer is addressing. The second revision makes the bodybuilders more distant. The reader does not feel as easily included. The tone is more formal. This writer must make a pronoun choice based on the audience and purpose, and then must be consistent.

---

*[See the section on sexism in pronouns for alternatives to the use of *he*.]

STEP TWO: READ AND REVISE FOR GRAMMAR AND PUNCTUATION

EXERCISES

Answers in back of book: 2a-d
Answers in instructor's manual: 2e-f

2. In the following sentences, revise for pronoun usage. For each paragraph, make two revisions, using two different pronoun choices. Then, in a paragraph, discuss the differences in tone, audience, and purpose that each revision implies.

(Sample revisions in back of book.)

   a. If you are coming from Towson, Dundalk, Essex, Owings Mills, or Loch Raven, the Kennedy Expressway is the main access road. If one is coming from the south, east, or west of the stadium, the person has to go through the city.
   b. The nightmare will haunt one for the rest of your life.
   c. With no intention of hurting anyone's feelings, many times one would rather not share one's clothes with roommates. For example, how do you tell a friend that you really don't want her wearing your favorite sweater because it's too tight on her and you don't want it stretched?
   d. In high school I learned that losing is a team effort and that when you play for a high caliber team, people took for granted that we would win.

(Sample revisions in instructor's manual)

   e. To the college commuter, your car is your home. Since the commuter spends more time in his car than in the classroom, he must find ways to entertain himself.
   f. Procrastination is a common disease that seems to affect each one of us at one point or another during your life.

LESSON 2F: SELECT PRONOUNS

SET A POLICY ABOUT SEXISM IN PRONOUNS.

You should adopt a thoughtful policy, geared to your own convictions and your audience. There are three possible options. Options one and two are unacceptable in a large number of publications. Whichever policy you choose, be consistent.

Option One: Use *he* for all instances where a pronoun is meant to refer to both sexes.

Anyone beginning the training session tomorrow should bring his calculator.
A hunter's rifle is his most important piece of equipment.
Space flight is one of man's greatest achievements, but he has not yet solved the problem of how to use space cooperatively and peaceably.

The last sentence shows how pronoun usage is linked to some other choices, such as whether to use *man* or a neutral term such as *humankind*. In Option One, terms that refer to *man* are freely used.

Option Two: Use *he* in instances where the meaning is obviously applicable to both sexes; however, where use of *he* might indicate bias, replace the term by one of the methods under Option Three. In this policy, the first sentence and third sentences under Option One would remain as they are, since the pronoun clearly refers to *anyone* of either gender or to *man* in the meaning of *humankind*. The second sentence, however, would be changed, so as not to imply that all hunters are male.

Option Three: Avoid *he* except when referring only to males. The following are some suggestions for avoiding *he*.

STEP TWO: READ AND REVISE FOR GRAMMAR AND PUNCTUATION

ALTERNATIVES TO *HE*

1. Use plural rather than singular:

   Draft: A chemist may seriously limit his career options.
   Revision: Chemists may seriously limit their career options.

2. Use *their* with a singular noun. Follow conversational rather than formal written rules, using *their* or *they* with a singular noun or pronoun. This is not acceptable in some situations. Ask your instructor.

   When someone contacts their legislator....

3. Omit the pronoun:

   Draft: A chemist may seriously limit his career options.
   Revision: A chemist may seriously limit career options.
   Draft: A merchant, if he sells produce, must have a license.
   Revision: A merchant who sells produce must have a license. OR A merchant selling produce must have a license. (Using *who* and *-ing* words are the most common formulas for eliminating pronouns.)

4. Use combined masculine and feminine pronouns:

   If problems arise, please call the manager. He or she will be happy to help you.
   Everyone must have his or her own supplies.
   A technician will never make that mistake if s/he has been well trained.

   Since these compounds sometimes sound awkward, you may want to adopt the first three practices wherever possible.

5. Substitute *she* for *he:*

Substitute *she* and *her* in each case where you would use *he/his/him* to refer to people of either gender.

A technician will never make that mistake if she has been well trained.

EXERCISES

(Note: Exercises 1–2 appear earlier in the lesson.)
Answers in back of book: 3a–e, 4
Answers in instructor's manual: 3f–g

3. Revise the following, using the strategies under Option Three, to avoid the masculine pronoun.
   (Sample revisions in back of book)
   a. It is important for a child to know that his parents are there to listen to his problems.
   b. With practice, experience, curiosity, enthusiasm, and legwork, even a mediocre writer can produce an acceptable feature story. While some writers may be particularly gifted and talented, hard work and practice will help the writer sharpen and develop his feature writing skills.
   c. The boater who has become confident about his ability to maneuver his craft may risk his life foolishly in bad weather.
   d. Ask a farmer what he thinks of the President's farm policy.
   e. Once the athlete begins to eat proper foods, he will find his strength and endurance improving.
   (Sample revisions in instructor's manual)
   f. Once the student learns all the formulas, then he must know the various ways to apply them in an industrial context, where he may be called on to produce solutions quickly.
   g. The life of a politician necessitates public access. The

STEP TWO: READ AND REVISE FOR GRAMMAR AND PUNCTUATION

voters need to be aware of a candidate and believe that he will be available to hear their complaints.

4. In the paragraph on bodybuilding, p. 283, revise the paragraph without using *you,* employing the strategies under Option Three to avoid the masculine pronoun.
(Sample revision in back of book)

REVISING YOUR OWN WRITING

In the space provided, enter passages from your own writing where you have missed problems with pronoun choices. Write the revision. Then write five other sentences that follow similar patterns, forming pronouns appropriately.

Your Sentence(s)

_____
_____
_____
_____
_____

Your Revision

_____
_____
_____
_____
_____

Five Other Sentences in the Same Pattern

_____
_____

LESSON 2F: SELECT PRONOUNS

_____
_____
_____

GRAMMATICAL TERMS IN THIS LESSON

Pronoun: A word that substitutes for another word or group of words
Antecedent: The word to which the pronoun refers
Adjective: A word or words that modify a noun

LESSON FOR STEP 2G

SOLVE THE WHO/WHOM, HIM AND ME DEBATE

PREVIEW OF THE LESSON

Choosing between *who* and *whom* is a choice about the *case* of the pronoun. The debate about whether to use *she and I* or *her and me* is also a question of case. If necessary, see Step 2F to learn how to identify pronouns. To decide case questions, this lesson presents two procedures. They are summarized in Figure 2G.1.

1. ISOLATE THE PRONOUN

If pronouns are paired with other pronouns (he and I) or with nouns (Jerry and I), say the sentence with a single pronoun by itself. Your ear will usually tell you which form is correct.

Problem:	He gave Jerry and (I, me) a job.
Isolate the pronoun:	He gave (I, me) a job.
Solution:	He gave Jerry and me a job.

290

LESSON 2G: SOLVE THE WHO/WHOM, HIM AND ME DEBATE

```
Him and Me
Decisions
    │
    ▼
Isolate the pro-
noun and listen

Who/Whom
Decisions
    │
    ▼
Isolate the          Substitute              he/they
who/whom    ──▶      he/they or      ──▶     sounds
clause               him/them                right—
                     in place of             Use who
                     who/whom
                                             him/them
                                    ──▶      sounds
                                             right—
                                             Use whom
```

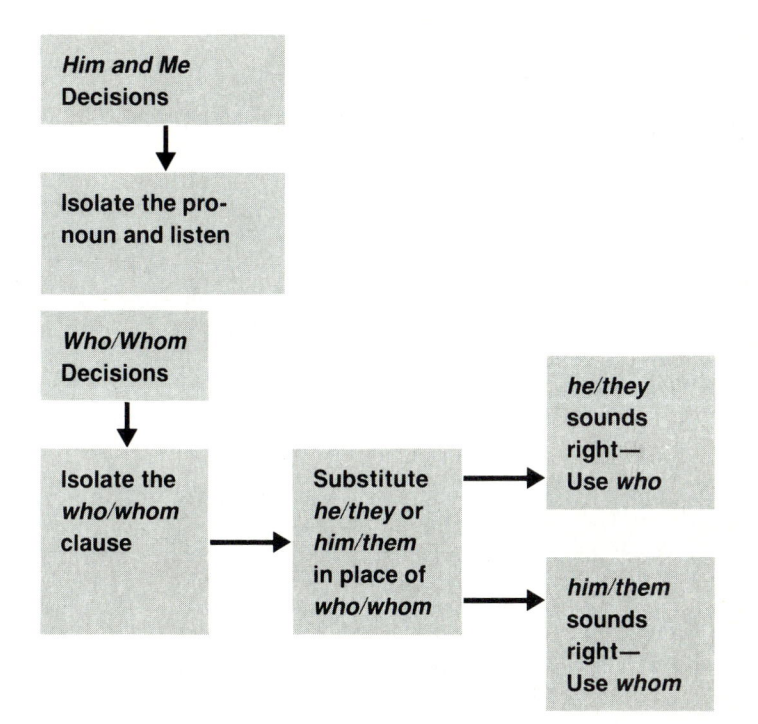

FIGURE 2 G.1   Making *Who/Whom, Him and Me* Decisions

2. ISOLATE THE CLAUSE AND SUBSTITUTE *HE/HIM* or *THEY/THEM* FOR *WHO/WHOM*

Say the *who/whom* clause by itself, ignoring the rest of the sentence. (To identify clauses, see Introductory Lesson B.) Now, wherever you have *who* or *whom,* substitute whichever pronoun sounds right—*he, him, they,* or *them.* Change word order if necessary so the clause makes a normal sentence. If *he* or *they* sounds right, use *who.* If *him* or *them* sounds right, use *whom.*

STEP TWO: READ AND REVISE FOR GRAMMAR AND PUNCTUATION

Problem:	There was no doubt about (who, whom) wrote the paper.
Isolate the Who/Whom Clause:	(Who, Whom) wrote the paper.
Substitute:	*He* wrote the paper.
Solution:	There was no doubt about *who* wrote the paper.
Problem:	The man (who, whom) I saw was at the library.
Isolate the who/whom clause:	(who, whom) I saw.
Substitute:	I saw *him*.
Solution:	The man *whom* I saw was at the library.

Pronoun Substitutions

If *he* or *they* sounds right, use *who*.
If *him* or *them* sounds right, use *whom*.

Sometimes even when you choose the right pronoun, the passage sounds awkward. In the next sentence, the combination of the pronouns with an *-ing* word sounds clumsy. The writer will want to rewrite the sentence.

Draft:	My father had always pampered and spoiled me. I will always remember he and I seeing a black velvet dress at Sears that I had wanted.
Isolate the pronoun:	I will always remember him.
Revision:	I will always remember him and me seeing. . . . (sounds awkward)
Further revision:	I will always remember the time he and I saw. . . . OR The time we saw. . . .

LESSON 2G: SOLVE THE WHO/WHOM, HIM AND ME *DEBATE*

In the example, you might be tempted to isolate *he and I seeing*. However, that is not a clause because *seeing* is not acting as a verb (see p. 00). Say the pronoun *in its clause*. The revision constructs a new clause, *he and I saw*.

DO NOT OVERUSE PRONOUNS WITH *SELF*

Use *myself, herself,* and other pronouns with *self* only when:

1. the same person is the subject

   I *cut* myself.
   Mrs. Robbins *cut* herself.

OR 2. you want to emphasize something.

   I *gave the letter to the ambassador* myself.
   (Emphasizes that I and no one else gave the letter.)

   I *gave the letter to the ambassador* herself.
   (Emphasizes that I gave the letter to the ambassador and no one else.)

Incorrect: A dinner and a movie made a lovely evening for my date and myself.

Correct: A dinner and a movie made a lovely evening for my date and me.

EXERCISES

Answers in back of book: 1a-k
Answers in instructor's manual: 1l-p

1. For each sentence, write the appropriate pronoun: (Answers in back of book)

    a. I remembered the times he had sneaked up on Megan and (I, me, myself).

STEP TWO: READ AND REVISE FOR GRAMMAR AND PUNCTUATION

b. Parting was very difficult for my friends and (I, me, myself) because we had been together since kindergarten.
c. People must defend themselves against this small minority (who, whom) is trying to take charge.
d. It's the coaches (who, whom) set the rules, but it's the players (who, whom) the rules are hurting.
e. To (who, whom) should I send the report?
f. He never seemed to forget that he was once a corporal and had to obey the generals (who, whom) he felt were incompetent.
g. Just last month a UFO passed Sandy and (I, me) as we walked down Cowenton Avenue.
h. It was important for my coworkers and (I, me) to coordinate our tasks.
i. She came from the same background as (I, me) though she proved to be very sophisticated.
j. By keeping her dream alive and creating a dream for (me, myself), we enriched our friendship.
k. I can't tell (who, whom) was more excited—(me or him, he or I).

(Answers in instructor's manual)

l. The ambassador presented small momentoes to my friend and (me, I, myself).
m. In each case a different approach was necessary for the other patients and (I, me) to develop strength.
n. From the story she told, it sounded like (her, she) and her parents were not getting along well.
o. I remember at one point, as I stumbled up the beach, a friend asked (who, whom) was driving home, and when I told him it was (I, me), he started to worry.
p. The news of the doctor's mistakes and malpractice devastated not only my family but (I, me, myself) as well.

LESSON 2G: SOLVE THE WHO/WHOM, HIM AND ME DEBATE

REVISING YOUR OWN WRITING

In the space provided, enter passages from your own writing where you've had problems with pronoun case. Write the revision. Then write five other sentences that follow similar patterns.

Your Sentence(s)

_____
_____
_____
_____
_____

Your Revision

_____
_____
_____
_____
_____

Five Other Sentences in the Same Pattern

_____
_____
_____
_____
_____

GRAMMATICAL TERMS IN THIS LESSON

Pronoun: A word that substitutes for another word or group of words

Antecedent: The word or group of words to which a pronoun refers

STEP TWO: READ AND REVISE FOR GRAMMAR AND PUNCTUATION

Pronoun Case: The form of the pronoun that reflects its relationship to other words in the sentence

Noun: A word or group of words that names a person, place, concept, or thing

Subject: A word or group of words that names the person or thing that is performing the action or that is in the state of being named in the verb

Verb: The one to four words that name the action or the state of being of the subject

Clause: A subject-verb unit plus that unit's modifiers and complements

LESSON FOR
STEP 2H

GIVE PRONOUNS CLEAR ANTECEDENTS

PREVIEW OF THE LESSON

To understand what this lesson will cover, read the following paragraph:

> Being a good friend is not always easy. At times a friendship is really tried, and it's difficult to overlook things they've done that might have upset us.

In the preceding paragraph, *they* has no clear antecedent. The writer means *friends,* but the word *friends* does not appear. The lack of a clear antecedent frustrates the reader and interrupts the smooth flow of the writing. A pronoun must have an immediately apparent antecedent so the reader can understand it the first time.

In this substep, go through your draft and be sure that each of the pronouns has a clear antecedent. See the beginning of Lesson 2F to review identification of pronouns and antecedents if needed. The procedures for this substep and the next are summarized in Figure 2H.1.

STEP TWO: READ AND REVISE FOR GRAMMAR AND PUNCTUATION

```
┌─────────────────────────────┐
│ Does the pronoun have an    │         ┌──────────────────┐
│ antecedent?                 │   No    │ Provide an       │
│                             │────────▶│ antecedent or    │
│                             │         │ revise to        │
│                             │         │ eliminate the    │
│                             │         │ pronoun          │
└─────────────────────────────┘         └──────────────────┘
           │ Yes
           ▼
┌─────────────────────────────┐
│ Do intervening words        │   Yes
│ obscure the relationship    │────────▶   Revise
│ between the pronoun and the │
│ antecedent?                 │
└─────────────────────────────┘
           │ No
           ▼
┌─────────────────────────────┐
│ Do *that*, *this*, and      │   Yes
│ *which* refer vaguely to    │────────▶   Revise
│ a preceding idea?           │
└─────────────────────────────┘
           │ No
           ▼
┌─────────────────────────────┐
│ Can the sentence be         │   Yes
│ tightened?                  │────────▶   Revise
└─────────────────────────────┘
           │ No
           ▼
┌─────────────────────────────┐
│ Does the pronoun agree with │   No
│ antecedent?                 │────────▶   Revise
└─────────────────────────────┘
           │ Yes
           ▼
┌─────────────────────────────┐
│ Are the pronouns, nouns,    │   No
│ and verbs consistent?       │────────▶   Revise
└─────────────────────────────┘
           │ Yes
           ▼
         O.K.
```

FIGURE 2H.1   Revising Pronouns and Antecedents
(Lessons 2H, 2I)

TIGHTEN TO ELIMINATE UNNECESSARY PRONOUNS

Identifying pronouns is often a good way to spot wordiness. Lesson 1E shows how to tighten to eliminate wordiness in your writing. However, even if you have already revised for wordiness, when you focus on pronouns specifically, you may find more unnecessary words. So take a moment to consider whether all of the pronouns you have identified in your draft are really necessary. The following are some guides to revision for unnecessary pronouns.

1. Sentences with *it is* and *there are* can frequently be shortened.

Draft: There are fifteen steers in this lot.
Revision: Fifteen steers are in this lot.

You might tighten your writing even more if you combine the fifteen steers sentence with the next sentence.

Further Revision: The fifteen steers in this lot are all too small.

2. Phrases like *It seems to me* can often be omitted or shortened. If you write something, readers assume that it seems to you to be so.

Draft: It seems to me that the governor is making a mistake.
Revision: The governor is making a mistake. OR Apparently the governor is making a mistake. OR I believe the governor is making a mistake (only when you need to emphasize that this is your belief, not someone else's, or that it is a belief, not a certainty—see p. 282).

3. A series of pronouns may indicate that sentences can be combined.

Apocalypse Now *is a powerful movie. It is about the Vietnam War. Its stars are Marlon Brando and Martin Sheen.*

BECOMES Apocalypse Now, *a powerful movie about the Vietnam War, stars Marlon Brando and Martin Sheen.*

Sometimes a pronoun is not strictly necessary but adds a desirable emphasis.

Draft: Practice is rough. It is usually three miles of swimming a day. That is 216 laps.

In the previous passage, two sentences in a row begin with pronouns—*it* and *that*. The writer can shorten the middle sentence to avoid the weak beginning *it is* and to make the sentence more economical. However, the emphasis provided by the short last sentence works nicely.

Revision: Practice is rough. We usually swim three miles a day. That is 216 laps.

In the next sentence, the first *it* can be eliminated, but the second provides needed emphasis.

Draft: It appears from present day evidence that the suspect was unjustly imprisoned. It is such injustices that the new procedures are designed to eliminate.

Revision: Judging by present day [or *contemporary*] evidence, the suspect was unjustly imprisoned. It is such injustices that the new procedures are designed to eliminate.

REVISE WHEN INTERVENING WORDS MAKE THE ANTECEDENT UNCLEAR

Sometimes so many words intervene between the pronoun and its antecedent that the reader becomes confused.

Draft: To keep the car on the track, it has a tiny peg that sticks out the bottom which fits into the slit.
(*It* is closest to *track* but actually refers back to *car*. *Which* is closest to *bottom,* but actually refers back to *peg*.)

Revision: To keep the car on the track, a tiny peg sticks out of the car's bottom and fits into the slit.
(One pronoun is eliminated, and *car's bottom* is substituted for another pronoun.)

REVISE VAGUE PRONOUNS

Avod using *it, this, that,* or *which* to refer vaguely to a preceding idea.

One way to revise vague pronouns is to eliminate them by the methods discussed earlier in this lesson; however, if a pronoun is needed, you can revise a vague reference by two basic methods:

1. substituting a noun for a pronoun to make the meaning clear OR
2. writing a sentence to make the reference clear

Both methods are shown in the following draft.

Draft: Each force had its own commanders and supply lines, with little communication or coordination between them. This resulted in a catastrophe.

Revision Method 1: Each force had its own commanders and supply lines. The lack of communication or coordination between them resulted in a catastrophe.

Revision Method 2: A catastrophe resulted because each force had its own commanders and supply lines, with little communication or coordination between them.

In the following draft and revision, problems with pronouns have been revised.

STEP TWO: READ AND REVISE FOR GRAMMAR AND PUNCTUATION

Draft: The Constitution, as it was originally framed in 1787, evolved out of obvious inadequacies in the Articles of Confederation, which clearly indicated the necessary transition of major political power into the hands of a unified central government.

The sentence does not make clear whether *inadequacies* or *Articles* is the antecedent of *which*. The writer also could tighten the first half of the sentence by removing the *it*.

Revision: The original Constitution of 1787 evolved from obvious inadequacies in the Articles of Confederation. These inadequacies clearly indicated. . . .

In the next passage, pronouns without clear antecedents and vague phrases such as *there are* and *it is* are in italics.

Draft: The initial central nervous system reaction to alcohol is stimulation, but as the blood alcohol level increases, *it is* followed by drowsiness and can eventually lead to coma and death if consumption has been extreme. Alcohol is often used to induce sleep by its effects on the central nervous system, but *it is* not considered normal sleep. During alcohol–induced sleep *there is* a decrease in the REM stage, a stage of normal sleep characterized by rapid eye movements. *It is* considered a necessary part of healthy sleep. *This* would normally be compensated during the next sleep period, unless *it* also is alcohol induced. The chronic drinker is deprived of REM sleep so often that *it* can develop into daytime hallucinations.

Revision: As the blood level of alcohol increases, initial stimulation is followed by drowsiness, which can eventually lead to coma and death if consumption has been extreme. Because of its effects on the central nervous system, alcohol is often used to induce sleep, though that sleep is not considered normal because of a decrease in the REM stage—a

LESSON 2H: GIVE PRONOUNS CLEAR ANTECEDENTS

necessary part of normal sleep, characterized by rapid eye movements. This decrease would normally be compensated during the next sleep period, unless that sleep is also alcohol induced. The chronic drinker is deprived of REM sleep so often that he or she can develop daytime hallucinations.

EXERCISES

Answers in back of book: 1a-d, 2a
Answers in instructor's manual: 1e-g, 2b

1. Revise pronouns and antecedents in the following items. (Sample revisions in back of book)

   a. Mammography and xeromammography are examples of a procedure that takes an X-ray image of the tissue, which exposes the breast to X-ray radiation.
   b. Out of these taxes the full cost of death row inmates is being paid, who, in return, give nothing back to society.
   c. The Chicano population is bound by "carnalismo," a type of brotherhood with its origin in the Chicano heritage. It is this common cultural heritage which has allowed the Chicano population to band together politically.
   d. Annmarie amused herself in her hideaway of boulders that separated the neighbors' yard from ours, which was redefined as her "house."

   (Sample revisions in instructor's manual)

   e. [From an essay about the importance of diet for athletes] The mediocre athlete thinks that the great athletes are skilled and gifted, which they may be, but they never see them behind the dinner table, a new kind of playing surface.
   f. [From an essay about obscene rock music lyrics] Without a contract, a band's music could never reach the record stores shelves where the kids get them. It would also encourage the band to clean up its lyrics so that it could sign a contract.

STEP TWO: READ AND REVISE FOR GRAMMAR AND PUNCTUATION

  g. Some men may feel threatened by their wives if they earn more pay or get a higher position.
2. In the following passages, revise for overuse of *it* and *there was* and clarify pronoun references as needed. Sentences are numbered for reference.
  (Sample revision in back of book)
  a. [This is the end of an essay in which the writer describes a one-day encounter with a small girl who was blind. Hint: begin by circling every *it* in the passage.]
  (1)I can't quite figure out what it was about Kelly that made her seem so much older than the rest of the children. (2)But I know that it was another aspect of Kelly's personality that made her special. (3)There was much inside of Kelly—her courage, her authority, and her maturity, but most of all her sense of humor. (4)It was the finishing touch. (5)She had a way of making people smile, making me smile. (6)It was not that she was always telling jokes or things like that, but rather a natural wit. (7)Kelly was able to laugh just as much as she made other people laugh. (8)She was a happy child and it showed on her face and in everything she did. (9)Maybe it was her mission in life to put laughter into other people's eyes. (10)It was something she did well and easily. (11)It took me one day to feel as if I knew Kelly for a lifetime. (12)She was warm and giving to everyone she met. (13)Yes, Kelly was blind but she learned to see not with her eyes but with her heart. (14)I will always remember Kelly and her special gift for appreciating life. (15)If it's one thing I learned from that memorable day is that the heart truly sees better than the eyes.
  (Sample revision in instructor's manual)
  b. [The passage is part of an essay on the difficulties of competitive swimming.]

LESSON 2H: GIVE PRONOUNS CLEAR ANTECEDENTS

You have to focus all your attention on armstrokes, flip-turns, and starts. It is very easy to become bored and distracted when you have done fifteen laps of freestyle and have fifteen more to go. In times like this, which happens often at practice, it takes as much work to concentrate as to physically swim.

REVISING YOUR OWN WRITING

In the space provided, enter passages from your own writing where you have missed problems with pronoun antecedents. Write the correction. Then write five other sentences that follow similar patterns, giving each pronoun a clear antecedent.

Your Sentence(s)

_____
_____
_____
_____

Your Revision

_____
_____
_____
_____

Five Other Sentences in the Same Pattern

_____
_____
_____
_____
_____

STEP TWO: READ AND REVISE FOR GRAMMAR AND PUNCTUATION

GRAMMATICAL TERMS IN THIS LESSON

Pronoun: A word that substitutes for another word or group of words

Antecedent: The word or group of words to which a pronoun refers

LESSON FOR
STEP 21

MAKE THE PRONOUN AGREE WITH ITS ANTECEDENT

PREVIEW OF THE LESSON

Once you have tightened to eliminate unnecessary pronouns and have made certain that each pronoun has a clear antecedent (Step 2H), one more step remains for pronouns—making sure that the pronoun agrees with its antecedent. These combined procedures for revising pronouns are summarized in Figure 2H.1, p. 298. If necessary, see Lesson 2F to identify pronouns.

THE AGREEMENT RULE FOR PRONOUNS

A singular antecedent takes a singular pronoun. A plural antecedent takes a plural pronoun.

An antecedent is singular if it signifies one, plural if it

signifies more than one. Most words are obvious: cow is singular, cows is plural. You would use *it* to refer to a single cow, *they* to refer to several cows. However, a few words may puzzle you — words like *group, crowd,* and *jury.* For those words, see Lesson 2C, pp. 242–44, on subject-verb agreement. If, by those rules, the subject would take a plural verb, then that same word as an antecedent would also take a plural pronoun. For example, those rules tell you that *jury* may be singular or plural, depending upon whether the jury is acting as a single body or whether members are acting individually. Thus, the pronoun that refers back to *jury* will be singular or plural according to those rules.

The foreman told the jury they *could leave* their *coats in the jury room when* they *went out on a break.*
(Members act individually; pronouns are plural.)

The jury returned its *verdict.*
(Jury acts as a single body; pronoun is singular.)

IDENTIFY THE ANTECEDENT

Sometimes it will be difficult to determine the real antecedent, especially if the antecedent contains a prepositional phrase such as "for the woman" or "to the store." (For more on prepositional phrases, see p. 47). Your perception can also be thrown off when a number of words separate the pronoun from its antecedent. For example, plural words between a pronoun and its singular antecedent can make you think you need a plural pronoun.

Any girl from the Group B Majorettes who has extra tickets should bring them to her section leader.

Girl, which is singular, is the antecedent of *her.* Thus, *to their section leader* would be incorrect. Do not be distracted by intervening plural words such as *Majorettes, tickets,* and *them.*

LESSON 21: MAKE THE PRONOUN AGREE WITH ITS ANTECEDENT

CHOOSE A SINGULAR OR PLURAL PRONOUN

Once you have determined whether the antecedent is singular or plural, you can, if necessary, turn to the list of pronouns at the beginning of Lesson 2F to find whether a pronoun is singular or plural. Only pronouns like *I, it* and *they* change for singular and plural. Pronouns such as *who, that,* and *which* do not change form with singular or plural antecedents.

MAKE PRONOUNS, NOUNS, AND VERBS CONSISTENT

Sometimes it is necessary to review several elements in a sentence or a passage—verbs, nouns, and pronouns—to achieve consistency in singular or plural forms. In the following examples, the elements that must be consistent are in italics.

Draft: The safety *record* of nuclear power plants here *speak* for *themselves.*

Revision: The safety *record* of nuclear power plants here *speaks* for *itself.*
(Subject, *record,* is singular; it takes a singular verb—*speaks*—and a singular pronoun—*itself.*)

Draft: Each of the women in this novel *face* a major problem in *their lives.*

Revision: Each of the women in this novel *faces* a major problem in *her life.*

Draft: I do know that in order to be a division one power in athletics the *university* must lower *their* standards for most of their athletes. The NCAA must design a universal policy requiring certain academic achievements, and perhaps also prohibiting *freshmen* from sports until *he proves himself* in school.

STEP TWO: READ AND REVISE FOR GRAMMAR AND PUNCTUATION

Revision: ... the *university* must lower *its* standards for most of *its* athletes. ... prohibiting *freshmen* from sports until *they prove themselves* in school.

EXERCISES

Answers in back of book: 1a-h
Answers in instructor's manual: 1i-l

1. For each sentence, revise the pronoun to agree with its antecedent. When a singular pronoun refers to people of either sex, use *he or she,* or *him or her,* or *his or her.* (See Lesson 2F.)

   (Answers in back of book)
   a. The crowd left for their homes.
   b. The jury announced their verdict.
   c. Anyone who needs a wheelchair should contact their group leader.
   d. Each girl was asked by the leaders to bring their uniform to the next meeting.
   e. Every sandwich was checked to be sure that they had no glass in them.
   f. Someone who has the number 347 on their ticket may come forward to claim their prize.
   g. One of the doctors should take this plant to their office.
   h. The books that the library had recently acquired were on display, each with their own little card acknowledging the donor.

   (Answers in instructor's manual)
   i. The jury stood and delivered their verdict.
   j. The jury went to their hotel rooms.
   k. Everyone who came to the meeting received a plaque with their name on it.
   l. Each of the elephants were ridden at least once a week.

LESSON 21: MAKE THE PRONOUN AGREE WITH ITS ANTECEDENT

EXERCISES FOR ALL PRONOUN LESSONS (LESSONS 2F-2I)

Answers in back of book: 2a-e

Answers in instructor's manual: 2f

2. Revise the following sentences. When a singular pronoun refers to people of either sex, use *he or she,* or *him or her,* or *his or her.* (See Lesson 2F).

   (Sample revisions in back of book)

   a. Who did you meet at the party?
   b. She gave the instruments to him and me.
   c. Each character reveals the physical and spiritual values of their lives.
   d. If women are qualified and can perform the same work that a man does, she receives equal pay.
   e. Being a good friend is not always easy. It can be as hard as being a parent. There are times when a friendship is severely tested and it's difficult to overlook things they've done that might have upset us. But those times are when one has to look deep inside himself to realize the true value of what they have.

   (Sample revisions in instructor's manual)

   f. If a voter is not familiar with a candidate, he will not pull the lever for him. When I voted for the first time, I casually scanned the ballot. Upon seeing a name I had heard before, I promptly pulled the appropriate lever. I did not take into consideration the opponent's qualifications. I thought that because I did not know of the candidate he must not be very active or serious about the position. Many people who I have encountered think along these lines. Consequently, candidates spend a great portion of their time promoting their public image. They accomplish this by attending numerous civic meetings,

STEP TWO: READ AND REVISE FOR GRAMMAR AND PUNCTUATION

various fund raisers, coffees, and public affairs such as local festivals and fairs.

REVISING YOUR OWN WRITING

In the space provided, enter sentences or paragraphs with pronoun agreement problems you've missed in your own writing, and write the revision. Then write five other passages that follow similar patterns, making the pronoun agree with its antecedent.

Your Passage

_____
_____
_____
_____
_____

Your Revision

_____
_____
_____
_____
_____

Five Other Passages in the Same Pattern

_____
_____
_____
_____
_____

LESSON 21: MAKE THE PRONOUN AGREE WITH ITS ANTECEDENT

GRAMMATICAL TERMS IN THIS LESSON

Pronoun: A word that substitutes for another word or group of words

Antecedent: The word or group of words to which a pronoun refers

Preposition: A word, usually short, that shows direction or relationship and that is accompanied by an object

Object of a Preposition: The word that completes the preposition, answering the question *for what? to what? near what?*

Prepositional Phrase: A preposition plus its object and modifiers

APOSTROPHE, -S AND -ES

LESSON FOR STEP 2J

USE APOSTROPHE, -S, AND -ES APPROPRIATELY

PREVIEW OF THE LESSON

In Step 2J, you will check all the places where you need to use an apostrophe and/or -*s* and -*es*. As you read a draft, note all the places where you have already used an apostrophe, -*s,* or -*es,* or where you think you should. Then check those spots using the following guidelines. The checking process is diagrammed in Figure 2J.1.

1. Use apostrophes correctly with contractions.
2. Eliminate apostrophes with verbs and pronouns.
3. Use -*s* and -*es* correctly to form the plural of nouns. Use apostrophe to show plural in only three circumstances. Choose between -*s* and -*es.*
4. Use -*s* or -*es* with apostrophe for the possessive of a singular or plural noun.

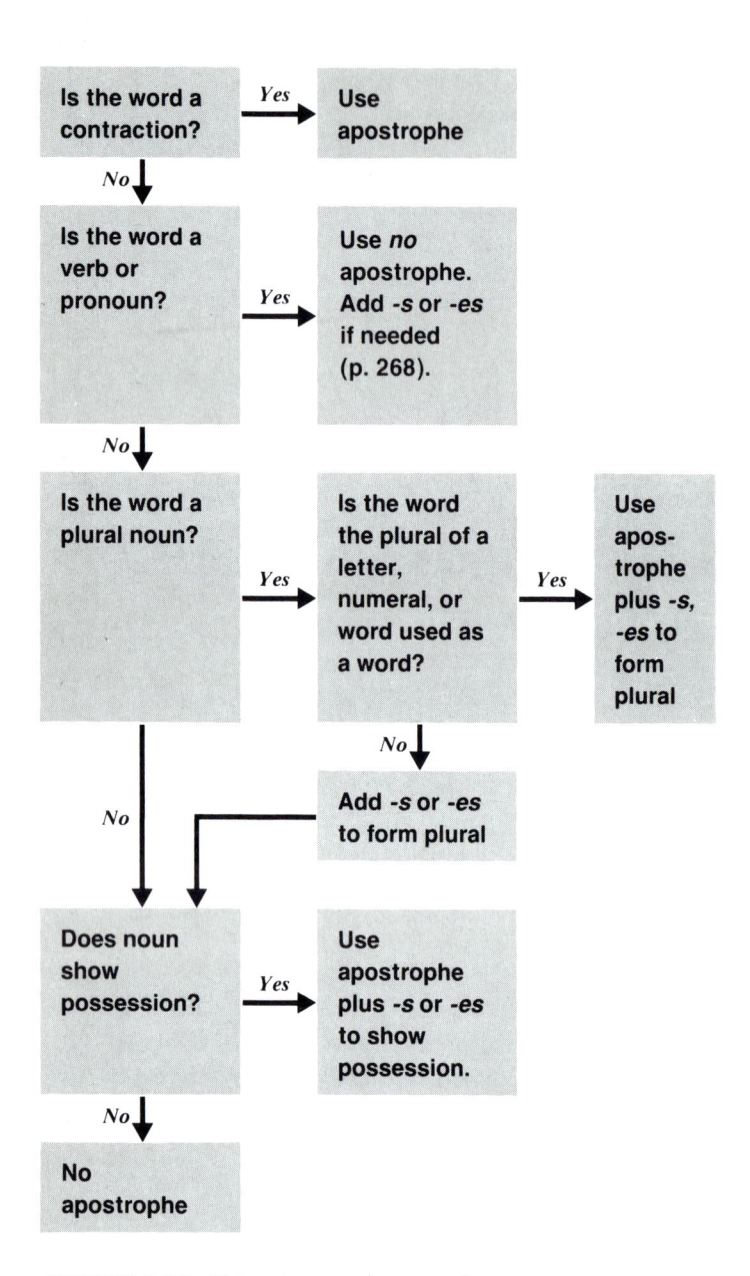

STEP TWO: READ AND REVISE FOR GRAMMAR AND PUNCTUATION

```
Is the word a contraction?  ──Yes──▶  Use apostrophe
        │
        No
        ▼
Is the word a verb or pronoun?  ──Yes──▶  Use no apostrophe. Add -s or -es if needed (p. 268).
        │
        No
        ▼
Is the word a plural noun?  ──Yes──▶  Is the word the plural of a letter, numeral, or word used as a word?  ──Yes──▶  Use apostrophe plus -s, -es to form plural
        │                                                │
        No                                               No
        │                                                ▼
        │                                        Add -s or -es to form plural
        ▼                                                │
Does noun show possession?  ◀───────────────────────────┘
        │  ──Yes──▶  Use apostrophe plus -s or -es to show possession.
        No
        ▼
No apostrophe
```

FIGURE 2 J.1   Using Apostrophe, *-s,* and *-es*

USE APOSTROPHES CORRECTLY WITH CONTRACTIONS

Locate each word that combines two words (the combination is called a contraction), and use an apostrophe in place of the missing letters. Leave no blank spaces.

don't (do not)
they're (they are)
who's (who is)
it's (it is)
she's (she is)
he'll (he will)
won't (will not)

Contractions are too informal for some kinds of writing. If in doubt, check with your instructor.

EXERCISES

Answers in back of book: 1a-c
Answers in instructor's manual: 1d-e

1. In the following sentences, create contractions wherever possible.
   (Answers in back of book)
   a. There is a small tear that will get bigger if we do not fix it.
   b. I would like to know whether they have eaten, or whether they are hungry.
   c. I have given so much time that I am exhausted.
   (Answers in instructor's manual)
   d. It is time that you are leaving.
   e. I have gone to the store to get your camping supplies, so you will not have to go.

STEP TWO: READ AND REVISE FOR GRAMMAR AND PUNCTUATION

ELIMINATE APOSTROPHES WITH VERBS AND PRONOUNS

If the apostrophe you are wondering about is not a contraction, go on to ask whether you have used an apostrophe with a verb or pronoun.

Never use an apostrophe with a verb (except when one of the words in a contraction is a verb, as in "let's go"). If you are not sure how to recognize when a word is a verb, see Introductory Lesson A.

Incorrect: He treat's his employees well.

If you have a question about adding *-s* or *-es* to a verb, see Lesson 2E, p. 268.

Never use an apostrophe with a pronoun (except the pronouns *either, neither, everyone, someone, anyone,* and *no one*). If you are not sure how to identify a pronoun, see Lesson 2F. Pronouns may be followed by an apostrophe if they are part of a contraction:

Pronoun	*Showing Possession*	*In a Contraction*
Its	Its coat was shiny.	It's cold out.
Hers	The bat was hers.	(*Her's* is not a word.)
Theirs	The car was theirs.	(*Their's* is not a word. *There's* is a contraction for *there is.*)
Whose	The boy whose arm was broken is not here.	Who's here?
Yours	These seats are yours.	(*Your's* is not a word.)
Someone	Someone's coat is here.	Someone's coming.

EXERCISES

Answers in back of book: 2a-b
Answers in instructor's manual: 2c-d

LESSON 2J: USE APOSTROPHE, -S, AND -ES APPROPRIATELY

2. Remove any apostrophes that are used incorrectly with verbs or pronouns. Leave apostrophes that are used correctly with contractions.
   (Answers in back of book)
   a. He eat's more than she'll ever dream of eating. In fact, more than once, when he finished eating his own dinner, he'd eat her's.
   b. The weather announcer predict's that Boston's weather will turn bad. That's natural for February.
   (Answers in instructor's manual)
   c. The weather announcer's prediction about Boston's weather didn't come true.
   d. The boy who's arm was broken say's he won't be able to play in any of this season's game's.

USE -S AND -ES CORRECTLY TO FORM THE PLURAL OF NOUNS

If the word you are reviewing is not a contraction, verb, or pronoun, check next whether it is a plural noun. If so, review your use of -s, -es, and apostrophe according to the following guidelines.

Definition: A NOUN names a person, place, concept, or thing.

Definition: A PLURAL NOUN names more than one person, place, concept, or thing.

Definition: A SINGULAR NOUN names just one person, place, concept, or thing.

Ignore for the moment whether your noun also shows possession (that is for the next stage). If the word is a singular noun, go directly to p. 323 of this lesson. If it is plural, the following rules will help you form the plural correctly.

STEP TWO: READ AND REVISE FOR GRAMMAR AND PUNCTUATION

USE APOSTROPHES TO SHOW PLURAL IN ONLY THREE CIRCUMSTANCES

Never use an apostrophe to make a noun plural, except in three particular circumstances:

1. Plurals of letters. (Her report card was full of A's.)
2. Plurals of numerals (The animals marched by 2's.)
   But if the number is spelled out, use regular rules for forming the plural—no apostrophe. (The animals marched by twos.)
3. Plurals of words used as words. (The speaker peppered her presentation with "you know's.") Use of quotation marks for words used as words is covered in Lesson 2R.

In all other cases, form the plural of a noun *without* using an apostrophe. That leaves only the problem of whether to form the plural with *-s*, *-es*, or a special plural form.

CHOOSE BETWEEN *-S* AND *-ES*

Most nouns form their plurals by adding *-s* or *-es*. The procedures for choosing between *-s* and *-es* to form plurals of nouns is summarized in Figure 2J.2.

Nouns ending in a sound that can be smoothly united with *-s* usually form their plurals by adding *-s*.

singular	plural
book	books
taxi	taxis
race	races
radio	radios

An exception is *some* words ending in *o*. These use *-es*. (But see *radios*, in the plural column.)

| zero | zeroes |

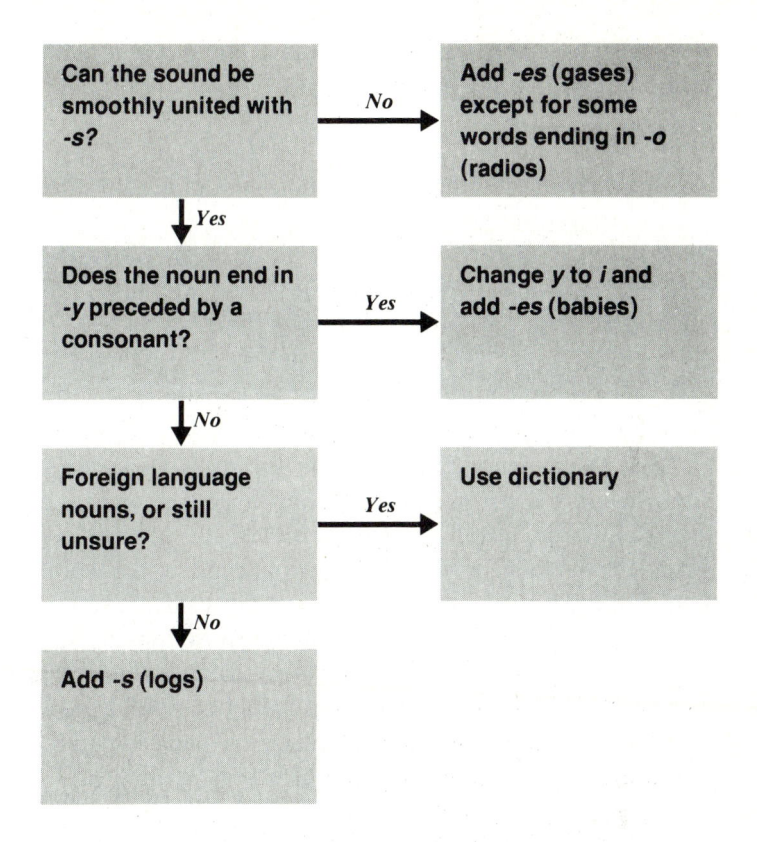

LESSON 2J: USE APOSTROPHE, -S, AND -ES APPROPRIATELY

```
Can the sound be smoothly united with -s?
  --No--> Add -es (gases) except for some words ending in -o (radios)
  |Yes
Does the noun end in -y preceded by a consonant?
  --Yes--> Change y to i and add -es (babies)
  |No
Foreign language nouns, or still unsure?
  --Yes--> Use dictionary
  |No
Add -s (logs)
```

FIGURE 2 J.2 Adding *-s* and *-es* to Form Plural Nouns

Nouns ending in a sound that cannot be smoothly united with *-s* form their plurals by adding *-es*. If, in saying the word aloud, you can hear that you have to make an "eh" sound between the last letter of the word and the added *-s,* then probably that word forms its plural by adding *-es*.

singular	plural
pouch	pouches
flash	flashes
ax	axes
mess	messes

STEP TWO: READ AND REVISE FOR GRAMMAR AND PUNCTUATION

Nouns that end in *y* preceded by a vowel *(a, e, o,* or *u)* form their plurals by adding *-s* only.

singular	*plural*
ray	rays
boy	boys

Nouns that end in *y* preceded by a consonant (any other letter except vowels, *a, e, i, o, u*) change *y* to *i* before adding *-es*.

singular	*plural*
ally	allies
candy	candies

Some nouns form their plurals irregularly *(mouse, mice)*. Some nouns are borrowed from foreign languages, and form their plurals according to the rules of those languages. For any words about which you are not sure, you can find the plural form in a dictionary. Look up the word in its singular form. Immediately after the initial listing of the word, look for the little letter *n* (for noun). If it says *v*, skip that listing and look for the same word labeled *n*. Immediately after the *n* will appear the abbreviation *pl.* (for plural), and then the plural form. For example, here is the first part of the listing for "pony."

be sure you have   plural
the *noun* form of the word   spelling
po·ny (pō'ni), *n.* [*pl.* PONIES (-niz)] [Scot. *powny;* prob.

EXERCISES

Answers in back of book: 3a
Answers in instructor's manual: 3b

3. Change all the words in parentheses to plural.
   a. The (pony) came across the (field) in (pair), their white (mane) streaming in the summer (breeze), their (hoof) pounding through the thick (grass). The men followed them in (3).

LESSON 2J: USE APOSTROPHE, -S, AND -ES APPROPRIATELY

b. In our town, when we were (child), (summer) meant (circus). First there would be the parade down Main Street, with the (elephant) marching by (2), and (horse) prancing lightly with spangled (lady) on their (back). A man ran along after the parade to scoop up the huge elephant (mess)—a sight just as entertaining to us as any other part of the parade.

USE -*S* OR -*ES* WITH APOSTROPHE FOR THE POSSESSIVE OF A SINGULAR OR PLURAL NOUN

You have identified all your contractions and used apostrophes correctly in them. You have eliminated apostrophes from verbs and pronouns. For nouns, you have used apostrophes to form the plural only in the few allowable instances. In all other instances, you have formed the plural of a noun by using -*s*, -*es*, or a special plural form. If the noun was singular, you skipped the preceding section and came here. Now you are ready for the last part: regardless of whether the noun is singular or plural, does it show possession? If it does not, then you are finished. If none of the rules so far have asked you to add an apostrophe, do not add one. If you have not added -*s* or -*es* up to this point, do not add it.

If the word *does* show possession, then you must use an apostrophe, usually together with -*s* or -*es*. The following are some examples to help you distinguish whether a noun is possessive or not.

A word that shows possession answers the question, "whose?" In addition, a word that shows possession can be turned into an "of" phrase.

The bear's den was large.

Does the word *bear* answer the question "Whose den was large?" Yes.

STEP TWO: READ AND REVISE FOR GRAMMAR AND PUNCTUATION

Can the word *bear* form an "of" phrase? The den of the bear was large. Yes.

Conclusion: *bear's* is possessive.

The <u>bond's</u> maturity date is August 7.

Underlined word addresses the question, "whose maturity date," so it is possessive. *Of* phrase: the maturity date of the bond.

This estimate is <u>Jane's</u>.

Underlined word answers the question, "Whose estimate?" *Of* phrase: the estimate of Jane.

The <u>Orioles'</u> batting average was high.

Underlined word answers the question, "Whose batting average?" *Of* phrase: batting average of the Orioles.

Later, you'll see the rules for forming possessives. Meanwhile, look at some words that are *not* possessive nouns, so you can tell the difference in your own writing.

WORDS THAT ARE NOT POSSESSIVE NOUNS

The chemical (<u>bonds</u> <u>bond's</u>) were puzzling to me.

Underlined word does not answer the question, "Whose?" It is merely a plural. The *of* phrase, *of the bonds* does not fit the sense of the sentence. The correct choice is *bonds*.

The company (<u>distributes</u> <u>distribute's</u>) parts for lawn mowers.

Underlined word is a verb, not a noun. The correct choice is *distributes*.

The coat was (<u>hers</u> <u>her's</u>).

LESSON 2J: USE APOSTROPHE, -S, AND -ES APPROPRIATELY

Underlined word is possessive, but it is a pronoun, so does not use an apostrophe. The correct choice is *hers*.

Once you have determined that you need an apostrophe to show possession, there are rules to form the possessive correctly. They are summarized in Figure 2J.3.

Usually, a noun adds an apostrophe and *-s* or *-es* to show possession. The following rules tell which to use and in what order.

Does the noun, as you are using it (singular or plural), end in -s? — No → **Add -'s**

Yes ↓

Is noun singular or plural?

Plural → **Add '**

Singular → **Would a second -s make pronunciation difficult?**
- Yes → **Add '**
- No → **Add -'s**

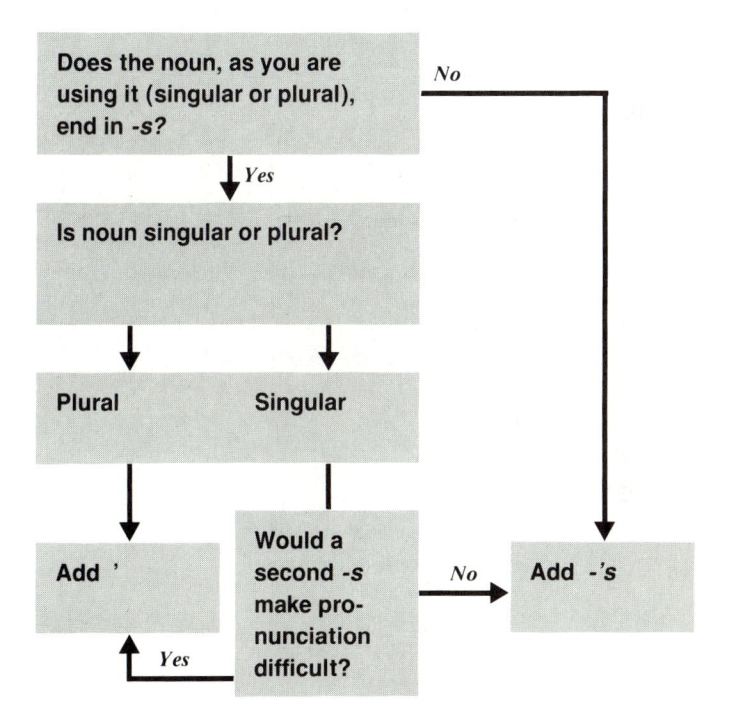

FIGURE 2J.3 Adding Apostrophe and *-s* to Form Possessive of a Noun

RULES FOR SEQUENCE OF -S, -ES, AND APOSTROPHE

1. If a noun as you are using it (singular or plural) does not end in -s, add an apostrophe plus -s to form the possessive.

   the beaker's lip
   the tire's rim
   the men's work

2. If the noun is singular and ends in -s, add an apostrophe plus -s unless the second -s makes pronunciation difficult; in such cases add only the apostrophe.

   Ross's book but
   Sophocles' drama

3. If the noun is plural and its plural form ends in -s, then add only the apostrophe.

   the animals' diets (more than one animal)
   the foxes' lair (more than one fox)

4. In compounds (words linked to form a single term), make only the last word possessive.

   the attorney general's ruling
   my father-in-law's business

5. In cases of joint possession, make only the last noun possessive; in individual possession, make both nouns possessive.

John and Jerry's restaurants (They own the restaurants jointly.)
John's and Jerry's restaurants (They each own a restaurant.)

EXERCISES

(Note: Exercises 1-3 appear earlier in the lesson.)
Answers in back of book: 4a-l
Answers in instructor's manual: 4m-p

4. In the following sentences, choose the correct form.
   (Answers in back of book)
   a. (It's Its) a cold day.
   b. The bell gave (its it's) last long toll.
   c. This ring is (hers her's).
   d. It is not your (mother's mothers) business to pack the trunks of fifteen-year-old (girls girl's).
   e. The (axes axe's axes') had sharp blades.
   f. The handles of both (axes axe's axes') were broken.
   g. The (axes' axe's axes) handles were broken.
   h. Only one of the (axes axe's) had a broken handle.
   i. You will be paid for each (days days' day's) work.
   j. The (sawfish's sawfishes' sawfishs') beak (looks look's looks') like a saw.
   k. My grandmother said the idea for the (plantings' plantings) was not (her's hers) but her (husband's husbands' husbands).
   l. The rose bushes march in (pair's pairs) up the walk, but the forsythia are planted in (3's 3s).

(Answers in instructor's manual)
   m. (It's Its) handle was red.
   n. The wind (churn's churns) the (lake's lakes) surface.
   o. Is the scarf (her's hers)?
   p. The (girls girl's) found a (robin's robins) nest that had blown down from a tree. They brought the nest to (they're their) school. The teacher took advantage of the (class' class's classes' class'es) interest to begin a unit on (animals' animals animal's) homes. The children studied (foxes' fox's) lairs, (wolves' wolves) dens, and (bird's birds' birds) nests.

STEP TWO: READ AND REVISE FOR GRAMMAR AND PUNCTUATION

REVISING YOUR OWN WRITING

In the space provided, enter mistakes you've made in using -s, -es, and apostrophes in your own writing, and write the correction. Then write five other sentences that follow similar patterns, forming and punctuating them correctly.

Your Draft

_____
_____
_____
_____
_____

Your Revision

_____
_____
_____
_____
_____

Five Other Sentences in the Same Pattern

_____
_____
_____
_____
_____

GRAMMATICAL TERMS IN THIS LESSON

Contraction: Two words connected to make one word, with an apostrophe in place of the missing letters

Noun: A word or group of words that names a person, place, concept, or thing

Plural: Referring to more than one

LESSON 2J: USE APOSTROPHE, -S, AND -ES APPROPRIATELY

Possessive case: The form of a noun or pronoun used to show possession

Pronoun: A word that substitutes for another word or group of words

Antecedent: The word or group of words to which a pronoun refers

Verb: The one to four words that name the action or the state of being of the subject

INTERIOR SENTENCE PUNCTUATION

LESSON FOR STEP 2K

AVOID COMMAS THAT SEPARATE THE SUBJECT FROM ITS VERB OR THE VERB FROM ITS OBJECT

PREVIEW OF THE LESSON

In Steps 2A and 2B, you checked for sentence boundary punctuation. In Steps 2C–2I, you checked the forms of verbs and pronouns—two types of words that change their form, depending on their role in a sentence. In Step 2J, you checked your use of apostrophe, *-s,* and *-es.* Now you are ready to begin the fourth major group of guidelines for revision of grammar and punctuation—the group that shows how to use punctuation to separate elements within a sentence. The process of choosing interior sentence punctuation is summarized in Figure 2K.1. The various situations and marks of punctuation are summarized in Figure 2K.2. Use whichever seems easiest for you—the process diagram or the list.

STEP TWO: READ AND REVISE FOR GRAMMAR AND PUNCTUATION

Identify pauses, links, or places you think need punctuation, then ask. Do I have a . . .

- link between two independent clauses? (Step 2B) → **Yes** → Use options pp. 224–255
- **No** ↓
- comma separating subject from its verb or verb from its object? (Step 2K) → **Yes** → No Commas
- **No** ↓
- introducer? (Step 2L) → **Yes** → Use commas
- **No** ↓
- modifier or interrupter? (Step 2M) → *Nonrestrictive* → Use commas / *Restrictive* → No commas
- **No** ↓
- strong interrupter? (Step 2N) → **Yes** → Use dash or ( )
- **No** ↓
- series of adjectives? (Step 2O) → **Yes** → Use commas except between last adjective and noun, or between adjective-noun as single term
- **No** ↓
- list or series? (Step 2P) → **Yes** → When items have interior commas, use semicolons to separate items. If statement introducing list is complete, introduce list with a colon.
- **No** ↓
- explanation or enumeration? (Step 2Q) → **Yes** → Introduce with a colon or dash

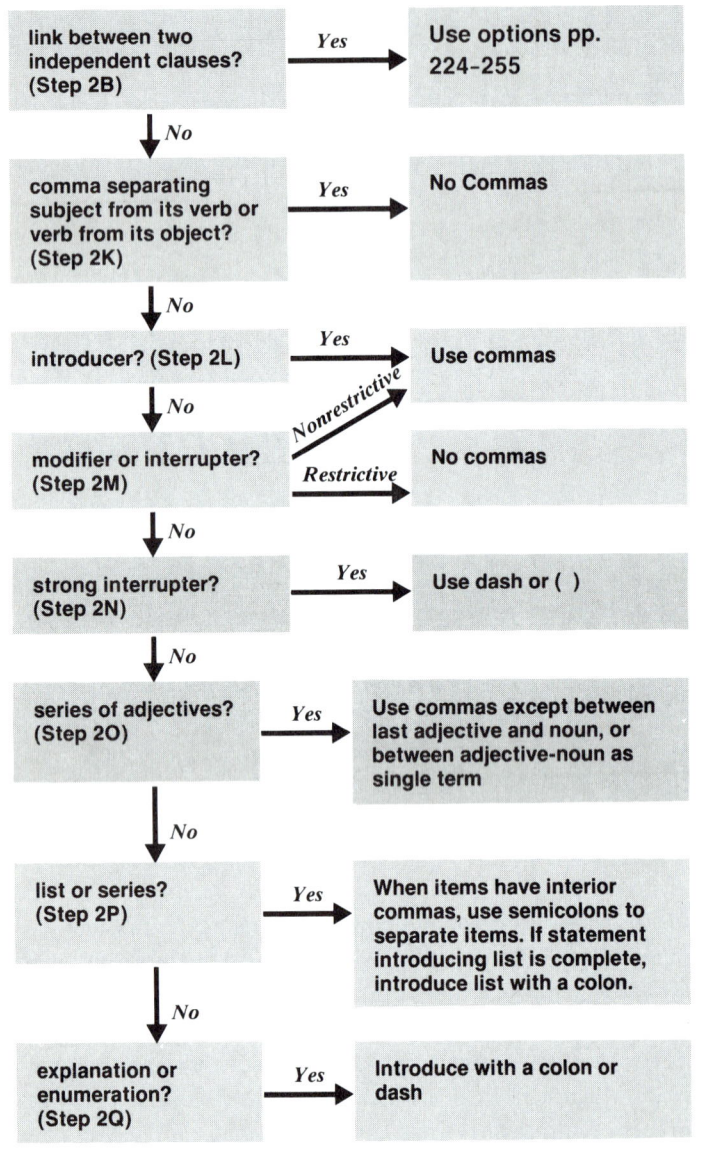

FIGURE 2 K.1 Interior Sentence Punctuation (Steps 2B, 2L-2Q)

LESSON 2K: AVOID COMMAS THAT SEPARATE THE SUBJECT FROM ITS VERB

FIVE MARKS FOR SEPARATING ELEMENTS WITHIN THE SENTENCE

For interior sentence punctuation, the writer has a number of marks available:

the comma	,
the colon	:
the semicolon	;
the dash	— (on your typewriter, two hyphens)
the parentheses	( ) (just one is called a parenthesis)

Independent Clauses Joined in Certain Ways (Lesson 2B)	Comma, Semicolon
Introducers (Lesson 2L)	Comma
Nonrestrictive Interrupters and Modifiers (Lesson 2M)	Comma
Elements That Strongly Interrupt the Flow of a Sentence (Lesson 2N)	Dash, Parentheses
Adjectives in a Series (Lesson 2O)	Comma
Elements in a List or Series (Lesson 2P)	Semicolon, Colon, Comma
Words that Announce an Explanation or Enumeration (Lesson 2Q)	Colon

FIGURE 2K.2: A Summary of Interior Sentence Punctuation

The following lessons offer guidelines for interior sentence punctuation using these marks of punctuation.

RELY ON YOUR EAR AND YOUR KNOWLEDGE OF RULES

When placing commas, most writers rely to some extent on their ears—on their sense of where a reader would pause. However, many comma problems stem from writers placing commas solely by ear, without knowing the appropriate rules for comma placement. This section tries to help you use your ear appropriately, together with a knowledge of the rules.

When punctuating by ear, usually the most serious mistake, is to put a comma where it doesn't belong. For example, the sentence immediately preceding this one has a misplaced comma after *mistake,* even though some readers might pause slightly at that point. You will understand why the comma is misplaced after reading the rest of this lesson. Because misplaced commas are often the most disturbing comma problem for readers, this lesson begins by telling you where *not* to put commas. One of those problems—the run-on—is treated in Lesson 2B. This lesson offers more guidance about where *not* to put a comma. Begin your revision by checking to make sure that you have not put commas in wrong places. Then rely on Lessons 2L–2Q to refine your use of commas and show you how to use colons, semicolons, and dashes.

DO NOT USE A COMMA TO SEPARATE A SUBJECT FROM ITS VERB

Never use a comma to separate the subject from its verb unless the intervening words are a unit that interrupts the flow, and that therefore is set off by a *pair* of commas, dashes, or parentheses, as explained in the next lessons.

You may be tempted to break this rule when the subject of a sentence is composed of several words. (For help determining the subject, see Introductory Lesson A.)

Leaving his mother behind in Ireland was a great sorrow to him.

What was a great sorrow to him? "Leaving his mother behind in Ireland" is the subject. No comma between subject and the verb *was.*

LESSON 2K: AVOID COMMAS THAT SEPARATE THE SUBJECT FROM ITS VERB

To get out of his difficulty cost him $500.
(What cost him $500?)

You will notice that multi-word subjects often begin with an *ing* word or with *to* plus an action word (to get, to run).

In the following examples, a *pair* of commas is used to mark off an interrupting word or group of words that fits between the subject and the verb.

Exercising in normal ways gives him no trouble.
Pushing himself in a competitive situation, however, brings on his asthma.

In the previous example, the first sentence's subject is *exercising in normal ways*. A comma should not separate the subject from its verb. In the second sentence, the subject is *pushing himself in a competitive situation*. The word *however* interrupts the flow, and is set off by a *pair* of commas (see Lesson 2M).

You must distinguish multi-word *subjects* from multi-word units that introduce a sentence but are not the subject, and that often *do* get marked with a comma. Use the strategies in Introductory Lesson A to identify your sentence's subject.

Exercising in normal ways, he usually has no asthma.

He is the subject. *Exercising in normal ways* is an introductory group of words that is marked by a comma. See Lesson 2L.

When a sentence opens with *it is* or *there are* you may be tempted to place a comma between the subject and verb.

Incorrect: It is of great importance, that Congress reconsider this bill.

It is postpones the real subject of the sentence. The subject is *that Congress reconsider this bill.* The verb is *is*. In constructions with *it is,* do not use a comma to separate the verb from the subject.

Correct: It is very important that Congress reconsider this bill.

STEP TWO: READ AND REVISE FOR GRAMMAR AND PUNCTUATION

DO NOT USE A COMMA TO SEPARATE VERBS THAT SHARE THE SAME SUBJECT

When a sentence has two or more verbs that belong to the same subject, do not use a comma to separate one verb from the next.

Correct: They discovered the treasure in the evening and worked all night to dig it up. (The subject *They* has two verbs: *discovered* and *worked*.)

Also correct: They discovered the treasure in the evening, and a crew of seven worked all night to dig it up. (Two independent clauses, each with its own subject-verb unit, are separated by a coordinating connector and a comma—see Lesson 2B.)

Incorrect: They discovered the treasure in the evening, and worked all night to dig it up.

Exception: Sometimes a comma is needed to assure clarity or to prevent misreading.

DO NOT USE A COMMA TO SEPARATE A VERB FROM ITS OBJECT

The same guidelines about separating subjects from verbs also apply to separating verbs from objects. For help identifying verbs, see Introductory Lesson A. For help identifying objects, see p. 135. You may be especially tempted to break this rule when the object comes before the verb.

Incorrect: Many a mile, we had travelled.

The subject of the sentence is *we*. The verb is *had travelled*. The object—the thing that tells *what* we had travelled—is *mile*, or, more broadly, *many a mile* (object plus its modifiers—for modifiers, see p. 41). Because the object precedes the verb and because it has modifiers attached to it, the writer was tempted to use a comma to separate the object and verb; however, the sentence should not have a comma.

You may also be tempted to place a comma between a verb and its object when the object is long or complex, or when it is the object of a second verb in the sentence:

Incorrect: We are in what could be called, a financial crisis.

The direct object of the second verb, *could be called,* is *financial crisis* because it is the thing that *gets called*—that receives the action of the verb *called.* So the writer should not use a comma.

In the following sentence, the writer incorrectly places a comma between the verb and its indirect object—the person or thing that indirectly receives the action of the verb. In the following sentence the indirect object is underlined:

He threw <u>me</u> the ball.

Sometimes the indirect object is preceded by a preposition—a word that shows relationship or direction *(to, of, beyond).*

He threw the ball <u>to me</u>.

Incorrect: I often wanted very much to mail a package or letter, to my girlfriend.

In this example, *package or letter* is the direct object and *to my girlfriend* is the indirect object, expressed as a prepositional phrase. A comma should not separate the direct or indirect object from the verb.

DO NOT USE A COMMA BETWEEN A VERB AND A PREPOSITIONAL PHRASE THAT FOLLOWS THE VERB

Definition: A PREPOSITIONAL PHRASE is a group of words opening with a preposition—a word that shows relationship or direction.

Examples: *to* the pool, *against* the enemy, *behind* the lines.

Place no comma between a verb and a prepositional phrase that follows the verb. If the prepositional phrase precedes the verb, however, it may be set off by commas as an introducer (see Lesson 2L).

Incorrect: Pacing yourself is the best way of winning, in this marathon.

Correct: Pacing yourself is the best way of winning in this marathon.

Also Correct: In this marathon, pacing yourself is the best way of winning.

EXERCISES

Answers in back of book: 1a-h
Answers in instructor's manual: 1i-k

1. In the following sentences, delete the commas that separate subject from verb, verb from object, or verb from a prepositional phrase that follows the verb. Leave all other commas alone. They are correct. Rules about them will appear in Lessons 2L-2M.

   (Answers in back of book)

   a. Racing to the finish line, she heard her blood pounding in her ears.
   b. Racing to the finish line, is the most exciting part of the competition.
   c. To be in competition with some of the best talent in the country, was his greatest delight.
   d. The firefighters were tired, since they had been on the job for twelve hours.
   e. It was very dangerous, to climb up on that steep roof.
   f. The very steep flights of steps, he finds difficult to climb.
   g. The stacks of dirty dishes and piles of dirty laundry, he had yet to tackle.

LESSON 2K: AVOID COMMAS THAT SEPARATE THE SUBJECT FROM ITS VERB

    h. It was not difficult at all, to attach the swing to the tree limb.

(Answers in instructor's manual)

    i. Carrying the baby in a backpack, she had her hands free to hold the toddler and the groceries.

    j. Carrying the baby in a backpack, is very convenient.

    k. To sail across the bay, had been his ambition.

REVISING YOUR OWN WRITING

In the space provided, enter passages from your own writing where you've placed commas inappropriately. Write the correction. Then write five other sentences that follow similar patterns, punctuating appropriately.

Your Sentence(s)

_____
_____
_____
_____
_____

Your Revision

_____
_____
_____
_____
_____

Five Other Sentences in the Same Pattern

_____
_____
_____
_____
_____

STEP TWO: READ AND REVISE FOR GRAMMAR AND PUNCTUATION

GRAMMATICAL TERMS IN THIS LESSON

Subject: A word or group of words that names the person or thing that is performing the action or that is in the state of being named in the verb

Verb: The one to four words that name the action or the state of being of the subject

Object: The person or thing that receives the action of the verb

LESSON FOR STEP 2L

USE COMMAS AFTER INTRODUCERS

PREVIEW OF THE LESSON

This lesson shows how to place commas after words or phrases that introduce sentences. See how this lesson fits within the process of interior sentence punctuation—Figure 2K.1, p. 332. (For dependent and independent clauses, see Introductory Lesson B.)

HOW TO PUNCTUATE INTRODUCERS

A word, phrase, or dependent clause that introduces a sentence should be followed by a comma, unless the introducer is short and there is no danger of misreading.

The rule about commas with introducers does *not* hold true when the introductory material is an independent clause. When an independent clause precedes another independent clause, a comma after the first clause will create a run-on (Lesson 2B).

STEP TWO: READ AND REVISE FOR GRAMMAR AND PUNCTUATION

TYPES OF INTRODUCERS

The introducer may take a number of forms and may be short or long. The introducer, however, never contains the sentence's *main* subject(s) or verb(s)—that is, the subjects or verbs of independent clauses (see Introductory Lesson A). An introducer may be a *dependent* clause and thus may contain the subject(s) and verb(s) of that clause. The introducer may be:

1. a single word:

   Sadly, *we closed the shop.*
   However, *the clamps were nearly rusted through.*

2. a group of words beginning with a word like *after* or *when:*

   After dinner, *the negotiations resumed.*
   At the same time, *the documented success rate of small businesses has plummeted.*
   After the first earthquake destroyed much of the town, *the aftershock caused additional damage.*
   However, because most residents had been evacuated, *loss of life was minimal.*

   The sentence combines an introductory word, *however,* and then an introductory dependent clause.

3. a verbal (verb-like word often ending in *-ing* or *-ed*), or a phrase containing a verbal (see p. 44):

   Smiling, *the boss came toward me.*
   Plagued by strikes, *the government became increasingly ineffective in providing elementary services.*

4. an infinitive (a verb with *to*):

   To get free, *he had to post bail.*

   Note that *to get free* is not the subject of the sentence, but an introducer. The subject is *he*. Thus *to get free* is different from the subjects beginning with *to* covered on p. 335.

  5. a prepositional phrase (see p. 47):

Without personal identification, *they could not prove they owned the car.*

A COMMA IS OPTIONAL AFTER A SHORT INTRODUCER

If the introducer is short, and if there is no chance of misreading, the comma may be omitted.

After dinner the patient felt better.
After heating, the water is transferred to another vat.
(Comma needed to prevent misreading as *after heating the water....*)

EXERCISES

Answers in back of book: 1a-i
Answers in instructor's manual: 1j-n

1. In the following sentences, add commas as needed. (Answers in back of book)
   a. Nevertheless I took the boat out on the lake.
   b. After the storm debris covered the yard.
   c. When the mechanic opened the hood she gasped.
   d. If a truck comes by flag it down.
   e. If you are going to spend money however why not do it in a big way?
   f. If you have to ask how much it costs you can't afford it.
   g. In 1779 while not yet three Carl Friedrich Gauss watched his foreman father tally up the payroll for a group of

STEP TWO: READ AND REVISE FOR GRAMMAR AND PUNCTUATION

bricklayers. When the child pointed out an error the father was amazed to find that his son was right.
h. Passing certain tests of skill enabled the medieval craftsman to join a guild.
i. Yesterday I came back to the stables. Since I had been away for a year my return was something of an occasion. Of course I had not told Henry. Wiping his hands on his overalls he came to the stable door when I shouted and look quizzically at me. Surprised and for a moment taken back he stood there looking at me.

(Answers in instructor's manual)

j. After the movie we went out to eat.
k. Once the mess was cleared away we could begin to work.
l. Raising the money to visit Scotland was easy.
m. However coming home we got stuck in Le Havre and had to spend two extra nights in a hotel.
n. Last year I visited my old grammar school. Because I have become a famous athlete I was the center of awed attention. In the cafeteria preventing food fights as usual Mrs. Mentink looked up distractedly. Still holding a young ruffian by the arm she gazed at me in surprise. Then releasing the fortunate prisoner she came toward me joyfully in greeting.

REVISING YOUR OWN WRITING

In the space provided, enter passages from your own writing where you've missed commas after introducers. Write the revision. Then write five other sentences that follow similar patterns, punctuating appropriately.

Your Sentence(s)

LESSON 2L: USE COMMAS AFTER INTRODUCERS

_____
_____
_____

Your Revision
_____
_____
_____
_____
_____

Five Other Sentences in the Same Pattern
_____
_____
_____
_____
_____

GRAMMATICAL TERMS IN THIS LESSON

Clause: A subject-verb unit plus that unit's modifiers and complements

Dependent Clause: A clause that cannot stand alone

Subject: A word or group of words that names the person or thing that is performing the action or that is in the state of being named in the verb

Verb: The one to four words that name the action or state of being of the subject

LESSON FOR STEP 2M

USE COMMAS WITH NON-RESTRICTIVE INTERRUPTERS AND MODIFIERS

PREVIEW OF THE LESSON

The previous lesson showed how to place commas after introducers. The same sorts of words and phrases, when sandwiched within sentences, are called interrupters and modifiers. Sometimes they are set off with commas, sometimes not. This lesson explains how to decide. See how this lesson fits within the process of interior sentence punctuation—Figure 2K.1, p. 332.

Definition: An INTERRUPTER is a word or group of related words that interrupts the flow between related elements such as the subject and the verb or the verb and its object.

LESSON 2M: USE COMMAS WITH NONRESTRICTIVE INTERRUPTERS

Definition: A MODIFIER describes or limits the meaning of some other word or words.

You need not be concerned with the difference between a modifier and other kinds of interrupters. Your only concern is to identify those groups of words that function as interrupters/modifiers of a certain type—nonrestrictive—because those are the ones that should be set off by commas. The same sorts of words, phrases, and dependent clauses that can be introducers (p. 342) can also be interrupters/modifiers if they appear within the sentence rather than at its beginning.

Begin by relying on your ear. You can usually hear interrupters; if you were reading the sentence aloud your voice would pause slightly. In the following sentences, interrupters are underlined.

The secretaries, <u>who all lived nearby</u>, volunteered to come to work despite the storm.
The beach, <u>however</u>, was very clean.
The children had fun, <u>in their high rubber boots</u>, wading in the creek.

GENERAL GUIDE FOR PUNCTUATING INTERRUPTERS/MODIFIERS

Though practices vary, and some situations are matters of judgment, the general rule for interrupters/modifiers is that they should be set off by commas if they merely add information but do not affect the essential meaning of the sentence (called *nonrestrictive*). Interrupters/modifiers should *not* be set off if they affect the essential meaning of the sentence (called *restrictive*). This is how to remember the terms: *non*restrictive interrupters/modifiers do *not restrict* the essential meaning; restrictive interrupters *do* restrict the essential meaning. The punctuation rule makes sense if you think about the sentence.

Any group of words that affects the essential meaning of the sentence needs to be seen by the reader as an integral part of that sentence, not separated from the sentence by punctuation; however, if a word or group of words is not essential to the central meaning, it is separated from the essence of the sentence by punctuation. With practice, you will develop a sense of how this rule is interpreted. In general, when in doubt, do not use a comma unless confusion might result.

Once you know that only nonrestrictive interrupters are marked off with punctuation, your next problem is to decide what sort of punctuation marks to use. Commas are the most common. Elements that strongly interrupt the sentence may be set off by dashes or parentheses, explained in the next lesson. Often a writer has a choice between commas, parentheses, and dashes to set off nonrestrictive interrupters. This lesson explains commas.

USING PUNCTUATION IN PAIRS

When the nonrestrictive interrupter/modifier has other parts of the same sentence on both sides, like a sandwich, then the interrupter/modifier must be set off by a *pair* of commas, dashes, or parentheses. If the interrupter/modifier has a part of the sentence on only one of its sides, it just needs one comma or dash. Parentheses, however, are always used in pairs, no matter where the interrupter/modifier is placed.

IMPORTANCE OF THE NONRESTRICTIVE PRINCIPLE

The rest of this lesson discusses several kinds of nonrestrictive interrupters and modifiers, all of which are set off by commas. Do not be intimidated by the grammatical names—concentrate on seeing how each type is nonrestrictive. If you know the nonrestrictive rule, and have been exposed to the various types of nonrestrictive elements that may turn up in sentences, you can punctuate with confidence even though you do not remember the grammatical terms for the various kinds of nonrestrictive interrupters and modifiers.

COMMAS AROUND NONRESTRICTIVE ADVERBIAL PHRASES AND CLAUSES

An adverbial phrase or clause modifies the verb of a sentence. (For more on verbs and modifiers, see Introductory Lesson A.) Adverbial phrases and clauses are set off by commas if they merely add information to the main sentence. If they restrict its meaning in an essential way, they are not set off by any punctuation.

These plants will not grow well **unless the soil is quite porous.**

The *unless* phrase is an essential restriction on the meaning of the main sentence. The writer's essential meaning is not captured within *these plants will not grow well.*

These plants will not grow well in this soil, **even though you are giving them the right amount of sun and water.**

The *even though* phrase introduces additional information, but that information does not restrict the essential meaning of the main sentence. The basic assertion, *these plants will not grow well,* remains true. Thus the modifying phrase that begins *even though* is nonrestrictive and is set off with a comma.

COMMAS AROUND NONRESTRICTIVE MODIFIERS OF NOUNS

Groups of words that modify a noun should be set off with commas only if the modifier does not restrict the essential meaning of the noun it modifies. (A noun names a person, place, concept, or thing.)

Restrictive modifier (no commas): The man *who cooked the steaks* is our company manager.
(There are several men visible. The phrase *who cooked the steaks* is necessary for the reader to identify which man is meant.)

Nonrestrictive modifier (commas): The man, who cooked the steaks, is our company manager.
(There is only one man visible. The phrase *who cooked the steaks* is not necessary to establish which man; it merely adds information about the man.)

COMMAS AROUND NONRESTRICTIVE MODIFIERS THAT RENAME A NOUN (APPOSITIVES)

A word, phrase, or clause, usually appearing beside a noun, that identifies or describes the noun by renaming it is called an *appositive*.

> The contractor, <u>Jean Rhodes</u>, *says she hopes to complete the building by next November.*
> This slide rule, <u>my best one</u>, was very expensive.

In the examples, the appositive does not change the meaning of the sentence. *The contractor says she hopes to complete the building by next November* retains its meaning. This is the most common type of appositive.

In a few cases, however, the appositive is essential to the sentence's meaning.

> The fantasy **Alice in Wonderland** *is one of my favorite books.*

LESSON 2M: USE COMMAS WITH NONRESTRICTIVE INTERRUPTERS

Without the appositive *Alice in Wonderland,* the sentence would read *The fantasy is one of my favorite books.* The meaning of the sentence changes or becomes unclear. In such cases, the appositive is restrictive and is *not* set off by commas.

The following are several other types of interrupters that are set off by commas. All of them are typically nonrestrictive. Thus all these guidelines fall under the general rule that nonrestrictive interrupters and modifiers are set off by commas.

COMMAS AROUND INTERRUPTERS SUCH AS *HOWEVER*

There are many different nonrestrictive phrases that may be inserted in a sentence—phrases such as *however, nevertheless, after all, at the same time, despite her wishes,* and *finally.* When nonrestrictive, such phrases are set off by commas.

He tried, at the same time, to keep the other restaurant going.
The cat, however, was breathing freely.
It was a poor choice, however.
The princess realized that, however she tried, she could not please the nobles.

The *however* is not an interrupter on its own; it is part of the interrupter, *however she tried.*

COMMAS WITH DIRECT ADDRESS

When the writer addresses someone by his or her name or title, the name or title is set off by commas. The name or title is nonrestrictive; it does not change the basic meaning of the sentence.

After all, Joan, someone has to take the late shift.

COMMAS WITH INTERJECTIONS

An interjection is a *grammatically independent* element that is used to express emotion. Grammatically independent means that it does not act as a subject, verb, modifier, or serve any other grammatical role in the sentence. Common interjections are *yes, no, alas, aha,* and *oh.*

The juice, **alas,** *had stained her gown.*

COMMAS WITH ELEMENTS SHOWING OPPOSITION

Commas are used to separate elements that are in opposition to one another. The word *or* by itself is not enough. The words that usually signal opposition that require commas are *not* and *but;* however, sometimes contrasting elements have no such markers, as in the following second example.

The room was either too hot or too cold.

Words and phrases joined by *or* do not require commas. However, two independent clauses separated by *or* do require a comma—see Lesson 2B.

We ordered the number 2 valves, not the number 3 valves.
We were not only hot, but also tired.
The fever made her cold, then hot again.

COMMAS TO CLARIFY MEANING

If a sentence could mislead a reader, insert a comma, even though no rules call for it.

LESSON 2M: USE COMMAS WITH NONRESTRICTIVE INTERRUPTERS

Managers who like to see their staff, eat in the company lunchroom.

Who like to see their staff is restrictive, so normally would get no commas; however, a comma is needed to prevent the reader from thinking that the managers like to see the staff eat.

EXERCISES

Answers in back of book: 1a-n
Answers in instructor's manual: 1o-u

1. Add commas to the following sentences according to the guidelines in this lesson. Use Lesson 2K to avoid misplaced commas and Lesson 2B to avoid run-ons.
   (Answers in back of book)
   a. The recruits after marching five miles will be allowed a fifteen-minute break.
   b. They may not however leave their places in the line of march.
   c. The cockroach used in laboratory research is the American cockroach which is about 2 inches long or more and can fly.
   d. Hunting the most aggressive outdoor sport repels him.
   e. Elijah Johnson whose great grandparents were slaves now owns a corporation worth several hundred million dollars.
   f. Put the toys on the shelves children not on the rug.
   g. The lamps since we had them rewired have given us no trouble.
   h. The local police fortunately got more help once the National Guard arrived.
   i. The photographs must be enlarged still more despite the cost.
   j. Politics and war too have cast their shadows over Cambodia once again.

STEP TWO: READ AND REVISE FOR GRAMMAR AND PUNCTUATION

k. Today says the director Nguyen van Nghi fifty people both experts and local villagers are active in the restoration project.
l. The old torch from the Statue of Liberty when its restoration is finished will be exhibited in a special museum in the statue's base.
m. Students learning to pilot aircraft meet dangers not in a jet 100 feet above the ground where a mistake can mean a fiery death but in a flight simulator where errors result in no more than a flashing red signal and a chance to try again.
n. Rare coins and jewels had fallen in price art was holding steady.

(Answers in instructor's manual)

o. Bring your uniforms please and check them at the desk.
p. We always when travelling on the train brought a hamper full of food.
q. We would swap chips and sandwiches with any of the other children who had brought food.
r. We wanted to invite them if possible to go sailing with us.
s. Fifteen bands all in uniform marched in the parade which was the grandest display that little village buried deep in the mountains had ever seen.
t. That brass will never shine unless you use the special refinisher not the ordinary metal polish.
u. Bears were last seen in those mountains more than twenty years ago wildcats have been gone for thirty years.

REVISING YOUR OWN WRITING

In the space provided, enter passages from your own writing where you've placed commas inappropriately. Write the correc-

LESSON 2M: USE COMMAS WITH NONRESTRICTIVE INTERRUPTERS

tion. Then write five other sentences that follow similar patterns, punctuating appropriately.

Your Sentence(s)
_____
_____
_____
_____
_____

Your Revision
_____
_____
_____
_____
_____

Five Other Sentences in the Same Pattern
_____
_____
_____
_____
_____

GRAMMATICAL TERMS IN THIS LESSON

Adverb: A word or group of words that describes or limits the meaning of a verb, an adjective, another adverb, or the sentence as a whole

Clause: A subject-verb unit plus that unit's modifiers and complements

Verb: The one to four words that name the action or the state of being of the subject

Modifier: A word or group of words that describes or limits the meaning of another word or group of words in the same sentence

STEP TWO: READ AND REVISE FOR GRAMMAR AND PUNCTUATION

Noun: A word or group of words that names a person, place, concept, or thing

Appositive: A word or group of words that modifies a noun by renaming it.

Interjection: A word or group of words that has no grammatical role in the sentence

LESSON FOR	**USE**
STEP 2N	**PARENTHESES**
	AND DASHES
	TO SET OFF
	INTERRUPTERS

PREVIEW OF THE LESSON

The previous lesson showed how to set off interrupters and modifiers with commas. When an element strongly interrupts the flow of the sentence, however, a writer may set it off with parentheses or with one or a pair of dashes. See how this lesson fits within the process of interior sentence punctuation—Figure 2K.1, p. 332.

PARENTHESES AND DASHES

Parentheses always appear in pairs (like this). Just one is called a parenthesis. The dash is formed on your typewriter by two hyphens: —. There is no space between the dash and words preceding or following it.

We cruised the main street—or what passed for the main street in that one horse town—feeling like kings of the road.

There are two differences between parentheses and dashes:

Parentheses	Dashes
always used in pairs	used in pairs only when sandwiched between parts of the same sentence; otherwise used singly;
used only to set off interrupters	used to set off interrupters or to announce an explanation or enumeration (Lesson 2Q)

USE PARENTHESES TO EXPLAIN TERMS OR REFER TO ANOTHER ITEM

Use parentheses rather than dashes for an explanation of terms or for referral.

The NEH (National Endowment for the Humanities) funded the project.
Be sure all the parts are included (Figure 1) before you begin assembly.

USE DASH FOR DESCRIPTIVE EXPLANATIONS AND SHARP SHIFTS

The dash is not used often, but it has specific functions. In some situations, a dash is the most appropriate form of punctuation. Therefore, don't be afraid to use the dash, even in formal writing, for the situations described in this chapter. Some writers like to use the dash as a wildcard, substituting it for periods and commas or using it to create a string of linked phrases. In creative writing, or for informal situations, this can be effective;

however, for most writing in school and in professions avoid using the dash except for the specific functions described in this lesson.

When the explanation is a business-like clarification of the meaning of a term or a reference to some other part of the paper, as in the previous examples, use parentheses; however, explanations that are more like a description or a new thought may be set off by either parentheses or dashes.

Correct: Her job (which included doing all her own typing) was more than one person could handle. (Interrupter set off with parentheses)

Also Correct: Her job—which included doing all her own typing—was more than one person could handle. (Interrupter set off with dashes)

Use dash marks to introduce a sharp shift in thought. When the shift in thought is not drastic, a writer may have a choice between dashes and commas, depending on the purpose and context.

Believe me, as a player and as a coach I did my share of abusing referees—that is, until I became a referee.

(This is a sharp shift; use a dash.)

Dismay marked her features—but she laughed. OR Dismay marked her features, but she laughed.

The shift is not sharp; use a dash or comma, depending on your purpose, meaning, and context.

REVISE PARENTHESES OR DASHES FOR EASIER READING IF NECESSARY

Sentences with long parenthetical phrases in the middle are often hard to read. When possible, use one of the following three alternatives. Each is a revision of the sentence about typing.

STEP TWO: READ AND REVISE FOR GRAMMAR AND PUNCTUATION

1. Rewrite the sentence so the parenthetical material is at the end. Then use a dash or comma to set it off.

No one person could handle all the responsibilities of her job, which included doing all her own typing.

2. Incorporate the parenthetical material more directly into the passage, so parentheses are not needed.

A job that included doing all her own typing was more than she could handle.

3. Make the parenthetical elements a separate sentence or clause.

Her job was more than one person could handle. She even had to do all her own typing.

PUNCTUATE WITHIN AND AROUND PARENTHESES AND DASHES

If the material within the parentheses is a grammatically complete sentence, and if it comes at the end of the larger sentence, treat the parenthetical material as a separate sentence and enclose it all, even its period, in parentheses. To review grammatically complete sentences, see Step 1A.

The patients were exhausted. (Nancy, though, was as lively as usual.)
The patients were exhausted (except Nancy, who was as lively as usual).

(The words in parentheses are not a grammatically complete sentence.)

If the material in parentheses is a full sentence, but the parentheses come in the middle of a sentence, omit the capital letter and period.

LESSON 2N: USE PARENTHESES AND DASHES

The patients were exhausted (they had been up all night), and they wanted to go to bed immediately.

If the material in parentheses requires an internal comma, colon, semicolon, or quotation marks, use them as you normally would and keep them within the parentheses.

The investigation dragged on. (The EPA, which had been called in near the end, needed time to review the facts.)

Never place a comma, colon, or semicolon directly in front of a parenthesis. If the sentence demands punctuation at that point, place the punctuation mark after the closing parenthesis.

Thoroughly exhausted (except for Nancy), the patients returned to the clinic.

As an introducer, *thoroughly exhausted* should be followed by a comma, but the comma is placed after the parenthesis.

Kenny (who calls himself "Flash"), screeching at the top of his lungs, zoomed around the room.

Screeching at the top of his lungs should be surrounded by commas on both sides because it is a nonrestrictive modifier for the noun *Kenny*. See Lesson 2M. The first comma appears after the parenthesis, not before it.

Richardson handed in his resignation (actually he was fired), and his family left for a vacation in the Great Smokies.

Two independent clauses are separated by a comma plus *and*. The comma is placed after the parenthesis. For punctuation between independent clauses, see Step 1B.

Do not use other punctuation before or after a dash. If the interrupter set off by dashes is at the end of the sentence, use only a period at the end.

Her glittering eyelids—blue, mauve, magenta—adver-

STEP TWO: READ AND REVISE FOR GRAMMAR AND PUNCTUATION

tised a young girl's strident grasp at womanhood. The first thing one noticed about her was her glittering eyelids—blue, mauve, magenta.

EXERCISES

Answers in back of book: 1a-h
Answers in instructor's manual: 1i-m

1. Insert commas, parentheses, and dashes as needed in the following sentences. Where you think there is a choice, indicate all possibilities.
   (Sample revisions in back of book)
   a. The IRS Internal Revenue Service has published this material.
   b. My son the rascal went off with my scissors.
   c. The tape believe it or not has disappeared.
   d. The street sounds bells, sirens, shouts of children playing came dimly through the dark curtains.
      [*Bells, sirens, shouts of children playing* is an explanation of *street sounds.*]
   e. Museum lists of trustees who tend to be generous donors as well as collectors do not contain many Hollywood names. [*who tend to be generous donors as well as collectors* is an explanation of *trustees.*]
   f. The university's director of foreign programs Milton Radisson calculates that altogether the college's engineers have supplied about sixty-seven years of professional service teaching and consultation to Peruvian engineering schools. [*Teaching and consultation* are an explanation of *service.*]
   g. The bobcat only wanted to reach dry ground so did I.
   h. I had wanted to see Mitchell again but not behind bars.
   (Sample revisions in instructor's manual)

LESSON 2N: USE PARENTHESES AND DASHES

i. Icelanders produce one third of the world's cod liver oil including a new mint flavor.
j. Crossing Baker Stream is a bridge of two cables one for your hands, one for your feet.
k. Only in the most remote regions such as Tsingey National Reserve defended by huge rocks does the country's national wildlife still survive.
l. Iceland's city of Reykjavik finds itself in a strategic location see map, p. 193.
m. The yellow-billed spoonbills *Platalea flavipes* feed together and breed in loose colonies. [*Platalea flavipes* is the scientific name for yellow-billed spoonbills.]

REVISING YOUR OWN WRITING

In the space provided, enter passages from your own writing where you've omitted dashes and parentheses or used them inappropriately. Write the correction. Then write five other sentences that follow similar patterns, punctuating appropriately.

Your Sentence(s)
_____
_____
_____
_____
_____

Your Revision
_____
_____
_____
_____
_____

STEP TWO: READ AND REVISE FOR GRAMMAR AND PUNCTUATION

Five Other Sentences in the Same Pattern

_____
_____
_____
_____
_____

GRAMMATICAL TERMS IN THIS LESSON

Independent Clause: A clause that can stand alone
Nonrestrictive Modifier: A modifier that does not change the basic meaning of the sentence

LESSON FOR STEP 20

USE COMMAS TO SEPARATE ADJECTIVES IN A SERIES

PREVIEW OF THE LESSON

This lesson and the next treat elements that appear in a series. This lesson shows how to use commas to separate adjectives. See how this substep fits within the process of interior sentence punctuation—Figure 2K.1, p. 332. The process for placing commas with adjectives is summarized in Figure 20.1.

Definition: An ADJECTIVE is a word or group of words that modifies (describes or limits the meaning of) a noun.

Definition: A NOUN names a person, place, concept, or thing. (For more on nouns and modifiers, see p. 42.)

Check all series of two or more adjectives:

```
Do two or more adjectives work together as one term?  --Yes--> Treat as one adjective
        |No
        v
Does adjective work with noun as one term?  --Yes--> No comma after adjective
        |No
        v
Is adjective a number?  --Yes--> No comma after adjective
        |No
        v
Is this the last adjective before a noun?  --Yes--> No comma after adjective
        |No
        v
Place comma after adjective
```

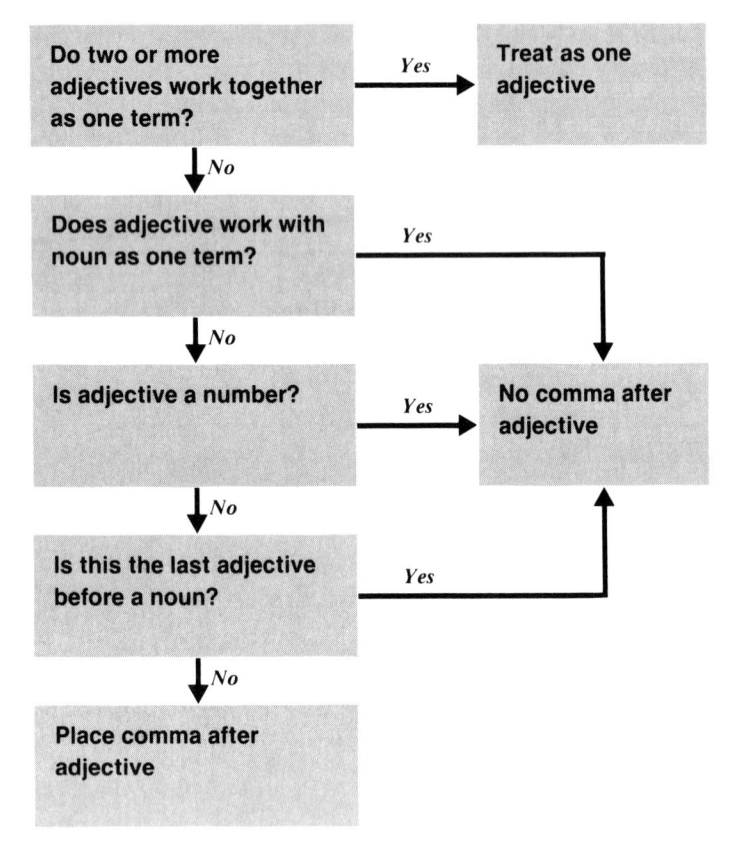

FIGURE 2 O.1   Using Commas to Separate Adjectives in a Series

THE RULE FOR USING COMMAS WITH ADJECTIVES

In a series of two or more adjectives, use a comma to separate adjectives from one another. Do not insert a comma between the last adjective and the noun. The rest of the lesson explains the fine points and exceptions to this rule.

>**He moved into a tiny, shabby house.**
>(Adjectives are *tiny* and *shabby*.)

NO COMMA BETWEEN ADJECTIVES THAT WORK TOGETHER AS ONE TERM

Do not use a comma between adjectives that work together as one term. A helpful technique is mentally to insert *and* between the adjectives. If the meaning is still preserved, insert a comma (except between the last adjective and the noun). If the *and* destroys the meaning, the two words are functioning together as one term, so do not place a comma between them.

>**The imaginative, highly tasteful decor suited the elegance of the building.**

No comma between *highly* and *tasteful,* because they work together as one unit to describe the noun, *decor.* It would make no sense to say, *The imaginative and highly and tasteful decor.* There is no comma after *tasteful* because it is the last adjective before the noun.

NO COMMA AFTER AN ADJECTIVE THAT WORKS TOGETHER AS ONE TERM WITH A NOUN

If the last adjective is so closely associated with the noun that they work together as one term, treat the adjective as part of the noun. That means do not place a comma between the next-to-last adjective and the adjective-noun unit.

STEP TWO: READ AND REVISE FOR GRAMMAR AND PUNCTUATION

The animals were kept in small, filthy pig pens.

Pig pens is one concept, so treat *filthy* as the last adjective, omitting any comma after *filthy*.

The animals were kept in small, filthy, crowded pens.

Pens is the noun, modified by three adjectives. All adjectives but the last are separated by commas.

NO COMMA AFTER NUMBERS MODIFYING A NOUN

A number should not be followed by a comma.

Incorrect: two, lovely babies
Correct: two lovely babies

OPTIONAL COMMA BEFORE *AND, OR,* AND *NOR*

When using commas to separate items in a series, you may eliminate the comma before *and, or,* and *nor,* if the meaning is clear.

Correct: The patient was fretful, feverish and thirsty.
Also Correct: The patient was fretful, feverish, and thirsty.

EXERCISES

Answers in back of book: 1a-h
Answers in instructor's manual: 1i-l

1. In the following sentences, supply commas between adjec-

LESSON 20: USE COMMAS TO SEPARATE ADJECTIVES IN A SERIES

tives as needed. If a comma is optional, underline it in your revision.

(Answers in back of book)

a. The firm was fortunate to have a talented bright efficient management team.
b. The sales staff was weak inefficient and poorly organized.
c. There were twenty-two violent destructive tornadoes in Kansas last year.
d. Sweaty thirsty and bone weary, the runners crossed the finish line.
e. The museum was full of historic fire engines.
f. Our car was rusty drafty and battered, but the engine was still reliable smooth and efficient.
g. These bright third grade youngsters had won the city spelling contest.
h. Randy's John's and Billy's coats were piled up in the hallway.

(Answers in instructor's manual)

i. The sandy unstable coastline proved unsuitable for building.
j. Randy Wood was a long legged red headed hiker from Tennessee.
k. Fans had sent two thousand get well cards to the injured singer.
l. We rescued Sue's Sandy's and Pat's umbrellas.

REVISING YOUR OWN WRITING

In the space provided, enter passages from your own writing where you've missed problems with commas between adjectives. Write the revision. Then write five other sentences that follow similar patterns, punctuating appropriately.

STEP TWO: READ AND REVISE FOR GRAMMAR AND PUNCTUATION

Your Sentence(s)

_____
_____
_____
_____
_____

Your Revision

_____
_____
_____
_____
_____

Five Other Sentences in the Same Pattern

_____
_____
_____
_____
_____

GRAMMATICAL TERMS IN THIS LESSON

Adjective: A word or group of words that modifies a noun
Noun: A word or group of words that names a person, place, concept, or thing
Modify: To describe or limit the meaning of

LESSON FOR STEP 2P

PUNCTUATE LISTS AND SERIES WITH COLONS, SEMICOLONS, AND COMMAS

PREVIEW OF THE LESSON

The previous lesson showed how to separate adjectives in a series. This lesson shows how to separate other elements that appear as lists or series. See how this lesson fits within the process of interior sentence punctuation—Figure 2K.1, p. 332. There are several types of lists and series. This lesson shows how to punctuate each type. The procedures are summarized in Figure 2P.1.

Definition: A LIST or SERIES is a list of items or a series of clauses or phrases.

Definition: A PHRASE is a group of related words without a subject–verb unit.

371

STEP TWO: READ AND REVISE FOR GRAMMAR AND PUNCTUATION

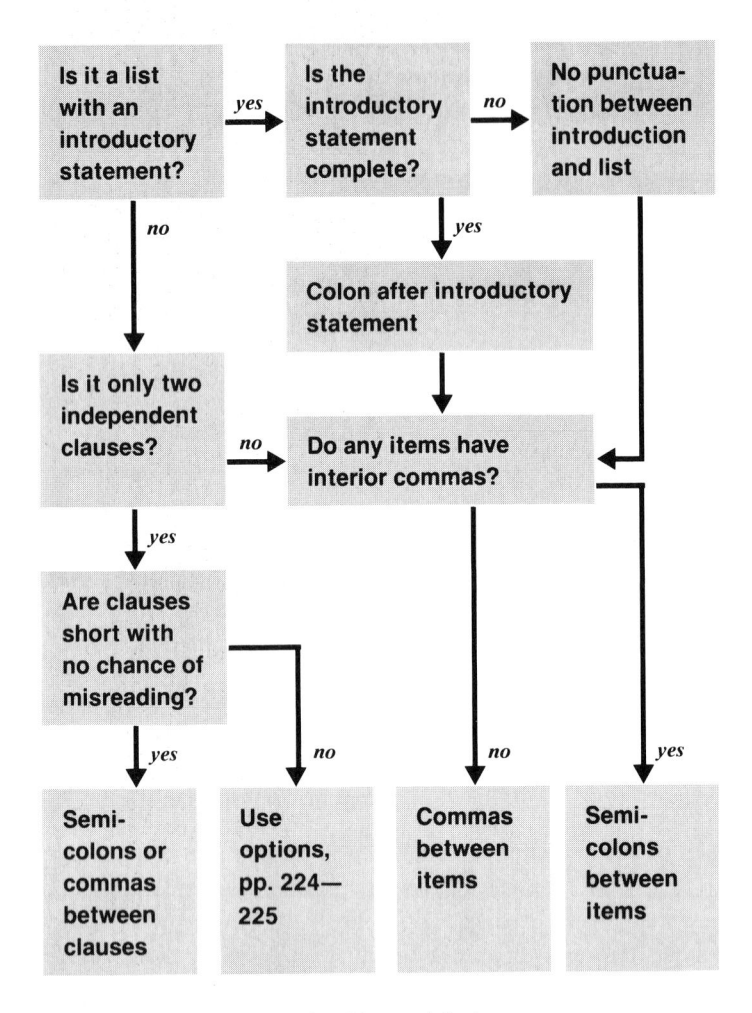

```
┌─────────────┐       ┌─────────────┐      ┌─────────────┐
│ Is it a list│       │ Is the      │      │ No punctua- │
│ with an     │  yes  │ introductory│  no  │ tion between│
│ introductory├──────►│ statement   ├─────►│ introduction│
│ statement?  │       │ complete?   │      │ and list    │
└──────┬──────┘       └──────┬──────┘      └─────────────┘
       │ no                  │ yes
       ▼              ┌──────▼──────────────────┐
                      │ Colon after introductory│
                      │ statement               │
                      └──────┬──────────────────┘
┌─────────────┐              │
│ Is it only  │              ▼
│ two         │       ┌─────────────┐
│ independent │  no   │ Do any items│
│ clauses?    ├──────►│ have interior◄────────┐
└──────┬──────┘       │ commas?     │         │
       │ yes          └──────┬──────┘         │
       ▼                     │                │
┌─────────────┐              │                │
│ Are clauses │              │                │
│ short with  │              │                │
│ no chance of│              │                │
│ misreading? │              │                │
└──────┬──────┘              │                │
   yes │  no                 │ no        yes  │
       ▼  ▼                  ▼                │
┌──────────┐ ┌──────────┐ ┌──────────┐ ┌──────────┐
│Semi-     │ │Use       │ │Commas    │ │Semicolons│
│colons or │ │options,  │ │between   │ │between   │
│commas    │ │pp. 224—  │ │items     │ │items     │
│between   │ │225       │ │          │ │          │
│clauses   │ │          │ │          │ │          │
└──────────┘ └──────────┘ └──────────┘ └──────────┘
```

FIGURE 2 P.1 Punctuating Lists and Series

Definition: A CLAUSE is a subject-verb unit together with that unit's complements and modifiers (See Introductory Lesson B.)

TYPES OF LISTS AND SERIES

1. A list of items:

   The menu is as follows: beef, mashed potatoes, and carrots. OR
   The menu is beef, mashed potatoes, and carrots.

2. Two or more words or phrases that have similar form and function (called *coordinate* words or phrases):

   We pulled away from the rapids, paddling furiously, straining our muscles, calling on our reserves of energy.

   Coordinate elements are the *-ing* phrases: *paddling* furiously, *straining* our muscles, *calling* on our reserves of energy.

3. Three or more independent clauses:

   We scraped, we filed, we sanded, and we rubbed.

   The rules for joining *two* independent clauses in a sentence are covered in Lesson 2B.

USE A COLON AFTER A COMPLETE STATEMENT THAT INTRODUCES A LIST

Use a colon to introduce a list only when the statement before the colon is complete. Do not use a colon or any other punctuation when the list is introduced by a verb or a preposition. A verb names the action or state of being of its subject (see Introductory Lesson A). A preposition is a word showing direction or relation, such as *of, toward, above,* and *for.* (See p. 47.)

Incorrect: On October 15, the truck delivered: a washer and dryer, two sofas, six dining room chairs, and the dining room table.

STEP TWO: READ AND REVISE FOR GRAMMAR AND PUNCTUATION

Delivered is the verb. No punctuation should interrupt the flow between the verb and the list.

Correct: On October 15, the truck delivered a washer and dryer, two. . . .

Also correct: On October 15, the truck delivered the following items: a washer and dryer, two. . . .
(The statement before the colon is complete.)

Incorrect: In the bin were: staples, brads, nails, and tacks.

The subject is *staples, brads, nails, and tacks.* The verb is *were.* Do not use punctuation to interrupt the flow between subject and verb.

Correct: In the bin were staples, brads, nails, and tacks.

Also correct: In the bin were several types of fasteners: staples, brads, nails, and tacks.
(The statement before the colon is complete. Its subject is *types;* its verb is *were.*)

CHOOSE BETWEEN COMMAS AND SEMICOLONS TO SEPARATE ITEMS IN A LIST

To separate individual items of a list, use commas, unless one or more of the individual items has a comma within it. In that case, use semicolons (;) to separate items from one another. The comma before the final linking word (such as *and* or *or*) is optional; however, use the comma if the items are long and complex or if a misreading might result. A semicolon before the final linking word is *not* optional, but required.

Incorrect: We ordered the girders; jousts; and flooring.

(None of the items has a comma within it, so use commas to separate items.)

Correct: We ordered the girders, jousts, and flooring.

(Comma after *jousts* is optional.)

Correct: On October 10 we sent the following items to you for repair: a #10–40 fuel pump, which had a dent in its side; a #90–87 filter; and a single-blade rotary mower.

(If even one of the items has an interior comma, all items are separated by semicolons.)

Correct: Each hiker was equipped with food, water, and a blanket or sleeping bag.

(The final item, *blanket or sleeping bag,* is a single item, so no comma before "or.")

EXERCISES

Answers in back of book: 1a–j
Answers in instructor's manual: 1k–o

1. Punctuate the following sentences.
    (Answers in back of book)
    a. In this class, students will read several novels *The Invisible Man Wuthering Heights Jane Eyre* and *The Bostonians.*
    b. In this class, students will read *The Invisible Man Wuthering Heights Jane Eyre* and *The Bostonians.*
    c. In this class, students will read novels such as *The Invisible Man Wuthering Heights Jane Eyre* and *The Bostonians.*
    d. In this class, students will read novels such as *The Invisible Man* the story of a black man growing up in America *Wuthering Heights* a dark gothic novel about a twisted relationship on the forsaken British moors and *Jane Eyre*

STEP TWO: READ AND REVISE FOR GRAMMAR AND PUNCTUATION

the tale of a young woman's attempt to find autonomy in a repressive culture.
e. Every camper should bring at least the following a set of sheets and towels two blankets a pillow and personal toilet items.
f. Every camper should bring a set of sheets and towels, preferably marked with his or her name two thick, heavy blankets and a pillow.
g. The Chicano movement in the U.S. may move in three major directions the first is a continuous strengthening of the Raza Unida Party as a separate party the second is an alliance with other minority organizations to form a third national party and the third is an alliance with one of the two major national political parties.
h. Instead of watching TV, you could be grooming pets caring for children or collecting bottles newspapers or aluminum cans for recycling.
i. The possibilities for making money in your spare time are numerous, depending on how creative enterprising and conscientious you are.
j. Just remember that clerking in a store answering telephones or flipping hamburgers are not your only choices.
(Answers in instructor's manual)
k. Among the most talented and famous actresses of the day were Gibber Pritchard Clive and Woffington.
l. Part time work in the summer may mean bussing dishes bagging groceries pumping gas or standing behind a cash register.
m. Some enterprising students advertise through local newspapers club newsletters or the bulletin boards at local grocery stores laundromats and community centers.
n. When my parents were young, they were not allowed to date anyone their parents did not know go dancing stay out past 11 p.m. even on Saturday night or wear makeup.
o. The long-term effects of alcohol consumption can be classified into two broad categories social-emotional

effects, such as family work and driving problems, and physical effects, which include liver problems heart disease and damage to the central nervous system.

USE COMMAS TO SEPARATE THREE OR MORE COORDINATE WORDS, PHRASES, OR CLAUSES

Definition: COORDINATE means that the words, phrases, or clauses are similar in their form and in their role in the sentence.

For help identifying clauses, see Introductory Lesson B. As with adjectives (Lesson 2O), the final comma before *and, or,* and *nor* may be omitted provided the unit is short and no misreading is possible.

Correct:	The miners were cold, tired, and hungry.
Also Correct:	The miners were cold, tired and hungry.
Correct:	The courses were sewing, building and carpentry, stonemasonry, and bricklaying.

Building and carpentry is *one* course, so it gets no comma. A comma is needed after *stonemasonry* to prevent the reader from wondering whether stonemasonry and bricklaying combine in a single course or are two separate courses.

The following examples will illustrate various types of coordinate elements separated by commas. (Coordinate elements are underlined.)

Spontaneity, freedom, poise, and harmony seemed to increase.

(Comma after *poise* is optional.)

People who live in the northern states are used to ice, snow, sleet, and slush.

(Comma after *sleet* is optional.)

STEP TWO: READ AND REVISE FOR GRAMMAR AND PUNCTUATION

> *There's no use knowing a lot if you* <u>can't be happy</u>, <u>can't get along with people</u>, *or* <u>can't hold the kind of job you want</u>.

(Comma after *people* is desirable, since the units are long, and a misreading of *people or* is possible.)

> *The intern* <u>arrived</u>, <u>assessed the situation</u>, *and* <u>acted quickly</u>.

(Comma after *situation* is optional.)

> *The* <u>intern</u>, <u>the medic</u>, *and* <u>the nurse</u> *all arrived together.*

(Comma after *medic* is optional.)

> <u>*Torn by strife*</u>, <u>*economically bankrupt*</u>, *and* <u>*without political leadership*</u>, *the nation slid into chaos.*

(Comma after *leadership* because the coordinate phrases act as an introducer—see Lesson 2L.)

USE A COMMA TO SEPARATE THREE OR MORE INDEPENDENT CLAUSES

For help identifying independent clauses, see Introductory Lesson B. In the following sentence, each of the coordinate units is an independent clause. If there were only two independent clauses, a comma between them would create a run-on (See Lesson 2B). Only if two independent clauses are very short with no chance of misreading may you separate them with a comma. However, when independent clauses of any length appear in a series of three or more, they are treated as coordinate elements in a series and are separated by commas. If any of them have interior commas, or if commas might create confusion, use semicolons.

> <u>*We cleared the land, the builder put in the foundation, and the owners finished the home.*</u>
> *We cleared the land, once spring came; the builder, in May, put in the foundation; and by the time of the first snow, the owners had finished the home.*

LESSON 2P: PUNCTUATE LISTS AND SERIES

(Coordinate elements have interior commas, so they are separated by semicolons.)

UNDERSTOOD ELEMENTS

Sometimes pieces of the coordinate elements may be understood rather than stated. Separate by commas.

The inventory was low, the shop filthy, the help slovenly, and the manager dishonest.

(The verb *was* is stated in the first clause and understood in the rest.)

EXERCISES

(Note: Exercise 1 appears earlier in the lesson.)
Answers in back of book: 2a-j
Answers in instructor's manual: 2k-n

2. Punctuate the following sentences.
   (Answers in back of book)
   a. The producers of TV shipboard fantasy shows are reluctant to show the workers who clean repair and operate the ship.
   b. He turns fakes a shot beats the last defender and scores.
   c. Broke dressed in tattered clothes but triumphant, Bill turned up at Shady's Bar one afternoon.
   d. We shucked the oysters the boys peeled the shrimp and Mom steamed the crabs.
   e. Should I stay in study and ace my test, or do up the town socialize till dawn and maybe meet a promising specimen?
   f. I spent my day running to check on the greenhouse then back to see if the kids were safe then out to the barn to check on the cattle.

STEP TWO: READ AND REVISE FOR GRAMMAR AND PUNCTUATION

g. People would ask us whether our pet ferret would bite whether it was house trained and whether we let it run free in the house.
h. Fido's coat was ragged each of his ribs showed plainly along his skinny body and one ear was torn and bloody, but he had made it home.
i. The beach was warm the sand clean and the waves gentle.
j. When we rode the train, we children loved to visit the dining car for the creamiest oatmeal we had ever tasted talk to the other passengers, who often gave us mints and candy or curl up sleepily in the arms of our parents, who now had nothing to do but sit still and hold children on their laps.

(Answers in instructor's manual)

k. The manager was surprised that we had so quickly mopped the floor closed the bar done the dishes and set up the tables for tomorrow's breakfast.
l. Harry ran to get the bikes Mike found some sweaters in the closet Don packed a quick lunch and we were off.
m. We were exhausted by the long treks to the store the demands of the children and the many interruptions to our sleep.
n. To be properly equipped for a fishing trip you need a large yawning tackle box full of sinkers lures and extra line a regulation fishing hat with lures stuck in the band and a pair of green rubber wading boots.

REVISING YOUR OWN WRITING

In the space provided, enter sentences or passages from your own writing where you've missed or misused punctuation with lists or series. Write the correction. Then write five other sen-

LESSON 2P: PUNCTUATE LISTS AND SERIES

tences or passages that follow similar patterns, punctuating them correctly.

Your Sentence(s)

_____
_____
_____
_____

Your Revision

_____
_____
_____
_____

Five Other Sentences in the Same Pattern

_____
_____
_____
_____
_____

GRAMMATICAL TERMS IN THIS LESSON

Verb: The one to four words that name the action or state of being of the subject

Subject: A word or group of words that names the person or thing that is performing the action or that is in the state of being named in the verb

Phrase: A group of related words that does not contain a subject-verb unit

Clause: A subject-verb unit plus that unit's modifiers and complements

STEP TWO: READ AND REVISE FOR GRAMMAR AND PUNCTUATION

Independent Clause: A clause that can stand alone
Coordinate: Similar in form and function
Adjective: A word or group of words that modifies a noun
Run-on Sentence: A group of words punctuated as a single sentence where independent clauses are joined incorrectly with a comma alone (sometimes called a comma splice) or with no punctuation (sometimes called a fused sentence)

LESSON FOR STEP 2Q

USE COLON OR DASH TO ANNOUNCE AN EXPLANATION

PREVIEW OF THE LESSON

The previous lesson showed the use of the colon to introduce a list. The colon has one other function in interior sentence punctuation: to announce an explanation, as illustrated in this sentence. The last part of the sentence *(to announce)* explains what the *other function* is. A dash could also be used. This lesson shows how to use both marks. See how this lesson fits within the process of interior sentence punctuation—Figure 2K.1, p. 332.

Definition: A COLON is two dots (:).

Definition: A DASH, on the typewriter, is two hyphens with no space between them and no space before or after them (word—word).

STEP TWO: READ AND REVISE FOR GRAMMAR AND PUNCTUATION

USE A COLON OR A DASH INTERCHANGEABLY TO ANNOUNCE AN EXPLANATION

A colon or dash means "Explanation to follow" or "Here's what this means." Wherever you could insert such a phrase, it is fairly safe to use a colon or dash.

Colons may only be used singly, not in pairs. Thus the colon should be used only when the explanation is the last thing in the sentence. Dashes may be used either singly or in pairs. Thus if you have an explanation that is sandwiched between two parts of the same sentence, use two dashes to set it off.

The colon is limited in function, used only to announce and explain and to introduce a list—Lesson 2P. (Colons also appear in certain special forms such as citations). Do not use a colon in place of a semicolon or comma in other situations. The dash has one other use—to set off elements that sharply interrupt the flow of the sentence (see Lesson 2N).

The following are examples of the use of the colon and the dash to announce an explanation:

> *The fate of the play's hero is sealed: he has sinned and must die.*
> *The fate of the play's hero is sealed—he has sinned and must die.*
> *The inadequacies of the Articles of Confederation became increasingly clear during one event in particular: Shays's Rebellion in North Hampton, Massachusetts.*
> *The inadequacies of the Articles of Confederation became increasingly clear during one event in particular—Shays's Rebellion in North Hampton, Massachusetts.*
> *Anna's deepest wish—to marry Marvin—is not apparent until the very end of the play.*

Dashes are the only option when the explanation has other parts of the sentence on both sides.

LESSON 2Q: USE COLON OR DASH TO ANNOUNCE AN EXPLANATION

EXERCISES

Answers in back of book: 1a-f
Answers in instructor's manual: 1g-j

1. Punctuate each of the following sentences in two versions—one with a dash and one with a colon. If colons are not possible, explain why not.
   (Answers in back of book)
   a. Universal's best option is to move its plant to a more practical, profitable location Hunt Valley.
   b. We have a serious problem here the attitudes of the workers themselves.
   c. In every village, a healer has cures for everything malaria, dandruff, or the plague.
   d. The senators honored everyone who had helped in the train disaster the towns people, the fire fighters, and the police.
   e. At a resort, there are many ways to earn money while meeting new friends be a lifeguard, a restaurant server, a cashier, or a tour guide.
   f. The one agency that did not participate the National Science Foundation played a supporting role nonetheless.
   (Answers in instructor's manual)
   g. There was only one solution go find Henry.
   h. The kitten had survived experiences that should have killed it abandoned by its mother hungry cold and severely dehydrated.
   i. I was tired of the whole business the dirt the mess the constant bickering and decided to leave.
   j. The thunder always frightened Henry it reminded him of the bombs he had heard dropping around him as a child during the war.

STEP TWO: READ AND REVISE FOR GRAMMAR AND PUNCTUATION

REVISING YOUR OWN WRITING

In the space provided, enter sentences or passages from your own writing where you have missed or misused dashes and colons to introduce an explanation or enumeration. Write the revision. Then write five other sentences that follow similar patterns, punctuating them correctly.

Your Sentence(s)

_____
_____
_____
_____
_____

Your Revision

_____
_____
_____
_____
_____

Five Other Sentences in the Same Pattern

_____
_____
_____
_____
_____

EXERCISES FOR INTERIOR SENTENCE PUNCTUATION (LESSONS 2B, 2K–2Q)

Answers in back of book: 1a-v, 2a-d
Answers in instructor's manual: 1w-cc, 2e-f

1. Punctuate the following passages.
   (Answers in back of book)

LESSON 2Q: USE COLON OR DASH TO ANNOUNCE AN EXPLANATION

a. In the northern woods beech pine and maple are joined by white birches.
b. The slender ghostly birches lean silently together like elders at a town meeting.
c. Walking among birches in the winter with snow sifting silently down is like walking into some ancient magic circle.
d. Discovered quite recently the Amsterdam albatross *Diomedea amsterdamensis* is considered one of the rarest seabirds in the world.
e. Contrary to what you might think the Amsterdam albatross does not live in the Netherlands but on tiny remote Amsterdam Island in the southern Indian Ocean.
f. Nesting in the peat bogs the albatross mating pairs of whom there are only fifteen raise one chick every two years.
g. The albatross have slick black backs with white furry feathered edges like capes with white fur linings.
h. Pastrami is basically beef shoulder often kosher cured in brine and spices smoked and finally steamed.
i. Pastrami has a checkered past Romanians Turks and Greeks all claim to have invented it.
j. A delicatessen in my neighborhood in New York City makes its own pastrami from an old Romanian recipe as much as 2,000 pounds of it per week.
k. Maritoni's pastrami is delicious subtly spiced not too salty and buttery in texture.
l. When I asked the owner Joe Maritoni what his secret was he said it's the New York City tap water used in curing.
m. Lest you think he was making that up I read recently in *Consumer Reports* that in fact New York City tap water is as pure as any bottled mineral water on the market.
n. The Southeast's devastating record-breaking drought dried up wells pushed thermometers to 100 degrees and claimed more than forty human lives.

STEP TWO: READ AND REVISE FOR GRAMMAR AND PUNCTUATION

o. The damage by August of 1986 was disastrous more than $2 billion in agriculture and other business losses.
p. The states affected were the Carolinas Alabama Georgia Maryland Delaware Virginia West Virginia and Tennessee.
q. The drying up of hay and grains left farmers with little to feed their cattle.
r. However in addition to suffering and frustration for humans and animals alike the drought of 1986 surprisingly produced a great old fashioned neighborly outpouring of helpfulness that surprised many Americans.
s. Farmers in the midwest which had not been hit by the drought began sending bales of hay by the tens of thousands to their fellow farmers in the Southeast.
t. When I was young my uncle a farmer who had increasingly severe arthritis was one spring unable to plow his fields.
u. His neighbors as a matter of course simply came over and plowed and planted for him it was the custom in that small rural community to help each other.
v. What made the 1986 gifts so amazing is that people in one part of the country themselves hard pressed as most farmers are these days sent precious resources to folks they didn't even know folks in a different state.

(Answers in instructor's manual)

w. Although a panda mother often gives birth to two cubs she usually abandons one of them without attempting to care for it a waste that seems cruel until one knows more about how pandas among nature's most solicitous mothers raise their young.
x. For the entire first month of its life the infant panda is held yes literally held by its mother no matter whether she is sleeping sitting or feeding.
y. The mother holds the infant in her broad hairy paw and if she relaxes her hold squeezes too tightly or makes the

LESSON 2Q: USE COLON OR DASH TO ANNOUNCE AN EXPLANATION

       little one uncomfortable the baby lets out a tremendous squawk.
- z. Panda babies which are more than two months old before they can even stand up stay with their mothers for a year and a half.
- aa. Because a mother panda can raise a cub only once every two years the birth of a second cub is a kind of insurance if the first cub is born dead the mother will raise the second.
- bb. Much of what is known about pandas in the wild has been gathered by researchers who catch pandas in log traps tranquilize them fit them with radio collars release them and then follow their movements by radio signals.
- cc. The furry cuddly panda can be as dangerous as any wild animal experienced animal researchers are wary not complacent as they observe track and study the animals.

2. In each group, use all the ideas in some form to compose one sentence. Punctuate appropriately.
(Sample sentences in back of book)
- a. You are selecting an award
You must keep in mind
Your award travel must originate in the U.S. Canada or Hong Kong.
- b. The U.N. has a charter
The charter places responsibility
The responsibility is for keeping peace
The responsibility is on the Security Council
The Security Council has five members
The five members are wartime allies
The five members are the U.S. the U.S.S.R. Britain France and China
- c. Ship owners lose between $5,000 and $20,000 a day
Ship owners lose the money when they operate vessels
The vessels are idle
The vessels are loaded

STEP TWO: READ AND REVISE FOR GRAMMAR AND PUNCTUATION

     Some of the owners begin furloughing crews
     Some of the owners begin tying up their ships
d. This is an example
    Chess strategy is controlled by a computer program
    The strategy is long-term
    The program is called Oracle
    The program was created by Hans Berliner
    Hans Berliner is an artificial-intelligence expert
    Hans Berliner is a former world correspondence-chess champion
(Sample sentences in instructor's manual)
e. The craft had room
    The craft was a World War II landing craft
    The craft was battered
    The craft had room for half a dozen vehicles
    The vehicles included my rental car
    The craft had room for about fifty people
    The craft had room for the peoples' assorted animals
    The animals were goats chickens mules and a cow
    The cow had a calf
f. It was shortly before the storm
    David Hiser and I were rafting down the Uma River
    David Hiser is a photographer
    The Uma River forms a stretch of border between Mexico and Guatemala
    The stretch of border is isolated
    The Uma River is narrow
    The Uma River is turbulent
    The map that shows this stretch of the border is on p. 42

QUOTATIONS

LESSON FOR
STEP 2R

PUNCTUATE WITHIN AND AROUND QUOTATIONS

PREVIEW OF THE LESSON

This lesson shows how to identify everything in your writing that must be enclosed in quotation marks, as well as words and passages that need underlining or citations. These decisions are summarized in Figure 2R.1. The lesson also shows how to indicate changes, additions, and deletions within quotations, and punctuate accurately around and within quotation marks.

This lesson has four main sections. You may follow them as steps in a sequence or use them to locate parts of the lesson you need.

1. Identify material that needs to be in quotation marks.
2. Indicate changes, additions, and deletions within quotations.
3. Punctuate around and within quotation marks.
4. Establish spacing and margins for quotations.

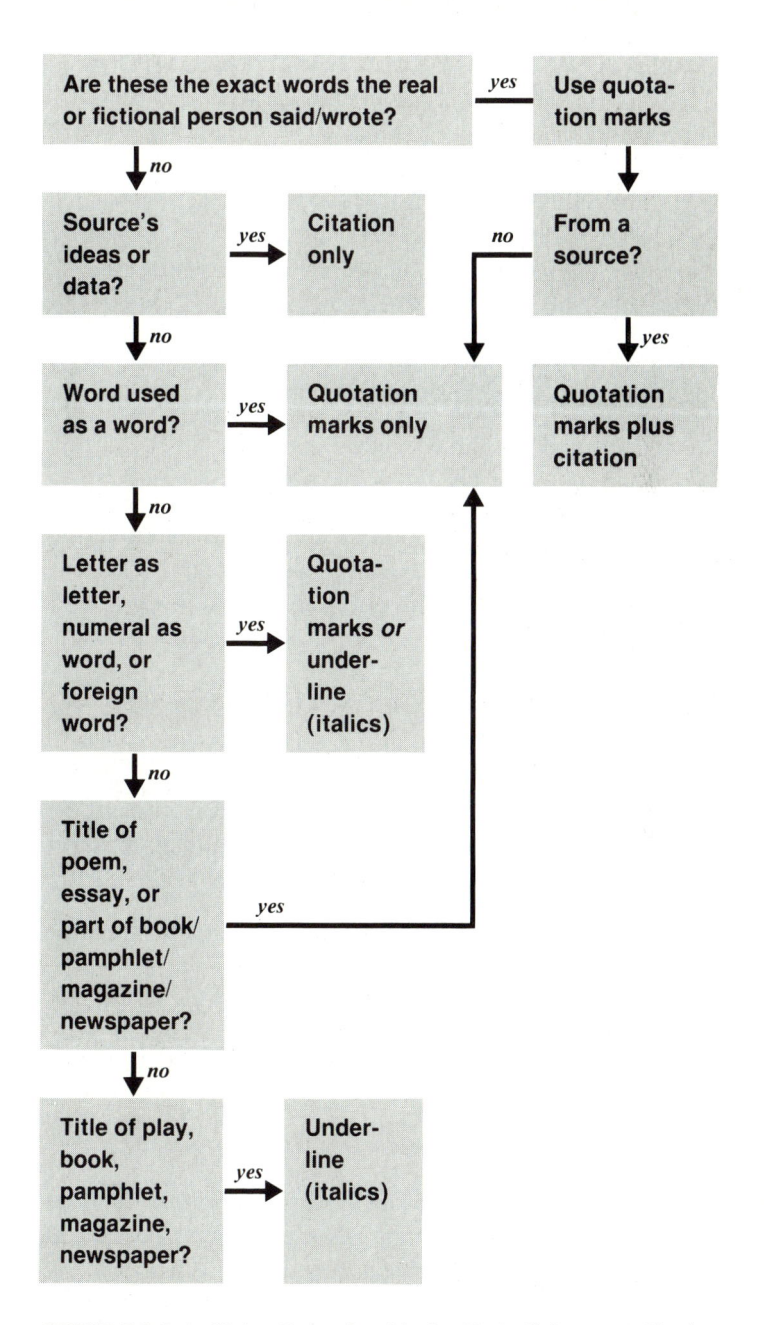

LESSON 2R: PUNCTUATE WITHIN AND AROUND QUOTATIONS

FIGURE 2 R.1 Using Quotation Marks, Underlining, and Citations

STEP TWO: READ AND REVISE FOR GRAMMAR AND PUNCTUATION

1. IDENTIFY MATERIAL THAT NEEDS TO BE IN QUOTATION MARKS

DIRECT QUOTATIONS TAKE QUOTATION MARKS; INDIRECT QUOTATIONS DO NOT

Definition: A DIRECT QUOTATION is the words the person actually said.

Definition: An INDIRECT QUOTATION is the writer's version of the words the person actually said.

Direct quotation: "I will go to the store."

Indirect quotation: He said he would go to the store.

The words of a direct quotation are set off with quotation marks. The words of an indirect quotation are not. The next section of this lesson explains applications and fine points of this basic rule.

WORDS OF CHARACTERS IN FICTIONAL DIALOGUE TAKE QUOTATION MARKS

In writing fictional dialogue, put quotation marks around the words a character speaks. All words inside the quotation marks must be the exact words the person said or would say:

Incorrect: Larry said "he would approach the director tomorrow."

Correct (indirect quotation): Larry said he would approach the director tomorrow. OR

Also Correct (direct quotation): Larry said, "I will approach the director tomorrow."

An advantage of direct quotation is that it can add vividness to your fictional dialogue. Skilled writers generally use direct quotation generously in fictional or personal narratives.

LESSON 2R: PUNCTUATE WITHIN AND AROUND QUOTATIONS

DIRECTLY QUOTED THOUGHTS TAKE QUOTATION MARKS

Reproducing a person's thoughts can be handled as though the person was actually speaking. If the actual words of the thought are reproduced, use quotation marks. If the thought but not the exact words are reproduced, do not use quotation marks.

Correct: I wondered, "Why are we having turkey?"
Correct: I wondered why we were having turkey.

DIRECT QUOTATION OF A SOURCE TAKES QUOTATION MARKS

The general rule is that when you are using words that someone else has said or written, you may not copy the words exactly without enclosing them in quotation marks. You must also include an acknowledgment of the original author. In some types of writing, that acknowledgment will be informal; in other types, you must use a formal citation. (See a handbook appropriate for your discipline.) The same rules for a written source apply also to a person's spoken words that you have taken down or taperecorded in a conversation or interview. Suppose, for example, that you have attended, or read the text of, a press conference in which the mayor said these words: "The savings and loan crisis is a genuine threat to the economy of the city." The following are some ways you might use the mayor's statement in your own writing.

> ***At the May 4 press conference, the mayor said the savings and loan crisis was dangerous.***

You have used the same common term, "savings and loan crisis," as the mayor, but you need not use quotation marks for common terms unless for some reason your readers need to know that the mayor used that term. As long as you use only common terms, not important terms, and as long as you do not

STEP TWO: READ AND REVISE FOR GRAMMAR AND PUNCTUATION

use more than a few words in a sequence from the source, you need no quotation marks.

At the May 4 press conference, the mayor for the first time referred to the savings and loan situation as a "crisis."

The word "crisis" is in quotation marks in this sentence because the reader needs to know that "crisis" was the exact word the mayor used. When you use even a single crucial or special word, use quotation marks.

At the press conference, the mayor said the savings and loan crisis was "a genuine threat to the economy of the city."

Since the writer has used more than the common terms, the mayor's exact words must be placed in quotation marks. The common term "savings and loan crisis," unless it is important, may be left out of the quotation marks if that seems more easily readable within your sentence. In the example, the writer wanted to begin the quotation marks after *was,* which is different from the quoted source. The word *was* may not be included in quotation marks unless it is marked by brackets (as explained later in this lesson) because the mayor did not say *was.*

Correct: At the May 4 press conference, the mayor said, "The savings and loan crisis is a genuine threat to the economy of the city."

Correct: By May 4, it was clear to the mayor that "the savings and loan crisis [was] a genuine threat to the economy of the city."

Incorrect: At the May 4 press conference, the mayor said the savings and loan crisis was a genuine threat to the economy of the city.

The incorrect version uses more of the mayor's words than merely the common phrases. Quotation marks are required.

LESSON 2R: PUNCTUATE WITHIN AND AROUND QUOTATIONS

For most academic writing, all of the versions of the savings and loan crisis sentence, even the ones that legitimately use no quotation marks, would need a footnote or other appropriate forms of citation.

COPY THE QUOTATION EXACTLY

Within a quotation, the writer must copy *everything* just the way it is. For example, in the following quotation, the writer must copy the commas within the quotation, even though those commas violate today's comma rules (Lesson 2K). For guidelines about making and indicating changes, see the following pages.

Original Source (The United States Constitution): A well regulated militia, being necessary to the security of a free State, the right of the people to keep and bear arms, shall not be infringed.

Direct Quotation: The United States Constitution guarantees that "the right of the people to keep and bear arms, shall not be infringed." (The quotation should be followed by a citation or footnote.)

USE SEPARATE SETS OF QUOTATION MARKS FOR INTERRUPTED QUOTATIONS

If you interrupt a quotation with words of your own, use a separate set of quotation marks for each part of the quotation.

"The improvement is impressive," said the governor, "but we cannot afford to be complacent."

STEP TWO: READ AND REVISE FOR GRAMMAR AND PUNCTUATION

CHECK ACCURACY OF QUOTATIONS FROM A SOURCE

Carefully check the accuracy of your quotations. If you have not checked with extreme care when you first copied the quotation, or if you've since recopied it, go back to the original from which you took the quotation and check every word and punctuation mark carefully.

Two good ways to avoid introducing typing errors into quotations as you reinsert them into successive drafts is to use a word processor or to type/write the quotation onto a notecard and lightly tape the original card into place in each successive draft. For both these methods, you should check for accuracy after you've typed from the original copy. Once you've finished drafting your paper, if you have not recopied the quotation, you can rely on its accuracy. If you have recopied quotations, however, go back to the original source or to your last checked copy to check accuracy before making your final copy of the paper. Protecting the accuracy of your quotations is summarized in Figure 2R.2.

A WORD USED AS A WORD TAKES QUOTATION MARKS OR UNDERLINING

A word used as a word may be enclosed in quotation marks or may be underlined to indicate italics. Choose either system, but follow the same policy throughout the whole paper.

The word "please" seldom falls on the ears of a fast food restaurant worker.
OR The word please seldom falls on the ears of a fast food restaurant worker.

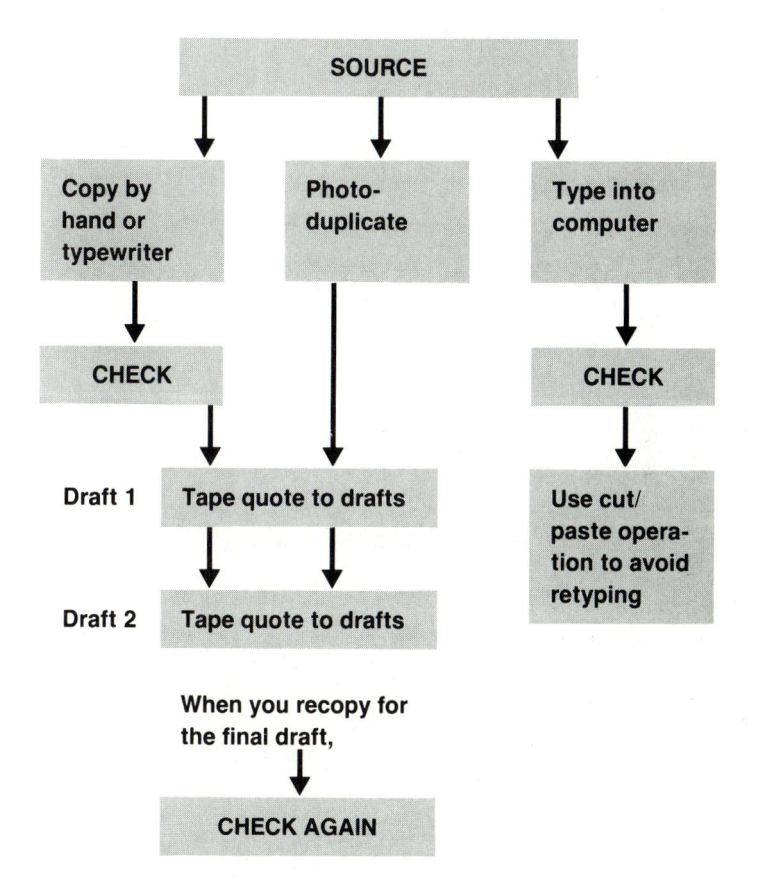

LESSON 2R: PUNCTUATE WITHIN AND AROUND QUOTATIONS

FIGURE 2 R.2 Protect the Accuracy of Quotations

QUOTATION MARKS CALL SPECIAL ATTENTION TO A WORD

You may want to set off a word because it is slang, or because it is being used in a special way, or because you want to call special attention to it.

> *Once the officer found the boy's "Teddy" in a nearby bush, the youngster stopped crying.*
>
> *Once a month they have "town leave," which means they can take the bus into town for the afternoon, but must be back by supper time.*

LETTERS, NUMERALS, AND FOREIGN WORDS TAKE QUOTATION MARKS OR UNDERLINING

Use quotation marks or underlining for a letter used as a letter, a numeral used as a word, or a foreign word. You may choose either quotation marks or underlining, but be consistent.

> *Please change "t" to "ed," and write "3" instead of "4."*
> *OR Please change <u>t</u> to <u>ed</u> and write <u>3</u> instead of <u>4</u>.*
> *The Pope spoke <u>ex cathedra</u>*
> *OR The Pope spoke "ex cathedra."*

SOME TITLES TAKE QUOTATION MARKS; SOME ARE UNDERLINED

Underline the title of a play or of any work published as a book or booklet with its own covers.

> *Shakespeare's <u>Hamlet</u> and Hemingway's <u>Farewell to Arms</u> were my favorite works in high school.*

Use quotation marks for any work that is published as part of a book: a poem, song, short story in a collection, or essay.

> *In "To My Last Duchess," we learn about the Duchess only through the voice of her murderer.*

For more on treating titles, see Step 3B.

EXERCISES

Answers in back of book: 1a
Answers in instructor's manual: 1b

1. In the following passage, place quotation marks or underlining where needed.

   (Answers in back of book)

   a. In a 1966 study, Schevill and Watkins recorded sounds they called strident screams from killer whales. Jones, in 1964, describing an attack by killer whales upon beluga whales, said, The beluga were torn to pieces. Other observers have commented that most other types of whales flee at the approach of killer whales. When the ice closes up, a situation known as a savssat in Greenland, killer whales have a field day because other whales are trapped and cannot flee.

   (Answers in instructor's manual)

   b. Hikers on the Appalachian Trail are greeted by the so-called ice cream lady, who has handed out more than a thousand free cones. One hiker told me, It warms your heart to see people help each other in good, old-fashioned ways.

2. INDICATE CHANGES, ADDITIONS, AND DELETIONS WITHIN QUOTATIONS

CHANGES THAT REQUIRE NO INDICATION

Anything that appears within quotation marks must be an *exact* copy of the original, with the three following exceptions. (See original, p. 397.)

1. You may change a lower case letter to a capital letter, or vice versa, in accordance with your own sentence:

"The right of the people to keep and bear arms" is guaranteed by the U.S. Constitution.

(Writer may change lower case *t* in the original Constitution to capital *T* without notice.)

2. When your own sentence ends, but the quotation does not, you may add a period, provided that doing so does not change the original writer's meaning.

The U.S. Constitution guarantees "the right of the people to keep and bear arms."

(Writer may add period after "arms" without notice.)

Only if it is important for the reader to know that the original author's sentence does not end with the part you quote, use ellipses—spaced dots. Use four spaced dots to indicate that the sentence continues (bear arms. . . ."), or three spaced dots to indicate that the sentence began before the words you quoted (. . . bear arms).

3. When the words you quote end with a mark of punctuation, you may change or omit that punctuation mark, in accordance with the demands of your own sentence.

Source:	Don't buy another computer.
Quoting the source:	"Don't buy another computer," the consultant advised.
	(The final period in the source changes to a comma without notice.)

Outside of the three exceptions, you may add, delete, or change parts of the quotation *only* if you so indicate to the reader by means of brackets or ellipses. The procedures for indicating changes, additions, and deletions within quotation marks are summarized in Figure 2R.3.

LESSON 2R: PUNCTUATE WITHIN AND AROUND QUOTATIONS

Have you changed the source by ...

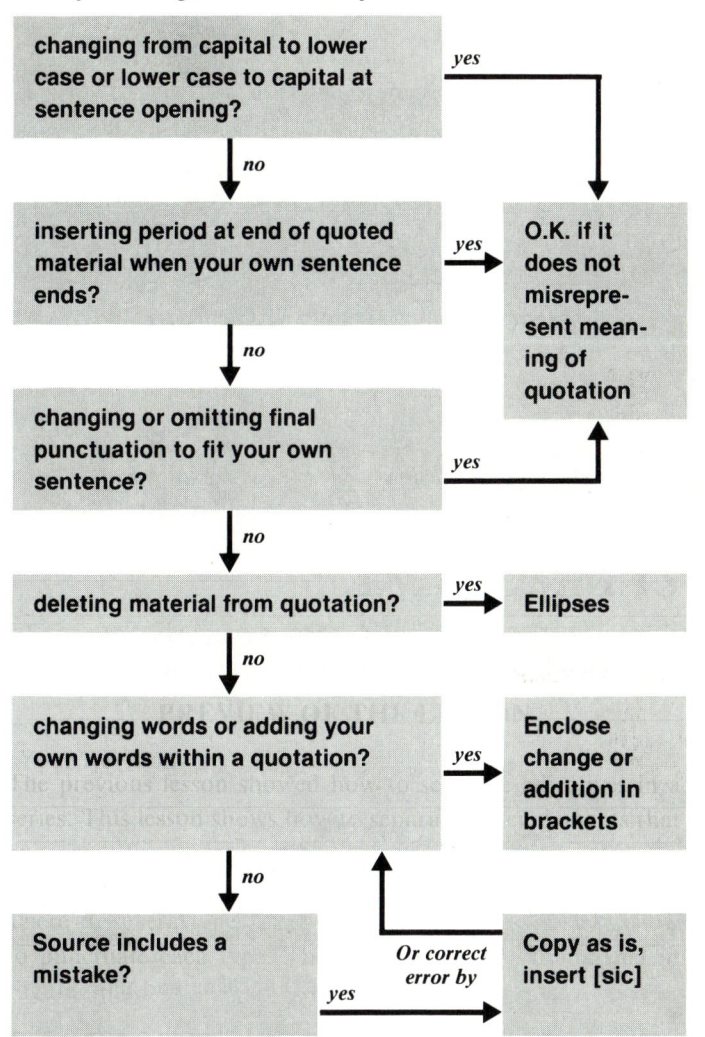

```
┌─────────────────────────────┐
│ changing from capital to    │   yes
│ lower case or lower case    │ ─────┐
│ to capital at sentence      │      │
│ opening?                    │      │
└──────────────┬──────────────┘      │
               │ no                  │
               ▼                     ▼
┌─────────────────────────────┐   ┌──────────────┐
│ inserting period at end of  │yes│ O.K. if it   │
│ quoted material when your   │──▶│ does not     │
│ own sentence ends?          │   │ misrepre-    │
└──────────────┬──────────────┘   │ sent mean-   │
               │ no               │ ing of       │
               ▼                  │ quotation    │
┌─────────────────────────────┐   │              │
│ changing or omitting final  │   │              │
│ punctuation to fit your own │yes│              │
│ sentence?                   │──▶│              │
└──────────────┬──────────────┘   └──────────────┘
               │ no
               ▼
┌─────────────────────────────┐
│ deleting material from      │yes   ┌──────────┐
│ quotation?                  │─────▶│ Ellipses │
└──────────────┬──────────────┘      └──────────┘
               │ no
               ▼
┌─────────────────────────────┐      ┌──────────────┐
│ changing words or adding    │ yes  │ Enclose      │
│ your own words within a     │─────▶│ change or    │
│ quotation?                  │      │ addition in  │
└──────────────┬──────────────┘      │ brackets     │
               │ no                  └──────────────┘
               ▼
┌─────────────────────────────┐  Or correct  ┌──────────────┐
│ Source includes a mistake?  │  error by    │ Copy as is,  │
│                             │─────────────▶│ insert [sic] │
└─────────────────────────────┘  yes         └──────────────┘
```

FIGURE 2 R.3 Changes, Additions, and Deletions within Quotations

INDICATE DELETIONS IN QUOTED MATERIAL BY SPACED DOTS (ELLIPSES)

Writers use a series of spaced dots to indicate deletions from quotations. If one or more periods are included in what you delete, use four spaced dots; otherwise, use three.

Original Source: [Thomas Jefferson's assessment of George Washington's character]: In public, when called on for a sudden opinion, he was unready, short and embarrassed. Yet he wrote readily, rather diffusely, in an easy and correct style. This he had acquired by conversation with the world, for his education was merely reading, writing and common arithmetic, to which he added surveying at a later day.

Quotation with Deletions: Thomas Jefferson said, "In public, when called on for a sudden opinion, he was unready.... Yet he wrote readily . . . in an easy and correct style."

Notice that the comma Jefferson inserted after *unready* is replaced by the dots. Do not insert punctuation before the dots or between the last dot and the next quoted word.

YOUR ADDITIONS AND EXPLANATIONS WITHIN A QUOTATION ARE BRACKETED

You may want to shorten a quotation by paraphrasing some of the interior words, or you may want to insert an explanation within the quotation. Such additions and explanations must be placed in brackets: [ ]

George Washington's education, said Jefferson, was "merely reading, writing . . . common arithmetic [and] surveying.

The *and* serves as a paraphrase of the omitted material. No dots are necessary, because the brackets tell the reader there has been a deletion of some of the original author's words.

LESSON 2R: PUNCTUATE WITHIN AND AROUND QUOTATIONS

> *Jefferson describes Washington's formal boyhood education as "reading, writing and common arithmetic [not including fractions or geometry, which Washington learned on his own], to which he added surveying at a later day."*

(The writer adds an explanation not found in the original source.)

PUNCTUATION AROUND AND WITHIN ELLIPSES AND BRACKETS

Do not use punctuation before the ellipsis dots or between the last dot and the first word after the ellipsis. Punctuation around brackets follows the same rules as punctuation around parentheses (Lesson 2N, p. 360).

> *Jefferson describes Washington's formal boyhood education as "reading, writing and common arithmetic [he learned fractions and geometry on his own], to which he added surveying at a later day." [Washington was a paid surveyor's assistant by age 15.]*

USE [SIC] TO MARK A SOURCE'S MISTAKES IN QUOTED MATERIAL

When, in something you are quoting, the original author has made a mistake, or what the reader may take to be a mistake, you may change it, provided you put all the changed words in brackets. Alternately, copy it as it is, and, to let the reader know you've copied accurately, put the bracketed word [sic] just after the mistake.

> *Johnson's log reads, "Sent the files to Hanson via Express Male [sic], July 16."*

STEP TWO: READ AND REVISE FOR GRAMMAR AND PUNCTUATION

EXERCISES

(Note: Exercise 1 appears earlier in the chapter.)
Answers in back of book: 2a
Answers in instructor's manual: 2b

2. The following is an original passage and a condensation. The original is from *The Prince,* by the Italian Renaissance statesman, Niccolo Machiavelli, who is giving advice to monarchs. Correctly punctuate and capitalize the additions, deletions, and changes.

Original: Hence a prince should take great care never to drop a word that does not seem imbued with the five good qualities noted above; to anyone who sees or hears him, he should appear all compassion, all honor, all humanity, all integrity, all religion. Nothing is more necessary than to seem to have this last virtue. Men in general judge more by the sense of sight than by the sense of touch, because everyone can see but only a few can test by feeling. Everyone sees what you seem to be, few know what you really are; and those few do not dare take a stand against the general opinion, supported by the majesty of the government.
(Answers in back of book)

a. Machiavelli advises that the prince should seem to have religion. The word seem is important. Machiavelli has little faith in peoples' ability to discern show from reality. He says, everyone can see but only a few can test.

(Answers in instructor's manual)

b. Machiavelli defines five good qualities that a prince should appear to have. Notice he says appear. Cynically, Machiavelli believes that men in general judge more by the sense of sight than by testing what is really true.

3. PUNCTUATE AROUND AND WITHIN QUOTATION MARKS

The next section of this lesson shows how to punctuate around and within quotation marks. The procedures are summarized in Figure 2R.4.

USE COMMA OR COLON TO SEPARATE INTRODUCTORY WORDS FROM A QUOTATION

Use a colon if the introductory statement is complete and if "explanation follows" can logically be inserted after the introductory statement. This rule is a combination of the rule about using a colon to introduce a list (Lesson 2P) and an explanation (Lesson 2Q).

He said it again: "Andy, come here."

USE A COMMA TO SEPARATE ALL OTHER INTRODUCTORY WORDS FROM A QUOTATION

If you do not use a *colon* for the reasons explained in the preceding rule, then use a *comma* to separate your introductory words from a quotation. However, note the exception explained later in this lesson.

He said, "Andy, come here."

USE A COMMA TO SEPARATE A QUOTATION FROM THE WRITER'S SENTENCE

The two previous rules explain how to handle your introductory words that appear before a quotation. When your words

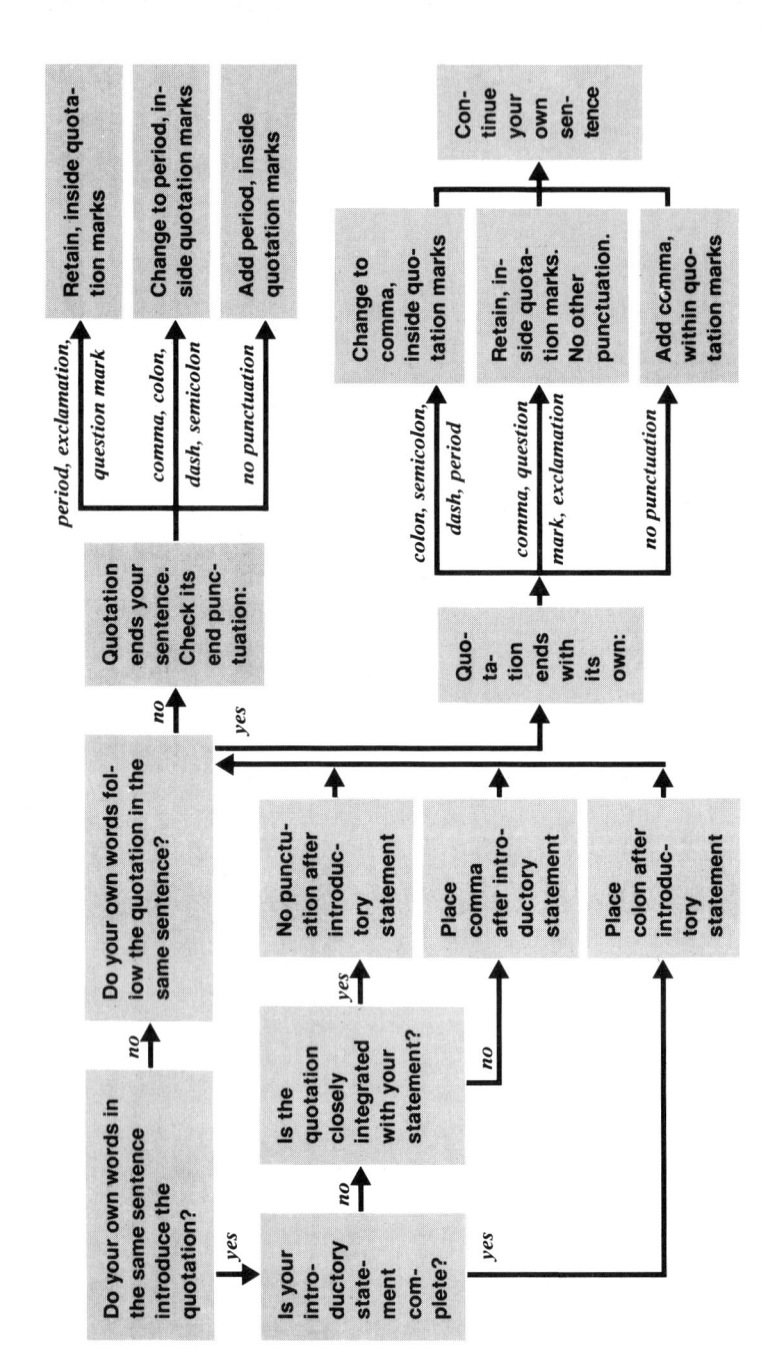

FIGURE 2 R.4 Punctuating Within and Around Quotation Marks

LESSON 2R: PUNCTUATE WITHIN AND AROUND QUOTATIONS

follow the quotation, likewise use a comma (but note the exceptions explained later).

Source:	The water was shiny with grease.
Quoting the source:	"The water was shiny with grease," reported the observers after the accident.
Quoting the source:	Observers reported, "The water was shiny with grease."

EXCEPTIONS TO THE COMMA RULE

There are two exceptions to the use of commas between your words and a quotation:

1. Do not use a comma when the quotation ends with a question mark or exclamation point.

"Is the foreign minister here?" asked the ambassador.

The comma after *here* has been replaced by the question mark.

2. Do not use commas to separate closely integrated quotations.
   When the quoted words are an integral part of a writer's sentence, do not separate them with commas unless regular punctuation rules call for commas.

Shaw said he was "humbled and honored" by the prize.

The quotation is closely integrated, so do not use commas.

Shaw said he was "humbled and honored," and he attributed his success to the help of his colleagues.
A comma is required by rules for joining independent clauses, Lesson 2B.

STEP TWO: READ AND REVISE FOR GRAMMAR AND PUNCTUATION

PLACE ALL COMMAS AND PERIODS INSIDE THE QUOTATION MARKS

The senator growled, "No comment."
"No comment," growled the senator.
I wanted to ask him whether he knew anything about the so-called "race horse scandal," but he brushed past me so quickly I had no chance.

(The comma is dictated by the joining of two independent clauses, but it is placed *inside* the quotation marks.)
The letter "g," which is more difficult for children to form, is postponed until later.

PLACE COLONS, QUESTION MARKS, AND EXCLAMATION POINTS OUTSIDE OR INSIDE QUOTATION MARKS

Place colons, question marks, and exclamation points outside the quotation marks when they belong to your sentence, but inside when they belong to the quoted source.

Source:	You're a crook!
Quoting the source:	"You're a crook!" he screamed.
Quoting the source:	He screamed, "You're a crook!"
Source:	I never knew him.
Quoting the source:	Did she say, "I never knew him"?
Source:	Is the acid solution ready?
Quoting the source:	The office asked, "Is the acid solution ready?"
	(Question is the original speaker's.)

LESSON 2R: PUNCTUATE WITHIN AND AROUND QUOTATIONS

Source: We located signs of illegal hunting even in the most isolated areas.

Quoting the source: The rangers reported, "We located signs of illegal hunting even in the most isolated areas": Baffin Bay, East Greenland, and the Davis Straits.
(The colon belongs to the writer's sentence.)

WHEN QUOTED MATERIAL IS A COMPLETE SENTENCE, CAPITALIZE ITS FIRST WORD

This rule applies even when the quoted sentence is merely a part of your sentence. In the previous example, *We* remains capitalized in the quotation because it is the first word of a quotation that is a complete sentence.

USE SINGLE QUOTATION MARKS FOR A QUOTATION WITHIN A QUOTATION

When your source quotes another source or uses dialogue, change the source's double quotation marks to single quotation marks. (Use the apostrophe key on your typewriter.)

Source: The old proverb "A penny saved is a penny earned" does not lead to prosperity in today's economy.

Quoting the source: Irving Fischer remarks, "The old proverb 'A penny saved is a penny earned' does not lead to prosperity in today's economy."

STEP TWO: READ AND REVISE FOR GRAMMAR AND PUNCTUATION

EXERCISES

Answers in back of book: 3a
Answers in instructor's manual: 3b

3. Insert punctuation and capitalization in the following passages.

   (Answers in back of book)
   a. Companies in California have found that so called "pickling acid" which is needed in metal-processing plants to remove scale, could be mixed with zinc sulfate and used to enrich citrus orchards. Despite its high cost, "the method holds great promise for recycling this toxic waste" said one plant manager.

   (Answers in instructor's manual)
   b. The new police commissioner announced his goal was to "reduce crime in the streets" Jones, however, was skeptical "how can he reduce crime in the streets when the budget forces cuts in police personnel" he said.

WHEN QUOTING POETRY, INDICATE LINE DIVISIONS

Whenever you are quoting more than one line of poetry, you must indicate the line divisions. You do this in one of two ways, depending on the length of the quotation. If the quotation is three lines of poetry or less, incorporate it within your text, using quotation marks as you would for any other quotation, and indicating the line breaks with a slash mark. (Put a space on each side of the slash.)

   Source:
   When I consider how my light is spent
     Ere half my days, in this dark world and wide,

LESSON 2R: PUNCTUATE WITHIN AND AROUND QUOTATIONS

> And that one talent which is death to hide,
>   Lodged with me useless, though my soul more bent
> To serve therewith my Maker, and present
>   My true account, lest he returning chide;
> "Doth God exact day-labor, light denied?"
>   I fondly ask; but Patience to prevent
> That murmur, soon replies, "God doth not need
>   Either man's work or his own gifts; who best
> Bear his mild yoke, they serve him best. His state
> Is kingly. Thousands at his bidding speed
>   And post o'er land and ocean without rest:
> They also serve who only stand and wait."
>   —John Milton,
>   "When I Consider How My Light Is Spent"

Quoting the Source: Milton's poem opens with a lament on his blindness, which has struck "Ere half my days." The speaker makes an excuse: "'Doth God exact day-labor, light denied?' / I fondly ask." The rest of the poem is an answer to that question.

Because the writer uses quotation marks, Milton's quotation marks change to single quotation marks. Because it is not important for the reader to know that the quoted part ends in mid-sentence, the writer replaces Milton's semicolon with a period for the writer's own sentence.

When you are quoting more than three lines of a poem, copy the lines exactly as they are in the original, including spacing and indentations. The line that extends farthest to the left in the original poem should be ten spaces from the left margin of your paper. If that spacing makes the poem look unbalanced, however, indent fewer spaces. Do not use quotation marks. If the poem contains quotation marks, copy them exactly. Double space between the poem and your paper. Also double space between the lines of the poem, triple spacing between stanzas.

STEP TWO: READ AND REVISE FOR GRAMMAR AND PUNCTUATION

Quoting the Source: Milton's poem opens with a description of the poet's state: he is blind, rendering useless the one talent—his writing—that he most wants to use in serving his maker. The middle of the poem is the poet's excuse for giving up and the answer to that excuse:

"Doth God exact day-labor, light denied?"
I fondly ask; but Patience to prevent
That murmur, soon replies, "God doth not need
Either man's work or his own gifts. . . .
They also serve who only stand and wait."

4. ESTABLISH SPACING AND MARGINS FOR QUOTATIONS

INDENT TEN SPACES FOR QUOTATIONS OF MORE THAN FOUR TYPED LINES

If your quotation is more than four typed lines in your own paper, indent the quotation ten spaces from the left margin. Type it double-spaced. Do not use quotation marks; the indenting shows the reader that the material is quoted. If you are quoting only a single paragraph or part of a paragraph, do not indent the first line more than the rest. If you are quoting more than one paragraph, indent the first line of each paragraph fifteen spaces. If the section you are quoting contains a quotation, use double quotation marks.

> Boswell draws a charming picture of the great Samual Johnson awakened by his friends for a midnight lark, just like any college student today:

LESSON 2R: PUNCTUATE WITHIN AND AROUND QUOTATIONS

> One night...about three in the morning, [two of Johnson's friends decided] to go and knock up Johnson, and see if they could prevail on him to join them in a ramble. They rapped violently at the door of his chambers...till at last he appeared in his shirt, with his little black wig on top of his head....he smiled, and with great good humor agreed to their proposal: "What, is it you, you dogs! I'll have a frisk with you." He was soon dressed, and they sallied forth.

EXERCISES

4. Using the Milton poem quoted in this section, write your own explanation in which you incorporate a quotation from the poem of three lines or less, and one of more than three lines. Also incorporate some lines that include the words that Milton encloses in quotation marks and some lines that he does not enclose in quotation marks.

EXERCISES FOR ALL OF STEP 2R

Answers in back of book: 5a
Answers in instructor's manual: 5b

5. In the following passages, add quotation marks and other punctuation and capitalization within and around the quotation marks as needed. Sentences are numbered for reference.

STEP TWO: READ AND REVISE FOR GRAMMAR AND PUNCTUATION

(Answers in back of book)

a. (1)On a cold morning in late October of last year, I heard, through the buzz of my hairdryer, the disc jockey of my favorite radio station blare out something about Black River High School. (2)I wonder why he's talking about Black River I said to myself as I turned off the hairdryer to find out why the D.J. was mentioning my school. (3)Black River quarterback, Edward Gladstone, was shot and killed last night in his Montego home the announcer continued in a monotone. (4)Edward Gladstone, Edward Gladstone I pondered, as I reached for my yearbook. (5)I don't know who he is. (6)As I paged through my *Riverdale,* I spotted Gladstone, Edward below a small photograph at the bottom of the page. (7)Oh, yeah I recalled as I glanced at his picture he's the guy who started the fight in the cafeteria last week. (8)It's really a shame. (9)I closed the yearbook and reached for my hairdryer as the thoughts of Edward Gladstone drifted to the back of my mind.

(10)Later that morning as I walked through the front doors of Black River High School and upstairs to my homeroom, I asked myself why is it so quiet (11)Then it hit me that the silence was the students' reaction to Edward Gladstone's death. (12)Groups of girls walked down the hall, huddled together and crying. (13)Boys stood by their lockers without speaking. (14)I found it hard to believe that all these people were so deeply affected by the death of Edward Gladstone. (15)Was I insensitive? (16)I found it even harder to listen to the morning announcements because the girl sitting next to me was whimpering and finding it difficult to catch her breath. (17)I'm sorry about Eddie I whispered to her. (18)How well did you know him? (19)I didn't she

LESSON 2R: PUNCTUATE WITHIN AND AROUND QUOTATIONS

responded sadly but he seemed like such a nice guy. (20)His life ended so quickly and he had so much going for him. (21)I thought it strange that a person unknown to me, who had started a fight in the school cafeteria, could have been so jovial and successful, but I figured it was possible.

(22)I knew it couldn't be possible that Eddie had been an outstanding quarterback, however, which was what the local newspaper said. (23)The team had just had a winless, practically scoreless season, and one of the reasons was what the same newspaper had earlier termed lack of talent. (24)I hadn't even known that Eddie was a member of the team. (25)But after his death, Eddie's athletic ability became legendary. (26)The newspaper mourned Edward Gladstone was an extraordinary quarterback who would have had a very bright future.

(Answers in instructor's manual)

b. [same paper continues] (27)The newspaper also remembered him as, in their words, a fine student with a steady C+ average who was well-liked by all the teachers and administrators. (28)My best friend, a member of the football team, told me that all the team members had had to keep after Eddie to study and complete his homework because he was in danger of failing. (29)He was also often late to practice because he was frequently given detention by his teachers for being disrespectful and using profanity in class. (30)I asked myself why do we have to remember Eddie as something he wasn't?

REVISING YOUR OWN WRITING

In the space provided, enter sentences or passages from your own writing where you have incorrectly punctuated within and around quotations. Write the revision. Then write five other

STEP TWO: READ AND REVISE FOR GRAMMAR AND PUNCTUATION

sentences or passages that follow similar patterns, punctuating them correctly.

Your Sentence(s)

_____
_____
_____
_____
_____
_____

Your Revision

_____
_____
_____
_____
_____

Five Other Sentences in the Same Pattern

_____
_____
_____
_____
_____
_____

GRAMMATICAL TERMS IN THIS LESSON

Direct Quotation: The words the person actually said

Indirect Quotation: The writer's version of the words the person actually said

Ellipses: Spaced dots that indicate deletions within a quotation

Independent Clause: A clause that can stand alone

LESSONS FOR STEP THREE

Spelling, Dates, Names, Titles, and Numbers

LESSON FOR STEP 3A

SPELLING

PREVIEW OF THE LESSON

This lesson gives you strategies for editing your writing effectively for words that you typically misspell. Some people seem to learn spelling automatically and effortlessly, while others can't write a paragraph without having to look up spelling. The difference is not due to intelligence. Some highly intelligent people are poor spellers. The ability to remember the spelling of a word you have read seems to depend on the way in which your eyes and your brain work together in perception. Some people are "wired" to remember spelling easily and some people are not.

In addition, the English language is a hard language for spellers. Some languages, such as French and German, have consistently phonetic spelling—that is, a certain sound or combination of sounds is always spelled the same way. But because English developed by adding words from early French, Anglo-Saxon, Latin, and other languages, a sound may be spelled several different ways. There are general rules that help with English spelling, but each rule has a number of common and important exceptions.

These two factors are the basis for a program to help yourself with spelling: try to improve your ability to register and remember the spelling of words you read, and, second, develop a fast and efficient system for looking up individual words. You can memorize a few of the most useful rules, but you may still have to look up a given word to make sure it's not one of the exceptions to the rules. Thus this section emphasizes perception, memory, and a fast reference system, rather than spelling rules.

IN DRAFTING, FREELY USE WORDS YOU CANNOT SPELL

Your campaign to become a good speller begins at the drafting stage. It's tempting to try to state an idea without using any words you're going to have to check for spelling. But such a practice puts a tight fence around the expansion of your vocabulary and your writing skill, at just the time when you should be pushing beyond old boundaries and experimenting boldly with language. So be bold. In drafting, concentrate on the most precise and effective words. If you can't spell the word, just put down an approximation and go on. If you stop to look it up, you may lose your train of thought. If you think you might later forget to check the spelling, put a check next to the word or underline it as a reminder. The time to check spelling is when you polish your final draft. At the drafting stage, deliberately tell your spelling worries to keep quiet.

USE A COMPUTER SPELL CHECK

If you use a word processor for your writing, investigate spellers. Sometimes a spelling program is part of a larger text analysis program (See Appendix A). Some spelling programs come attached to word processing packages, while others are sold separately.

A speller selects possibly misspelled words for you to check. But the speller can only identify those words that are contained in its "dictionary." Your speller may have a large or small dictionary, and the words in that dictionary may be more or less applicable to the writing you do. Thus if you are buying your own speller, be sure to examine what kind of dictionary it has, and for what kinds of writing the dictionary was developed and intended.

No dictionary will have all the words you use. Thus the program will *flag* a word—say, the name of your college—that is actually spelled correctly, just because that word is not in the computer's factory-made dictionary. Nearly all spellers, however, let you add words into the dictionary. Be sure to add new words systematically to your speller. That way, gradually you build a speller that accepts words you use and that flags only genuine misspellings. When you add a word to your speller's dictionary, be *sure* it is spelled correctly.

A limitation of some spellers is that when your misspelled word forms another word, the speller may accept it. For example, if the situation demands *there* but you write *their,* both are legitimate words (they are called *homonyms*—words that sound alike but are spelled differently). Some spellers will accept either spelling, without alerting the writer; however, the more useful software programs flag all homonyms for the writer's attention.

Some spelling programs can only be activated after your draft is written, allowing you to go back and correct misspelled words. But with some programs, you can ask the computer to flag words as soon as they are typed. This feature can be a monstrous distraction, however, when you are trying to concentrate, in early drafts, on meaning and organization. If you get too distracted by having misspellings flagged as you are typing, get a program where that feature is not present or can be disconnected.

Some programs actually change the spelling of the misspelled words. Some suggest a correct spelling and let you type it in; some merely flag the words. The programs that go ahead and fill in the correct spelling may not understand the meaning you want to convey and fill in the wrong word. You can be more sure of accuracy when the computer lets you decide. The programs that do not suggest correct spelling leave you thumbing through your dictionary. The ones that suggest one or more correctly spelled words that you may have meant are perhaps the most useful. You must choose, however, according to your own work habits and spelling problems.

If you work with a speller, then in Step 3 you will check your numbers, dates, and titles (computers don't do a thorough job on these aspects.) Then run your paper through the speller. It will flag for you all the words it thinks are misspelled. Correct them, using the dictionary for reference.

There will be times when you cannot run your writing through a computer. Therefore, the suggestions in this lesson, about the way to read so as to catch spelling errors and the way to gradually build your spelling competence, are still relevant.

TRAIN YOURSELF TO REMEMBER SPELLING

Consciously try to improve your memory for spelling. Be conscious of spelling particularly at these times:

1. when you have to look up a word's spelling;
2. when, in reading, you find a word you frequently misspell;
3. when, in studying for a course, you master vocabulary special to that course.

At these times, try to memorize spelling. Several techniques will help:

1. Divide the word into its syllables: for example, remember "curious" as cu – ri – ous.
2. Print the word in small letters, with the letter(s) you missed in caps: dEspite.
3. Make up a memory link: for example, remember the two "L's" in "finally" by thinking "That's final, Lee!"
4. Say the word to yourself in a way that reveals its spelling: for example, say "muscle" as "mus – kl," or "concede" as "kon – kee – dee."

DEVISE EFFICIENT WAYS TO LOOK UP WORDS

If you have frequent troubles with spelling, it will be worth your while to devise a fast, efficient system of looking up words. A speller's dictionary is faster than a regular dictionary because it has some features specifically designed for spellers. If you have frequent problems with spelling, you may want to purchase a speller's dictionary, in addition to the regular dictionary you own, for looking up the meanings, forms, pronunciation, and other aspects of words. A speller's dictionary does not spend time on anything except giving you the basic meaning so you can be sure you have the right word. Thus a speller's dictionary is less dense than a regular one, so you can find individual words more quickly. The words are in large, bold print so you can see them quickly. Typically, a speller's dictionary will contain frequently misspelled first syllables with a reference to the correct spelling. For example, the misspelling *preform* will be listed, with a note referring you to the correct spelling, *perform*. That feature helps when you don't know enough of the spelling to look for the word in the right alphabetical place.

In addition to a purchased speller's dictionary, you may be helped by your own speller's dictionary. Your own can be smaller, therefore more efficient. It will have in it only the words that you have misspelled in the past or know you must learn for the future. Here's how to make one. Buy a pocket-sized spiral notebook with alphabetized tabs. Every time you have to correct spelling before you hand in a paper, or have to learn the spelling of a new term, or get back a paper with misspellings you let slip by, enter the correct spelling under the appropriate tabs of your notebook. You can simply enter all the *t* words together under *t,* no matter what the next letter is. If you have many spelling troubles, however, and you think the *t* section may have more than ten or fifteen words in it, you create subsections, *ta-te, th-to,* and so on. Then, next time you proofread a paper for spelling, you can quickly look up any of the words you know are in your notebook. For words not yet in your notebook, use your speller's dictionary; then enter the word in your speller's notebook. Gradually you will build your speller's guide so that it includes most of the words you commonly have to look up. Putting the words in the notebook helps you begin to memorize them. You will select your most important notebook words for the program of memorization described in the next section.

MEMORIZE YOUR MOST IMPORTANT WORDS

In addition to consistently trying to remember spelling and entering words into your notebook, follow a systematic program to memorize your own most important words. In your notebook, described in the previous section, *star* those words that you would like to memorize most, either because you use them frequently or because they're most embarrassing to you when you misspell them (like your instructor's name, the name of the course, or key terms in a discipline). Many instructors are more offended on an essay test when you misspell key terms in that subject area than they are about other kinds of misspellings, so if a course has essay or short answer tests, memorize the technical words you may have to use on a test, where you can't look up their spelling. Each week, choose five *starred* words from your notebook to memorize. Write these words on your daily calendar next to the coming week, on the bulletin board by your phone, or on a notecard taped to your mirror—anyplace you frequently look. If it's a word that changes spelling with context—like *their* and *there*—write a definition or a sample sentence. That week, try to memorize those five words. Look at them as many times a day as you can. In addition, set aside ten minutes a day to concentrate on them. You can do this while you're exercising or walking to a class. Say the spelling out loud. Look at the word frequently, trying to etch each letter into your memory. Use the aids to memory discussed earlier. A good way to quiz yourself is to have someone else read the words to you while you write them down. You can tape yourself as your own reader: record yourself reading the words you're trying to memorize. Once a day, play the tape back to yourself, writing down the words as they're said. Then check whether you spelled them correctly. Once you have done this for three or four weeks, include a few minutes each day to review words from previous weeks.

USE SPELLING RULES

If you typically misspell several words that are all covered by the same rule, memorize the rule rather than each individual word. Go through the words in your notebook looking for any with the following five problems. If you find several under one category, memorize the relevant rule or write the rule in the opening pages of your notebook for easy reference.

1. *Choosing ie or ei.* Remember this guide:
   Write *i* before *e*
   Except after *c*
   And when sounded like *a*
   As in *neighbor* and *weigh.*

   > *i* before *e:* believe
   > *ei* after *c:* receive
   > *ei* when sounded like *a:* vein

Exceptions: leisure, weird, either, neither, seize, species

2. *Dropping or retaining e before a suffix.* Sometimes a word that ends in *e* is given an ending (called a *suffix*), and the writer wonders whether to retain or omit the original *e*. For example, when adding the suffix *ing* to *ride,* should it be *rideing* or *riding?* The rule: omit the final *e* before a suffix beginning with a vowel *(a, e, i, o, u).* Retain the final *e* before a suffix beginning with a consonant.

   e *omitted before vowel:* love + ing = loving
   e *retained before a consonant:* love + ly = lovely

Exception: *e* retained to keep *c* or *g* soft (formed in the front of the mouth) rather than hard (formed in the back of the mouth) before *a* or *o:* noticeable, changeable

3. *Changing y to i before a suffix.* Change *y* to *i* before a suffix, unless the suffix begins with *i.*

   Suffix does not begin with i: rely + ance = reliance
   Suffix begins with i: cry + ing = crying

4. *Doubling the consonant before a suffix.* Do *not* double the final consonant (any letter except *a, e, i, o, u*) unless
   a. *the suffix begins with a vowel, AND*
   b. *a single vowel precedes the consonant, AND*

c. the consonant ends an accented syllable or a one-syllable word.

begin + ing = beginning (All three conditions are met; consonant is doubled.)
boat + ing = boating (Condition b is not met; consonant is not doubled.)
develop + ing = developing (Condition c is not met; consonant is not doubled.)

5. *Adding -s or -es to a word.* See Lesson 2J.

ONE SEMESTER TO BETTER SPELLING

If for one semester you use memorization together with an efficient notebook and speller's dictionary, you can make significant improvement as a speller. During the semester, you should enter into your notebook every word you've misspelled during that semester. With your notebook and a speller's dictionary, you should be able to decrease the number of seconds it takes you to look up a word for spelling. In addition, if you memorize five of your most frequently misspelled words per week for a semester, that's seventy-five words you don't have to look up at all. Then you can draft confidently, using whatever words seem most precise and appropriate, knowing that you'll later be able to check spelling quickly and efficiently.

EXERCISES

1. Begin your speller's notebook. Hand in to your instructor either the notebook itself or a list of the words you have so far entered in it.
2. Each week, hand in to your instructor the five words you are memorizing for that week.

REVISING YOUR OWN WRITING

Enter your spelling errors in your notebook as described in the lesson.

GRAMMATICAL TERMS IN THIS LESSON

Suffix: An ending added to a word. Example: In the word *dryness,* the suffix *ness* is added to the word *dry.*
Vowels: The vowels are *a, e, i, o, u,* and sometimes *y* and *w*
Consonants: All letters that are not vowels

LESSON FOR
STEP 3B

CAPITALIZE, PUNCTUATE, AND ABBREVIATE DATES, NUMBERS, NAMES, AND TITLES

PREVIEW OF THE LESSON

This lesson covers dates, numbers, names, titles, and addresses. Under each of these headings, the section discusses aspects such as abbreviation, capitalization, punctuation, underlining, and quotation marks.

DATES

CAPITALIZING DATES

Capitalize the names of days, months, and holidays. However,

LESSON 3B: CAPITALIZE, PUNCTUATE, AND ABBREVIATE DATES

do not capitalize words like *day* or *holiday* unless they are part of the name of the holiday.

> ***January***
> ***Wednesdays***
> ***the Christmas holiday***
> ***New Year's Day***

ABBREVIATING DATES

Do not abbreviate dates or days. The exception is bibliographies and footnotes, where dates are abbreviated according to specific rules. See a handbook appropriate for your disciplines.

Correct: The board met Wednesday, November 11.
Incorrect: The board met Wed., Nov. 11.

PUNCTUATING DATES

Use a comma to separate numbers *within* a date. Do not put a comma *after* a date, unless required by other comma rules. However, if a date has a month or day, followed by a year, use commas to set off the year from the rest of the sentence.

> ***Jones was born on April 2.***
> ***The shipment was sent on July 22, 1978, from Honolulu.***

The day is followed by the year, so a comma separates the year from the rest of the sentence.

> ***The shipment was sent on April 22 from Honolulu.***

No commas needed because the year is not included.

> ***After January 1, we will cash no more checks.***

The comma is required by rules for commas after introducers, Lesson 2L.

STEP THREE: SPELLING, DATES, NAMES, TITLES, AND NUMBERS

USING NUMBERS IN DATES

Use numerals, not words, for numbers in dates. In dates, use numerals rather than words like *first* or *second,* unless there is good reason to emphasize the word.

Correct:	He died on May 22.
Incorrect:	He died on May twenty-second.
Special reason for writing first:	Ironically, he died on the first of May—the month in which he had been born and married, the month of his daughter's birth, the month of promises, of renewal.

EXERCISES

Answers in back of book: 1a-b
Answers in instructor's manual: 1c-d

1. Revise the following.

   (Answers in back of book.)
   a. On dec 24 1958 his daughter was born—almost a christmas baby.
   b. The shipment arrived on sept. the 2nd 1986 but it was not opened or inspected until the sixth of sept., after the labor day weekend.

   (Answers in instructor's manual)
   c. My package arrived from home on easter sunday in march 1984.
   d. On october 3rd 1984 I first met Johnny.

CHOOSING BETWEEN NUMERALS AND WORDS

You can decide between numerals and words according to the following guidelines:

LESSON 3B: CAPITALIZE, PUNCTUATE, AND ABBREVIATE DATES

Use words, not numerals:

1. Whenever a number opens a sentence
2. In nontechnical writing, if the number is less than one hundred, or the number has two words or less when written out (count hyphenated words as two)

Use numerals, not words:

1. For all numbers in scientific and technical writing
2. Whenever there are a great many numbers in your paper
3. In nontechnical writing, whenever a number has three or more words when written out (count hyphenated words as two)

nontechnical writing:	When the daycare center opened, it had twenty children.
nontechnical writing:	The state police reported two thousand injuries from the flood.
technical writing:	The state police reported 2,000 injuries from the flood.
technical or scientific writing:	We placed 18 g. of the powder into a beaker.
technical and nontechnical writing:	George Washington lost 133 men in that battle. (The number has three or more words when written out.)

Incorrect:	147 cranes were left in the flock. (The number opens the sentence.)
Correct:	One hundred forty-seven cranes were left in the flock, but 101 were badly undernourished.
Correct:	The flock had 147 cranes remaining, but 121 were badly undernourished. (Because it seems awkward to write out one number in words while its com-

435

panion number is in numerals, the writer revises so that neither number opens the sentence.)

NUMBERING ITEMS OR IDEAS

When numbering items or ideas, use *first, second, third,* rather than *1st, 2nd, 3rd,* except in very informal situations. When using numbers *(1* or *one, 2* or *two),* use *words* for thoughtful writing, *numerals* for informative or technical writing.

Correct: This is the second time the machine has broken.

Incorrect: This is the 2nd time the machine has broken.

Nontechnical writing: First, the theories of Jung form the basis for Carter's thought. Second, ...

Technical or nontechnical writing: Three advantages would be gained by this course of action: (1) The union would be satisfied; (2) the school board would save $560,000; and (3) severely handicapped children would receive better care.

Technical writing: There are three legal problems with this contract:
1. It does not specify which party pays the insurance between now and March 1.
2. It does not define the term *prepayment.*
3. It does not establish deadlines for payment.

USING *NO.* and

The word *number* may be abbreviated *no.* or # when used with the numeral, but not when used alone.

LESSON 3B: CAPITALIZE, PUNCTUATE, AND ABBREVIATE DATES

Incorrect: Please give me the no.
Correct: Please give me the number.
Correct: The item you requested is catalog no. 410–C.

USING *A.M.* AND *P.M.*

Use a.m. and p.m. only with numerals, not alone. Do not capitalize a.m. and p.m. except in headings or titles where all letters are capitalized. (Note: a.m. and p.m. are capitalized in the heading for this section because they are used as words in a heading.)

Incorrect: We arrived home in the p.m.
Correct: We arrived home in the afternoon.
Incorrect: We arrived home at two p.m.
Correct: We arrived home at 2 p.m.
Correct: We arrived home at 2:00 p.m.
Correct: We arrived home at two o'clock in the afternoon.

WRITING FRACTIONS

In nontechnical writing, common fractions such as *one half* or *one fourth* may be written as words. For fractions that are not common and for all fractions in scientific or technical writing, use numerals.

Correct: The baby spilled one half pint of milk.
Correct: The baby spilled a half pint of milk.
Correct: The baby spilled half a pint of milk.
Correct: The sound reached him in 1/64 second.
          (Not a common fraction.)
Scientific or technical: Each section was 1/2 m. long.

REPEATING A NUMBER IN PARENTHESES

Except in legal or commercial documents, do not repeat in parentheses a number that has already been spelled out.

STEP THREE: SPELLING, DATES, NAMES, TITLES, AND NUMBERS

Legal: We hereby authorize a change in the order from one hundred (100) bales of hay to fifty (50) bales.

Legal: The said John Jones shall be issued a check for one thousand dollars ($1,000).

Nonlegal: John Jones received a check for $1,000.

PUNCTUATING NUMBERS

Do not use commas between words in a number. Insert a hyphen between the words of a two-digit number in which the first word ends in *y (forty)*.

> **Three hundred forty steers were saved.**
> **Forty-two calves were saved.**

WRITING DOLLARS AND CENTS

When the numbers are written as words, also write out *dollars* or *cents*. When the numbers are written as numerals, use *$* and either *¢* or *cents*. Be consistent within a piece of writing. In formal documents, both the numbers and the dollars and cents should be written as words.

Correct: He inherited two thousand dollars. OR
He inherited $2,000. OR
He inherited 2,000 dollars.
(This version may be harder to read.

Incorrect: He inherited $two thousand.

Correct: She gave the child ten cents for candy. OR
She gave the child 10¢ for candy. OR
She gave the child 10 cents for candy.

Incorrect: She gave the child ten ¢ for candy.

Legal: The owner agrees to contribute two thousand dollars ($2,000) to the capital of said firm.

Formal: The owner contributed two thousand dollars.

LESSON 3B: CAPITALIZE, PUNCTUATE, AND ABBREVIATE DATES

EXERCISES

Answers in back of book: 2a-d
Answers in instructor's manual: 2e-h

2. Revise the following.

   (Answers in back of book)
   a. 500 trees were damaged in the 1st frost and an equal no. in the second frost.
   b. We lost one thousand (1,000) dollars on the deal.
   c. Between four and five P.M., drinks are 1/2 price, so we were all able to have a nice time for under twenty dollars.
   d. There were forty two caps in the 3rd shipment, making a total of one thousand five hundred forty two now in stock.

   (Answers in instructor's manual)
   e. We have fifty-seven varieties of ice cream at each of our 3 restaurants.
   f. 1,000 prospective students arrived for our 5th annual college-career day.
   g. I earned $five thousand dollars ($5,000) last year, working 2 different jobs part time.
   h. 500 workers arrive at the plant at six pm.

NAMES OF PEOPLE, PLACES, ORGANIZATIONS, LANGUAGES, EVENTS, NATIONALITIES

CAPITALIZING NAMES

Capitalize names of *specific* people (Jane Smith), places (New York), organizations (Alcoholics Anonymous), languages (French), events (The First Annual Hawkinsville Invitational Tournament), historical documents (the Constitution), religious terms (Sacrament of Holy Communion), nationalities

STEP THREE: SPELLING, DATES, NAMES, TITLES, AND NUMBERS

(Polish), and races (Jewish). The words *black* and *white,* referring to races, may be capitalized or not, but be consistent within a single piece of writing. (The project involved both Blacks and Whites. OR The project involved both blacks and whites.) Also capitalize a person's title when the title precedes the person's name (President McMurtrie), and capitalize a very important title at any time. (The President lives at the White House.) However, do *not* capitalize these terms when they are being used in a general sense or when they are used as part of a noun that otherwise would not be capitalized. The following chart shows the distinction between specific and general use.

Specific	*General*
France	Names of cities, counties, and countries, as nouns, are always capitalized.
the French boy	french bread (part of a noun that otherwise is not capitalized)
Father O'Malley	my father, Jack Gumas
First Methodist Church is on the corner of Main and Elm.	Blakely established the first Methodist church in Arkansas.
I don't know, Dad. *(Dad* is used like a name.)	I told my dad I didn't know.
The Department of Biology needs more faculty.	The biology department needs more faculty.
He grew up in the South Bronx. (South Bronx is the formal name of the area.)	The building faces south. He grew up in southern New York.
We went to the Green Tree Apple Orchard.	We passed an apple orchard.
His course is Biology 101.	He studies biology and English. *(English* is capitalized because it is the name of a language.)

Specific
President Wilson called.
The President called the Secretary of State.
Now Uncle Jack lives here.
The Constitution guarantees free speech.
Expanded trade helped bring about the Renaissance in Europe in the fifteenth and sixteenth centuries.
I attended Woodbrook Elementary School.
Hear, O Israel, the Lord our God is one.

General
The president of the rifle club called today.

Now my uncle lives here.
Every organization needs a constitution.
The United States is experiencing a renaissance of its cities.

I attended elementary school at Woodbrook.
The Greek gods were often portrayed as very human.

WRITING SCIENTIFIC TERMS

In scientific terms, capitalize genus, not species; underline both. In general, capitalize and underline other scientific terms. (Check with your science instructor for specific conventions in the discipline.)

We studied five specimens of the giant squid Taningia danae.

Our nearest galaxy is Andromeda Nebula.

WRITING NAMES OF ORGANIZATIONS AND AGENCIES

Capitalizing. Capitalize the first letter of each word of a formal name, except articles *(a, an, the),* conjunctions (linking words like *and* and *but,* also called connectors), and prepositions (words like *for* or *from* that show direction or relationship). However, if one of these words is the first word in the title,

STEP THREE: SPELLING, DATES, NAMES, TITLES, AND NUMBERS

capitalize it. If an initial article is part of the formal name, capitalize it; otherwise, do not.

> *We opened an account in the First National Bank of Jarrettsville.*
>
> (*The* is not part of the bank's official title.)
>
> *We attended a meeting of The Society for Civic Improvement.*
>
> (*The* is part of the organization's official title.)

Abbreviating. You may abbreviate names of agencies and organizations usually referred to by their initials. However, if any reader might not know the meaning of the abbreviation, provide an explanation in parentheses the first time you use the term. After the first time, you may use the abbreviation alone.

> *The IRS starts the investigations today.*
> (Use only when all readers will know what the IRS is.)
>
> *The IRS (Internal Revenue Service) starts the investigations today. However, Senator Blake said he did not trust the IRS to conduct a thorough probe.*

USING COMMAS WITH NAMES OF CITIES AND STATES

Set off a state name with commas only when a city name is also written.

> *The program began in Nebraska and expanded to neighboring states.*
> *The program began in Omaha, Nebraska, and expanded to neighboring states.*

NAMES WITH TITLES

This section covers use of titles in normal expository writing. The next section covers titles in addresses.

LESSON 3B: CAPITALIZE, PUNCTUATE, AND ABBREVIATE DATES

In all but the most formal situations, if you are using the person's name, you may freely abbreviate a title that indicates marital status (Mr., Mrs., Ms.), academic degree (Dr.,), a religious title (Fr., Sr.) or a title of sainthood (St. John). Titles that indicate a person's position (rather than marital status, degree, or religious position) should not be abbreviated (Professor, Director). When the title is being used alone, without the person's name, do not abbreviate.

Incorrect:	They paged the Dr.
Correct:	They paged Dr. Homes.
Incorrect:	Pres. Halsey gave the inaugural address.
Correct:	President Halsey gave the inaugural address.
Correct (in an essay):	The boys loved Father McInnis.
Correct (salutation of a letter):	Dear Fr. McInnis:
Correct (business memo):	The task was completed by Fr. Francis Koziol.
Correct:	Professor Anker chaired the committee.
Correct:	That day, in a meeting at St. John's Church, we heard a talk on the life of St. Teresa.

NAMES IN ADDRESSES

Abbreviating: State names may be abbreviated in addresses, in all but the most formal situations. However, do not abbreviate state names when they are part of the name of an agency (The University of Iowa). City names should not be abbreviated. For titles with names, follow the rules in the previous section.

Punctuating: Within an address, use a comma to separate the city from the state and a comma between a name and a title that follows the name.

(informal letter)
Prof. Julia Anker, Chair
Dept. of Sociology
Univ. of Maine
264 S. Bleaker St.
Presque Isle, ME 04769

(formal letter)
Professor Julia Anker, Chair
Department of Sociology
University of Maine
264 South Bleaker Street
Presque Isle, Maine 04769

EXERCISES

Answers in back of book: 3a
Answers in instructor's manual: 3b

3. Revise the following.

   (Answers in back of book.)
   a. On the north side of cleveland, a group of parents, meeting in an elementary school, organized a foreign exchange program with cleveland's japanese sister city, oheiko. hayato tokugawa, a japanese student, came to cleveland, lived with the arnold hansens, a local family, and attended richard brandson high school. He studied english, biology, history, and algebra. His father, a japanese manufacturer with international business interests, visited him occasionally. A local catholic school, st. jude's, was offering japanese language classes at the time. The japanese professor, fr. timothy hoyt, invited hayato and his father to talk to the class. The success of the exchange program

is amply proven in the Japanese sentence hayato chose to teach the saint jude's students: in Japanese, it says, "Hi, dad! I'm having a great time in america."
(Answers in instructor's manual)
b. A german exchange student, Nina Gottesman, stayed with us in chicago and attended the howard leary high school on bleaker street. The principal and the instructors were very glad to have her in the school, and the other students were very friendly. However, in the first weeks, she was homesick at times. Living in a small town in germany, she was astonished not only by american ways but by big city ways. But the president of the student council asked her for a date, she made some friends, she called her mom and dad once or twice long distance, and soon she was no longer homesick and enjoyed herself enormously.

TITLES OF LITERATURE, ART, AND MEDIA PRODUCTIONS

The rules in this section are for titles used in the text of a paper. For treatment of titles in footnotes, bibliographies, and other forms of citation, see a handbook appropriate for your discipline.

CAPITALIZING TITLES

Capitalize the first letters of all the words in the names of books, plays, poems, journals, newspapers, articles, and works of art. However, do *not* capitalize articles *(a, an, the),* conjunctions (linking words like *and, but, or,* also called connectors), or prepositions (words showing direction or relationships: *of, for, over*). Always capitalize the first and last words of the title and the first word after any colon, even if that word is an article, conjunction, or preposition.

Children Who Have Lost a Loved One: A Guide for Parents and Professionals

UNDERLINING TITLES

Underline the title of any work that is published separately (book, journal, newspaper). Underline titles of works of art such as paintings and statues, titles of plays, and titles of films or radio/television shows.

Shakespeare wrote the play <u>Hamlet</u>.
<u>Emma</u> is a fine novel.
On December 6, CBS aired a 60-minute documentary on drugs, called <u>Popping and Shooting</u>.

USING QUOTATION MARKS FOR TITLES

If a work is published as part of some other work, set off its title in quotation marks, but do not underline. An exception is the title of a play: underline it, even though it may be published as part of a book.

In an essay titled "The Electronic Newsroom," Eric Robinson fantasizes about the impact of information technology on journalism.

PUNCTUATING TITLES WITHIN TITLES

When a work's title includes another title, use regular rules for capitalizing the included title and for underlining it or placing it in quotation marks. However, if the main title and the included

LESSON 3B: CAPITALIZE, PUNCTUATE, AND ABBREVIATE DATES

title both take quotation marks, put the included title in single quotation marks.

> *His essay was titled "<u>Hamlet: Shakespeare's Masterpiece</u>."*
> *Brooks' first book of poems was "<u>Arise" and Other Poems</u>.*
> *In her essay, "John Milton's 'On His Blindness,'" Sarah Killins reviews critical interpretations of the poem.*

PUNCTUATING AROUND TITLES

Do not set off titles with commas unless required by other comma rules. When regular rules of usage call for a comma or period following a title in quotation marks, place the mark inside the quotation marks. Place colons, semicolons, question marks and exclamation points outside the quotation marks (unless they are part of the title).

Correct:	Hemingway's <u>A Farewell to Arms</u> is one of the best war novels I've ever read. (Subject is <u>A Farewell to Arms</u>. Verb is *is*. A comma should not separate subject from verb: Lesson 2K.)
Incorrect:	Hemmingway's, <u>A Farewell to Arms</u>, is one of the best war novels I've ever read.
Correct:	Hemingway's novel about the Crimean War, <u>A Farewell to Arms</u>, is one of the best war novels I've ever read. (The comma is required by rules for setting off appositives: Lesson 2M.)
Correct:	"Cats," a poem for children, held the class spellbound. (The comma is required by rules for setting off appositives: Lesson 2M. Comma is placed inside quotation marks.)
Correct:	Murphy opened a book and began to read "Cats"; the children quieted down at once. (The semicolon is placed outside the quotation marks.)

STEP THREE: SPELLING, DATES, NAMES, TITLES, AND NUMBERS

Correct: Have you ever read the poem "Crossing the Bar"? (The question is the writer's.)
Correct: Angie loved the poem "Why?" (The question mark is part of the title.)

REFERRING TO CHAPTER AND VOLUME

Do not abbreviate words like *chapter* and *volume,* except in citations, footnotes, and bibliographies. (See a handbook appropriate for your discipline.) Use numerals, not numbers (Chapter 1). Capitalize the first letter when referring to a specific chapter or volume, but do not capitalize when the word is used in a general sense.

In the first chapter, Brown discusses the causes of the problem.
In Chapter 1, Brown discusses the causes of the problem.

EXERCISES

(Note: Exercises 1-3 appear earlier in the lesson.)
Answers in back of book: 4a, 5a-b, 6a-b
Answers in instructor's manual: 4b, 5c-d, 6c

4. In the following paragraph, insert punctuation and capitalization as needed.

   (Answers in back of book)
   a. herman melville's short story billy budd, foretopman, contains the classic philosophical argument about whether the end justifies the means. melville introduces captain vere as the character who must decide whether it is right to sacrifice a man innocent before god to preserve law and order. Although vere is an intellectual man who at times

LESSON 3B: CAPITALIZE, PUNCTUATE, AND ABBREVIATE DATES

seems swayed by idealism, in the end he is a devoted realist who finds his answers in the law.

(Answers in instructor's manual)
- b. On monday, june 20th, just twenty days after sailing, the spanish armada ran into a terrible storm shortly after midnight. At this time part of the fleet was anchored at corunna. During the storm, one ship broke loose from its anchorage and ran into another ship. The other ships scattered. After the storm was over, the captain of the fleet, the duke of medina sidonia, sent out boats to find the missing ships. Three days later, twenty had been found, but 30 were still missing. 6,000 men were still on those thirty vessels. The spanish ships that had survived the storm suffered great damage.

5. In the following sentences, make changes in abbreviations as needed.

   (Answers in back of book)
   - a. The dr. phoned mister Haines with the good news.
   - b. All freshmen must take bio. A freshman not majoring in science may substitute environmental science for bio, but must have the permission of the head of the dept and the prof teaching the course.

   (Answers in instructor's manual)
   - c. My dr taped the ankle and told me not to put much weight on it.
   - d. These hoses should be delivered to the engineering dept in the main bldg on Elm st.

6. In the following passages, revise titles, names, dates, and numbers as needed. Follow the requirements for formal situations.

   (Answers in back of book)
   - a. [The following is a memo from a college staff member to an instructor. The *S. J.* means Society of Jesus, but is always abbreviated in titles.]

STEP THREE: SPELLING, DATES, NAMES, TITLES, AND NUMBERS

To: prof magnum and sister mary jacques
From: fr john reilly, S. J., office of student personnel
Please excuse alice jones from her eng and bio classes for the 1st 2 weeks of the spring semester, monday jan 15 through friday feb 2 1987. ms jones has had 2 operations and has been at home under a dr's care since the christmas holiday. She expects to attend classes again beginning feb 5. She intends to attempt only 2 courses—english and bio—in spring semester. She will drop her other 3 courses. We hope that, with your help, she will be able to have a successful spring semester despite her medical difficulties.

b. [a letter from the instructor to the student mentioned in Exercise 6a]

ms alice jones
103 s elm st
last chance, nebraska 99999
Dear ms jones:
fr reilly in the student personnel office has told me that you have been having medical problems and will not attend classes until feb the fifth. I hope you will make a speedy recovery. I will do anything I can to help you make up your work and get a good start for the new semester in modern lit class. In case you are able to begin some of the semester's reading, enclosed is a syllabus and copies of the 1st texts we will use. The cost of these texts was twenty two dollars nineteen cents. The bookstore has agreed to let you pay for the books when you return to school, or you may mail me a check made out to furman college bookstore. I suggest you begin james joyce's novel portrait of the artist as a young man. You might also read chap 1 of the poetry anthology, particularly t s eliot's the wasteland, which begins on p 57. On sun feb 4, the day before you return to class, the theater dept is presenting its last performance of samuel beckett's play waiting for godot. Performance begins at 8 pm in goodwin theater. I

LESSON 3B: CAPITALIZE, PUNCTUATE, AND ABBREVIATE DATES

have asked the class to attend. If you have returned to campus and are not too tired that evening, please plan to see the play. Admission is free to students and no reservation is necessary.

(Answers in instructor's manual)

c. Tryouts for eugene ionesco's play rhinoceros will begin at 7 pm on mon oct 4 1987 in the theater dept rehearsal room, halley hall room 412. For those who wish to try out, copies of the play are available in the college bookstore for six dollars ninety-five cents. There are also 3 copies of the play on reserve at the library. Be ready to read lines from act one. If you wish to try out but are unable to come on oct 4, please contact prof thompson at once.

7. Read the memo and letter in Exercise 6a-b, above. Then write a letter from the student back to her instructor. The letter should:

> Report her medical condition (make up something that includes a reference to a disease or operation as well as references to medical personnel)
>
> Thank him for sending the books
>
> Tell him she is enclosing a check for the cost of the books (include amount and date of the check)
>
> Report what she has been able to read (mention titles and authors)
>
> Say that she will try to attend the play (mention it by its title and author)

REVISING YOUR OWN WRITING

In the space provided, enter mistakes you've made in using names, number, dates, and titles. Write the correction. Then write five other sentences that follow similar patterns, forming and punctuating them correctly.

STEP THREE: SPELLING, DATES, NAMES, TITLES, AND NUMBERS

Your Draft

_____
_____
_____
_____
_____

Your Revision

_____
_____
_____
_____
_____

Five Other Sentences in the Same Pattern

_____
_____
_____
_____
_____

GRAMMATICAL TERMS IN THIS LESSON

Article: a, an, the

Conjunction: A linking word (examples: *and, so*)

Noun: A word or group of words that names a person, place, concept, or thing (examples: France, Idaho, bag)

Preposition: A word, usually short, that shows direction or relationship and that is accompanied by an object (examples: *of* Seattle, *for* the retarded)

APPENDIX A How to Use this Book with a Computer

Computers offer three types of help for revisers: word processing, which makes physical production and revision easier; spelling programs, which help you locate misspelled words; and text analysis programs, which help you identify some (but not nearly all) of the stylistic and grammatical problems.

USING THIS BOOK WITH WORD PROCESSING

Word processing helps writers because it makes the mechanical part of revising easier. It can create a clean copy of a paper at any time and it encourages writers to revise because revisions do not entail retyping a whole paper. Suggestions for using a word processor in the revising process are incorporated into the section on "The Revising Process," pp. 12–14.

In addition to making revision easier, a word processor can help you locate some kinds of problems in your drafts. The "search/find" operation, available on nearly all word-processing programs, can locate constructions you know are troublesome for you. For example, if you consistently have trouble with "who" and "whom," ask your computer to locate all instances of those two words in your manuscript. Then you can check your use of them, using the guidelines in Lesson 2G.

USING THIS BOOK WITH SPELLERS

A computer program that checks spelling can be very useful to a writer. See Lesson 3A on spelling for more information about how to use one. The remainder of this appendix covers how to

APPENDIX A

use this book with computer text analysis programs. These may be included with your word processing programs or purchased as separate packages.

USING THIS BOOK WITH COMPUTER TEXT ANALYSIS PROGRAMS

This book focuses on two operations: (1) reading to find problems, and (2) revising the problems. Computer *text analysis programs* help you find certain types of problems and may help in revising your writing. However, it is a mistake to think that a computer can do the work for you. As yet, computer text analysis programs are very limited. Nonetheless, a program can be useful. The following are suggestions for using text analysis programs in conjunction with this book.

WHAT TEXT ANALYSIS PROGRAMS DO

Text analysis programs are intended to help you with grammar, punctuation, and style. However, since many of those elements depend upon context and the writer's intention, the computer can do only a few limited aspects of the job. The computer can *flag* some questionable constructions, such as the passive voice, or places where you have used only one pair of quotation marks or one parenthesis. The second thing the computer does is *count*—it counts the percentage of your verbs that are passive, the average number of words in your sentences, and other features. However, the computer program cannot determine for you whether passive voice is an appropriate choice in a particular sentence; you must still decide. This book's guidelines will help.

You still must also prioritize your attention. A text analysis program gives you a list of information about your writing, but, unlike this book, it does not tell you which problems are most serious, or which to address first.

STRUCTURE YOUR REVISION ACCORDING TO THE THREE STEPS

Because text analysis programs are limited, you should use this book's steps to structure your revision. When one of this book's steps or substeps calls for you to identify a certain type of problem, find the relevant item on the computer's program and let it help you with that substep. You'll find that for many of the most important substeps, the computer is unable to help because programmers have not yet figured out how to provide the computer with the judgment that people use in making decisions about language.

The following procedure is suggested for when you use a text analysis program:

1. Run the program and view the information either on the screen or as a printout.
2. Follow this book's three steps and substeps in order, just as you would if you were not using the program.
3. As you follow the steps, use the appropriate parts of the text analysis to help you find problems in your draft.

For example, at the beginning of Step 1, when this book directs you to check for passive voice verbs, consult the program, either to find the percentage of passive voice verbs, or to flag each passive voice verb (different programs perform different operations).

KNOW THE MEANING OF THE PROGRAM'S TERMS

Be sure you consult the program or its guidebook carefully so you know just what the various function titles mean, and what the functions can and cannot do. For example, when a text analysis program has an item simply called "punctuation," do not be misled. No computer text analysis program covers more than just a few of the many aspects of punctuation that writers

APPENDIX A

need, and that are covered in this book's Step 2. For example, a computer program can flag instances where you have placed a period (end of a sentence) that is not followed by a capital letter. This helps with carelessness in punctuating beginnings and ends of sentences, but it does not help with the essential task of deciding whether you have fragments and run-ons (Step 2A and 2B).

The following is a list of revisions covered in this book that some computer text analysis programs can do (terminology may differ).

TYPICAL COMPUTER PROGRAM	*STEP IN THIS BOOK*
SENTENCE STRUCTURE prints sentences with passive verbs and tells whether the percentage of passive verbs is appropriate.	1A
Also tells whether the percent of nominalizations is appropriate (A *nominalization* is a verb and a noun used where just a verb would serve: i.e. "make a decision" instead of "decide.")	1E
FINDBE: prints weak *to be* verbs so the writer can substitute action verbs	1E, 1F
UNSPECIFIC: gives the percentage of unspecific words, lists them, and suggests the writer substitute specific words	1F
ABSTRACT: gives percentage of abstract words, suggests whether the percentage is too high, and prints the words	1F
DICTION: prints wordy phrases, long words, trite words, and sexist words	1F 2F

APPENDIX B   *Essays for Revision*

INSTRUCTIONS FOR REVISING THE ESSAYS

This appendix contains drafts of three student essays. Use the following procedures to practice or test your ability to revise for style and for grammar/punctuation.

1. *To test your ability to revise for style:* Revise the paper for the aspects discussed in the lessons for Step 1. You may see broader changes you'd like to make, but for this exercise, keep the same content and organization for the paper and for each paragraph. A discussion of the major stylistic problems of the first two essays is included at the back of the book to help you evaluate your revisions on your own. Discussion of the third essay is in the instructor's manual.

2. *To test your ability to revise for grammar and punctuation:* Go through the *original* draft (not your revised draft) making changes only for grammar, punctuation, and capitalization/abbreviation of numbers, dates, and titles (Step 2 and Step 3B). The essays have no spelling errors. Even if you note an awkward sentence, revise it only for grammar, punctuation, capitalization, and abbreviation. Doing this allows you to see how many of the grammar and punctuation errors you can catch, without the changes that would occur if you revised the passage for style. For the first two essays, you can score yourself using the answers in the back of the book. Answers for the third essay are in the instructor's manual.

ESSAY ONE

LOOKING LIKE A MILLION

(1)Americas unemployment tips the scale at 9.5%. (2)Nearly two million of the jobless being teenagers.

APPENDIX B

(3)Being young and unemployed, combined with the value of the dollar being equal to the price of a plain hamburger, create a scary situation for those who dont have "money to burn". (4)But you need not worry. (5)As a teenager, with few responsibilities and many advantages, a little ingenuity and resourceful thinking can make the ordinary Poor Richard live like a Prince Rainier.

(6)I have been a statistic on the unemployment chart for two years now, partially through sheer laziness and partially because of my preoccupation with the social aspects in life. (7)Yet I have developed certain "tricks of the trade", that are not very complex, and permitting me to maintain my desired way of life.

(8)Major financial obligations, such as owning a car, may be first on most teenager's minds, it certainly is a primary concern of mine. (9)Therefore, I purchased a $200 Ford torino from my brother. (10)Buying such an automobile from a relative, made the car reasonable and more affordable than a $30,000 Mercedes, however, there are others who prefer to use the family car. (11)A friend of mine found this way the most economical, with repair bills already paid, but was often bound in a struggle for access to the car. (12)He often had other people drive, by relating to us his sad tales of broken pumps and dead batteries, while his sister used the car with friends.

(13)Regardless of whether you own the car or merely share one, all teenagers face another problem gas money. (14)But that is really nothing that a few loopholes can't solve. (15)First of all, I charged a gas fee for transporting my brothers or sisters to destinations beyond walking distances. (16)Logically a fee can be imposed, after convincing them of their great need for my services and their consumption of my precious time and gas. (17)The revenue was saved for gas and repairs. (18)The second loophole is never fuel up if the tank is over one-eighth full. (19)Chances are someone will need to borrow the car, and it is only fair to let them foot the bill.

(20) Another financial obligation, which confronted me, was that of supporting an active social life, or dating. (21) Being male, I am subject to the tradition that the boy always picks up the tab. (22) Women's lib has helped in recent years, however, with the size of the tab, a night out on the town can really put you in the red. (23) Don't let this stop you, the creative mind can easily overcome such problems.

(24) A dinner date, for instance, was one evening I wanted to avoid. (25) However, my girlfriend felt that a dinner for two was romantic. (26) Having only enough money for a small meal at McDonalds, I decided to try my hand at creating my own cuisine. (27) An Italian meal was prepared from a box of spaghetti, a jar of Ragu from the cabinet, a loaf of bread from the bread box, and some red wine from the liquor cabinet. (28) It is the thoughtfulness that counts and, a rewarding evening can be accomplished.

(29) Unfortunately, this is not your only problem. (30) Going out for entertainment, such as a movie a concert or a ball game, can be another costly evening. (31) I, for one, believe that such evenings are necessary in male/female relationships. (32) But I also found it important to avoid frequent nights like these, keeping them to a minimum by introducing alternatives. (33) A night, with friends at a party, is relatively inexpensive and was usually a lot of fun for my girlfriend and I. (34) This may only work to an extent, so I used a second alternative. (35) I have found a way to provide a quite enjoyable evening on the couch. (36) You may develop different means to accomplish similar results.

(37) With the suitable lifestyle accomplished, all I need is proper attire. (38) Being of that age where my mother will no longer clothe me, such "novelty shops" as Bamburger's and Sears contained only birthday and Christmas presents.

(39)Second-hand stores and discount stores such as Marshall's, where I frequent, supply a fashionable wardrobe at a very reasonable price. (40)By selling my old clothes to my family, I can buy my new ones. (41)I look like a million, but I'm worth about thirty bucks.

(42)So now you have seen how one person has overcome, what you could call, a financial crisis. (43)Common knowledge and resourceful thinking were the main tools used, and a relatively enjoyable lifestyle was preserved. (44)Just remember as teenagers, with few responsibilities and many advantages, a little ingenuity can go a long way.

ESSAY TWO

JOHN

(1)It's been over two years now since Johns horrible and senseless death, but memories of him interrupt my thoughts to this very day. (2)Hearing his name I still find myself turning around hoping to see his attractive face. (3)However, I never see it though, only memories are visible. (4)Memories like this rekindle the pain that was felt at the time of John's death. (5)John was two years ahead of me in high school so I did not know him well, but he was in my spanish class when I was a freshman (he being a junior) and an acquaintance of my older brother. (6)Ralph, my brother, was a senior in High School when John was a sophomore. (7)They often associated with the same circle of friends, so it was not uncommon for Ralph to bring John, who was not of driving age, home from parties and soccer practices.

(8)Ralph once told my sister and I that John had a reputation of being the 'Town Drunk' around school because of his excessive drinking. (9)At first, this was hard to believe. (10)To look at this seemingly happy and healthy

17-yr.-old, one would never guess, he had a drinking problem that often lingered past the weekend parties. (11)He seemed so innocent of his cruel surroundings. (12)Maybe this and his drinking problem were foreshadows of his tragic ending.

(13)John and I rarely talked to one another in Spanish class; but when we did, our conversation was usually limited to how Ralph was progressing in college. (14)However, he always made a point to acknowledge my presence in the crowded noisy, hallways between classes with either a barely audible greeting or just a slight nod of the head. (15)In either case, having an upperclassman, especially one with John's status, acknowledge you was a great accomplishment for a freshman. (16)John's kindness was enough to relieve some of the tension formed from the junior high to senior high school transition.

(17)Although he may not have realized it, John had a lot going for him, good grades, true friends, great looks, a sense of humor, popularity, school involvement, President of the National Honor Society, a soccer player, a varsity wrestler and self-confidence, or so I had thought. (18)He was the type of guy that could always be found at the 'right' parties. (19)At the parties, one could usually find him living up to his infamous reputation. (20)Holding a mug of beer in each hand, and with the corners of his mouth turned up into a goofy smile. (21)John seemed deserving of the title 'Town Drunk'.

(22)Dressed as though he just stepped out of the pages of GQ (Gentlemen's Quarterly magazine), John's sandy blonde hair and brown eyes, captured the envy of almost every girl—or at least those ignorant of his drinking problem. (23)Although Sally, well aware of his problem, was still his girlfriend. (24)Like any couple though, his drinking began to put a strain on their eight-month relationship. (25)Eventually, the strain outweighed the romance. (26)The summer

APPENDIX B

following their 1984, graduation, Sally severed the relationship with John. (27)Could this be another cause for the event that was to take place in the near future? (28)No one will ever know. [Essay continues with discussion of how and why John committed suicide and the writer's feelings about him.]

ESSAY THREE

ONE DOCTOR'S MISTAKE

(1)I received six years of radiation treatment in an attempt to shrink the bubbled birthmark on the upper half of my right arm. (2)Five long years of routine treatment passed. (3)Before the doctor showed reluctance to administer the radiation any further. (4)No one suspected the doctor committed any crime.

(5)In the event of my parents curiosity, I visited other doctor's to obtain several second opinions. (6)These visits revealed that the area of skin, containing the somewhat reduced birthmark, displayed severe radiation burn. (7)Every physician recommended the birthmark be removed immediately to prevent future skin cancer. (8)This news of the doctor's mistake and malpractice not only devastated my family but myself as well.

(9)Uneasiness and constant mood swings became common as the date of my surgery December 27th, quickly approached. (10)My Christmas spirit became noticeably dampened, while doubt and fright filled my body when I pictured needles, nurses, and doctors.

(11)Two days after my surgery I entered the world of reality where simple tasks, such as eating, sleeping, and showering, became chores. (12)Because my arm had to constantly be propped up on a pillow to circulate the blood properly, eating and sleeping proved to be extremely difficult. (13)Many times during the night my arm slid off the pillow causing me to wake up crying in pain. (14)Some nights my arm throbbed so badly with pain it felt as if someone dropped a load of bricks on it. (15)Even though sometimes I didn't think I would survive my doctor still refused to prescribe pain killers because of the side effects and me being so young. (16)Showering while keeping my stitches dry turned out to be impossible, water always managed to make it's way to this specific area. (17)The sight of my huge ugly black and blue mark with at least one hundred stitches, sent me into hysterics. (18)How was I suppose to cope with this situation?

(19)The following year proved the hardest due to the doctor restricting me from any physical or strenuous activity that could injure my healing process. (20)These restrictions really meant no roller skating, sledding, or ice skating until further notice. (21)I dreaded sitting home on the weekends while all my friends went ice skating and sledding; it just was not fair! (22)Depression as well as embarrassment struck me hard. (23)I refused to wear any type of short sleeve shirt because of the noticeable discoloration and rude comments thrown at me; the day I did wear a short sleeve shirt to school I encountered the worst experience of my life. (24)The many piercing remarks, advanced toward me, showed in my tearful eyes and unstable emotions.

(25)Although I still came across many difficulties as I matured, I started to accept my scar and I became more concerned about my cosmetic appearance. (26)Trying to cover up my scar turned out to be of utmost importance. (27)During the bathing suit season, my girl friends reminded me, through hurtful comments, how discolored and unattractive my arm appeared which lowered my self image and triggered me to continuously wear a beach cover up or tee shirt while laying out in the sun. (28)While my friends

APPENDIX B

were gallivanting about the beach meeting tons of people I sat on the blanket for fear someone would notice my arm.

(29)Throughout my high school years, problems arose around prom time when I tried to find a gown that covered my scar. (30)As I trudged through thousands of stores, I fell in love with countless gowns, none of which I bought. (31)The pressure and frustration of a fruitless search caused tears to burst from my eyes. (32)This task filled other girls with excitement and anxiety, but for me it seemed as just another hassle. [Essay continues with discussion of how the writer has begun to accept and overcome the effects of her scar.]

ANSWERS TO EXERCISES

INTRODUCTORY LESSON A

2. a. F; b. F; c. T; d. T; e. F; f. T; g. F
3. a. V: went; S: Roger
   b. V: brought; S: Alice
   c. V: has acquired; S: zoo
   d. V: will resume; S: players
   e. V: have been; S: children (*quiet* is a modifier)
   f. V: has been mowed; S: lawn
   g. V: have been selected; S: apples
   h. V: will take; S: Rachel
   i. V: will have been; S: we
   j. V: arrived; S: we
4. a. V: played; S: we
   b. V: lay; S: costumes
   c. V: had caught; S: can
   d. V: returned; S: workers
      V: could rest; S: they
   e. V: can come, [can] eat; S: you, Bob (*Can* is understood with the second verb.)
      V: finish; S: you
   f. V: can provide; S: computers
      V: must know; S: management
   g. V: installed; S: they
      V: have been able; S: companies
   h. V: experienced; S: which
      V: acknowledged; S: firm
      V: were; S: computers
   i. V: has entered; S: business
   j. V: are using; S: towns
      V: are recorded; S: that

ANSWERS TO EXERCISES

    k. V: does; S: computer
       V: can spend; S: officers
    l. V: provides; S: device
       V: have ignored, owe; S: who
    m. V: punches in; S: officer
       V: searches; S: machine
    n. V: matches; S: license
       V: beeps, flashes; S: device
    o. V: go; S: I
       V: have; S: I
       V: is; S: no one
    p. V: was; S: pair
       V: had seen; S: I
    q. V: had jumped; S: who
       V: started; S: shooting
       V: ran, leapt; S: officer
    r. V: was; S: to hold, [to] go, [to] take (*To* is understood with subjects after its first use. The *it* serves to postpone the subjects.)
    s. V: said; S: boss
       V: would be recommended; S: I

5. a. (1) V: was; S: pier
     (2) V: were waiting; S: men
         V: were running; S: children
         V: kept; S: parents
     (3) V: felt; S: I
         V: were; S: I
     (4) V: was; S: it
     (5) V: creaked, shifted; S: pier
     (6) V: stood; S: we
         V: would be; S: maintaining our relationship
     (7) V: felt; S: to be in his arms
         V: was; S: I
     (8) V: would survive; S: love
         V: were; S: we

(9) V: was; S: year
(10) V: streamed; S: tears
V: had; S: we

7. (Sample answers; other versions are possible.)
   a. As verb: The elk were running fast.
      V: were running; S: elk
      As subject: Running is difficult in snow.
      V: is; S: running
      As something else: Running fast, the elk escaped.
      V: escaped; S: elk
   b. As verb: Many times I have laughed.
      V: have laughed; S: I
      As subject: To have laughed would have been rude.
      V: would have been; S: to have laughed
      As something else: I wanted to have laughed.
      V: wanted; S: I
   c. As verb: He could track any animal in the woods.
      V: could track; S: he
      As subject: The track was clear.
      V: was; S: track
      As something else: The plow cleared the track.
      V: cleared; S: plow

8. (Sample answers; other versions are possible.)
   a. He laughed so hard he fell against a table.
   b. After the children brushed their teeth and washed their faces, they were ordered to bed.
   c. The little dog was teased by some children, so it came home and hid.

9. (Sample answers; other versions are possible.)
   a. The farm hands had been practicing with their guns; they were shooting at tin can targets.
      V: had been practicing; S: hands
      V: were shooting; S: they
      The farm hands, practicing with their guns, had been shooting at tin can targets.
      V: had been shooting; S: hands

ANSWERS TO EXERCISES

    b. The farm hands did not realize they were so near the horses grazing in a nearby pasture.
       V: did realize; S: hands
       V: were; S: they
       Unknowingly, the farm hands were near the horses grazing in a nearby pasture.
       V: were; S: hands
    c. The horses ran into the woods; then they scattered through the trees.
       V: ran; S: horses
       V: scattered; S: they
       The horses ran into the woods and scattered through the trees.
       V: ran, scattered; S: horses
    d. The farm hands ran after the horses and called to them, but the horses were panicked.
       V: ran, called; S: hands
       V: were; S: horses
       The farm hands ran after the panicked horses and called to them.
       V: ran, called; S: hands
    e. Finally the farm hands gave up; they stopped the chase, left open the barn door, and put oats into the mangers in the barn.
       V: gave up; S: hands
       V: stopped, left, put; S: they
       Finally giving up, the farm hands stopped the chase, left open the barn door, and put oats into the mangers in the barn.
       V: stopped, left, put; S: hands
    f. The night was dark and cold, and there was no food or water in the woods.
       V: was; S: night
       V: was; S: food, water
       On that dark, cold night, there was no food or water in the woods.
       V: was; S: food, water

ANSWERS TO EXERCISES

g. The horses came slowly into the yard; they stamped their feet and snuffled softly to each other.
V: came; S: horses
V: stamped, snuffled; S: they
The horses came slowly into the yard, stamping their feet and snuffling softly to each other.
V: came; S: horses

h. The horses smelled the grain in the barn and saw the open door; they slipped into their stalls.
V: smelled, saw; S: horses
V: slipped; S: they
The horses, smelling the grain in the barn and seeing the open door, slipped into their stalls.
V: slipped; S: horses

INTRODUCTORY LESSON B

5. (Sample answers; other versions are possible.)
   a. After they left, we finished the meal.
      After dinner, we went to a movie.
   b. Because the paint was chipping, we had to scrape the woodwork.
      Because of the chipping paint, we had to scrape the woodwork.

8. a. The Titanic was a British steamer that was supposed to be unsinkable.
             S-I V-I   S-D V-D

   b. However, the Titanic sank on its first voyage.
                        S-I V-I

   c. On the night of April 14–15, 1912, as it was sailing through icy seas about 1600 miles northeast of New
                                        S-D V-D

ANSWERS TO EXERCISES

                              S-I   V-I
York City, the ship struck an iceberg.
           S-DV-D   S-I   V-I
d. When it tore through the ship's hull, the iceberg made

a 300–foot gash.
                      S-I   S-I   V-I
e. On board ship, crew members and passengers struggled

to fill and release the lifeboats.
      S-I   S-D   V-D
f. The lifeboats, which had room for less than half the
                 V-I
passengers, took on mostly women and children,

leaving fathers and husbands behind.
        S-I   V-I
g. Launching the lifeboats was risky and difficult
         S-D   V-D
because the decks were sloping and wet.
   S-I   V-I   S-D   V-D
h. No one knows exactly how many lives were lost.
   S-I   V-I
i. The sinking of the Titanic was one of the greatest

tragedies in shipping history.
    S-I   V-I   S-I   V-I
9. a. Worms are wet and slimy, (but) snakes are dry.
              S-I   V-I
b. A transparent cap keeps a snake's eyes always open, (so)
    V-I   S-I   S-D   V-D
it is impossible to tell whether a snake sleeps.
     S-I V-I   S-I V-I
c. The snake is deaf to sound carried by air, (;) it hears

by sensing vibrations from the ground.

ANSWERS TO EXERCISES

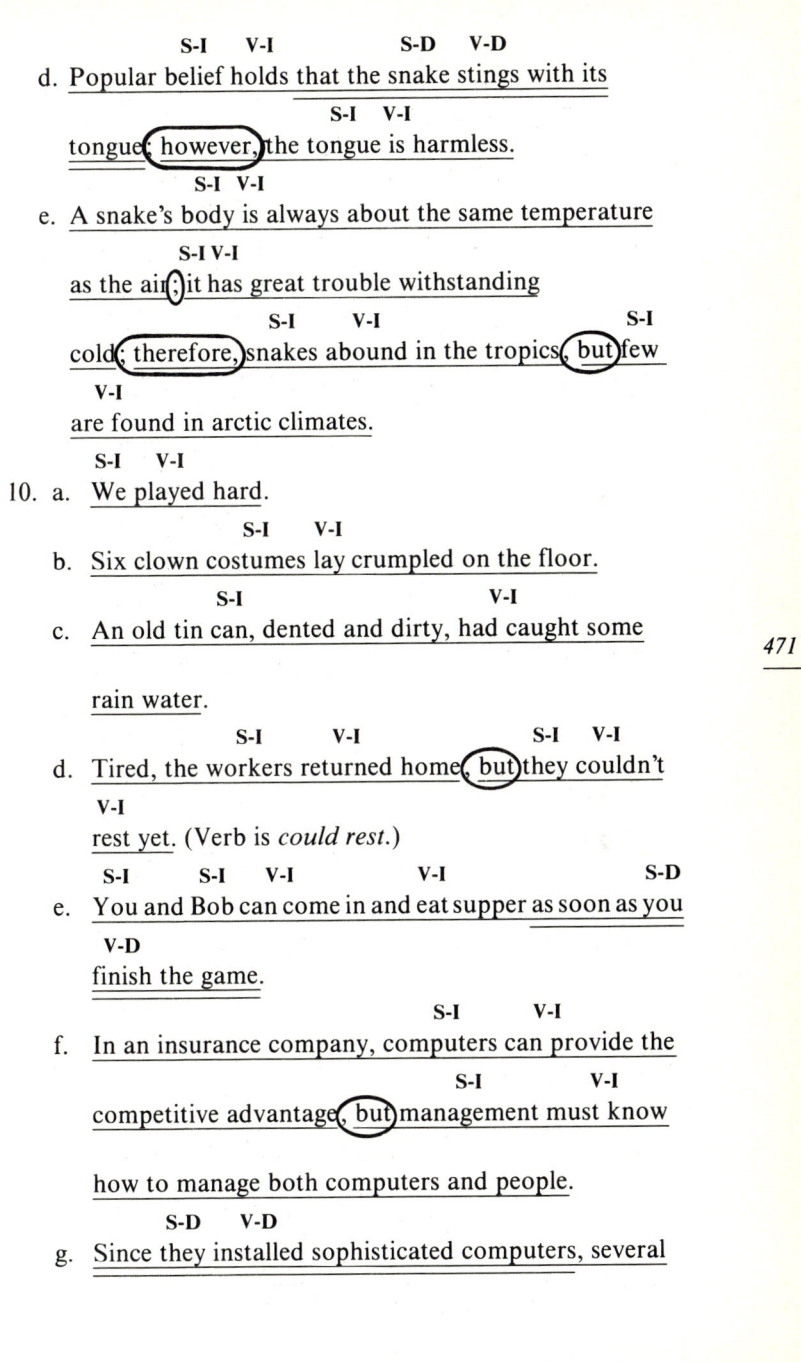

          S-I   V-I   S-D V-D
d. Popular belief holds that the snake stings with its
                      S-I V-I
   tongue; *however,* the tongue is harmless.
      S-I V-I
e. A snake's body is always about the same temperature
         S-I V-I
   as the air; it has great trouble withstanding
                  S-I   V-I   S-I
   cold; *therefore,* snakes abound in the tropics, *but* few
   V-I
   are found in arctic climates.

       S-I   V-I
10. a. We played hard.
                S-I   V-I
   b. Six clown costumes lay crumpled on the floor.
              S-I   V-I
   c. An old tin can, dented and dirty, had caught some
      rain water.
                   S-I   V-I   S-I V-I
   d. Tired, the workers returned home, *but* they couldn't
      V-I
      rest yet. (Verb is *could rest*.)
           S-I   S-I   V-I   V-I   S-D
   e. You and Bob can come in and eat supper as soon as you
      V-D
      finish the game.
                         S-I   V-I
   f. In an insurance company, computers can provide the
                                        S-I   V-I
     competitive advantage, *but* management must know
     how to manage both computers and people.
          S-D   V-D
   g. Since they installed sophisticated computers, several

471

ANSWERS TO EXERCISES

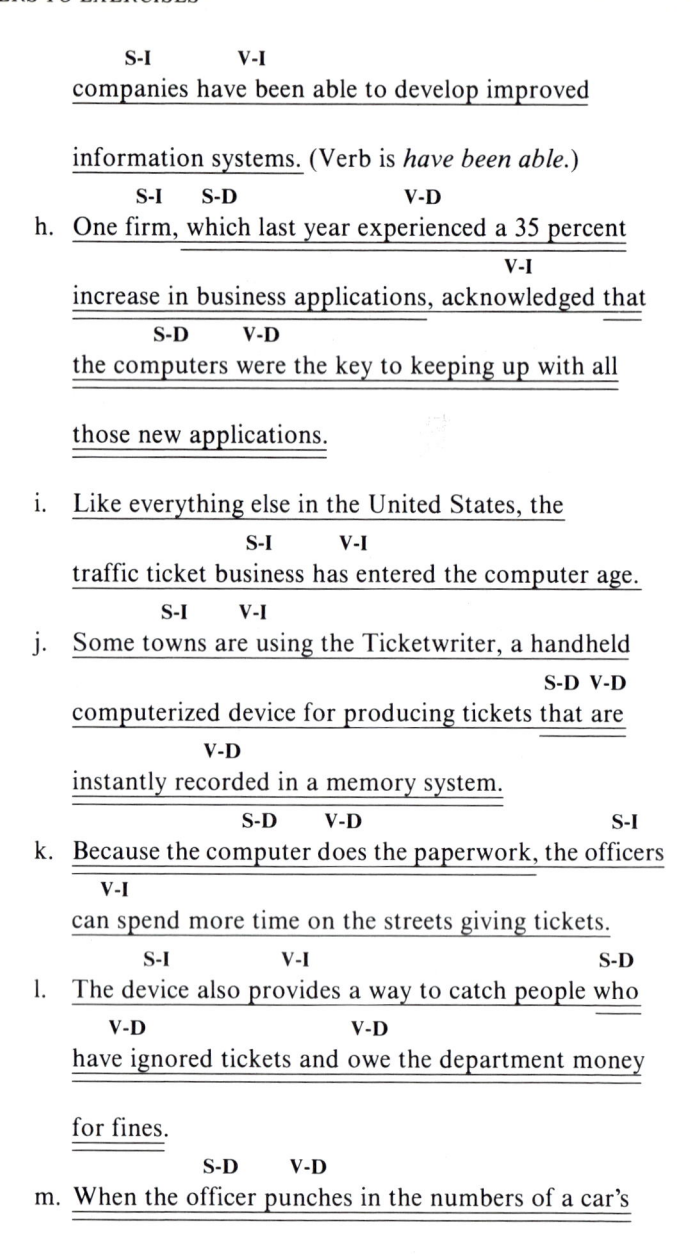

          S-I   V-I
companies have been able to develop improved
information systems. (Verb is *have been able*.)

      S-I   S-D   V-D
h. One firm, which last year experienced a 35 percent
                                     V-I
increase in business applications, acknowledged that
    S-D   V-D
the computers were the key to keeping up with all
those new applications.

i. Like everything else in the United States, the
             S-I   V-I
traffic ticket business has entered the computer age.

   S-I   V-I
j. Some towns are using the Ticketwriter, a handheld
                                 S-D V-D
computerized device for producing tickets that are
    V-D
instantly recorded in a memory system.

         S-D   V-D   S-I
k. Because the computer does the paperwork, the officers
  V-I
can spend more time on the streets giving tickets.

    S-I   V-I   S-D
l. The device also provides a way to catch people who
   V-D   V-D
have ignored tickets and owe the department money
for fines.

        S-D   V-D
m. When the officer punches in the numbers of a car's

ANSWERS TO EXERCISES

             S-I   V-I
license, the machine automatically searches the list of delinquent fine payers.

      S-D   V-D   S-I   V-I
n. If the license matches a delinquent, the device beeps
    V-I
and flashes.

     S-D V-D   S-I   V-I
o. Whenever I go camping, I always have to take along
                    V-D S-D
my sister because there's no one else to stay with her.

(Dependent clause verb is *is*.)

            V-I   S-I
p. There in the window was the most beautiful pair of
   S-D V-D   V-D
gold earrings I had ever seen.

   S-I   S-D   V-D
q. The officer who had jumped out of the car when the
  S-D   V-D   V-I
shooting started now ran zigzagging between the walls
  V-I
and leapt up onto the roof.

  V-I   S-I   S-I
r. It was hard for me to hold down a job, go to school,
  S-I
and take care of my children.

    S-I V-I   S-D   V-D
s. The boss said that I would be recommended for a promotion. (Dependent clause verb is *would be recommended*.)

ANSWERS TO EXERCISES

11. a. <u>Spices</u> <u>were used</u> by the Egyptians 4500 years ago to
            S-I   V-I

embalm bodies.

  b. Today, even <u>cat litter</u> and <u>dolls</u> often <u>contain</u> scent.
                     S-I   S-I   V-I

  c. The <u>smell</u> of smoke that <u>has permeated</u> <u>a building</u>
        S-I   S-D   V-D

after a fire <u>can linger</u> for years.
            V-I

  d. In today's market, <u>companies</u> <u>have discovered</u> that
                              S-I   V-I

<u>consumers</u> <u>will</u> more readily <u>buy</u> a <u>product</u> that <u>smells</u>
   S-D   V-D   V-D   S-D V-D

<u>nice</u> than <u>a product</u> that <u>has</u> no smell.
               S-D V-D

  e. <u>Dogs</u> leased by private owners <u>help</u> find drugs,
      S-I   V-I

termites, and lost children.

  f. The <u>campers</u> wisely <u>set</u> up tents and <u>slept</u> out the
          S-I   V-I   V-I

blizzard.

  g. When a <u>recipe</u> <u>calls</u> for vanilla, the <u>chef</u> <u>inserts</u> a
             S-D   V-D   S-I   V-I

knife into a long vanilla bean and <u>scrapes</u> tiny seeds
                                          V-I

into the pot.

  h. The <u>tent</u> <u>was crowded</u>; <u>tempers</u> <u>flared</u>.
         S-I V-I   S-I   V-I

  i. About 65 million years ago, large <u>numbers</u> of living
                                             S-I

ANSWERS TO EXERCISES

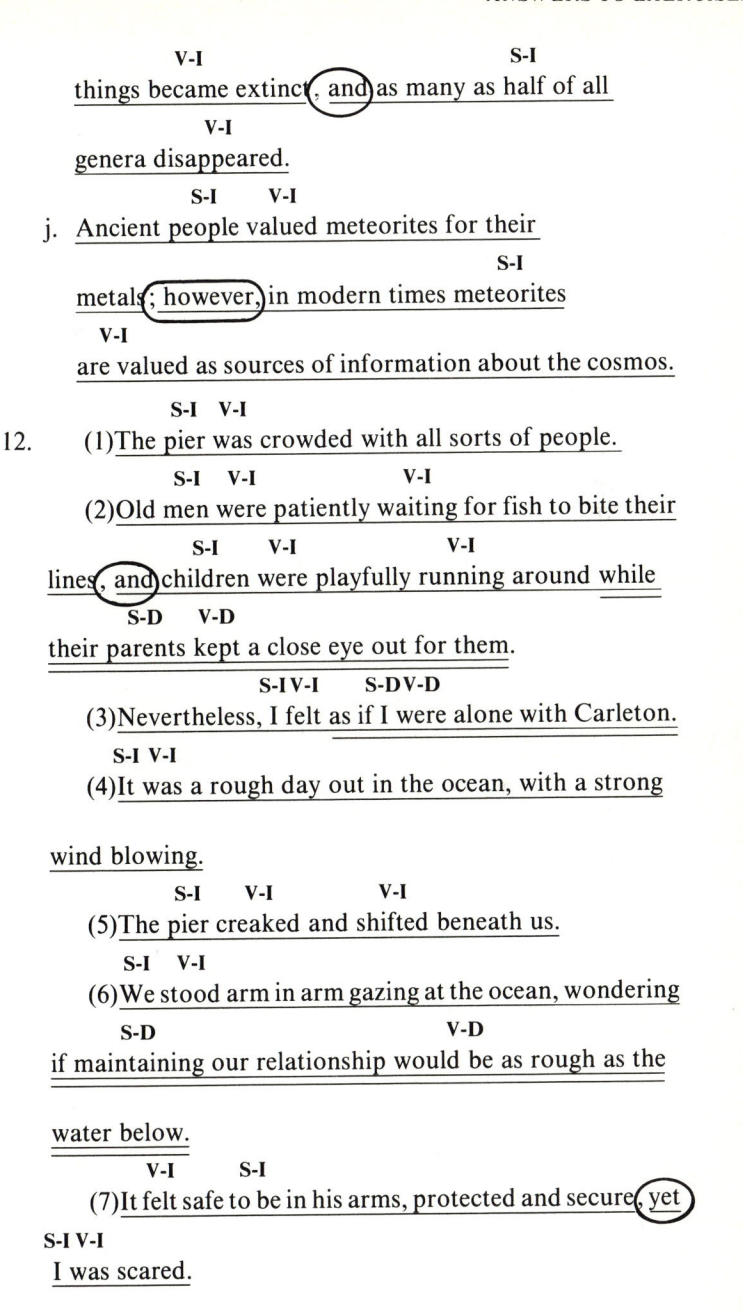

     V-I   S-I
 things became extinct, and as many as half of all
       V-I
 genera disappeared.

    S-I   V-I
j. Ancient people valued meteorites for their
            S-I
 metals; however, in modern times meteorites
  V-I
 are valued as sources of information about the cosmos.

      S-I V-I
12. (1) The pier was crowded with all sorts of people.
     S-I   V-I   V-I
  (2) Old men were patiently waiting for fish to bite their
       S-I   V-I   V-I
 lines, and children were playfully running around while
   S-D   V-D
 their parents kept a close eye out for them.
       S-I V-I   S-D V-D
  (3) Nevertheless, I felt as if I were alone with Carleton.
     S-I V-I
  (4) It was a rough day out in the ocean, with a strong

wind blowing.
      S-I   V-I   V-I
  (5) The pier creaked and shifted beneath us.
     S-I V-I
  (6) We stood arm in arm gazing at the ocean, wondering
    S-D   V-D
 if maintaining our relationship would be as rough as the

water below.
     V-I   S-I
  (7) It felt safe to be in his arms, protected and secure, yet
S-I V-I
 I was scared.

ANSWERS TO EXERCISES

                S-I   V-I   V-I
(8) <u>Perhaps our love would not survive the separation</u>
S-D V-D
<u>we were about to face.</u>

             S-I   V-I
(9) <u>An entire year of college 1200 miles away was an</u>

<u>overwhelming thought.</u>
      S-I   V-I
(10) <u>Tears streamed down my face that day on the pier,</u>
    S-D V-D
<u>the day we had to say goodbye.</u>

20. (Sample answers; other versions are possible.)
    a. 1. The Freedman's Bureau was a federal agency that was created by Congress.
       2. The Freedman's Bureau was a federal agency created by Congress.
    b. 1. The Freedman's Bureau staffed hospitals, which were the only source of medical treatment for many Blacks.
       2. The Freedman's Bureau staffed hospitals, the only source of medical treatment for many Blacks.
    c. 1. The Freedman's Bureau distributed food to many Blacks in the war-torn South who were hungry. OR In the war-torn South, the Freedman's Bureau distributed food to many Blacks who were hungry.
       2. The Freedman's Bureau distributed food to many hungry Blacks in the war-torn South.

21. (Sample answers; other versions are possible.)

    a. Three independent: <u>At the end of the Civil War, only</u>
               S-I   V-I   V-I
    <u>10 percent of U.S. Blacks could read and write; five</u>
              S-I   V-I   V-I
    <u>years later, 21 percent could read and write; the</u>

ANSWERS TO EXERCISES

    S-I   V-I
difference was largely due to the Freedman's Bureau

schools.

                                               S-D
Two independent, two dependent: As the Civil War
  V-D   S-I   V-I
ended, only 10 percent of U.S. Blacks could read or
 V-I   S-I   V-I
write; the Freedman's Bureau schools were largely
                                        S-D
responsible for the fact that five years later, 21 percent
  V-D   V-D
could read and write.

Two independent, one dependent: At the end of the
                 S-I   V-I
Civil War, only 10 percent of U.S. Blacks could read
   V-I   S-I   V-I
or write; the Freedman's Bureau schools were largely
                                        S-D
responsible for the fact that five years later, 21 percent
  V-D   V-D
could read and write.

Two independent: At the end of the Civil War, the
   S-I   V-I
percentage of literate Blacks went from 10 percent to

21 percent in five years; the Freedman's Bureau
  S-I   V-I
schools were largely responsible for the difference.

One independent, one dependent: At the end of the
             S-I   S-D   V-D
Civil War, the percentage of Blacks who could read

477

ANSWERS TO EXERCISES

        V-D   V-I
and write went from 10 percent to 21 percent in five years, largely due to the efforts of the Freedman's Bureau schools.

One independent: At the end of the Civil War, the
        S-I   V-I
percentage of literate Blacks went from 10 percent to 21 percent in five years, largely due to the efforts of the Freedman's Bureau schools.

LESSONS FOR STEP 1

Note: Sentence answers and revisions in Step 1 are suggested only. Other versions are possible.

LESSON FOR STEP 1A

1. a. Gail hit the ball.
   b. A
   c. A
   d. A
   e. A
   f. A
   g. The company hired them all.
   h. A
   i. She wanted to know whether the personnel office had hired all salespeople.
   j. A
   k. A routine the school generally has followed is to allow the children into the hallway only when someone is presenting an assembly. OR only when there is an assembly.

2. The company decided to dispose of all wastes according to federal regulations. However, the government has recently closed the only nearby approved toxic waste dump, so the company faces a problem. OR However, the recent government closing of the only nearby approved toxic waste dump presents a problem for the company. (No change in last sentence.)

LESSON FOR STEP 1B

3. a. Who is afraid of New York City? Of course you know what a great city it is—the Empire State Building, Madison Square Garden, Broadway, Chinatown, Fifth Avenue, Carnegie Hall. *Most people would love to visit New York City, but* the average tourist does not want to experience or witness the disgusting violence on the six-o'clock news. It is true that the city is filthy, congested, and overpopulated with thieves, murderers, and other unpleasant elements. *However,* your chances of surviving a day in the city are not as delicate as a game of Russian roulette. *Despite your fears,* New York City may be both safe and exciting if you know how to travel and how to act like a New Yorker. (The original paragraph is not badly fragmented. However, a few added transitions, such as those in italics, can help to smooth the reader's progress through the various switches between the fearful aspects and the enticing aspects of New York City.)

LESSON FOR STEP 1C

1. a. Since the present site for the new stadium is city owned, financial arrangements are not necessary. (Since financial *arrangements* may in fact be necessary, perhaps the real meaning is: money to purchase a site is not necessary.)
   b. The progress of alcoholism has been classified into four stages: the pre-alcoholic stage (rest as is)

ANSWERS TO EXERCISES

    c. The candidate who adopts a fake personality usually doesn't get elected (rest as is)
    d. Under Rochester's rule, Jane would be a puppet, which would (rest as is)
    e. The record industry cannot control what songs play on the radio because the FCC has that jurisdiction.

2. a. Clearly teens have sex without birth control, and many become pregnant. In fact, every thirty seconds, another unwed teenager becomes pregnant. Naturally, this challenges the Church's stand on premarital sex and its teaching against birth control. (Replace inappropriate verbs *hurt* and *damage,* and the awkward *and without.*)

3. a. So-called "killer Route 9" has always been recognized as life-threatening, especially in Howell. Yet while other highways were dualized, Route 9 was not. Now, with the new development in the area, Route 9 will be a dual highway. Maybe this will finally stop the Route 9 killer. (Use subjects and verbs to move the "killer" aspect of Route 9 to the opening of the sentence and to highlight the fact that new developments will diminish the slaughter.)

4. (1) In planning an article, Ms. G. must always keep the audience in mind. OR When Ms. G. plans an article, she must always keep the audience in mind.
   (2) Ms. G. must carefully handle touchy subjects, such as
   (3) (4) Last two sentences may be left as is, or opening of paragraph 3 may be revised with Ms. G. as subject: for example, "Ms. G. must be concerned about the durability of the magazine articles."

5. Lead for article on growth of *MM: MM* has more than quadrupled its circulation in the past decade. In 1972, when staff editor Brenda Gottesman arrived, the magazine had a trickling circulation of 9,000, and was owned by the Milwaukee Chamber of Commerce. Growth began in 1977, when the *Capital News* purchased the magazine. With

growth came an increase in staff responsibility. For example, Ms. Gottesman, who had been typing, filing, phoning, and doing research, gradually assumed her present responsibilities, which include writing her own monthly column, editing the articles submitted by freelancers, and planning articles for the magazine. Careful planning is the key to the future growth of the magazine, Ms. Gottesman believes.

LESSON FOR STEP 1D

1. a. We need to discover who is in control and what their goals are. OR We need to discover the controllers and their goals.
   b. The college student must often hold down a job at night and borrow money to stay in college.
   c. As I drive over the bridge connecting the island to the mainland, I remember my family's long drives to our beach home and our arrival with armloads of luggage.
   d. The 1940's also saw the rise of political organizations in addition to the formation of youth groups for juvenile problems and the achievement of education reform for the Chicano.
   e. At the beginning of the night, there may be more than enough students to build stage sets, but as it gets later, students leave either because they have class the next day or because they have other things to do.
2. a. According to the final thoughts of the general convention, which included delegates from all the colonies, the purpose of the new government was to provide for (rest as is)
3. a. The massive quantities of drugs consumed have caused severe medical problems, complicated by malnutrition.
   b. Brief periods of forgetfulness, called amnesia, become frequent during or after the trauma.
   c. ... businesses, like restaurants and hotels, that are geared to serve the public.

ANSWERS TO EXERCISES

    d. On the vanity I have a two week old cup of tea, in which the also two week old lemon has begun drawing fruit flies by the swarm.

4. a. Do you often wonder what makes us appreciate certain things more when they're not around than when they are?
   b. Well once at college, you realize, after only three days (rest as is)

EXERCISES FOR ALL OF LESSON 1D

5. a. Tossed into the center of the raft as we rode over a partially submerged rock, I was very lucky to get only a bruise on my knee and a bump on my head. OR I was tossed into the center of the raft as we rode over a partially submerged rock, but I was very lucky to get only a bruise on my knee and a bump on my head. (Reduce the number of independent clauses linked with *and.* Use parallel construction for *bruise* and *bump.*)
   b. When my mom called me to dinner with that stern, strict tone, I knew something was wrong. As I sat down, Dad would slowly look up from his plate and send a bleak smile in my direction. OR look up from his plate, sending a bleak smile in my direction. (First verb changes to active voice—Step 1A—to eliminate awkward placement of *with* and *by* phrases. Use parallel form.)
   c. In the years ahead, we will face many of the same problems that arose for many of these women as they provided and cared for their children. OR In providing and caring for their children, many of these women faced the same problems we will face in the years ahead. (Revise to shorten distance between *problems* and *which.* Eliminate awkward *and.* Change to active voice verb—Step 1A.)
   d. If the raters used the same warning labels for records as for movies, the "R" label on a record would force distributors to think twice about restricting their sales by carrying

ANSWERS TO EXERCISES

the particular album. (Revise for dangling modifier, *using*. Make clearer the relationship of *and therefore restricting sales* to the rest of the sentence.)

6. a. When Ralph Morrison, a ship analyst at the U.S. Naval intelligence Center in Feester, Virginia, noticed three photos of a Soviet aircraft carrier lying on a colleague's desk, he thought the photos might be of interest to the press, so he gave them to the *American Defense Weekly*.
   b. The Digital Equipment Corporation achieved national recognition by winning the Business in the Arts Award, which is jointly sponsored by the Business Committee for the Arts and *Forbes Magazine,* and which is the only national program to honor businesses for sponsoring the arts.

LESSON FOR STEP 1E

1. a. The Chicano Service Organization still exists, but, because of its nonpartisan platform, it holds little power within the Chicano community.
   b. If the source of electricity is near the stadium, wiring costs will be less. OR A source of electricity near the stadium will reduce wiring costs.
   c. A solution being discussed is to require a C average for all students receiving federal assistance.
   d. Due to the harsh treatment my car experiences daily, I found myself petting and consoling my faithful companion. OR Because my car experiences harsh treatment daily, I would pet and console my faithful companion.
   e. Traffic is a major consideration, so the stadium must be accessible by major roadways. OR Accessibility by major roadways is a major consideration for the stadium.
   f. Lack of parking at the existing stadium causes transportation problems. OR causes problems.
   g. Although probably no ideal stadium location exists, the

media and city officials must consider many factors before deciding anything.

LESSON FOR STEP 1F

1. a. The lack of space at concession stands is absolutely horrendous. OR The quality of the space at concession stands is absolutely horrendous. OR Space at concession stands is horrendously cramped.
   b. The last irritation was little Bobbie asking to play. (Revise for trite phrase *last straw*.)
   c. By building the new stadium in a less congested area with more parking, we could avoid inconveniences for residents when fans park on the streets. OR . . . we could avoid having sports fans take residents' parking spaces.
   d. Within the last six to eight years, the Chicano population has become substantially more sophisticated, both educationally and legally. OR Within the past six to eight years, the educational and legal sophistication of the Chicano population has grown substantially.
2. a. Half of the cases of dyslexia are inherited.
   b. The first symptom of dyslexia is reduced vision and hearing.
   c. Dyslexia is a symptom of one or more nervous system problems.
   d. Even with adequate emotional and educational stimulation, the dyslexic reverses and scrambles letters and words when reading, writing, and spelling.
3. a. Sources reflecting the history and development of our Constitution are filled with degrading descriptions of the inability of the common people to participate in their government, specifically through election.

EXERCISES FOR ALL OF STEP 1

1. a. In the best definition of loneliness I have ever read, poet May Sarton says that people are lonely when they have no

one with whom to exchange the deepest part of themselves.
- b. The definition helps to explain why married people may feel lonely and single people may not.
- c. Sometimes, when I have no private time, I lose sight of myself; then when I talk with others, I hear myself parroting their views—a lonely and depressing experience.
- d. My hours alone do not make me feel lonely; they keep me from feeling lonely because they help me know an essential self which I can share with others.

2. a. I had always been impressed and attracted by French culture and wanted to study it first hand. In my fourth year of studying French, the opportunity to visit France made me elated but then a bit apprehensive. Everyone I knew who had visited France told me how awful their trips were because the French were so rude and nasty. So the French hate Americans. What do I do now?

3. a. Imagine being swept down a river by rushing white water totally under nature's control—exhilarating and exciting, but also dangerous. Three years ago in June, on the Snake River, I went white water rafting for the first time. I was very frightened but I was looking forward to a physical challenge.

   My parents, my brother and I left for Wild Rock State Park on a Saturday morning with almost forty other people, all very excited but very weary because no one knew what to expect. After nearly four hours, we arrived at our campground, pitched tents, and prepared for sleep. First, however, we had a meeting around the fire. There were only eight experienced people in this group, so everyone listened intently.

   First the guide told us that, in this very dangerous sport, carelessness and stupidity cause many deaths. The guide said never to get excited or frightened because you will do dumb things.

   Water, we were told, is very dangerous. In the rock-covered river, many accidents can occur. Never kneel or

ANSWERS TO EXERCISES

sit on the bottom of the raft because if the raft rides over rocks, you can be injured. Also, hold your hand over the end of the paddle because if the other end hits a rock, the end you are holding might be knocked into your face.

Careless white water rafters have caused many drownings. Very often people are thrown from their raft—a crucial time. You must not try to get back into the raft because you may get sucked under it, caught between the raft and a rock. You must float on top of the water with your feet downstream to push off rocks. You must not try to stand up because if your feet become wedged between rocks in the bottom, the water's force will push you under and you will drown.

LESSONS FOR STEP 2

LESSON FOR STEP 2A

1. Fragments are a, c, e, f, h, i.
2a. Fragments are 2, 3.
4. Fragments are a, b, c, d, e, f, g, h, i, j, m.
5. Fragments are a: 2; b: 4; c: 2, 3; d: 2.
6a. Fragment is 1.
7. (Sample answers; other versions are possible.)
   a. The airplane was damaged.
      We knew that the airplane was damaged.
   b. Someone wanted my scarf.
      She was the woman who wanted my scarf.
   c. I loved the puppy.
      We went to the beach, which I loved.
   d. However, he laughed.
      Even though he laughed, I did not think the joke was funny.

ANSWERS TO EXERCISES

   e. The ice was too thick.
      We gave up because the ice was too thick.
   f. The customers became too demanding.
      Whenever the customers became too demanding, I took a coffee break.
   g. The pennies were tossed into the fountain.
      The pennies that were tossed into the fountain were given to charity.
   h. I dearly loved my brother.
      Joe was my brother, whom I dearly loved.
   i. The guard wanted my scarf to use as a flag.
      Tim talked to the guard who wanted my scarf to use as a flag.
   j. The danger was going too far.
      We were well aware of the danger of going too far.
   m. As we sailed jauntily into the harbor, the flags waved and the people cheered.
      Sailing jauntily into the harbor, while the flags waved and the people cheered, Jones relished his victory.
8. (Sample answers; other versions are possible.)
   a. This forces a shoot-out, which has the spectators hanging on the edges of their seats.
   b. This is very difficult when other servers have used all the silverware, plates, and glasses.
   c. For some reason, many people think that louder and slower speech is the key to understanding different languages, when in fact shouting makes the situation seem almost ridiculous, especially if you're the "foreigner" watching a person yelling in vain and getting nowhere.
   d. How we handle the pollution of our lakes is an important political issue that each individual must consider carefully and knowledgeably. OR
      Our approach to lake pollution is an important political issue. . . .
9. a. The director of the county animal shelter told me that

ANSWERS TO EXERCISES

   the rabies epidemic had increased greatly during the past decade, especially in the city's wild animal population.
10. a. Fragments are 6, 8. Sample revisions: But since so many people go to Tio Rancho restaurant, the bread doesn't get enough time to heat, making the server take a tray of bread to the ovens that the cooks use in the kitchen. Then the cooks protest that the server is interfering with their jobs.
   b. Fragments are 5, 9. Sample revisions: (5)It contains sulfur and some metals, which are very expensive to remove. (8)The burning of coal and other fossil fuels emits carbon dioxide that can accumulate in the atmosphere, holding heat on the earth's surface and leading to the Greenhouse Effect—a great meltdown of the polar ice caps, which would cause destruction and cost many lives.

LESSON FOR STEP 2B

1. a. The dogwood died this spring; it
      The dogwood died this spring. It
   b. while; unfortunately, it
   c. while, and
   d. bankers; Monica
      bankers. Monica
   e. bankers, but
   f. Europe; however, most
   g. Americans; mushroom
      Americans. Mushroom
2. a. Run-on is 2. Sample revision: He had no choice; he was dealing OR choice. He (Colon or dash are also possible to join the two clauses, since the second is an explanation or enumeration of the first—see Step 2Q.)
   b. Run-on. Don't get me wrong; Americans do not hate their country; they OR Don't get me wrong. Americans

do not hate their country. They (You may use any combination of semicolons and periods as links. The clauses are not similar in form and function, so cannot qualify as a series to be separated by commas.)
- c. Run-on. herself; she OR herself. She
- d. Run-on. business; you OR business. You
- e. Misplaced semicolon. smile, of (Second part of sentence is not an independent clause.)
- f. Run-on. cheating; it OR cheating. It
- g. Run-on. yes. However OR yes; however
- h. (Not a run-on because three clauses are similar in form and function.)
- i. Run-on. diabetes; it OR diabetes. It
- j. Run-on. down; she OR down. She
- k. Run-on. people; he OR people. He
- l. Misplaced semicolon. power, I (Second part of sentence is a dependent clause, *that I can be happy*.)
- m. Run-on. believe; you OR believe. You
- n. Run-on is 3. month; then OR month. Then
- q. Misplaced semicolon. ended, the (First part of sentence is not independent clause, but dependent.)

3. (Sample answers; other versions are possible.)
   a. The settlers arrived in a cold February with very little food; that winter, 30 percent of them died. OR Arriving in a cold February, the settlers had very little food with them; 30 percent of them died that winter. OR That winter, 30 percent of the settlers died; they had arrived in a cold February with very little food. OR When the settlers arrived, in a cold February, they had very little food; 30 percent of them died that winter.
   b. The June rain filled the mountain gullies, causing flash floods and mud slides; the rangers went out to look for the three parties known to be camping in the mountains. OR Three parties were known to be camping in the mountains; when the June rain filled the mountain gullies and

ANSWERS TO EXERCISES

caused flash floods and mud slides, the rangers went out to look for the campers. OR June rain caused flash floods and mud slides; floods filled the mountain gullies; the rangers went out to look for the three parties known to be camping in the mountains.

LESSON FOR STEP 2C

1. a. V: is; S: subject
   b. V: could obtain; S: she
   c. V: moved; S: management
   d. V: lives; S: doctor; V: is; S: Gordon
   e. V: hands down, signs, may play; S: jury
   f. V: has influenced; S: decision
   g. V: is; S: body; V: is; S: it/ transmission and engine; V: cost; S: that
   h. V: was; S: reasoning; V: gave; S: that; V: must; S: neutrinos
   i. V: resemble; S: Leaders; V: fail, try; S: who; V: stood, commanded; S: who
   j. V: may be shared, [may be] developed; S: task; V: remains, can be delegated; S: it

2. Singular: f, g, h, i, k, l, q. Plural: a, b, d, e, n, p. Either: c, j, m, o.

3. a. gets (Subject: *any*)
   b. has (Subject: *every one*)
   d. meets (Subject: *group*)
   e. need (Subjects: *trails, lookout*)
   h. wins (Subject: *team*)
   i. goes (Subject: *group*)
   j. go (Subject: who, referring to *men*. Meaning is clarified by sentence i.)
   k. separate (Subject: *that*, referring to *boulders*. If *that* is read as referring to *one*, then *separates* is correct.)
   l. has (Subject: *profit*)

m. has been . . . that is under (Subjects: *results; that,* referring to *area*)
n. survives (Subjects: *cactus, plant*)
o. gives (Subject: *recollection. Happen* is correct because its subject is *dates.*)

LESSON FOR STEP 2D

1. All verbs are in past except the following, which are in present: *concerns, moves, struggles, alerts, runs, shoot.* These verbs are in present because they describe the events of the short story. However, past tense is dominant. It is used to describe Tuinstra's actions, which are the topic of the passage.
2. a. had been read . . . already had answered
   b. because I had been involved
   c. It had been expertly
   d. She had studied (*Had* before *decided* is optional. It may be understood.)
   e. She had made
3. Make present tense dominant, since you are discussing a still existing work of art. Paragraph 1, since it refers to events before "this scene," should be in present perfect:

   Aslaksen has come out to support Dr. S. to enhance his own reputation in the community. A. also has supported Dr. S. because he knows (in present, because it's still true) S's proposal to improve the baths will eventually improve A's own business (*will improve* is future tense, to be consonant with present tense *knows.*)

   Paragraph 2: he is also
4. (1) received OR has received OR receives (8) has always wondered if the waves freeze (9) wants . . . simply cannot OR could not (10) batter (11) happen (12) it is a bit late (Sentence 1 is cast in present tense—*today.* Thus the verb may be in

ANSWERS TO EXERCISES

present—*receives*. However, the action may be interpreted as having happened before the present moment in which the writer is locating the narrative. Thus *has received* is appropriate to describe action completed. Most readers in this context would probably not object to simple past—*received*. Sentence 8 needs present perfect to describe continuing action in the past, and present tense—*freeze*—to describe something still true.)

5. Bob . . . begins by reading. . . . Then he reads the story . . . can answer best

LESSON FOR STEP 2E

past: slunk. perfect: slunk. No archaic, obsolete, rare, or dialect forms. No forms equally acceptable.
Present: she slinks
Future: she will slink
Past: she slunk
Present perfect: she has slunk
Past perfect: she had slunk
Future perfect: she will have slunk

2. a. lie; b. sitting; c. sitting; d. laid; e. set; f. rose; g. chose; h. choose; i. led; j. lose

3. a. might have gone; b. could have happened d. If I had not (OR hadn't) caught him, he would (OR he'd) have fallen

4. (2) awaking (6) lay (7) I had to have awakened OR I had to have waked up OR I had to have woken up (See dictionary for definitions and principal parts of *wake, awaken,* and *awake.*)

5. Every day when I hear the mail carrier come around the neighborhood, I am waiting (OR I wait) to see if anything has come (OR will come) for me. Usually nothing comes. But yesterday a big, fat envelope came rattling into the mail chute. I opened it. What was it? Nothing but a piece of

cardboard. Every once in awhile, Samantha sends me a picture she has taken of the kids. (*Has taken* is present perfect, to reflect action completed before the present tense but impacting on it. *Sends* is in present because it's still true—Lesson 2D.)

LESSON FOR STEP 2F

1. (Antecedents are in brackets.)
   a. (1) my [speaker understood] me [speaker understood] (2) it [to bike], my [speaker understood] (3) I [speaker understood] (4) it [to bike], we [speaker and friend understood], ourselves [speaker and friend, understood]. (5) which [trip], it [trip]
2. (Sample answers; other versions are possible.)
   a. Option 1: For a person coming from Towson. . . . When coming from the south . . . the person
      Option 2: If you are coming. . . . If you are coming from the south, east, or west of the stadium, you must go through the city.
   OR eliminate pronouns: Coming from Towson, . . . road. Coming from the south . . . stadium, go through the city. (This version leaves out the concept "has to" or "must" in the last sentence, so, though it is the most economical, it may not be the most desirable, if the writer wants to retain the "has to" idea.)
      The first version is more distant and objective. It would be appropriate if the writer were describing the transportation routes in an objective or formal context. The second option sounds more like the writer is giving directions to the reader face to face. It is more conversational, less formal.
   b. Option 1: The nightmare will haunt you for the rest of your life.
      Option 2: The nightmare will haunt a person for the rest

of his life. (To avoid the masculine pronoun—haunt a person for life.)

Option 1 includes the reader as one of those who might be haunted. Option 2 is more distant and formal.

c. Option 1: With no intention of hurting anyone's feelings, many times you would rather not share your clothes with roommates. For example

Option 2: With no intention of hurting anyone's feelings, many times one would rather not share one's clothes with roommates. For example, how does one tell a friend not to wear one's favorite sweater because it's too tight on her and it may stretch?

Option 1 sounds conversational and natural. Option 2 sounds more formal and requires revision to avoid frequent and awkward *one*.

d. Option 1: In high school I learned that losing is a team effort and that when one plays for a high caliber team, people take for granted that the team will win.

Option 2: In high school I learned that losing is a team effort and that when you play for a high caliber team, people take for granted that you (OR the team) will win.

Option 3: In high school I learned that losing is a team effort and that when I played for a high caliber team, people took for granted that we would win.

Option 1, using *one*, forces the writer into the neutral *the team* because the statement now is a general truth. Option 2 phrases the general truth using *you*, so as to include the reader. This version sounds more conversational. In fact, strictly speaking, it breaks this lesson's guideline about not using *you* for general truths. Option 3 makes the entire lesson that was learned specific to the reader. The writer loses something of the universality of the lesson learned, and focuses instead upon the writer's experience in his/her particular high school.

3. (Sample answers; other revisions are possible.)

ANSWERS TO EXERCISES

a. Change to plural: It is important for children to know that their parents are there to listen to their problems.
b. Change to plural: Hard work and practice will help writers sharpen and develop their feature writing skills.
Also possible—omit pronoun: will help the writer sharpen and develop feature writing skills.
c. Change to plural: Boaters who have become confident about their ability to maneuver their crafts may risk their lives foolishly in bad weather.
d. Ask a farmer what he or she thinks.
e. An athlete who begins to eat proper foods will find strength and endurance improving. (OR will improve strength and endurance.)

4. Eliminate pronouns where possible; use *a person* or *one:* Of course, bodybuilding is not easy. Maintaining concentration and discipline is necessary when beginning to train. At times a person doesn't feel like pushing anymore, feels depleted of energy and listless. (You may substitute *one* for *a person.*)
Use plural: Of course, bodybuilding is not easy. People must maintain concentration and discipline when they begin to train. At times they won't feel like pushing anymore; they will feel depleted of energy and listless.

LESSON FOR STEP 2G

1. a. me; b. me; c. who; d. who, whom; e. whom; f. who; g. me; h. I; i. I; j. me; k. who, he or I

LESSON FOR STEP 2H

1. a. ... tissue, exposing. ... OR ... tissue. This procedure exposes OR For example, mammography and xeromammography take an X-ray image of the tissue, exposing the breast to X-ray radiation.
b. Out of these taxes is being paid (OR These taxes are

ANSWERS TO EXERCISES

paying) the full cost of death row inmates, who, in return, give nothing back to society. OR Out of these taxes the full cost of death row inmates is being paid. The inmates, in return, give

c. a type of brotherhood originating in the Chicano heritage. This common cultural heritage has allowed (The writer may have reasons for retaining *It is this common cultural heritage,* for emphasis.)

d. Annmarie amused herself in her "house," a hideaway of boulders that separated the neighbors' yard from ours. OR Annmarie amused herself in her hideaway—redefined as her "house"—among the boulders that separated the neighbors' yard from ours.

2. I can't quite figure out why Kelly seemed so much older than the rest of the children. But I know another aspect of Kelly's personality that made her special. Kelly had courage, authority, maturity, but most of all she had a sense of humor—the finishing touch. She had a way of making people smile, making me smile. Not that she was always telling jokes, but she had a natural wit. Kelly was able to laugh just as much as she made other people laugh. Her happiness showed on her face and in everything she did. Maybe her mission in life was to put laughter into other peoples' eyes—something she did well and easily. After one day I felt I had known Kelly for a lifetime. She was warm and giving to everyone she met. Yes, Kelly was blind, but she learned to see not with her eyes but with her heart. I will always remember Kelly and her special gift for appreciating life. One thing I learned from that memorable day is that the heart truly sees better than the eyes.

LESSON FOR STEP 21

1. b. its verdict
   c. his or her group leader

d. her uniform
e. that it had no glass in it
f. on his or her ticket may come forward to claim his or her (A smoother version would be created by eliminating pronouns: Anyone with ticket number 347 may come forward to claim a prize.)
g. his or her office
h. its own

EXERCISES FOR ALL PRONOUN LESSONS

2. a. Whom did
   c. of his or her life.
   d. If women are qualified and can perform the same work that a man does, they receive equal pay. OR If a woman is qualified and can perform the same work that a man does, she receives equal pay.
   e. Being a good friend is not always easy. It can be as hard as being a parent. At times a friendship is severely tested, and it's difficult to overlook things the friend has done that might have upset us. But at those times we have to look deep inside ourselves to realize the true value of what we have.
   OR Being a good friend is not always easy. It can be as hard as being a parent. At times a friendship is severely tested, and it's difficult to overlook upsetting things the friend has done. But at those times one must look deep inside to realize the true value of what one has.
   OR Being a good friend is not always easy. It can be as hard as being a parent. At times a friendship is severely tested, and it's difficult to overlook things the friend has done that might have upset you. But at those times you must look deep inside yourself to realize the true value of what you have.

ANSWERS TO EXERCISES

LESSON FOR STEP 2J

1. a. There's a small tear that'll get bigger if we don't fix it.
   b. I'd like to know whether they've eaten, or whether they're hungry.
   c. I've given so much time that I'm exhausted.
2. a. eats, hers
   b. predicts
3. ponies, fields, pairs, manes, breezes, hooves, grasses, 3's
4. a. It's; b. its; c. hers; d. mother's, girls; e. axes; f. axes; g. axes'; h. axes; i. day's; j. sawfish's, looks; k. plantings, hers, husband's; l. pairs, 3's

LESSON FOR STEP 2K

1. Delete commas from b, c, e, f, g, h.

LESSON FOR STEP 2L

1. a. Nevertheless, I
   b. storm, debris
   c. hood, she
   d. by, flag
   e. money, however,
   f. costs, you
   g. In 1779, while not yet three, ... error, the father
   i. (Optional commas are in parentheses)
      Yesterday(,). . . . year, my. . . . Of course(,) I. . . . overalls, ...taken back, he

LESSON FOR STEP 2M

1. (Optional commas are in parentheses.)
   a. The recruits, after marching five miles, will
   b. They may not, however, leave

ANSWERS TO EXERCISES

- c. American cockroach, which . . . long(,) or more(,) and (Commas around *or more* are optional because the oppositional element is so short.)
- d. Hunting, the most aggressive outdoor sport, repels him.
- e. Elijah Johnson, whose great grandparents were slaves, now
- f. shelves, children, not
- g. lamps, since we had them rewired, have
- h. police, fortunately, got more help(,)
- i. more, despite
- j. Politics and war, too, have . . . Cambodia once again.
- k. Today, says the director, Nguyen van Nghi, fifty people, both experts and local villagers, are
- l. Liberty, when its restoration is finished, will
- m. dangers not . . . ground, where . . . death, but . . . simulator, where
- n. price, but art OR price; art (Original version is a run-on. See Step 2B)

LESSON FOR STEP 2N

1. a. The IRS (Internal Revenue Service) has published this material. (This is the only option. The interruption is too sharp for mere commas; do not use dashes to set off an explanation of terms in the kind of official or formal setting this statement implies.)
   b. My son—the rascal—went off with my scissors. OR My son, the rascal, went off with my scissors. (Parentheses would be inappropriate because the interrupter is a shift, rather than a businesslike explanation.)
   c. The tape, believe it or not, has disappeared. OR The tape—believe it or not—has disappeared. (Parentheses inappropriate for same reason as b.)
   d. The street sounds—bells, sirens, shouts of children playing—came dimly (Dashes are more appropriate than

ANSWERS TO EXERCISES

commas, since the interrupter has interior commas that could cause confusion. Parentheses not appropriate for same reason as b.)

e. Museum lists of trustees (who tend to be generous donors as well as collectors) do not contain many Hollywood names. OR use dashes in place of parentheses. (Topic and tone are businesslike, so parentheses are appropriate for the explanation. However, dashes would also be appropriate. Commas are less satisfactory since the interrupter is quite long and quite sharply different from the flow of the sentence.)

f. programs, Milton Radisson, calculates that, altogether, the college's engineers have supplied about sixty-seven years of professional service (teaching and consultation) to Peruvian engineering schools. (Dashes are also appropriate.)

g. ground—so (Semicolon would also be acceptable. Comma would create run-on—Step 2B.)

h. again—but (Comma would also be acceptable.)

LESSON FOR STEP 2O

1. (Optional commas are in parentheses.)
   a. talented, bright,
   b. weak, inefficient(,)
   c. violent,
   d. Sweaty, thirsty(,) and bone weary, (Comma after weary, because it is an introducer. See Step 2L.)
   f. rusty, drafty(,) . . . reliable, smooth(,) (Comma after *battered* to link two independent clauses joined by coordinating connector—see Step 2B.)
   g. bright,
   h. Randy's, John's(,)

LESSON FOR STEP 2P

1. (Optional commas are in parentheses.)
   a. novels: *The Invisible Man, Wuthering Heights, Jane Eyre*(,) and
   b. *Man, Wuthering Heights, Jane Eyre*(,) and
   c. *Man, Wuthering Heights, Jane Eyre*(,) and
   d. *Man,* the story of a black man growing up in America; *Wuthering Heights,* a dark, gothic novel about twisted relationships on the forsaken British moors; and *Jane Eyre,* the tale of a young woman's attempt to find autonomy in a repressive culture.
   e. following: a set of sheets and towels, two blankets, a pillow(,) and
   f. towels, preferably marked with his or her name; two thick, heavy blankets; and
   g. directions: ... separate party; the second ... third national party; and (Commas might replace the semicolons, but semicolons are advisable because the elements are long and complex.)
   h. pets; caring for children; or collecting bottles, newspapers(,) or (Semicolons are used because one of the elements has interior commas.)
   i. creative, enterprising(,) and
   j. store, answering telephones(,) or
2. (Optional commas are in parentheses.)
   a. clean, repair(,) and
   b. He turns, fakes a shot, beats the last defender(,)
   c. Broke, dressed in tattered clothes, but
   d. oysters, the boys peeled the shrimp(,) and
   e. Should I stay in, study, and ace my test, or do up the town, socialize till dawn, and maybe meet a promising specimen?
   f. greenhouse, then ... safe, then
   g. bite, whether it was house trained(,) and

ANSWERS TO EXERCISES

    h. ragged, each . . . body(,) and
    i. warm, the sand clean(,) and
    j. tasted; talk . . . candy; or

LESSON FOR STEP 2Q

1. a. location—Hunt Valley OR location: Hunt Valley
   b. here—the OR here: the
   c. everything—malaria OR everything: malaria
   d. disaster—the OR disaster: the
   e. friends—be OR friends: be
   f. participate—the National Science Foundation—played (Colon is not possible because the explanation has part of the sentence on both sides. Commas would also be acceptable. Parentheses would be appropriate only if the NSF was not central to the writer's point.)

EXERCISES FOR ALL INTERIOR PUNCTUATION

1. (Optional punctuation is in parentheses.)
   a. In the northern woods, beech, pine(,) and maple are joined by white birches. (Comma after *woods* separates the introducer—Lesson 2L. Other commas separate items in a series—Lesson 2P.)
   b. The slender, ghostly birches lean silently together(,) like elders at a town meeting. (Comma after *slender* separates adjectives in a series—Lesson 2O. Optional comma after *together* sets off nonrestrictive modifier—Lesson 2M. Comma is optional because the modifier is closely related to the sentence and there is no chance of misreading.)
   c. Walking among birches in the winter, with snow sifting silently down, is like walking into some ancient, magic circle. (Commas set off the nonrestrictive modifier *with*

snow sifting silently down—Lesson 2M. Comma after *ancient* separates adjectives in a series—Lesson 2O.)

d. Discovered quite recently, the Amsterdam albatross *(Diomedea amsterdamensis)* is considered one of the rarest seabirds in the world. (Comma after *recently* separates the introducer—Lesson 2L. The scientific name of the albatross is in parentheses because it is a strong interrupter—a formal, business-like explanation—Lesson 2N.)

e. Contrary to what you might think, the Amsterdam albatross does not live in the Netherlands but on tiny, remote Amsterdam Island in the southern Indian Ocean. (Comma after *think* separates the introducer—Lesson 2L. Comma after *Netherlands* might be inserted to separate oppositional elements with *but,* because the elements are long and complex. Comma after *tiny* separates adjectives in a series—Lesson 2O. No commas after *southern* or *remote* because in both cases the last two words—*Indian Ocean* and *Amsterdam Island*—act as one noun—Lesson 2O.)

f. Nesting in peat bogs, the albatross mating pairs—of whom there are only fifteen—raise one check every two years. (Comma after *bogs* separates the introducer—Lesson 2L. Dashes set off the strong interrupter—Lesson 2N. Parentheses or commas would also be acceptable. Colon would not be acceptable because there are parts of the same sentence on both sides of the interrupter.)

g. The albatross have slick, black backs with white, furry, feathered edges, like capes with white fur linings. (Final comma separates the nonrestrictive modifier—Lesson 2M. All other commas separate adjectives in a series—Lesson 2O.)

h. Pastrami is basically beef shoulder—often kosher—cured in brine and spices, smoked(,) and finally steamed. (Dashes set off strong interrupter—Lesson 2N. Parentheses would also be acceptable. Commas are not as

ANSWERS TO EXERCISES

good because the interrupter is too strong and because, with the other commas and the length of the sentence, confusion could result. The commas separate items in a series—Lesson 2P. Comma before the last item is optional.)

i. Pastrami has a checkered past: Romanians, Turks(,) and Greeks all claim to have invented it. OR past; Romanians (Semicolon is acceptable to separate two independent clauses—Lesson 2B. Colon is also appropriate because second clause is explanation of the first—Lesson 2Q. Commas separate items in a series—Lesson 2P.)

j. A delicatessen in my neighborhood in New York City makes its own pastrami from an old(,) Romanian recipe—as much as 2,000 pounds of it per week. (Comma after *old* is optional, though comma rules call for it (Lesson 2O), because in actual usage a comma in this type of phrase that includes a nationality is often omitted. Dash marks strong interrupter—Lesson 2N. No commas to mark *in my neighborhood in NYC* because it is a restrictive modifier—Lesson 2M.)

k. Maritoni's pastrami is delicious, subtly spiced, not too salty, and buttery in texture. (Commas separate items in a series—Lesson 2P. Last comma is necessary to prevent misreading as *not too salty and buttery*. A colon or dash could follow *delicious* if the other descriptions were taken as explanations of *delicious*.)

l. When I asked the owner, Joe Maritoni, what his secret was, he said it's the New York City tap water used in curing. (Commas set off the modifier *Joe Maritoni*—Lesson 2M (noun in apposition). Comma after *was* separates the introducer—Lesson 2L. No comma after City, because *tap water* acts as one term. No comma separates *used in curing* because the modifier is restrictive—Lesson 2M.)

m. Lest you think he was making that up, I read recently in

Consumer Reports that, in fact, New York City tap water is as pure as any bottled mineral water on the market. (Comma after *up* separates the introducer—Lesson 2L. Commas separate the nonrestrictive interrupter *in fact*—Lesson 2M.)

n. The Southeast's devastating, record-breaking drought dried up wells, pushed thermometers to 100 degrees(,) and claimed more than forty human lives. (Comma after *devastating* separates adjectives in a series—Lesson 2O. Other commas separate elements in a series—Lesson 2P. Comma before the last item is optional.)

o. The damage, by August of 1986, was disastrous—more than $2 billion in agriculture and other business losses. (Commas set off the nonrestrictive modifier. A dash introduces the enumeration. A colon would also be acceptable—Lesson 2N.)

p. The states affected were the Carolinas, Alabama, Georgia, Maryland, Delaware, Virginia, West Virginia(,) and Tennessee. (Commas separate items in a series—Lesson 2P.)

q. (No punctuation. Avoid the temptation to place a comma after *grains,* between subject and verb—Lesson 2K.)

r. However, in addition to suffering and frustration for humans and animals alike, the drought of 1986, surprisingly, produced a great, old fashioned, neighborly outpouring of helpfulness that surprised many Americans. (The first two commas separate two introducers—Lesson 2L. The next two commas set off the nonrestrictive modifier, *surprisingly*—Lesson 2M. Commas after *great* and *old fashioned* separate adjectives in a series—Lesson 2O. No commas separate *old* and *fashioned* because they act as one term.)

s. Farmers in the midwest, which had not been hit by the drought, began sending bales of hay by the tens of thousands to their fellow farmers in the Southeast. (Commas set off the nonrestrictive modifier—Lesson 2M. Commas are possible to set off *by the tens of thousands* if the phrase is interpreted as nonrestrictive—Lesson 2M.)

t. When I was young, my uncle, a farmer who had increasingly severe arthritis, was(,) one spring(,) unable to plow his fields. (Comma after *young* separates the introducer—Lesson 2L. Commas set off the nonrestrictive modifier *a farmer who had increasingly severe arthritis*—Lesson 2M. No comma after *increasingly* because it works with *severe* as a single adjective—Lesson 2O. No comma after *farmer* because *who had increasingly severe arthritis* is a restrictive modifier to farmer—Lesson 2M. Also, comma after *who* would multiply commas perhaps to the point of confusion. Commas are optional to set off the interrupter *one spring* because the interrupter is closely integrated, is short, and because the sentence already has a number of commas; more might cause confusion.)

u. His neighbors, as a matter of course, simply came over and plowed and planted for him—it was the custom in that small rural community to help each other. (Commas separate nonrestrictive interrupter *as a matter of course*—Lesson 2M. Dash marks strong interrupter—Lesson 2N. Semicolon after *him* is also possible, since the rest of the sentence is an independent clause—Lesson 2B.)

v. What made the 1986 gifts so amazing is that people in one part of the country, themselves hard pressed, as most farmers are these days, sent precious resources to folks they didn't even know—folks in a different state. (No comma after *amazing* because it would separate subject from verb—Lesson 2K. Commas separate nonrestrictive interrupters *themselves hard pressed* and *as most farmers are these days*—Lesson 2M. Dash marks the strong interrupter—Lesson 2N. A comma would also be accept-

able, since the interrupter is not highly separate from structure of rest of the sentence.
2. a. When selecting an award, keep in mind that your award travel must originate in the U.S., Canada, or Hong Kong. OR you must keep in mind
   b. The U.N. charter places peace keeping responsibility on the Security Council, whose members are five wartime allies—the U.S., the U.S.S.R., Britain, France(,) and China. (A colon would also be acceptable after *allies*.)
   c. Since ship owners lose between $5000 and $20,000 a day when they operate idle, loaded vessels, some owners begin furloughing crews, and some begin tying up their ships. OR Operating idle, loaded vessels, owners lose between $5000 and $20,000 a day, so some of them begin furloughing crews, and some begin tying up their ships. OR begin furloughing crews or tying up their ships.
   d. For example, long-term chess strategy is controlled by a computer program called Oracle, created by Hans Berliner, who is an artificial-intelligence expert and a former world correspondence-chess champion. (*Who is* may be omitted.)

LESSON FOR STEP 2R

1. a. "strident screams" "The beluga were torn to pieces." "savssat" OR *savssat*
2. a. Machiavelli advises that the prince should "seem" to have religion. OR should "seem to have [religion]." OR should "seem" to have "religion." The word "seem" is important. Machiavelli has little faith in peoples' ability to discern show from reality. He says, "Everyone can see but only a few can test." (Note that the original does not contain a comma to separate independent clauses linked by a coordinating conjunction—Lesson 2B. When quoting, copy original exactly as it is. If the error were more distracting,

the writer would place [*sic*] next to it, but since the omitted comma here does not interfere with meaning, and probably would not be noticed by most readers, no [*sic*] is needed. No dots are needed at the end of the final quotation, since the reader does not need to know that the quotation continues with more in the same sentence. The rest of Machiavelli's sentence does not change the meaning of what the writer quotes.)

3. a. Companies in California have found that so-called "pickling acid," which is needed in metal-processing plants to remove scale, could be mixed with zinc sulfate and used to enrich citrus orchards. Despite its high cost, "The method holds great promise for recycling this toxic waste," said one plant manager. (Comma after *acid* sets off the nonrestrictive modifier that begins *which*. . . . Comma after *waste* separates the quotation from writer's following words in the same sentence. Both commas are placed within the quotation marks. *The* is capitalized because the quoted words are a complete sentence.)

5. a. (2) "I wonder why he's talking about Black River?" I
(3) "Black River quarterback, Edward Gladstone, was shot and killed last night in his Montego home," the announcer
(4) "Edward Gladstone, Edward Gladstone," I
(5) "I don't know who he is."
(6) spotted "Gladstone, Edward,"
(7) (8) "Oh, yeah," I recalled as I glanced at his picture, "he's the guy who started the fight in the cafeteria last week. It's really a shame." (This version considers the first two quoted sections as one sentence: "Oh yeah, he's the guy . . ." Also possible: "Oh, yeah," I recalled as I glanced at his picture. "He's the guy. . . .")
(10) myself, "Why is it so quiet?"
(15) (No quotation marks because these are not the exact words the writer would have said to herself. She would have said, "*Am* I insensitive?")

(17) (18) "I'm sorry about Eddie," I whispered to her. "How well did you know him?"
(19) (20) "I didn't," she responded sadly, "but he seemed like such a nice guy. His life ended so quickly and he had so much going for him."
(22) Optional quotes: "outstanding quarterback,"
(23) termed "lack of talent."
(26) The newspaper mourned, "Edward Gladstone was an extraordinary quarterback who would have had a very bright future."

LESSONS FOR STEP 3

LESSON FOR STEP 3B

1. a. On December 24, 1958, his daughter was born—almost a Christmas baby.
   b. The shipment arrived on September 2, 1986, but it was not opened or inspected until September 6, after the Labor Day weekend.
2. a. Five hundred trees were damaged in the first frost and an equal number in the second frost.
   b. We lost $1000 on the deal. OR We lost one thousand dollars on the deal.
   c. Between 4 and 5 p.m., drinks are half price, so we were all able to have a nice time for under $20. OR for under twenty dollars.
   d. There were 42 caps in the third shipment, making a total of 1542 now in stock. (Business or technical context implied by the topic of this sentence would probably use numerals throughout.)
3. a. On the north side of Cleveland . . . Cleveland's Japanese . . . Oheiko. Hayato Tokugawa, a Japanese student, came to Cleveland . . . Arnold Hansens . . . Richard Brandson

ANSWERS TO EXERCISES

High School. . . . English . . . Japanese manufacturer . . . Catholic school, St. Jude's, was offering Japanese. . . . The Japanese professor, Fr. Timothy Hoyt, invited Hayato . . . Hayato . . . St. Jude's students . . . Dad . . . America."

4. a. Herman Melville's short story *Billy Budd, Foretopman,* . . . . Melville introduces Captain Vere . . . God . . . Vere
5. a. The doctor phoned Mr. Haines
   b. biology. . . . biology . . . department . . . professor
6. a. To: Professor Magnum and Sister Mary Jacques
   From: Father John Reilly, S.J., Office of Student Personnel

   Please excuse Alice Jones from her English and biology classes for the first two weeks of the spring semester, Monday, January 15 through Friday, February 2, 1987. Ms. Jones has had two operations and has been at home under a doctor's care since the Christmas holiday. She expects to attend classes again beginning February 5. She intends to attempt only two courses—English and biology—in spring semester. She will drop her other three courses. [Remainder as is.]

   b. Ms. Alice Jones
   103 South Elm Street
   Last Chance, Nebraska 99999
   Dear Ms. Jones:
   Father Reilly in the Student Personnel Office has told me that you have been having medical problems and will not attend classes until February 5. I hope you will make a speedy recovery. I will do anything I can to help you make up your work and get a good start for the new semester in modern literature class. In case you are able to begin some of the semester's reading, enclosed is a syllabus and copies of the first texts we will use. The cost of these texts was $22.95. The bookstore has agreed to let you pay for the books when you return to school, or you may mail me a

ANSWERS TO EXERCISES

check made out to Furman College Bookstore. I suggest you begin James Joyce's novel *Portrait of the Artist as a Young Man*. You might also read Chapter 1 of the poetry anthology, particularly T.S. Eliot's "The Wasteland," which begins on page 57. On Sunday, February 4, the day before you return to class, the theater department is presenting its last performance of Samuel Beckett's play *Waiting for Godot*. Performance begins at 8 p.m. in Goodwin Theater. [Remainder as is.]

APPENDIX B

1. The following are corrections for grammar, punctuation, capitalization, and abbreviation. (Lesson numbers are included for reference.) Give yourself one point for every correct revision. Optional punctuation is in parentheses.

SENTENCE	CORRECTION	LESSON
1	America's	2J
2	Nearly two million of the jobless are teenagers. (Fix fragment.)	2A
3	(You may use both commas or no commas to set off *combined . . . hamburger*.)	2M
3	creates (Subject is *being*.)	2C
3	don't	2J
3	"burn." (OR delete quotation marks)	2R
5	(Comma after *teenager* may be omitted if modifier is interpreted as restrictive, but comma after *advantages* must remain to follow introducer.)	2M
		2L

ANSWERS TO EXERCISES

SENTENCE	CORRECTION	LESSON
7	trade(,)"	2R
7	complex and permitting OR permit	2K
8	teenagers'	2J
8	minds; it (Fix run-on.)	2B
8	a car certainly is (Give *it* a clear antecedent.)	2H
9	Torino	3B
10	relative made	2K
10	Mercedes; OR Mercedes. However, (Fix run-on.)	2B
12	(You may omit comma after *drive*.)	2M
13	whether they own (OR some version that does not mix *you* and *all teenagers* in the same sentence.)	2F
13	problem—gas OR problem: gas	2Q
16	Logically(,)	2L
16	(Comma after *imposed* may be omitted.)	2M
19	Chances are other people will . . . them foot OR Chances are someone . . . him or her foot (See Step 2F on sexism.)	2I
20	obligation which confronted me was	2M
22	years; OR years. However	2B
23	you; OR you. The	2B
26	McDonald's	2J
28	counts, and a	2B

ANSWERS TO EXERCISES

SENTENCE	CORRECTION	LESSON
29	food is not (Fix vague antecedent for *this*.)	2H
30	movie, a concert(,) or	2O
30	(Commas after *entertainment* and *game* may be omitted.)	2M
33	night with . . . party is	2M
33	and me.	2G
34	Parties may (Fix vague *this*.)	2H
38	contain	2D
42	overcome what you would call a	2K
44	remember, OR remember—	2Q
44	(You may omit comma after *teenagers*.)	2M

The following are some of the most obvious style problems. You may wish to make other changes.

SENTENCE	PROBLEM	LESSON
1–3	overuse of the awkward *being*	1F
3	too much between subject *being* and verb *creates*	1D
5	*As a teenager* dangles	1D
7	parallelism: *that* and *permitting*.	1D
10	unnecessary *there are*	1E
12	verb choice: *had*	1C
14	Can a *loophole solve*?	1C
16	passive: *can be imposed*	1A
16	*convincing them of their consumption* is awkward	1F
18	subject-verb words: *loophole is never fuel up*	1C

513

ANSWERS TO EXERCISES

SENTENCE	PROBLEM	LESSON
20	unnecessary words: *that of*	1E
27	passive	1A
28	passive	1A
28	omit *It is* and *that*	1E
31	omit *for one*	1E
32	repetitious: *avoid* and *keeping to a minimum*	1E
38	awkward *being*	1F
39	word choice: *where*	1F
43	*used* is unnecessary	1E
43	passive	1A
44	*as teenagers* dangles	1D

2. The following are corrections for grammar, punctuation, capitalization, and abbreviation. (Lesson numbers are included for reference.) Give yourself one point for every correct revision. Optional punctuation is in parentheses.

SENTENCE	CORRECTION	LESSON
1	John's	2J
2	name,	2L
2	around,	2M
3	though; only OR though. Only (Fix run-on.)	2B
5	school, so	2B
5	Spanish	3B
6	high school	3B
8	my sister and me	2G
8	"town drunk"	2R
10	seventeen-year-old	3B
10	guess he	2K

ANSWERS TO EXERCISES

SENTENCE	CORRECTION	LESSON
12	Maybe his innocence and his drinking (Fix vague antecedent of *this*.)	2H
13	class, but	2B
14	crowded, noisy hallways	2O
15	acknowledge one was	2F
17	him—good OR him: good	2Q
17	president	3B
17	Retain comma after *confidence* or replace it with a dash.	2N
18	"right" OR right (Quotation marks are optional, but using single quotation marks is incorrect.)	2R
20	smile, John (Fix fragment.)	2A
21	"town drunk."	2R
22	he had just	2D
22	GQ (Gentleman's Quarterly magazine),	3B
22	eyes captured	2K
23	However, Sally, (Fix fragment.)	2A
26	1984 graduation	3B

The following are some of the most obvious style problems. You may wish to make other changes.

SENTENCE	PROBLEM	LESSON
1	unnecessary *very*	1E
3	unnecessary repetition: *however, though*	1E
3	word choice: can a *memory* be *visible*?	1C

ANSWERS TO EXERCISES

SENTENCE	PROBLEM	LESSON
4	passive	1A
5	material in parentheses awkwardly placed; *he being* is awkward word choice; parallel two situations: *in my class* and *an acquaintance of my brother*	1F, 1D
8	*had the reputation of being* is wordy	1E
12	*were foreshadows of* is wordy	1E
16	*formed from* is wordy and awkward	1E
17	parallel form for John's qualities	1D
22	opening modifier dangles; John's hair is not dressed	1D
24	*Like any couple* dangles	1D

ACKNOWLEDGMENTS

pp. 116-18, pp. 124-25 From "I Have a Dream" by Martin Luther King, Jr. Copyright © 1963 by Martin Luther King, Jr. Reprinted by permission of Joan Daves.

pp. 121-123, pp. 256-57 Copyright © Writing: Strategies for All Disciplines, Barbara Fassler Walvoord, Prentice-Hall, 1985.

pp. 144-46 From "Access to Computing Facilities" by Loyola College Academic Computing Service. Reprinted by permission.

pp. 188-91 From Dyslexia Defined by Macdonald Critchley and Eileen A. Critchley. Copyright © 1978 by M. Critchley and E. A. Critchley. Reprinted by permission.

p. 215 Copyright © 1987 by Eastern Air Lines Inc. Reprinted by permission.

p. 264, p. 322 "Swim" and "pony" from Webster's New World Dictionary, second college edition. Copyright © 1984 by Simon & Schuster, Inc. Reprinted by permission of Simon & Schuster, Inc.

p. 404 From a letter written in 1814 by Thomas Jefferson to Dr. Jones.

The author would like to thank the following students for allowing segments of their essays to be reprinted in her text:

Erik Batt	Stacey Kraft
Chrissy Borkowski	Brian McGowan
Joseph Davis	Lenore Pasqualucci
Triana D'Orazio	Jill Pickett
Mary Kay Dougherty	Christine Prime
Stuart Earhart	Kelly Reichart
Jeffrey Forwood	Christine Russell
Tamatha Furman	Gina Sapnar
Mike Gabrielle	Maritoni Sarmiento
Bryan Groll	Johnny Walker
Billy Keene	Francis Weber

INDEX

Abbreviation
and dates, numbers, names, and titles, 432–52
exercises, 434, 439, 444–45 448–51
ABSTRACT, 456
Abstract words, 185–86
"Access to Computing Facilities," 144
Accuracy, and quotation, 389, 399
Action words, 44–45
Active verb, 104–14
exercises, 110–13
Active voice, defiined, 105, 114
Additions, and quotations, 401–5, 406
Address, direct. *See* Direct address
Addresses, 443–44
Adjective
defined, 365, 370, 382
exercises, 368–69, 386–90
predicate. *See* Predicate adjective
and pronoun, 280
and series, 365–70
See also Modifier
Adjective clause, 76–78, 349–50
See also Dependent clause *and* Modifier, restrictive
Adventures of Huckleberry Finn, 28, 29, 30, 34, 35, 252, 253
Adverb, defined, 355
See also Modifier
Adverbial clause, 79–80, 349
See also Dependent clause
Adverbial connector, 79–80
See also Movable connector
Adverbial phrase, 349
See also Adverbial clause
Agreement
exercises, 240–41, 244–46
rule for pronoun and antecedent, 307–8
rule for subject and verb, 237
of subject and verb, 236–48
A.M., 437
And, 368
Antecedent
defined, 277, 295, 306, 313, 329
exercises, 303–5, 310–12
and pronoun, 297–306
and pronoun agreement, 307–13
Antonym, defined, 183, 194
A person, 282–83
Apostrophe
and contraction, 317
exercises, 317, 318–19, 322–23, 327
-s and -es, 315–29
and verb and pronouns, 318

518

Appositive, 350–51
Article, defined, 452
Audience, 9
Auxiliary verb. *See* Helping verb
Awkwardness, 17

Being, states of. *See* States of being
Be. *See* To be
Boswell, James, 414
Brackets, 404–5, 406
But, and not, 156

Capitalization, 411
  and dates, numbers, names, and titles, 432–52
  exercises, 434, 439, 444–45, 448–51
Case
  of pronouns, 290–94
  possessive of nouns, 323–26
  possessive of pronouns, 318
Cents, 438
Changes, and quotations, 401–5, 406
Choose, 265
Chose, 265
Citation, 10, 393
City, 442
Clarity, and sentence opener, 128–52
Clause
  adjective clause. *See* Adjective clause
  adverbial. *See* Adverbial clause *and* Adverbial phrase
  coordinate, 377–78
  defined, 68, 99, 152, 182, 220, 234, 248, 262, 296, 345, 355, 372, 381
  dependent, *See* Dependent clause
  and fragment test, 205–6, 212–13
  identifying, 70
  independent. *See* Independent clause
  and run-on, 222–25
Clemens, Samuel. *See* Twain, Mark
Clue, topic. *See* Topic clue
Coherence, 9
Collective noun, 241–44
Colon, 333, 410
  defined, 383
  exercises, 375–77, 379–80, 385, 386–90
  and explanation, 383–90
  and series and list, 371–82
Comma
  and adjectives in series, 365–70
  and city and state, 442
  and clarity, 352–53
  and direct address, 351
  exercises, 338–39, 343–44, 353–54, 368–69, 375–77, 379–80, 386–90
  and interjections, 352
  and interrupters and modifiers, 346–56
  and introducer, 341–45
  and opposition, 352
  and series and lists, 371–82
  and subject and verb and object, 331–40
Comma splice. *See* Run-on
Complement

519

defined, 68, 99, 220
and modifier, 69–70
Complex sentence,
　punctuation of, 224
Compound sentence,
　punctuation of, 224
Computer
　and spelling, 423–25, 453–54
　use with text, 6, 453–56
Concrete words, 185–86
Conjunction, defined, 452
　See also Connector
Connective. *See* Connector
Connector
　adverbial. *See* Adverbial
　　connector
　coordinating. *See*
　　Coordinating connector
　defined, 75–76, 234
　and dependent clause, 79
　movable. *See* Movable
　　connector
　nonmovable. *See*
　　Nonmovable connector
　types of, 79–81
　See also Conjunction
Connotation, 186
　defined, 194
Consonant, defined, 429, 431
Contraction
　and apostrophe, 317
　defined, 328
Coordinate, defined, 377, 382
Coordinate elements,
　punctuation of, 373
　See also Parallelism
Coordinating connector, 79
　defined, 100, 234
Correlative, 156

Dangling modifier
　defined, 175
　exercises, 168–69, 172–74
　revising, 166–67
Dash, 333
　defined, 383
　exercises, 385, 386–90
　and explanation, 383–90
Dashes
　exercises, 362–63
　and interrupters, 357–64
Dates, 432–34
　exercises, 434, 439, 444–45,
　　448–51
Deletions, and quotations,
　401–5, 406
Demonstrative pronoun, 78
Denotation, 186
　defined, 194
Dependent clause
　and connector, 79
　defined, 70, 99, 152, 220, 234,
　　262, 345
　exercises, 87–99
　and functions, 72–75
　identifying, 81–87
　and independent clause,
　　67–100
　and nonmovable connector,
　　81
Development, 9
Diagrams, use of, 23–24
Dialect verb forms, 268–70
Dialogue, 394
Diction
　exercises, 191–93
　revising, 183–99
DICTION, 456
Direct address, and commas,
　351
Direct object, defined, 114,
　194, 266
Direct quotation, 394–400
　defined, 394, 418

exercises, 401, 415–17
See also Quotation
Distracting material
 exercises, 163
 and subject and verb, 159–63
Dollars, 438
D'Orazio, Triana, 28–40
Dyslexia, 188–91

Economy, 176–82
 exercises, 180–81
-ed, and verb forms, 270
Either/or, 156
Ellipses, 404, 405, 406
 defined, 418
Emancipation Proclamation, 117
Emphasis, and sentence opener, 128–52
Engfish, 189–90
-es
 and apostrophe and -s. *See* Apostrophe, -s, and -es
 and nouns, 319
Essays, revising, 457–64
Exclamation point, 410
Explanation
 and colon and dash, 383–90
 exercises, 385, 386–90
Expletive, 49

FINDBE, 456
Foreign words, and quotation marks, 400
Fractions, 437
Fragment
 and complete sentence, 216–17
 complicated, 211–12
 defined, 100, 203, 220

and dependent clause, 75
exercises, 206–7, 213–15, 217–19
purposeful, 215–17
revising, 203–20
tests, 204–6, 208–9, 210–11
Fused sentence. *See* Run-on

Gender, of pronouns, 285–87
Gerund, 44–45
Gettysburg Address, 116
Grammar
 overview and introduction, 1–7
 and punctuation, 201–418
 understanding, 19–21

Have, 263
He, 291–93
 alternatives to, 286–87
Helper, 14–15, 106
Helping verb, 43–44
 defined, 65–66, 114
Him, 290–96
Homonym, 424
However, 351

I, 281–82
Idea
 main. *See* Main idea
 parallel. *See* Parallel ideas
"I Have a Dream," 116–18
Indefinite pronoun, 242, 279
Independent clause
 and commas, 378–79
 defined, 70, 99, 152, 220, 234, 364, 382, 418
 and dependent clause, 67–100

INDEX

and fragment, 208-9
and functions, 72
identifying, 81-88
and movable connector, 80
and run-on, 222-25
and sentence opener, 129
Indirect object, defined, 135, 194
Indirect quotation, 394-400
  defined, 394, 418
  exercises, 401, 415-17
  See also Quotation
-ing, 45, 155
  and verb forms, 270
Infinitive, 45
Interjection
  and commas, 352
  defined, 356
Interrupter
  and comma, 346-56
  defined, 346
  exercises, 362-63, 386-90
  and parentheses and dashes, 357-64
Introducer
  and commas, 341-45
  exercises, 386-90
Irregular verb, 269
It, 49

Jargon, 187-91
Johnson, Samuel, 414
Jungle Books, 51, 82, 85

Kagan, J., 121, 123
Khan, Shere, 51, 57, 58, 82, 86
King, Martin Luther, Jr., 116-18
Kipling, Rudyard, 51, 52, 57, 82, 85, 86

Language, understanding, 19-21
Large-scale questions, 8-10
Lay, 266-68
Letters, and quotation marks, 400
Lewis, M., 121, 123
Lie, 266-68
Lincoln, Abraham, 116, 117, 118
Linking verb. *See* Helping verb
List
  exercises, 375-77, 379-80, 386-90
  punctuation of, 371-82
Listening, 17
Local revising, 15-16
Loose, 265
Lose, 265

Macrorie, Ken, 189
Main clause. *See* Independent clause
Main idea, 9
Margins, and quotations, 414
Me, 290-96
Meaning, reading for, 102-99
Milton, John, 412-13
Miscue
  exercises, 172-74
  revising, 169-72
Modifier, 163-67
  and comma, 346-56
  and complement, 69-70
  dangling. *See* Dangling modifier
  defined, 42, 66, 68, 99, 152, 163, 175, 220, 248, 347, 355
  exercises, 168-69, 172-74, 386-90

522

and fragment, 212-13
nonrestrictive, 349-51
 defined, 364
restrictive, 349-51
and subject, 47
Modify, defined, 152, 370
Money, 438
Movable connector, 79-80

Names, 432, 439-44
 exercises, 434, 439, 444-45, 448-51
Neither/nor, 156
Nominalization, 456
Nonmovable connector, 79-80
 defined, 234
 and fragment, 209-10
Nonrestrictive principle, 348-51
Nor, 368
 and neither, 156
Not/but, 156
Noun
 collective. *See* Collective noun
 and consistency with pronouns and verbs, 309-10
 defiined, 42, 66, 99, 194, 220, 234, 296, 319, 328, 355, 365, 370, 452
 and nonrestrictive modifiers, 349-50
 predicate. *See* Predicate noun
 singular and plural, 319-22, 323-24
 defined, 319
 exercises, 322-23
Numbers, 432, 434-38
 and commas, 368
 exercises, 434, 439, 444-45, 448-51
 and quotation marks, 400
 See also Agreement *and* Plural *and* Singular

Object, 106
 and comma, 331-40
 defined, 135, 152, 194, 340
 direct. *See* Direct object
 exercises, 386-90
 indirect. *See* Indirect object
 of preposition defined, 313
 and subject and verb, 135-38
Of, 263
One, 282-83
Opener
 defined, 75-76
 sentence. *See* Sentence
Opposition, and commas, 352
Or, 368
 and either, 156
Organization, 9

Parallel, defined, 175
Parallel forms, 154-58
 exercises, 158-59, 172-74
Parallel ideas, 154-58
 exercises, 158-59, 172-74
Parallelism, 154-58
 exercises, 158-59, 172-74
 See also Coordinate elements
Parentheses, 333
 exercises, 362-63, 386-90
 and interrupters, 357-64
 and numbers, 437
Participial phrase, 166
 defined, 175
Participle, 45, 47, 166
 defined, 175

INDEX

Passive verb, 104-14
  exercises, 110-13
Passive voice, defined, 105, 114, 182
Person, 282-83
  of pronoun, 285-87
  of verb, 268-70
Personal pronoun, 279
Phrase, defined, 381
Plural, 237, 244, 309
  defined, 248, 328
Plural noun, defined, 319
P.M., 437
Poetry, and quotation, 412-13
Possessive
  case defined, 329
  of singular or plural noun, 323-25
Possessive pronoun, 318-19
Predicate. *See* Complement *and* Modifier *and* Verb
Predicate adjective, 106-8
Predicate noun, 106-8
Preposition
  defined, 47-48, 66, 248, 313, 452
  object defined, 313
Prepositional phrase, defined, 248, 313, 337
Principal parts, of verb, 264-65
Process diagrams, use of, 23-24
Progressive tenses, 270
Pronoun, 275-313
  and adjective, 280
  and antecedent, 297-306
  and antecedent agreement, 307-13
  and apostrophe, 318
  case defined, 296
  and consistency with nouns and verbs, 309-10
  defined, 48-49, 66, 182, 277, 289, 295, 306, 313, 329
  demonstrative. *See* Demonstrative pronoun
  exercises, 280-81, 284, 287-88, 293-94, 303-5, 310-12
  gender. *See* Gender
  and him/me, 290-96
  indefinite. *See* Indefinite pronoun
  memorizing, 278-80
  person. *See* Person
  personal. *See* Personal pronoun
  possessive. *See* Possessive pronoun
  reflexive. *See* Reflexive pronoun
  relative. *See* Relative pronoun
  select, 276-89
  and self, 293
  and sexism, 285-87
  substitution, 292
  and substitution test, 277-78
  and who/whom, 290-96
Punctuation
  and dates, numbers, names, and titles, 432-52
  exercises, 434, 439, 444-45, 448-51
  and grammar, 201-418
  interior sentence, 330-90
  and interrupters/modifiers, 347-48
  and introducers, 341
  overview and introduction, 1-7

pairs of, 348
and quotation marks, 407–11
and quotations, 392–418
and sentence boundaries,
  202–34
of series and list, 365–70,
  371–82
understanding, 19–21

Question mark, 410
Questions, large-scale, 8–10
Quotation, 10, 391–418
  and accuracy, 393, 399
  and changes, deletions, and
    additions, 401–5, 406
  direct. *See* Direct quotation
  exercises, 401, 406, 411–12,
    415–17
  indirect. *See* Indirect
    quotation
  and poetry, 412–13
  single, 411
  and spacing and margins,
    414
Quotation marks, 393, 398–99,
  400
  exercises, 401, 411–12,
    415–17
  and punctuation, 407–11

Raise, 266–68
Reading, 17
  for grammar and
    punctuation, 201–418
  for meaning, 102–99
  exercises, 195–99
Reflexive pronoun, 279, 293
Relative clause. *See*
    Dependent clause *and*
    Relative pronoun

Relative pronoun, 76–78, 279,
  290–93
  defined, 100, 234
  and fragment, 209–10
Revising
  essays, 457–64
  exercises, 38–40
  for grammar and
    punctuation, 201–418
  and large-scale questions,
    8–10
  local. *See* Local revising
  overview and introduction,
    1–7
  process, 8–40
  and sentence opener, 129–30
  for style, 102–99
  exercises, 195–99
Revision. *See* Revising
Rewrite, 18
Rise, 266–68
Run-on, 221–34
  acceptable, 226–27
  defined, 221, 234, 382
  exercises, 228–33, 386–90
  revising, 227–28

-s
  and apostrophe and -es. *See*
    Apostrophe, -s and -es
  and nouns, 319
  and verb forms, 244, 268–69
Scientific terms, 441
Self, and pronouns, 293
Semicolon, 333
  exercises, 375–77, 379–80,
    386–90
  and series and list, 371–82
Sentence
  boundaries and punctuation,
    202–34

INDEX

complex. *See* Complex
  sentence
compound. *See* Compound
  sentence
  defined, 99
  exercises, 172–74
  and fragments, 203–20
  fused. *See* Run-on
  opener
    exercises, 146–51
    and subject/verb, 128–52
  parts related clearly, 153–75
  punctuation, 330–90
  run-on. *See* Run-on
  subordinating elements,
    133–34
  topic. *See* Topic sentence
SENTENCE STRUCTURE,
  456
Series
  exercises, 368–69, 375–77,
    379–80, 386–90
  punctuation of, 365–70,
    371–82
Set, 266–68
Sexism, and pronouns, 285–87
Sic, 405, 406
Singular, 237, 244, 309
  defined, 248
Singular noun, defined, 319
Sit, 266–68
Sixty Minutes, 140, 142
Spacing, and quotations, 414
Spelling, 422–31
  and computer, 423–25,
    453–54
  exercises, 430
  overview and introduction,
    1–7
  rules, 428–30

Standard English
  verb forms, 263–74
  exercises, 270–73
State, 442
States of being, 44–45
Steps, overview and
  introduction, 1–7
Style
  defined, 16–17
  overview and introduction,
    1–7
  revising for, 102–99
Subject
  agreement exercises, 240–41,
    244–46
  agreement with verb, 236–48
  and comma, 331–40
  defined, 41, 65, 99, 114, 152,
    194, 220, 234, 247, 274, 296,
    340, 345, 381
  and distracting material,
    159–63
  exercises, 59–65, 146–51, 163,
    172–74, 386–90
  finding, 51–58
  identifying, 41–66
  and pronoun, 48–49
  and sentence opener, 128–52
  singular or plural, 241–44
  with verb and object, 135–38
Subordinate clause. *See*
  Dependent clause
Subordinating connector. *See*
  Nonmovable connector
Subordinating sentence
  elements, 133–34
Substeps, use of, 18–19, 22,
  24–27
Substitution test, for
  pronouns, 277–78

Suffix, defined, 429, 431
Syllable, 426
Synonym, defined, 183, 194

Technical words, 187–91
Tense
  combining, 254–55
  defined, 262
  dominant, 250–51
  exercises, 258–61, 270–73
  past, 264–65
  perfect, 264–65
  progressive. *See* Progressive tenses
  and research data, 256–57
  Standard English system, 249–50
  verb, 249–62
That, 78, 244
Them, 291–93
There, 49
Thesaurus, using, 183–84
They, 291–93
Tightening, 176–82
  exercises, 180–81
Time, 437
Titles, 432, 442–43, 445–48
  exercises, 434, 439, 444–45, 448–51
  and quotation marks, 400
To be
  and tense, 250
  and voice, 106
Tone, 10
Topic, 119, 120, 122
Topic clue, 119, 120
  defined, 127
Topic sentence, 119
Transition, 115–27

defined, 115, 127
exercises, 124–26
Transitive verb, 105–7, 266–68
Trite words, 184–85
Twain, Mark, 28, 30, 34, 252
Twenty-Twenty, 178, 179, 180
Typing, and quotations, 414

Underlining, 393, 398–99, 446–48
  exercises, 401, 415–17
Understood elements, 379
UNSPECIFIC, 456

Verb, 235–74
  active. *See* Active verb
  adding -s to singular form, 244, 268–69
  agreement exercises, 240–41, 244–46
  agreement with subject, 236–48
  and apostrophe, 318
  and comma, 331–40
  and consistency with pronouns and nouns, 309–10
  defined, 41, 65, 99, 114, 152, 182, 194, 220, 234, 247, 274, 296, 329, 340, 345, 355, 381
  dialect forms. *See* Dialect verb forms, 268–70
  and distracting material, 159–63
  exercises, 59–65, 146–51, 163, 172–74, 386–90
  finding, 51–58
  helping. *See* Helping verb

identifying, 41-66
irregular. *See* Irregular verb
linking. *See* Helping verb
passive. *See* Passive verb
patterns, 43
person. *See* Person
principal parts. *See* Principal parts
and sentence opener, 128-52
and singular or plural subject, 241-44
Standard English exercises, 270-73
Standard English forms, 263-74
and subject and object, 135-38
tenses. *See* Tense
transitive. *See* Transitive verb
Verbal, 44-45, 47
Verbal phrase. *See* Verbal
Voice. *See* Active verb *and* Active voice *and* Passive verb *and* Passive voice
Vowel, defined, 429, 431

Which, 244
Who, 244, 290-96
Whom, 290-96
Will, George, 136
Word choice. *See* Diction
Word processing, 12-13, 453

Yes/no question test, 210-11
You, 282-83